The Triumph of The Goddess

Durgā Mahiṣa-Mardinī, Bhadgaon, Nepal, Seventeenth century. Photo by the Author.

Sri Garib Dass Oriental Series-No. 134

The Triumph of The Goddess

The Canonical Models and Theological Visions of the Devī-Bhāgavata Purāṇa

C. Mackenzie Brown

SRI SATGURU PUBLICATIONS
A DIVISION OF
INDIAN BOOKS CENTRE
DELHI-INDIA

Published by :

Sri Satguru Publications
Indological and Oriental Publishers
A Division of
Indian Books Centre
40/5, Shakti Nagar,
Delhi-110007
(INDIA)

First Indian Edition : Delhi, 1992

ISBN 81-7030-305-2

PRINTED IN INDIA

For Nisha and Nathan

Contents

Part III The Two *Gītās*: The Harmonization of Traditions and the Transcendence of Gender

Preface

Interest in the feminine dimensions of transcendence as revealed in mythologies, theologies, and cults of goddess figures throughout the world has been keen in recent years both among those concerned with "Women Studies" and among religion scholars generally. The Hindu tradition in particular has attracted considerable attention because of its rich development of religious perspectives that emphasize the feminine aspect of ultimate reality.

The Great Goddess, or Mahā-Devī as she is known in India, burst onto the Hindu religious stage in the middle of the first millennium of the Christian era. Prior to that time, there were many goddess traditions in India. But it is in the *Devī-Māhātmya* (c. A.D. 500-600) of the *Mārkaṇḍeya Purāṇa* that the various mythic, cultic, and theological elements relating to diverse female divinities were brought together in what has been called the "crystallization of the Goddess tradition." After that time, there were few if any attempts by Hindus to elucidate the nature of the Goddess and her activities that did not take the *Devī-Māhātmya*'s vision of the Devī directly or indirectly into account. This study is concerned with a text, the *Devī-Bhāgavata Purāṇa*, composed and compiled some five to ten centuries later, whose roots are deeply embedded in the soil of the *Devī-Māhātmya*. The *Devī-Bhāgavata* in many ways represents a justification or vindication of the Goddess tradition, as well as an elaboration of it.

I came to this work from somewhat the opposite direction of the historical development indicated above. My original immersion into the world of the Hindu Goddess came with an investigation into a late Kṛṣṇaite text, the *Brahmavaivarta Purāṇa* (c. fourteenth to sixteenth century). While the supreme reality, according to this work, is the cowherd god Kṛṣṇa, the primary soteriological figure is that of his amorous consort Rādhā, who emanated from her spouse's left side at the beginning of creation. Through worshipping her, one may attain salvation quickly and easily, while devotion to Kṛṣṇa is arduous and timeconsuming. In developing the soteriological dimensions of the divine feminine, the *Brahmavaivarta* availed itself of many older Śākta notions, identifying Rādhā with *śakti* (power), *māyā* (illusion), and especially *prakṛti* (nature). The *Brahmavaivarta* clearly was familiar with many of the themes and stories of the *Devī-Māhātmya*, but assimilated them into a Vaiṣṇava-Kṛṣṇaite framework that ontologically if not devotionally subordinated the feminine to the masculine.

One of the most intriguing sections of the *Brahmavaivarta Purāṇa* is its second book, the "Prakṛti Khaṇḍa," which serves as a kind of encyclopedia of goddesses, telling their major myths and providing a comprehensive structure that unites all the goddesses as manifestations of Prakṛti. My earlier study of the *Brahmavaivarta* focussed on this book. An interesting fact I stumbled upon in the course of the research was that the "Prakṛti Khaṇḍa" had been taken over, in large part verbatim, by another Purāṇa, the *Devī-Bhāgavata*, forming the latter's ninth book. Here was my introduction to this Śākta text. I immediately formed in my mind the idea of someday comparing the conception of the divine feminine in these two Purāṇas, the Kṛṣṇaite text emphasizing the amorous side of the feminine, the Śākta work stressing the maternal.

As I began work on the *Devī-Bhāgavata*, I soon found my focus of attention shifting. The ninth book (the "Prakṛti Khaṇḍa" slightly adapted to its new Śākta context) was in many ways anomalous, representing a very late addition to a more fundamental core. As I became familiar with the older parts of the text, it became evident, from a historical point of view at least, that a comparison of the *Devī-Bhāgavata* with the famous Vaiṣṇava *Bhāgavata Purāṇa* (c. tenth century A.D.) would prove more illuminating. For the original portions of the *Devī-Bhāgavata*, I concluded, were composed in part as a reponse to the *Bhāgavata*. Moreover, the inspirational seed of the *Devī-Bhāgavata* was clearly the *Devī-Māhātmya*, suggesting the need for a careful comparison between these two texts. This double shifting of focus is reflected in the first two parts of this book, constituting the bulk, which are devoted to elucidating the relationships between the *Devī-Bhāgavata* on the one hand, and the *Bhāgavata* and *Devī-Māhātmya* respectively on the other.

My interest in examining these relationships was not purely, nor even primarily, historical but theological. That is, I wished to evoke from the comparison of these texts, especially from their mythological materials, the distinctive vision of the Goddess that is the *Devī-Bhāgavata*'s. My use of a text-historical approach thus differs in intent from that of certain scholars in the past who utilized such a method in hopes of discovering some pristine, original version of a myth or myths, enabling these scholars (they thought) to discard later additions as irrelevant accretions. Today, however, for an increasing number of students of mythology, the "later additions" may represent interesting and valid new insights into the older versions, or even reveal new insights into aspects of reality obscured in the earlier myths.

Admittedly, the application of a text-historical method in the realm of Purāṇic studies is fraught with difficulties, given the fluid nature of the Purāṇic tradition, partly oral and partly written. Some Purāṇas are largely compilations, made over many centuries by many hands. Others may represent relatively integrated and "original" creations of a single composer, though always rooted in previous tradition as the very name Purāṇa ("ancient happenings") implies, and always subject to later additions and revisions. Moreover, for many Purāṇas, there is no single recognized text as such, but rather multiple versions, the published editions representing only one small number of the total available in manuscript form, which in turn may represent only a part of all versions, including oral. In the present case, however, the major texts involved, that is, the *Devī-Bhāgavata*, the *Bhāgavata*, and the *Devī-Māhātmya* (part of a Purāṇa), are fairly well integrated texts and their individual text histories are not entirely obscure. These circumstances make feasible a historical reconstruction of the development of various mythic themes and motifs that culminate in the grand vision of the Goddess appearing in the *Devī-Bhāgavata*.

My interest in this magnificent theological vision extended beyond simply observing what this vision was for the *Devī-Bhāgavata* composer(s) or what it meant to later Hindu listeners or readers. There is a sense, then, in which I have grappled with what this vision might mean, could mean, even does mean for myself, for my relationships with wife and children, for my teaching and interaction with students, and for my response to the world and cosmos at large. If it has the ability to move my Hindu brother or sister, am I not less of a scholar, less of a valid interpreter of Hindu life, less of a human, if I am unable to find within myself a similar capacity to be inspired by the grandeur of the *Devī-Bhāgavata*'s vision? I do not claim to be moved in the same way as those among us who are Hindus, or more specifically Śāktas. I am sure I have understood less than they, and have undoubtedly misunderstood much of what the Goddess is in herself, and what she signifies to her Hindu worshippers. Whatever limited understanding I have gained, however, has been increased, not diminished, by the personal struggle to engage her directly.

I do not wish to enter into an extensive defense of such an approach. On the one hand, most of my personal reflections on the Goddess have entered into the following pages only indirectly, manifesting primarily in a sympathetic orientation that takes the text, and the Goddess, seriously. On the other, this personalist approach to the *Devī-Bhāgavata* is not, in my view, a compromise with "objectivity," but rather a going beyond it. As Geoffrey Parrinder has affirmed in the context of discussing another great Hindu scripture, the *Bhagavad Gītā*, "Should not those who teach such scriptures sometimes consider their religious value, not only to their Indian readers but also to themselves? They are not just antiquarian pieces, to be dissected or debunked, and it makes a difference if we can appreciate their religious teachings."[1] And as my own mentor, Wilfred Cantwell Smith, has argued, the personalist nature of truth as found in Islam—and I would add, in the Hindu tradition—"itself requires that that distance, that non-*engagé* objectivity and neutralist observationism [often characteristic of earlier scholarly approaches to others' religiousness], be replaced with an existential concern, a wrestling with the implications for oneself. The very suggestion that truth is not an inert and impersonal observable but that truth means truth for me, for you, is challenging. Let us face the challenge."[2]

While many scholars of Hindu goddesses in recent years have increasingly turned to the *Devī-Bhāgavata* as a rich source to mine, quoting a few lines or passages here and there to illustrate certain aspects of the Devī or her cult (see, e.g., D. Kinsley, *Hindu Goddesses*, pp. 133, 137-39 and passim; W. D. O'Flaherty, *Women, Androgynes, and Other Mythical Beasts*, p. 129 and passim), there has not been any systematic and critical attempt to comprehend the text's vision of the Goddess as a whole. Often the text is simply alluded to as a great Śākta exposition of the female principle as mother. Not infrequently, specific references to the *Devī-Bhāgavata* are primarily or exclusively to its ninth book, which as indicated above is not necessarily representative of the work in general (see e.g., J. N. Tiwari, *Goddess Cults in Ancient India*, pp. 32-33; W. C. Beane, *Myth, Cult and Symbols in Śākta Hinduism*, pp. 61-65).

More attention has been given to the *Devī-Bhāgavata*'s particular view of the Goddess in works or chapters of books that focus on specifically Purāṇic images of the Devī. Here mention may be made of P. C. Chakravarti's *Doctrine of Sakti in Indian Literature* ("Śakti in the Purāṇas," esp. pp. 84-86) and S. Mukhopadhyay's *Caṇḍī in Art and Iconography* ("Caṇḍī in Purāṇic Tradition," esp. pp. 12-15). Far more comprehensive than either of these is U. Dev's *The Concept of Śakti in the Purāṇas*, which relies throughout on four Śākta Purāṇas including the *Devī-Bhāgavata*. Such studies have tended to be primarily descriptive rather than analytical or interpretive.

Of special relevance for those interested in Women Studies is Kinsley's article, "The Image of the Divine and the Status of Women in the *Devī-Bhagavāta-Purāṇa* [sic]" (*Anima* 9:50-56, 1982). Kinsley contrasts the *Devī-Bhāgavata*'s exalted vision of the Goddess with the Purāṇic author's traditional, low view of women.

A number of articles, mostly by Indian scholars, have been written on the *Devī-Bhāgavata* regarding, on the one hand, its historical origins and date, and on the other, the related question of its scriptural status within the larger corpus of Purāṇic works, specifically its connection to the famous Vaiṣṇava *Bhāgavata Purāṇa.* Among such articles, the most thorough are those by R. C. Hazra ("The Devī-bhāgavata," *Journal of Oriental Research, Madras* 21:49-79, 1953; a slightly revised version of this article appears in his *Studies in the Upapurāṇas*, II, 284-361) and N. C. Sanyal ("The Devī-Bhāgavata as the Real Bhāgavata," *Purāṇa* 11:127-58, 1969).

There has been one book-length study of the *Devī-Bhāgavata*, that by P. G. Lalye, dealing with historical, mythological, philosophical, and literary aspects of the text. Lalye's work is an invaluable source of reference for a wide variety of topics relating to the *Devī-Bhāgavata*, but many of its historical conclusions are quite untenable, and its individual sections are often poorly and confusingly arranged. Nonetheless, I feel a great indebtedness to Lalye for helping me to find my way through a complex and labyrinthine text, and I offer this work in the same spirit of furthering the empathetic, scholarly understanding of this important Śākta testimony to the greatness of the Devī.

Translations from Sanskrit are by the author, unless otherwise noted.

Regarding the illustrations in the book, the frontispiece was photographed by the author on a trip to Nepal in 1974. It reveals many of the central motifs of this study, portraying the Goddess at the climactic moment of her most famous mythic triumph, her victory against the buffalo-demon, Mahiṣa. She stands with one foot on her own lion-mount, while her other foot pins down her elusive adversary. Mahiṣa, well-known for his metamorphic abilities, is seen escaping out of the neck of his decapitated buffalo-form, whose sundered head lies at the feet of the lion. As the demon prepares to unsheathe his sword, the Goddess seizes his hair, ready to pierce his chest with her trident. In the midst of this violent combat, the Goddess appears hauntingly aloof and at peace. Her many arms, suggestive of her omnipotence, evoke images of her various cosmic roles as creator, protector, and destroyer of the universe. Her garland of severed heads may terrify, but she also removes the delusion that lies at the root of all fear, as she is the grantor of eternal wisdom, symbolized by her front, left hand raised in the gesture of teaching. A somewhat different rendering of the Goddess' victory may be found on p. 95. This ink drawing, bought at a market in Calcutta in 1974, dispenses with the gruesome adornment of severed heads, yet more forcefully suggests the dynamic power of the Goddess, as her body sways to the rhythm of battle. Her devotees may be assured that this particular victory against the forces of chaos will not be her last.

Acknowledgments

I would like to thank the following individuals for their help and inspiration during the ten years this work has been in progress. To my father, D. Mackenzie Brown, I am indebted for the example of his own humane scholarship in Indian studies, for his encouragement to keep this project moving, and for his critical observations about the manuscript at various stages of writing. To Thomas B. Coburn I owe my thanks for inspiring in me a fascination with the *Devī-Māhātmya* and a curiosity about its later history, as well as for his comments on an early draft of this book. I am grateful to Cynthia Humes for sharing with me the results of her fieldwork and her insights regarding the contemporary use and recitation of the *Devī-Bhāgavata Purāṇa* in North India. I appreciate the helpful suggestions and encouragement offered by Diana L. Eck and two other, anonymous readers for the State University of New York Press. Thanks are due to William O. Walker, Jr., Dean of Arts and Humanities at Trinity University, for his support and gentle encouragement over the years. My gratitude is also due to the interlibrary loan staff at Trinity University, especially to Maria G. McWilliams and Margie M. Roe for their patience in locating obscure materials. In addition, I wish to thank Kay Bolton, a most diligent copyeditor, and Marilyn P. Semerad, production editor at the State University of New York Press, for their assistance in turning the manuscript into this book. Claude Zetty deserves special credit for his invaluable help in proofreading the text.

The American Academy of Religion has kindly given permission to use, in modified form, my "The Origin and Transmission of the Two *Bhāgavata Purāṇa*s: A Canonical and Theological Dilemma," *Journal of the American Academy of Religion* 51:551-67 (1983). Trinity University has provided a semester's leave, as well as grants to purchase research materials and to expedite the final preparation of the manuscript.

Finally, I thank Metta Zetty, friend and wife.

Introduction

The Vindication of the Goddess in the Purāṇic Tradition

Goddess figures and feminine imagery appear in many of the world's religious traditions, but often such goddesses have fallen into eclipse and such imagery has become peripheral or subordinate to masculine metaphors of the divine. This was not the fate of the feminine in India. From one standpoint, the history of the Hindu tradition can be characterized as a reemergence of the feminine. This book addresses itself to certain later phases and aspects of this development within the Hindu world.

In the ancient, pre-Aryan period of India, the archaeological evidence, largely in the form of feminine figurines and ring-stones suggestive of the *yoni* (vulva), points to an early fascination with female powers of fertility and with female divinity. In the mid-second millennium B.C., Sanskrit-speaking Aryan invaders brought into the subcontinent a robust, martial world view that was predominantly masculine in its spiritual orientation. The goddesses (or the Goddess?) of the pre-Aryan culture fell silent.

The Aryan world view, however, was not without sensitivity to the feminine, as seen in its reverential attitude toward certain aspects of nature that were perceived as revelatory of feminine power or beauty: night, dawn, and the life-giving rivers such as the Sarasvatī. For the next millennium and a half, though, at least on the level of the official priesthood and religious elite, that is, within Sanskritic-Brahmanical circles, the most engaging deities were males: Indra, general of the gods; Varuṇa, overseer of cosmic order; Agni, the fire god who served as messenger between the human and divine; Soma, identified both with the moon and the sun, and with the divine food of the gods; Rudra, the wild mountain lord and precursor of Śiva. In the last centuries of the pre-Christian era, the great masculine gods of the later *bhakti* or devotional movements, Śiva and Viṣṇu, began to assert themselves.

What had happened to the female divinities of the pre-Aryan culture? Perhaps they were simply overwhelmed by the deities of the invaders. More likely, in my view, they went "underground," surviving in the hearts and minds of the nonliterate, "uncultured" peasants, eventually percolating back to the surface of orthodox Brahmanical spirituality and interacting with the fragments of feminine divinity never completely absent there. In any case, by the beginning of the first millennium A.D., we find a number of goddesses emerging from non-Sanskritic obscurity, often as the spouses of the long renowned male deities and thus largely subordinate. Hymns to goddesses in the late portions of the great *Mahābhārata* epic and in the *Harivaṃśa* (c. A.D. 100-300) reveal the increasing importance of female deities in Brahmanical devotional life.

Around the middle of the first millennium A.D., perhaps in northwestern India, the several individual goddesses with their somewhat fragmentary feminine symbolisms coalesced into the figure of the Great Goddess, the Mahā-Devī, independent of and far superior to any male god. This "crystallization" of the Goddess tradition, appearing in the *Devī-Māhātmya* of the *Mārkaṇḍeya Purāṇa,* was a powerful synthesis that has influenced the self-understanding of Hindus to the present day. Through it, millions of Hindus have apprehended something of what it means to be human in a universe that infinitely transcends the human and yet which is pervaded by the very human quality of a woman's care (and anger). The reemergence of the divine feminine in the *Devī-Māhātmya* was thus both the culmination of centuries-long trends and the inspirational starting point for new investigations into the nature of feminine transcendence.

The *Devī-Māhātmya,* in the fresh enthusiasm kindled by its integrating vision of the one Great Goddess, assumes rather than contends that she is supreme. While bearing witness to her transcendent status, the *Devī-Māhātmya* is disinclined "to pursue speculative matters, and it focuses instead on the myriad ways that the Goddess is operative within the world."[1] Thus, her absolute superiority to the historically most prominent male deities of the time, including the holy triumvirate (Trimūrti) of Brahmā, Viṣṇu, and Śiva—responsible for the creation, preservation, and destruction of the universe according to earlier, masculine conceptions of how the world works—is simply affirmed with little ado. Often, she just quietly assumes the place of her male "predecessors" or manifests herself as the controlling power behind their actions.[2] Thomas Coburn summarizes the situation succinctly:

"the DM [*Devī-Māhātmya*] does not argue that ultimate reality is feminine, nor does it propose it as a deliberate alternative to understanding ultimate reality as masculine. Feminine motifs are, of course, pervasive of the DM. But insofar as the DM is concerned to 'demonstrate' anything, it is that ultimate reality is really ultimate, not that it is feminine."[3]

Not all Hindus shared, or shared fully, though few if any were entirely unaffected by, the glorious vision of the Goddess propounded in the *Devī-Māhātmya*. Given the lack of philosophical justification or elaboration in this text, it is hardly surprising that later generations of Devī-worshippers, or Śāktas, attempted to explain more extensively their insights into the relationship between the feminine and masculine dimensions of cosmic reality and to articulate more persuasively their conviction that ultimate power and authority in the universe reside in the Goddess. One such endeavor, and the main subject of this study, is the *Devī-Bhāgavata Purāṇa*, a text whose initial composition probably stems from the eleventh or twelfth centuries, though its final redaction was not completed for four or five centuries.[4]

The *Devī-Bhāgavata*, in contrast to the *Devī-Māhātmya*, is far more studied, far more self-conscious in its deliberations on the nature of the Goddess. Certainly the *Devī-Bhāgavata* wishes to show that the ultimate reality is truly ultimate, but it also feels compelled to establish that this reality is, or at least is most adequately conceived of, or apprehended as, feminine. To understand how the *Devī-Bhāgavata* went about its task of vindicating the Goddess, it will be helpful to consider briefly the nature of Purāṇic literature, as well as the probable historical and social circumstances in which this particular Purāṇic text was composed.

Traditionalism and Originality in the Purāṇas

The word *purāṇa* as an adjective means "old, ancient, primeval." As a noun it refers to a past event, or to an account of ancient happenings. By extension, it came to signify a group of "sacred works" containing such accounts. These Purāṇic works are rooted in an ancient oral bardic and priestly culture, and even when committed to writing, they continued to interact with the ongoing oral traditions. They were not static texts but remained fluid, continuously expanding, incorporating an ever-increasing body of traditional lore. They thus came to include a vast variety of materials from widely different ages. In addition to accounts of the creation of the world and of the history of early royal dynasties, they provide models of the ideal society and the rules for the proper functioning of individuals within that community. The Purāṇas also describe the theory and practice of several arts and sciences, such as drama, medicine, and astrology. However, "the major component of today's Purāṇas is devotional material from the *bhakti* tradition of two distinct but interrelated kinds: stories about the gods who are the objects of people's loyalty, and practices of various kinds appropriate to the worship of these gods."[5] The extant Purāṇas thereby provide an invaluable record of the development of Indian civilization and of the religious transformations within Hindu culture.

The Purāṇas have frequently been characterized as "unoriginal." As Dimmitt and van Buitenen have expressed it, "by definition they [the Purāṇas] never contain novel materials; they merely repeat the stories of the old days."[6] Indeed it is their adherence to the ancient traditions that makes them religiously authoritative, for truth, in the Hindu perspective, is not something so much to be newly discovered as to be recovered. The ancient events and happenings between gods, demons, wise men, and kings are considered paradigmatic, revealing the essential nature of the cosmos and humankind's place in the universe. Moreover, the ultimate and eternal truth of the universe is felt to have been fully revealed to, or rather perceived by, qualified sages in ages past. The insights of these ancient seers constitute the divine knowledge (*veda*) that eventually was gathered together into four great collections known as "the Vedas." The sage responsible for the division of the Vedas, Vyāsa, is also generally held to be the author or compiler of the Purāṇas. The Purāṇas thus are regarded as elucidations and interpretations of the truths of the Vedas, made comprehensible for later times, or for those excluded from hearing the Vedas.[7] Yet the Purāṇas themselves are often called a fifth Veda.[8]

While it is true that the Purāṇas cleave to tradition, it is not quite accurate to describe them simply as lacking originality. We may first note that the term *original* itself has two somewhat opposed meanings, referring on the one hand to what is initial or primary, suggesting something old or even ancient, and on the other to what is fresh, new, innovative. In the former sense, then, the Purāṇas are strictly original, for "by definition" they deal with matters of origin, with the primary and initial events of the universe and of the human world. Their authority is bound up with their "originality," a word whose older sense, now archaic, of authenticity, would have been well understood by the Purāṇic composers, or Paurāṇikas.

The Purāṇas, at least at times, can also be quite original in the sense of being fresh and innovative. For in the process of retelling the old stories, they may provide new, even startling, interpretations of the ancient myths and legends. Older concepts, terms, and ideals may be taken over with new twists and surprising conclusions. The various materials or units of Purāṇic mythology and theology are more often than not steeped in tradition, but the way a given Purāṇa blends the elements together can itself be a radical revaluation of tradition.

Even more radically, the Purāṇas are original in introducing entirely new subject matter, though this is not usually acknowledged within the Purāṇas themselves.[9] New ritual and devotional practices (at least new to the Sanskritic/Purāṇic tradition), new hymns of praise to various deities, even new stories find their way into the texts, as they record the transformations within Hindu society and culture. The "Purāṇicization" of such innovations and developments helps to make the Sanskritic tradition contemporary, and contemporary practices traditional.[10] Or in different words, the duty of a Paurāṇika is to be simultaneously true to tradition and up-to-date.

Given the assimilative and conservative nature of the Purāṇas, much has been added over the millennia, and relatively little has been lost. Today the extant Purāṇic literature is massive—according to Ludo Rocher, its volume constitutes the "one characteristic . . . [that] stands out above all others."[11] One modern Indian scholar estimates the extent of the Purāṇas at some two million verses, distributed in approximately one hundred works, an estimate which Rocher considers "vastly" deficient.[12] Undoubtedly, the mass will continue to grow, as the Purāṇic activity continues in present times, adapting ancient stories to the modern world.

The Hindus themselves have attempted to bring some sense of order to this voluminous literature. They have classified the better known Purāṇas into two groups: the most prestigious eighteen major or Mahā-Purāṇas, and a like number of minor or Upa-Purāṇas. While most of the lists of the eighteen Mahā-Purāṇas, given in the texts themselves, are in basic agreement, there are a few discrepancies. There is no consensus, however, regarding the Upa-Purāṇas.

What distinguishes a Mahā-Purāṇa from an Upa-Purāṇa? That is, what is there about a particular Purāṇic text that gives it the necessary acclaim to be considered a major Purāṇa? Unfortunately, the Purāṇic tradition is not of much help, and there is little agreement among scholars.[13] A. S. Gupta gives a "minimalist" definition, arguing that "the only tenable distinction between them seems to be this that the Mahāpurāṇas are those which the Purāṇas mention in their lists of the eighteen Purāṇas . . . and the rest are the Upapurāṇas."[14] Even this minimal definition does not put an end to the controversy, as we shall see. In view of the problems with the traditional lists, and of the fluidity of the texts, many scholars today tend to dismiss the validity or importance of the Mahā- and Upā- categories, noting that eighteen is a highly sanctified number in Indian culture.[15] Nonetheless, the ideal of a canon of eighteen Mahā-Purāṇas has been of some theological and historical significance. Of particular concern to us is the fact that the *Devī-Bhāgavata* has been considered by some Hindus to be a great Purāṇa, and by others a minor. But before we return to the *Devī-Bhāgavata* and its disputed status, we first need to look at the position of the Great Goddess in the Mahā-Purāṇas overall.

The Goddess and the "Great Purāṇic" Tradition

One of the new, fresh visions that is articulated in the Purāṇas is that of the all-powerful Great Goddess. The Purāṇas (or parts of Purāṇas) composed after the *Devī-Māhātmya*, including those Purāṇas focussed on masculine deities, attest to the growing popularity of Śākta ideas. At the same time one can also observe in the Purāṇic tradition an increasing tension between feminine and masculine conceptualizations of the ultimate reality. As O'Flaherty has written with reference to Hindu hierogamies: "In the Purāṇas, male-dominated and female-dominated couples both occur, and one can occasionally find them side by side in a single text, as in the epics. But, by and large, Purāṇic sectarianism was developed in such a way that it was almost always necessary to stand up and be counted on the side of either the god or the goddess."[16] O'Flaherty further points out that on the mythological level, if not always on the theological, the Purāṇas often present the Goddess as the effective power behind any male consort.[17] This comment suggests that while the captivating force of the *Devī-Māhātmya*'s vision could not easily be denied in the less formal stories about the deeds of the Devī, that vision could be dimmed at times in the more conventional and rigid theological discourses of the Purāṇas.

With the exception of the *Devī-Māhātmya* of the *Mārkaṇḍeya Purāṇa* (universally accepted as a Mahā-Purāṇa), the "Great Purāṇa" tradition in fact seems largely to overlook the Great Goddess, however much, in its later phases, it may have been influenced by Śākta ideas. Dimmitt and van Buitenen, in their discussion of the deities appearing in the eighteen major Purāṇas, note the role of various goddesses, especially as the spouses of the gods of the famous Trimūrti (Brahmā, Viṣṇu, and Śiva). These two scholars also call attention to the exceptional position of the Goddess in the *Devī-Māhātmya*. But their final assessment is that "the main actors in most Purāṇic stories are the three major gods [of the Trimūrti]."[18]

The main actors can actually be narrowed even further. The cult of Brahmā seems to have seriously declined by the fourth or fifth centuries A.D., while those of Viṣṇu and Śiva flourished. It is not surprising, then, as Rocher contends, that the "two deities that dominate puranic literature are, without doubt, Viṣṇu and Śiva."[19] And even here, far more Purāṇas are focussed on Viṣṇu than Śiva, especially among the earlier texts. Or as more cautiously stated by Rocher: "it is Viṣṇu who is the dominant figure in those purāṇas which have been recognized as mahāpurāṇas."[20] Regarding the Goddess tradition, Rocher adds: "Śakti worship appears, though rather infrequently, in some of the mahāpurāṇas. It is far more prevalent in the upapurāṇas. In some of them it is so prevalent that they have been labeled 'Śākta upapurāṇas'."[21] Among these Upa-Purāṇas Rocher includes the *Devī-Bhāgavata*.[22]

A somewhat different assessment of the relation of the Goddess tradition to the Mahā-Purāṇas is provided by Nirmal Sanyal. He contends that

> when the Śaivas and the Vaiṣṇavas began to write Mahāpurāṇas for describing the glories and exploits of Siva and Vishṇu respectively, those Śāktas [of the time] naturally felt the need for writing at least one Mahāpurāṇa for describing the glories of Devī. Thus one of them wrote the *Devī-Bhāgavata*. It is of course incorrect to say that they felt this need when it was too late—when the age of the Mahāpurāṇas was gone.[23]

Unfortunately, Sanyal is rather vague about the "age of Mahāpurāṇas," though he accepts a common scholarly assumption that the Upa-Purāṇas generally belong to a later age.[24] While I shall challenge certain aspects of such an assumption, Sanyal's notion that the *Devī-Bhāgavata* is a Mahā-Purāṇa cannot be as readily dismissed as it sometimes is. In any case, it is time to look more closely at the role of the *Devī-Bhāgavata* in the development of the Goddess tradition.

The Goddess Tradition and the *Devī-Bhāgavata*

Given the fluid nature of Purāṇic literature and the twofold obligation of the Paurāṇikas to be authentically grounded in tradition and to be up-to-date, the mixture of old and new in the extant texts can easily become a text-historian's nightmare. The dating of individual Purāṇas, and parts of Purāṇas, has become something of a game, a game which some scholars, perhaps not unwisely, refuse to play. At the same time, Purāṇic texts, however fluid, exist in time and space, and were composed, edited, and redacted by specific individuals at specific times in response to particular situations. Moreover, some Purāṇic texts are more integrated than others, manifesting a relatively unified interpretive perspective throughout, suggesting that they are the work possibly of a single hand or at least of a closely knit community of like-minded scholar-devotees. These integrated works offer the textual scholar the tantalizing possibility of establishing relatively concrete historical contexts for them.

One such text is the *Bhāgavata Purāṇa*, a major Vaiṣṇava work that will figure prominently in our discussion. In his study of this text, Friedhelm Hardy notes, after commenting upon the meaninglessness of assigning any single date to the Purāṇas in general: "But to adopt such a critical attitude may sometimes be misleading; in the case of the BhP [*Bhāgavata Purāṇa*] it would ignore the pronouncedly homogeneous character of this text. . . . it may be assumed that the overall uniformity of the work is due to a very restricted milieu in space and time, if not to one author."[25] The *Devī-Bhāgavata*, with the exception of Books VIII and IX, is also such a text.

Despite the relative homogeneity of the bulk of the *Devī-Bhāgavata*, scholars have been far from unanimous in assigning it, even loosely, to a given time, though its place of composition is generally recognized as northeast India. Clearly a major factor in the lack of consensus regarding the date of this text has been the canonical question as to whether the *Devī-Bhāgavata* is one of the great or Mahā-Purāṇas, or whether this status belongs to the *Bhāgavata*. Scholars like Sanyal who support the *Devī-Bhāgavata* have tended to place it relatively early, perhaps in the seventh to ninth centuries A.D., and most significantly, prior to the *Bhāgavata*. Those who favor the *Bhāgavata* like R. C. Hazra date the *Devī-Bhāgavata* in the eleventh to twelfth centuries[26] or later, and after the *Bhāgavata*. There is a general consensus today that the *Bhāgavata* itself is from the ninth or tenth century.

One interesting alternative to the above polarized views is the theory of P. G. Lalye. He argues that both the *Bhāgavata* and the *Devī-Bhāgavata* are Mahā-Purāṇas. Lalye accepts Hazra's basic view regarding the relative dates of the two texts, but rejects the scholarly preoccupation with age as a valid criterion for determining canonical status.[27] In support of his position, Layle hypothesizes that there was an original "Bhāgavata," perhaps completed in the Gupta age (A.D. 300-500), devoted to glorifying Bhagavan (the Lord) and his supreme, mysterious power, Māyā. Sometime around the ninth century, he suggests, this text was split, following a division within the Bhāgavata sect. Those devotees who focussed primarily on the Bhagavan developed the extant *Bhāgavata* out of the original text, incorporating the childhood sports of Kṛṣṇa derived from the *Harivaṃśa*. The other group of Bhāgavatas, who came to worship Māyā herself as the supreme Goddess, adopted Śākta terminology in elaborating their own version of the original "Bhāgavata" text, a process completed perhaps a century or two after the final editing of the rival *Bhāgavata*.

Lalye's theory explains in its own way the many connections between the two extant *Bhāgavata*s and the relative dependence of the *Devī-Bhāgavata* on the Vaiṣṇava *Bhāgavata*. Lalye is to be commended for his recognition of the interconnectedness of the two texts, though his supposition of an original "Bhāgavata" that was the immediate root of both extant *Bhāgavata*s is dubious at best. While there may well be an earlier version of the Vaiṣṇava *Bhāgavata*, there is little reason for relating the *Devī-Bhāgavata* to such an original. The textual overlaps can be easily explained, even better explained, on the thesis that the *Devī-Bhāgavata* has relied directly on the extant *Bhāgavata*. Nonetheless, there is much merit in Lalye's overall view, for it affirms, quite correctly I believe, the later date of the *Devī-Bhāgavata* and its dependence, in whatever form, upon the *Bhāgavata*, without dismissing either Purāṇa as somehow inferior or less genuine. This perspective, in any case, informs the present study.

My own view regarding the history of the *Devī-Bhāgavata* and its place in the Goddess tradition is as follows.[28] The *Devī-Bhāgavata* was originally composed at a time when the Śākta movement, having grown rapidly since the time of the *Devī-Māhātmya*, was subject to vigorous competition from other Hindu theistic schools, especially the Vaiṣṇavas. Furthermore, Hindu Brahmanical society at large was faced with growing threats to its sense of proper social order both from within, through internal corruption, and from without, by Muslim invaders. The impending social chaos was seen by many as simply the reflection of the disintegration of cosmic order in general, due to the law of entropy that characterizes the Hindu view of time. In the *Devī-Bhāgavata*, however, we see the vision of the triumphant Goddess, victorious against the demonic forces threatening cosmic/social order. She is equally victorious against the impertinent godly forces who falsely arrogate to themselves the victories of the Goddess against the forces of chaos. In addition, the Goddess triumphs against those prejudices-

regarding her own person that limit her, or rather, limit the transcendence which shines through her.

Whether this vision of the Goddess was the inspiration of one man or several is not clear. The homogeneous nature of the text, excepting Books VIII and IX, allows for the possibility of a single author. Though there are differences in perspective of the basic text (outside Books VIII and IX), these are not so large that they cannot be accepted as part of a Purāṇic author's openness to variations within a tradition. In any case, Hazra goes so far as to argue for the author being a Bengali who migrated to Banāras, "probably because it was the best place of residence for a Devī-worshipper."[29] Given the apparent zeal of certain Vaiṣṇava kings of Bengal and Orissa in the twelfth century, Banāras may well have been a safer refuge in those days. The text's familiarity with the medieval culture and country of Bengal and Banāras makes Hazra's thesis quite plausible, though I am not sure one can rule out the possibility that a small group of Goddess devotees from Bengal might have migrated to Banāras and been responsible for the co-production of the text. I myself will in due course suggest, though quite tentatively, that such a group, or individual, may have moved once again to Ayodhyā, perhaps to escape Muslim persecution. These migrations would fit well, in any case, into the chaotic times of the eleventh and twelfth centuries in northeast India.

Given the uncertainty of single or multiple authorship of the bulk of the *Devī-Bhāgavata*, how is one to refer to its composer or composers? To avoid undue awkwardness, I shall usually refer to "the composer" or "the author" in the singular, with an occasional parenthetical reminder that the plural might in actual fact be more accurate.

As for the anomalous Books VIII and IX, both have been borrowed, in large part, from the *Bhāgavata* and *Brahmavaivarta* Purāṇas respectively.[30] Sanyal proposes that both books were added by the same pious hand sometime in the fifteenth to seventeenth centuries, in order to bring the text up to its traditionally reputed length of eighteen thousand verses. I am not so certain that Book VIII was necessarily such a late interpolation; it may have been borrowed by an earlier editor of the text, or even by the original composer. But clearly Book IX must be late, for the *Brahmavaivarta*, or at least that part borrowed by the *Devī-Bhāgavata*, comes from the fourteenth to sixteenth centuries. I shall refer to the person(s) responsible for the incorporation of Book IX as the "late redactor," without wishing to reject the possibility of his handiwork appearing in other parts of the Purāṇa as well, or to deny categorically the existence of other redactors. Our attention in this study will be focussed primarily on the original author and his composition, though we shall have occasions to refer to the late redactor, as he was responsible for certain systematic innovations in the conceptualization of the Goddess.

In concentrating on the original author of the *Devī-Bhāgavata*, we may note two main concerns or goals on his part: 1) to demonstrate the superiority of the Devī to all other deities, especially Viṣṇu; and 2) to articulate in new ways the manifold nature of the Goddess and her supernal powers as they are manifested in the historical process.

The *Devī-Bhāgavata* composer(s) employed two basic strategies to achieve the first goal. First, many ancient themes, motifs, and myths from older masculine theologies were taken over and incorporated into a thoroughly 'feminized' theological framework. Second, the *Devī-Bhāgavata* attempted in various ways to supplant older 'masculine' canonical authorities. In particular, the *Devī-Bhāgavata* asserts that it is "the *Bhāgavata*," a title more generally associated with the highly regarded Mahā-Purāṇa of the Vaiṣṇavas, probably composed, as already indicated, two or three centuries earlier. The *Devī-Bhāgavata*, then, was to be a (or the) Mahā-Purāṇa for the Śāktas. Moreover, the *Devī-Bhāgavata* contains a "Gītā" modelled after the famous Vaiṣṇava-Kṛṣṇaite *Bhagavad Gītā*. The *Devī-Bhāgavata*'s Gītā came to be known as the *Devī Gītā*, but interestingly enough, the text itself never uses such terminology, purporting instead simply to be "the *Gītā*."

To achieve his second main goal, the *Devī-Bhāgavata* composer reenvisioned his own Śākta heritage, examining and reinterpreting older mythological traditions about the Goddess and her mighty deeds, most specifically, those traditions assembled in the *Devī-Māhātmya*. In the process, the *Devī-Bhāgavata* created two new "Devī-Māhātmyas" of its own and confirmed the transformation of the Devī from a primarily martial and erotic goddess into the maternal world mother of infinite compassion.

The *Devī-Bhāgavata*'s own Gītā, referred to above, serves to fulfill the two basic goals of the Purāṇa simultaneously. Not only does it attempt to supplant the *Bhagavad Gītā* and its view of Kṛṣṇa as the ultimate reality, but it also looks back to earlier Śākta Gītās, revising and reinterpreting their visions of the Goddess as the supreme teacher of divine wisdom.

In carrying out these various strategies, the composer, like any good Paurāṇika, drew upon many other authoritative Sanskritic sources besides those already mentioned. Our author relied extensively upon the great epic, the *Mahābhārata*, though he considered it to be a work inferior to his own. He also drew upon the *Rāmāyana* and various Purāṇas, as well as upon specialized treatises on such subjects as drama, erotics, and politics. Not surprisingly, then, the Goddess emerges also as an expert in aesthetic sensibilities, skilled in the subtleties of seduction, and a master of diplomacy. In addition, the author has borrowed much ritual and devotional materials from relatively late texts like the *Śāradātilaka*, a Tantric work probably of the eleventh century. In all of this, however, our Śākta Paurāṇika claims only to be confirming the truths already revealed or intimated in the most sacred and authoritative of all Hindu scriptures, the Vedas and Upaniṣads. The Goddess is, after all, the mother of the Vedas,[31] though at the same time the Vedas are not able fully to explain her nature.[32]

I have provided a summary and schematization of my views of the text-history of the *Devī-Bhāgavata*, along with the views of Sanyal and Layle, in the Appendix for those readers interested in the details of such matters.

Structure of this Study

This book is organized along the lines of the major strategies adopted by the *Devī-Bhāgavata* composer(s). Part I ("The Two *Bhāgavatas*: Contending Revelations and Visions of the Divine") deals with the first goal of the Purāṇa by focussing on its self-conscious endeavor to supersede the Vaiṣṇava *Bhāgavata*. Chapter one looks at the general problem of scriptural authority as it pertains to Purāṇic works in general and to the two "*Bhāgavatas*" in particular. The *Devī-Bhāgavata* makes its claim for exalted canonical status in large part by modelling the account of its own divine origin and transmission on that of the Vaiṣṇava *Bhāgavata*. Inasmuch as the canonical problem is intricately intertwined with the theological and mythological dimensions of the text, we also meet in this chapter the first of many "Viṣṇu-motifs" taken over by the *Devī-Bhāgavata* to embarrass or dishonor the god, in this case the famous image of Viṣṇu as an infant floating on the cosmic ocean on a fig-leaf, sucking his toe.

Chapter two looks at perhaps the most embarrassing of all the ancient Viṣṇu-motifs, his decapitation by a sundered bowstring, eaten through by ants. It is typical of the *Devī-Bhāgavata* to search through the ancient literature, in this case the Brāhmaṇas, to find long-neglected motifs rich in potential for mortifying Viṣṇu. The motif of Viṣṇu's beheading is closely associated with his horse-headed form or *avatāra* (Hayagrīva), which in turn is connected with the promulgation of divine

.nowledge or Brahmavidyā. The *Devī-Bhāgavata* not only humiliates Iayagrīva, but equates the Goddess herself with the divine knowledge, he highest object or goal of the Upaniṣads.

If the decapitation of Viṣṇu is the most embarrassing of the arious ancient accidents suffered by the god, his most dishonorable eed is his role in the deceitful slaying of the demon Vṛtra, the subject of hapter three. Viṣṇu's deceitfulness, however, raises a number of uestions about the Devī's own powers of illusion and delusion as the upreme Māyā. The dilemma involved is partially resolved through the otion of the Devī's grace and compassion, an aspect that at times ppears in marked contrast with her traditional image as a wild and orrific, bloodthirsty slayer of demons. The tension between her orrific and benign aspects becomes a major theme in the next Part.

Part II (The Two *Devī-Māhātmyas*: Revisions Within the Tradition") urns to the *Devī-Bhāgavata*'s reenvisioning of the *Devī-Māhātmya*. Chapter four analyzes the three great demon-slaying deeds of the Devī hat are the mythological focus of the original *Devī-Māhātmya*. The *Devī-Bhāgavata*'s own "Devī-Māhātmyas" utilize not only the original *Devī-Māhātmya*'s versions of the three deeds but other traditions as well, raditions that are much more highly eroticized and which help to bring ut further aspects of Devī's role as Māyā. The martial-erotic tension r polarity in the Goddess' nature that is thereby developed is finally ranscended in an image of the Devī as the supremely compassionate vorld mother. At the same time, the androgynous character of the Goddess is revealed both on a mythological and philosophical level.

Chapter five focusses on the *Devī-Bhāgavata*'s symbolic interpretaon of the Devī's three incarnations in the three deeds. The three re envisioned as the three cosmic manifestations of the Goddess—as Iahā-Kālī, Mahā-Lakṣmī, and Mahā-Sarasvatī—responsible for the estruction, preservation, and creation of the universe. The correlation f the incarnations with these cosmic manifestations was extremely nportant in the later cult of the Goddess and was used to provide a 'edic sanction to certain Tantric aspects of her worship.

The three great deeds of the Goddess in the *Devī-Māhātmya* are ecounted within a frame story dealing with the worldly misfortunes of king and merchant. This frame story is itself an insertion into an xtended account of the fourteen Manus or world sovereigns who reside over one age of the world cycle. The frame story serves to ndicate something of the Devī's involvement in mundane affairs and olitics. Chapter six examines the frame stories in the *Devī-Māhātmya* nd the *Devī-Bhāgavata*, with particular attention to the latter's new perspective on history and the Devī's role in establishing social order, even in such perilous times as the present Kali Yuga. This chapter also elucidates the Purāṇa's emphasis on both enjoyment (*bhukti*) and liberation (*mukti*) as appropriate goals of human endeavor.

Part III, the final main section of the book, ("The Two *Gītās*: The Harmonization of Traditions and the Transcendence of Gender") brings together many of the diverse strands of Parts I and II. This final Part moves from "Māhātmya" (Glorification of the Goddess) to Gītā (the Self-Revelation of the Goddess). Like the *Bhagavad Gītā*, the *Devī Gītā* consists of two main parts: the spiritual teachings by the supreme God or Goddess, and the revelation of his or her cosmic form(s). Chapter seven compares these teachings and revelations in the two Gītās, as well as looking at other related Vaiṣṇava and Śākta Gītās that lie behind the *Devī Gītā*.

In chapter eight we turn to certain other theophanies of Viṣṇu and the Devī which take place on the mystic isles of the White Island and the Jeweled Island, respectively. While these theophanies occur outside the Gītās proper, they are parallel to them and have as their model, directly or indirectly, the vision of Kṛṣṇa in the *Bhagavad Gītā*. These visions on the mystic isles and their associated teachings complement and, in certain ways, complete the views of the Gītās themselves.

The *Devī Gītā* and the related revelations on the Jeweled Island, while still affirming that the ultimate power and authority in the universe is the divine mother, avow that her highest form as the divine light, encompasses and transcends all gender. Such a view, of course, is already intimated with regards to Kṛṣṇa in the *Bhagavad Gītā*. Indeed, at the highest levels, the teachings of the *Devī Gītā*, and the *Devī-Bhāgavata* as a whole, often become nearly indistinguishable from their Vaiṣṇava counterparts. There is a unity here, even if not fully acknowledged by the traditions themselves. This unity, in fact points to what we may call the ultimate triumph of the Goddess, to be discussed in the Conclusion.

Part I

The Two Bhāgavatas*: Contending Revelations and Visions of the Divine*

Chapter 1

The Origin and Transmission of the Two *Bhāgavata* Purāṇas: A Canonical and Theological Dilemma

I alone was, in the beginning; there was nothing else at all, manifest or non-manifest.
What exists now as the universe is I myself; what will remain in the end is also simply myself. (From the *Bhāgavata Purāṇa*)

All this universe indeed is just I myself; there is nothing else eternal. (From the *Devī-Bhāgavata Purāṇa*)

In these words the Great Lord (Bhagavan) and the Great Goddess (Devī) respectively declare their supreme and ultimate nature. In these same words lie, according to the texts themselves, the primordial seeds of the two celebrated *Bhāgavata Purāṇas*, the one exalting Bhagavan or Viṣṇu,[1] the other Devī.[2] The extant texts of the two *Bhāgavatas* both contain several thousand verses,[3] but each claims ultimately to be derived from a quintessential revelation spoken by the supreme reality him- or herself. Viṣṇu's germinal proclamation, in four verses (only the first of which is quoted above), describes himself as the ground of all being, whose nature has been obscured by *māyā* (the mystical power of creation and illusion), and whose reality must be discovered and understood by one seeking to know the truth of Ātman (Self). The lengthy work now known as the *Bhāgavata Purāṇa* is merely a detailed elaboration, explanation, and illustration of this "Four-Verse *Bhāgavata*." The *Devī-Bhāgavata*'s seed form is even briefer: The Devī speaks just half a verse (quoted above in its entirety) propounding herself as none other than that same ground of all being.

The theological controversy reflected in Viṣṇu's and Devī's seemingly exclusive claims is parallel to, and intertwined with, the canonical debate regarding which of the two *Bhāgavatas* is the Great or Mahā-Purāṇa,[4] listed usually as the fifth among the traditional eighteen. Modern scholars like R. C. Hazra have addressed themselves to the canonical question, but often from a text-critical standpoint that avoids the theological aspects of the problem.[5] The important and intriguing issue of what constitutes canonicity from the point of view of the religious community is largely ignored, the whole problem becoming rendered in purely historical terms. Such an approach, while admirable for its desire to be nonsectarian and objective, at the same time runs the danger of trivializing the texts themselves, of not comprehending them as serious interpretations of ultimate reality and humankind's relation to it. Implicit in the text-critical approach, frequently, is the assumption that the texts are merely compositions that one or another group of Purāṇic authors/editors has unscrupulously manipulated to advance purely sectarian interests. This assumption seemingly denies any "revelatory" nature to the Purāṇic texts, and in effect it would dismiss the two quotations at the beginning of this chapter as poetic fabrications at best.

I do not wish, any more than most other modern scholars, to try to arbitrate the theological issues involved. Yet as a historian of religion trained to read "sacred texts" with at least a sympathetic (though not necessarily a believing) eye, I am uncomfortable with a complete separation of the theological from the historical/text-critical studies. While the latter have tended to be reductionistic, they can be quite helpful in establishing the historical relation between the two *Bhāgavatas*. We simply must not be misled by historical considerations into making unconscious and unwarranted theological judgments about the texts. After considering the canonical question, we shall be better prepared to examine some of the implications of the theological differences between the two Purāṇas.

The Problem of Canonicity

As indicated in the Introduction, I agree with Hazra and Lalye that the Vaiṣṇava *Bhāgavata* is the older by a century or two and is almost certainly the one traditionally designated as belonging to the canonical eighteen.[6] I shall not go into all the evidence here for the earlier date of the *Bhāgavata* but will simply mention two rather compelling arguments. First, the *Bhāgavata* is largely innocent of any self-conscious attempt to establish itself as a Mahā-Purāṇa and is unaware even of the existence of the *Devī-Bhāgavata*, while the latter text devotes considerable effort to affirming its own claim to be among the canonical eighteen and explicitly states that the *Bhāgavata* belongs to the lesser class of minor or Upa-Purāṇas.[7] Indeed, the *Devī-Bhāgavata* asserts that it is the fifth Purāṇa[8] and refers to itself as the *Śrīmad* (famous or glorious) *Bhāgavatam*, an old, popular appellation for the Vaiṣṇava *Bhāgavata*.[9] Second, the *Devī-Bhāgavata* models the account of its own origin and transmission upon the *Bhāgavata*'s, and in various other ways has apparently fitted itself out to meet the traditional descriptions of the earlier work.[10]

The question of relative age is of some importance to us, for text-critics often cite it as a significant factor in determining the canonicity of a text. That is, the earlier a Purāṇic text, the greater its claim to being a Mahā-Purāṇa. There are serious problems in such a view, however, both historically and theologically. The extreme fluidity of the Purāṇic corpus means that the very earliest texts often contain sizable interpolations from a much later date, and fairly recent works may contain ancient materials. Also, some of the older Purāṇas have been largely or wholly replaced by later compositions that retain the original title. This may well be the case with the *Bhāgavata*, for as Hazra points out, the extant text of this title seems to have replaced an earlier prototype.[11] Accordingly, with regards to the two *Bhāgavata*s, the greater age of the Vaiṣṇava text does not mean that it is the "real *Bhāgavata*"[12] or genuine Mahā-Purāṇa, if this implies that the *Devī-Bhāgavata* is false, spurious, and a corruption or perversion of the earlier text. If the *Devī-Bhāgavata* is not genuine because it is not the original, then probably the *Bhāgavata* is not genuine either, for the same reason.

The discussion of age so far has been from the viewpoint of the academic, not religious, community. For the Paurāṇikas and their audiences, these historical considerations may be largely irrelevant. Both *Bhāgavata*s claim primordial origins, as we have seen, and both accept that they have been edited, expanded, and contracted by human hands (as well as divine). Human alteration of Purāṇic texts is an acceptable practice, provided that the humans involved are well versed in Vedic truth. To be sure, the Purāṇic text histories would differ from an academic history of the Purāṇas, but there is not necessarily a conflict in general principles. In any case, the Paurāṇikas would insist that the date of expansion or final editing of a text is far less important than the significance of the ancient events recorded in each.

If the early or original historical character of a text is not absolutely determinative for its canonical status from an academic viewpoint, and is somewhat irrelevant from the religious viewpoint, then what does constitute a genuine Mahā-Purāṇa? Text-critical historians have provided some further guidelines, in addition to age: (1) relative freedom from major alterations or destructive recasts; (2) nature of the contents, that is, the topics included, or not included; (3) traditional acceptance and respect; (4) general significance. The last two are of special importance, as they may help to bridge the gap between the academic and religious views of canonicity. Nevertheless, all four guidelines need interpretation and refinement.

One difficulty regarding freedom from major alterations is that a fairly early text may make significant changes in telling an older story, while a much later text may go back to the more original version. One example, of some interest for our present concerns, relates to the circumstances in which the two *Bhāgavatas* are recited, and specifically the events surrounding the death of King Parīkṣit.

According to the *Bhāgavata*,[13] when Parīkṣit receives word that he has been cursed to die by snakebite in a week's time, he immediately is penitent for his misdeeds, renounces wordly interests, and goes to the banks of the Ganges. There he listens to Śuka recite the whole of the *Bhāgavata* before he dies. This story is derived from the *Mahābhārata*,[14] but there, when Parīkṣit learns of the curse, he does not contemplate renunciation but rather makes every effort to save his own skin, taking refuge in an isolation chamber he has built high off the ground where even the wind, let alone a snake, cannot enter. Needless to say, through the magical powers of the snake Takṣaka, the curse is fulfilled, and the king ascends to heaven. Parīkṣit's son, Janamejaya, seeking revenge, performs a great snake-sacrifice. At the end of the sacrifice, prematurely closed, Janamejaya listens to the *Mahābhārata* recited by Vaiśampāyana.

The *Devī-Bhāgavata*[15] follows the *Mahābhārata* in describing Parīkṣit's attempt to avoid his own death. But the *Devī-Bhāgavata* then adds a few details of its own: Janamejaya is unconsoled by the interrupted snake-sacrifice, and he is still depressed even after hearing the *Mahābhārata* from Vaiśampāyana, for his father dwells in hell (not heaven!). Accordingly, Vyāsa recites the *Devī-Bhāgavata* to Janamejaya and advises him to perform Devī-Yajña (worship of the Goddess) after which Parīkṣit will attain to the highest heaven of Maṇi-Dvīpa (the Devī's abode).[16]

Granted that both *Bhāgavatas* have modified the *Mahābhārata*'s story of Parīkṣit's death, it can be easily argued that the *Bhāgavata*'s alterations are far more extensive and irreconcilable. Indeed, the *Devī-Bhāgavata* makes relatively few changes, avoiding as far as possible direct contradictions with the *Mahābhārata* (except in Parīkṣit's immediate after-death fate), simply supplementing the earlier account. It seems likely, in fact, that the *Devī-Bhāgavata* was fully aware of the *Bhāgavata*'s "tampering" and quite purposely went back to the more ancient standard to bolster its own authority. Which *Bhāgavata*, then, is more genuine?

Regarding the second guideline, the contents of an authentic Mahā-Purāṇa, there is an old definition of a Purāṇa as consisting of five topics or characteristics, the famous *pañca-lakṣaṇas*: creation, re-creation, genealogies, Manu-cycles, and dynastic histories.[17] In reality, the extant Purāṇas conform rather loosely or not at all to this definition. Some scholars have argued that the closer a Purāṇa adheres to the definition, the more likely it is to be old, and thus more likely to be a Mahā-Purāṇa. Such reasoning, of course, is simply a variation on the age argument.

I do not see the *pañca-lakṣaṇas* as offering much help in the canonical controversy, whether they are taken in an inclusive or exclusive sense.[18] That is, many late Purāṇas, including the *Devī-Bhāgavata*, deal with all the five topics, along with much other material on rituals, fruits of karma, and so forth; if taken in an exclusive sense, then many earlier Purāṇas would have to be deleted from the canonical eighteen, including the *Bhāgavata*, as they, too, exceed the five topics. Accordingly, I disagree with Hazra's contention that the "contents of the *Bhāgavata* are more befitting a principal Purāṇa than those of the *Devī-Bhāgavata*."[19] Moreover, the *Bhāgavata* itself is audacious enough to expand the old definition to include ten topics,[20] and even the original five can be construed in rather broad terms to cover many subjects beyond what a narrow and strict interpretation might allow.[21]

The bulk of the materials in the *Devī-Bhāgavata*, in any case, is similar to that in other Purāṇas generally accorded the status of Great. Lalye concludes that the *Devī-Bhāgavata* "abides by almost all the characteristics [*lakṣaṇas*], which are mentioned in various Purāṇas. Therefore, its claim to the title of Mahāpurāṇa, stands incontrovertible."[22] Lalye does not reject the *Bhāgavata*, but rather accepts both *Bhāgavatas* as Mahā-Purāṇas, making the *Devī-Bhāgavata* the nineteenth.[23] While I am not so bold as to expand the canon, I concur with Lalye that it is difficult to see a distinction in subject matter between the *Devī-Bhāgavata* and many of the commonly accepted Mahā-Purāṇas.

Turning to the third factor, traditional acceptance and respect, we can easily see how older Purāṇic texts are more likely to gain authoritative status than recent works. At the same time, the most popular and reverenced of all the Purāṇas is the *Bhāgavata*, which is far from being the earliest. Moreover, many of the most ancient have fallen into relative obscurity, even oblivion. Thus, the *Devī-Bhāgavata* is more popular, especially among the large number of Śāktas, than, say, the *Brahmavaivarta*, even among its own Kṛṣṇaite sectaries.[24] One may point out that the extant *Brahmavaivarta* is not the original Mahā-Purāṇa of that name, but that only further indicates the lack of "respect" which could allow such a fate to befall the prototype.

The fourth guideline, general significance, is usually meant to convey the historical importance and influence of a Purāṇa. It correlates closely with the previous factor and shares many of the same problems. However, general significance at times seems also to imply something about the worthiness or greatness of the philosophical/religious ideas themselves contained within the texts. Accordingly, we may regard this last aspect as a fifth guideline: theological and philosophical insightfulness. This fifth factor, for the Paurāṇikas themselves as well as for their audience, is the most crucial of all.

As indicated earlier, I would not wish to judge the ultimate validity, truth or falsity, of theological perceptions. At the same time, I am willing, with a critical yet empathetic approach, to see whether the various insights constitute a coherent, persuasive, even compelling, view of reality and humankind's place in it. One must further recognize that theological perceptivity is twofold, involving not only keenness of insight into the ultimate, but also understanding as to how such insight can be communicated to others, in diverse times and places. The Purāṇic corpus itself is a constantly ongoing attempt to interpret ancient yet eternal truths in ways accessible and comprehensible to changing generations. Perhaps what we need to acknowledge, then, is that the idea of a Mahā-Purāṇa, including the notion of the canon of eighteen, is a dynamic, not a static concept.

Paul Ricoeur has written, with reference to Christianity, "Preaching is the permanent reinterpretation of the text [the Bible] which is regarded as grounding the community."[25] In the Hindu tradition there is little or no preaching as such, but the Purāṇas have played an analogous role, ever reinterpreting the Vedic text that is the grounding of the Hindu community. Ricoeur also shies away from the notion of revelation as something static or "frozen in any ultimate or immutable text."[26] He argues, rather, that "the process of revelation is a permanent process of opening something that is closed, or making manifest something which was hidden. Revelation is a historical process, but the notion of sacred text is something antihistorical."[27] Ricoeur's comments about the notion of sacred text apply very well to the idea of sacred canon as well, at least in the Purāṇic instance, for the Purāṇic canon of eighteen is perhaps best seen as a *revealing process*, rather than as a fixed, unchanging ideal.

At this point we, as well as the tradition, may do well to remember that *purāṇa* originally meant not a book, but rather something ancient, specifically, the ancient events of history and prehistory[28] that have the power of disclosing the nature of the human predicament vis-à-vis divine reality. A Mahā-Purāṇa, then, might best be regarded not so much as a "great ancient text" as some text-critics would have it, but more as a record and interpretation of "great ancient events." Is it entirely unreasonable, in this light, to view the canon of eighteen as an ever-changing set of texts that contain the most perceptive interpretations and insights for any given age within a particular religious community? In any case, does not this viewpoint, implicitly at least, underlie the attitude of the composer of the *Devī-Bhāgavata*, who so boldly and earnestly pressed forward the claim of his Purāṇa to be "the fifth"?

It thus may be that the most relevant question to ask, with regards to the status of a Purāṇic text, is *to whom* has it appeared as a Mahā-Purāṇa? The *Bhāgavata* clearly has functioned as a Mahā-Purāṇa within the Vaiṣṇava community for a millennium. And given the Vaiṣṇava orientation of the majority of the traditionally accepted Mahā-Purāṇas, it may be that the very concept of a canon of eighteen came originally from Vaiṣṇava Paurāṇikas.[29] But the Vaiṣṇavas had no exclusive authority for determining what was included in the canon for other groups. While the Śāktas share a general Purāṇic heritage with the Vaiṣṇavas (and Śaivas), they have seen fit to define the exact character of that heritage in their own way. In view of the fluid, responsive nature of the Purāṇic tradition, such a redefinition does not seem, to this author, as inappropriate or inept.

If we are to accept both *Bhāgavatas* as Mahā-Purāṇas, thereby granting each a certain respect and authoritativeness, what are we to make of the historical contradictions between them? (I shall deal with the theological contradictions later.) We must accept that Purāṇic compilers are rather free in their "reconstruction of history." But part of the Purāṇic spirit is the constant attempt to update tradition and specifically to reveal more penetratingly truths that transcend mundane history. Actual concrete history, for the Purāṇic compilers, is not the primary locus of revelation as it has been for Western religions. This does not mean Purāṇic compilers did not take history as a whole seriously, for they show a tremendous respect for tradition, avoiding as far as possible direct contradiction in favor of reinterpretation of the "historical record." But in accord with Hindu tradition, history is seen as a playground, not a battlefield as often is the case in the West. More specifically, history is envisioned as the carrousel in the playground, whirling round and round. The actual details of any one cycle are regarded as less significant than the principles that govern the cycles as a whole. Accordingly, the outside hearer or reader needs to develop a playful, even humorous attitude toward the Purāṇic use of history (and prehistory), in order to appreciate the compilers' delight in "creative history" for the sake of salvific truth.

In harmony with the Purāṇic spirit, then, we may note without condemnation the *Bhāgavata*'s alteration of the story of King Parīkṣit's death and may genuinly admire its theological perceptiveness in advancing the ideal of humility, nonattachment, and acceptance in the face of death. Similarly, the *Devī-Bhāgavata* can be esteemed for building on the theological insights of the *Bhāgavata*, delving (from its own point of view) further into the mysterious nature of creation and specifically examining the feminine dimensions involved that are largely overlooked by the *Bhāgavata*, even if the *Devī-Bhāgavata* had to play around a bit with the received tradition.

We have already touched upon the "mundane" history of the transmission of the two *Bhāgavatas* as given by the texts themselves. What I wish to do now, however, is to concentrate on their divine or precreation histories, which brings us back to the quotations at the beginning of this chapter. In looking at these precreation histories, I wish not only to compare the basic outlines of the text-transmissions, but also to pay attention to some of the philosophical and theological ideas that are intertwined with the mythological accounts, to begin to see what different insights may be offered by each Purāṇa.

The Divine or Precreation History of the Two *Bhāgavatas*

The creator god Brahmā was floating alone on the primal waters of the dissolution, abiding on his lotus seat sprung from Viṣṇu's navel. Thus begins the *Bhāgavata*'s account of its own transcendent origin.[30] Brahmā, the story continues, was anxious to commence the work of creation but could not figure out how to proceed. A voice sounded out over the waters: "*tapa, tapa*" (practice creative asceticism). Brahmā, though failing to see the speaker, found the command so compelling that he at once began the austerities. After a thousand divine years, the Lord Viṣṇu became pleased with Brahmā's performance and revealed himself, surrounded by his attendants and endowed with his twenty-five *śakti*s or creative potencies, to the anxious but obedient creator. Brahmā, filled with humility and devotion, and with tears in his eyes, bowed down to the supreme Lord, who in a comforting, friendly gesture, touched the creator with his hand. Viṣṇu then explained that it was he himself who had commanded the austerities in order to help Brahmā carry out the work of creation.

Brahmā, suddenly afraid of becoming puffed up with the pride of achievement when he should complete his creative tasks, implored Viṣṇu to save him from such delusion. Appealing to Viṣṇu as a close friend, he enquired after that ego-destroying knowledge of the higher and lower forms of Viṣṇu, who himself is formless. Brahmā also sought to understand how Viṣṇu, through his *māyā*, playfully spins out the universe from himself and eventually reabsorbs it, like a spider letting out and taking back its own web. The supreme Lord, showing his favor, then relieved Brahmā's fears, disclosing the "Four-Verse *Bhāgavata*," summarized earlier. By constantly meditating on this seed *Bhāgavata*, Brahmā would never succumb to delusion. Viṣṇu disappeared, and Brahmā proceeded to create the universe.

The *Devī-Bhāgavata*'s account of its own transcendent origin also opens with a scene on the primordial ocean.[31] On the waters, we are told, there was standing a fig tree, on a leaf of which lay Viṣṇu in the form of an infant. He was pondering how he came into existence and who made him into a little babe, when suddenly he heard a voice declaring, "All this universe indeed is just I myself; there is nothing else eternal."[32] This was, in fact, the half verse revelation of the *Devī-Bhāgavata*, spoken by the Devī, but Viṣṇu failed to recognize the voice. Not being able even to determine whether the speaker was male, female, or neuter, Viṣṇu finally took up repeating the half verse in his heart. The Devī, pleased with his devotion, appeared before him in the auspicious form of Mahā-Lakṣmī (his own wife!), with all her attendant *śakti*s. Not recognizing Mahā-Lakṣmī, Viṣṇu wondered if she might be Māyā, or perhaps his own mother. While he was trying to make up his mind what to do or say, Mahā-Lakṣmī addressed the bewildered Lord. She asked him (somewhat disingenuously) why he was so disconcerted, and then explained to him that, through the enchantng power of Mahā-Śakti, he had forgotten who she (his own wife) was, even though he had come into existence time and again in each cosmic cycle, along with her. She herself, Mahā-Lakṣmī declared, is simply the *sāttvikī* (good, nurturing) *śakti* of the supreme, *nirguṇā* (unqualified) Śakti. Viṣṇu's spouse further described how Brahmā would soon arise from his navel-lotus, and by practicing austerities, Brahmā would obtain the necessary *śakti* to create the world. Mahā-Lakṣmī concluded by assuring Viṣṇu that she would reside always on his breast. Somewhat consoled, Viṣṇu still remained puzzled about the identity of the speaker of the half verse. Mahā-Lakṣmī then disclosed to her rather slow-witted husband that the meritorious (*Devī-*)*Bhāgavata*, in the form of that half verse, had been revealed to him by *nirguṇā* Devī out of her great compassion for him. Viṣṇu at once began meditating constantly on that half-verse mantra.

The *Devī-Bhāgavata*'s account of its own precreation history continues with the transmission of the seed text from Viṣṇu to Brahmā, at this point loosely paralleling the *Bhāgavata*'s primordial history. The *Devī-Bhāgavata* jumps ahead a little in time, to when Brahmā was born from Viṣṇu's navel-lotus. Brahmā, fearful of the two demons Madhu and Kaiṭabha, took refuge with Viṣṇu, who after slaying the demons began *japa* (repeated chanting) of the half verse.[33] Brahmā was puzzled as to whom Viṣṇu could be adoring with *japa* and asked him if there were anyone higher than he.[34] Viṣṇu, considerably wiser now, undoubtedly due to his repetition of the Devī's mantra, enlightened Brahmā with the profound insight that all power (*śakti*) in the universe, including himself, is simply the power of the supreme Śakti, also known as Bhagavatī. It is she who is the cause of liberating knowledge as well as bondage to *saṃsāra* (the world cycle). All beings are born from that Śakti, who is consciousness (*cit*) itself. Viṣṇu finally informed Brahmā that the half-verse mantra he was reciting had originally been proclaimed by the supreme Śakti and was the seed of the (*Devī-*)*Bhāgavata*. Thus, by hearing Viṣṇu's *japa*, Brahmā had received the divinely uttered, quintessential Purāṇa.

What are we to make of these two seemingly contradictory accounts? On further analysis of the mythological events themselves, one finds that in general the *Devī-Bhāgavata* has carefully avoided any absolute contradiction with the *Bhāgavata*. (This is not true of the post-creation history, where the *Devī-Bhāgavata* appeals as it were to a more ancient authority, the *Mahābhārata*.) One must remember that the *Devī-Bhāgavata*, after all, recognizes the existence of two *Bhāgavatas*, and thus the origins and transmissions of each would naturally be different. Indeed, the *Devī-Bhāgavata* leaves room for the *Bhāgavata*, most clearly in a secondary account of the precreation history.[35] Brahmā himself tells us how, after his birth from the lotus, he sought his origins, diving under the primal waters and searching for the ground in which the lotus grew. Unable to discover it even after a thousand years, he heard a disembodied voice commanding him to perform ascesis (*tapas tapa*), which he did for another thousand years on his lotus seat. Next, he heard the command to create (*sṛja*), but was confused as to how to proceed. Up to this point, the *Devī-Bhāgavata* has closely followed the *Bhāgavata*, with only minor alterations. To be sure, the *Devī-Bhāgavata* does not explicitly mention Viṣṇu's revelation of the "Four-Verse *Bhāgavata*," and in fact seems intentionally to ignore it, but anyone familiar with the *Bhāgavata* account would recognize that it fits in somewhere at this juncture.

When we turn from the mythological events surrounding the original disclosures of the *Bhāgavatas* to the actual contents of those revelations, the differences are less easily resolved. It is here that the two Purāṇas seem to contradict each other most critically, each claiming Viṣṇu or Devī respectively to be the ground of all being. Yet the *Devī-Bhāgavata* has a well-worked-out answer to account for such a contradiction: Viṣṇu's proclamation of supremacy is based on a self-delusion due to the *māyā* (deluding power) of the supreme Devī. At times, this *māyā* causes him to forget that he is a god, as during his various human and animal incarnations on earth.[36] At other times, *māyā* causes him to forget the true source of his power, misleading him into thinking he is the supreme.

The idea of Viṣṇu's forgetfulness appears throughout the *Devī-Bhāgavata*. We have already seen that he was unable to recognize his own wife while he rested as an infant on a fig leaf over the primal waters, having forgotten how this identical scene had occurred many times in the past. Similarly, the *Devī-Bhāgavata* records a somewhat later incident, referring back to those same waters.[37] Viṣṇu, along with the other members of the all-male trinity or cosmic triumvirate, Brahmā and Śiva, had gone to visit the Devī in her supreme abode. At first they did not know who the brilliant lady they encountered there was, but then Viṣṇu remembered: when he had been resting on his fig leaf on the primal ocean, playing like an ordinary babe, licking his big toe, it was she, this same lady, who had sung songs to him and rocked him gently, and who was the mother of all of them.

Viṣṇu's resting on the fig leaf in the form of an infant deserves further comment, for it adroitly introduces the Devī in her most important role—as mother. As is typical of the *Devī-Bhāgavata*, it did not come up with the Viṣṇu-as-infant motif on its own but has borrowed it, in this case from the *Bhāgavata* itself, from the story of the sage

Mārkaṇḍeya.[38] The sage praised the Lord Nārāyaṇa (Viṣṇu) as a friend of the soul (*ātma-bandhu*) and supreme creator who spins out and reabsorbs the universe like a spider. Mārkaṇḍeya, granted a boon by Viṣṇu, requested to see the *māyā* (cosmic illusion) by which the one reality appears as many. Viṣṇu consented, and sometime later while the sage was meditating on the Lord in his hermitage, a terrible wind arose followed by a deluge that swallowed up the whole universe, leaving only Mārkaṇḍeya alive. Drifting alone for what seemed to him millions of years, the sage at last espied a fig tree on a slight elevation in the midst of the ocean. On a leaf of the tree, he saw a babe curled up, sucking on its foot. Mārkaṇḍeya approached and was suddenly swept up like a gnat by the breath of the babe into its body. There in the belly he beheld the whole universe, with all its stars, oceans, gods, and so forth, including even his own hermitage. Soon he was exhaled from the body and again saw a babe, smiling on the fig leaf. As Mārkaṇḍeya attempted to embrace the infant—who was none other than Viṣṇu—the babe, tree, and ocean all disappeared, leaving the sage sitting as he had been back in his hermitage.

Mārkaṇḍeya certainly had an intimate and terrifying experience of *māyā*. But whose *māyā* is it? Who ultimately controls it? Does it belong to the baby, or to the baby's mother? The *Bhāgavata*, naturally, assumes the baby is self-existent, i.e., has no mother, and thus *māyā* is fully Viṣṇu's. The *Bhāgavata* refers to it as Viṣṇu-*māyā*,[39] and calls Viṣṇu himself Māyeśa (Lord of *māyā*).[40] Yet the same text refers to *māyā* as *yoga-māyā* (the mystical power attained through yoga),[41] and thus it would appear to belong to any adept yogi. Indeed, in the concluding part of the story of Mārkaṇḍeya, the god Śiva enters the sage's heart by his own *yoga-māyā*.[42] Is, then, Viṣṇu the ultimate master of *māyā*, or is he, along with other gods, merely able to use on occasion this power which actually stems from a higher source?

Before dealing with this question directly, it is worth noting in the *Bhāgavata* that *yoga-māyā*, though usually appearing as an impersonal power wielded by various gods or yogis, occasionally is personified as a goddess.[43] Further, this goddess is closely identified with the power of sleep (*nidrā*).[44] The association of *yoga-māyā* with *nidrā* is highly significant, for the answer to the question of whether or not Viṣṇu is the ultimate master of *māyā* depends in large part on the precise nature of sleep, specifically, the cosmic sleep of Viṣṇu while he rests on the serpent Śeṣa, floating on the primal waters during the *pralaya* (cosmic dissolution).

In both *Bhāgavatas*, Viṣṇu's cosmic sleep is referred to as *yoga-nidrā*, the "sleep of yoga," an entranced state that is readily connected with the mystical, enchanting power of *yoga-māyā*. The *Bhāgavata* insists that this *yoga-nidrā* of Viṣṇu's is not like ordinary sleep but is a transcendent (*turya*) state of consciousness, also called *samādhi*.[45] The *Devī-Bhāgavata* gives a very different interpretation, which is most clearly seen in the Madhu-Kaiṭabha story mentioned above.

This myth has a complex history and appears in many variations.[46] In its earlier forms Viṣṇu is the hero and protagonist. In one typical version from the *Mahābhārata*,[47] Viṣṇu lies on the primal waters in his *samādhic* or yogic "sleep" during the period of dissolution. Prior to his awaking, Brahmā arises from his navel-lotus, shortly followed by the appearance of the two demons Madhu and Kaiṭabha, who steal the Vedas from Brahmā. The latter, terrified, takes refuge with Viṣṇu, who when aroused from his slumber, restores the Vedas and slays the demons.[48]

This basic story, briefly referred to in the *Bhāgavata*,[49] undergoes a remarkable reinterpretation in the *Devī-Māhātmya* of the *Mārkaṇdeya Purāṇa*. By an intriguingly simple reevaluation of Viṣṇu's cosmic sleep, the *Devī-Māhātmya* uses the notion of *yoga-nidrā* to attest not to Viṣṇu's yogic skill in attaining trance, but rather to his succumbence to the stupefying, benumbing power of the supreme Devī in her manifestation as sleep.[50] Brahmā is able to arouse Viṣṇu only after he has praised the Devī beseeching her to withdraw from the sleeping god.

The *Devī-Bhāgavata* follows the *Devī-Māhātmya*, personifying *yoga-nidrā* as a manifestation of the supreme Devī who brings about Viṣṇu's helpless stupor. Thus Brahmā concludes, upon failing to awaken Viṣṇu, "It is not sleep who is under Viṣṇu's control, but Viṣṇu who is under sleep's control . . . . He sleeps helpless, like an ordinary man."[51] The *Bhāgavata*, in already personifying *yoga-māyā/nidrā*, prepared the way for the *Devī-Bhāgavata*, making the latter's interpretation of Viṣṇu's sleep seem like a natural and obvious step.[52]

In accord with my theological neutrality, I do not wish to decide which *Bhāgavata*'s interpretation of *yoga-nidrā* is the correct or superior one (rather both are valid in their own ways). But I do wish to point out some of the new insights made possible by the *Devī-Bhāgavata*'s particular perspective. The interpretation of Viṣṇu's cosmic sleep is integrally involved in the problem of the nature of consciousness in general. An important aspect of this problem, as perceived by the Purāṇic philosophers, is whether consciousness is a purely spiritual entity, or whether it is also closely related to, even identified with, material force. Another way of stating the problem is whether or not matter is entirely void of consciousness. One major point of departure for the Purāṇic thinkers in dealing with these questions was the ancient Sāṃkhya school, according to which spirit (*puruṣa*) alone was conscious, though inactive while matter or nature (*prakṛti*), though active, was insentient and unconscious.

This dualism was taken over by the Purāṇas and adapted to various theistic frameworks from an early period. Such adaptation was facilitated and complicated by non-Sāṃkhyan, Vedic images of *puruṣa*, such as that of the "Puruṣa Sūkta" in the *Ṛg Veda*, where *puruṣa* is the sacrificial cosmic person whose diverse parts constitute the elements of the universe. The Vedic *puruṣa* thus includes both material and spiritual aspects. In the *Bhāgavata*, where several notions of *puruṣa* have become inextricably intertwined and coalesced, we find the relation of Viṣṇu to *puruṣa* variously depicted, according to whether Sāṃkhyan or Vedic imagery prevails.[53] Sometimes Viṣṇu is referred to as the supreme or great Puruṣa (*puruṣottama, mahā-puruṣa*) in apparent contrast to the lesser (Sāṃkhyan) *puruṣa*.[54] At other times, he is identified with *puruṣa* (with or without such modifiers as *ādi* [primal], *purāṇa* [ancient], or *para* [supreme]) in contrast to *prakṛti*.[55]

The matter is further complicated by the frequent Advaitic (non-dualistic) perspective of the *Bhāgavata*, so that occasionally Viṣṇu is said to be beyond *puruṣa* and *prakṛti*[56] or to include both.[57] Nonetheless there is a general feeling that emerges from the text that on the cosmic created level at least, Viṣṇu is to be closely identified with spirit (*puruṣa*, *mahā-puruṣa*, etc.) alone. Though he enters into material creation, and the material world in some sense is none other than he, still he is often regarded as distinct from and above *prakṛti*.[58] The Advaitic impulse of the *Bhāgavata* does lead to a transcendence of the *puruṣa/prakṛti* dualism but only on the ultimate level, and at the expense of *prakṛti*, which becomes largely illusory. Though occasionally called "divine,"[59] *prakṛti* on the wordly level is seen as distinctly inferior, full of faults,[60] and merely the material cause of the universe. In any case, *prakṛti*, like *māyā* and *śakti*, in the *Bhāgavata*, is something Viṣṇu possesses and controls. There thus remains a dualism, somewhat modified but reminiscent of the Sāṃkhya, between the possessor of matter and what is possessed, or between spirit/consciousness on the one hand and material nature on the other.

We find the breakdown of this dualism on the cosmic level beginning with the personification of the notion of *śakti*, feminine in gender, whereby a god's active power (*śakti*) became represented by, or identified with, his spouse. The Śākta school perceived even more in the idea of *śakti*, making the female force dominant over the male counterpart. In the process, a series of feminine concepts, including *māyā* and *prakṛti*, came to be seen as fully conscious, living forces.[61] With *prakṛti* becoming a goddess, or even identified with *the* Goddess, Devī, the old Sāṃkhyan dualism between a conscious spirit-person and an active but insentient material force was basically transcended "from the ground up."

The *Devī-Bhāgavata*, expounding the Śākta perspective, explicitly rejects the Sāṃkhyan view of matter, *prakṛti*. Brahmā, in praising the Devī after failing to rouse Viṣṇu from sleep, declares: "The Sāṃkhya philosophers say that of the two principles, Puruṣa and Prakṛti, it is Prakṛti, the creatrix of the world, that is devoid of consciousness (*caitanya*). But can you (Devī, identified with Prakṛti) really be of such nature, for (if this were so,) how could the abode of the world (Viṣṇu) be made unconscious by you today?"[62]

Though the composer of the *Devī-Bhāgavata* was certainly not "scientific" in his approach to discovering the nature of reality, his preliminary insight into the unitary relation between consciousness and matter on the cosmic level has an interesting parallel to the view of certain modern physicists who have begun to argue "that the explicit inclusion of human consciousness may be an essential aspect of future theories of matter."[63] Given the Hindu cultural situation and its presuppositions about the nature of masculinity and femininity, the *Devī-Bhāgavata* was able to arrive at its insight about consciousness-matter by emphasizing the feminine aspects of reality on the divine level.

The use of feminine and specifically maternal imagery in suggesting the nature of the supreme power in the universe has led to many other insights with far-reaching implications, psychological, sociological, soteriological, as well as ontological. For example, the maternal metaphor for the Goddess emphasizes the intimate relationship between her and her devotees, a bond transcending but not necessarily negating the social and moral structures of *varṇāśrama-dharma* (the order of society based on class and stage of life). Viṣṇu or Kṛṣṇa in the *Bhāgavata*, however, is rarely referred to as father,[64] possibly because the paternal metaphor, in contrast to the maternal, would suggest a greater distance between God and his children. Accordingly, the most intense and intimate relationship with Kṛṣṇa is that of lover and beloved, especially outside the marital tie. Loving Kṛṣṇa often entails forsaking society and its laws. Loving the Devī, as portrayed in the *Devī-Bhāgavata*, does not.

Not surprisingly, then, the model of a devotee frequently set forth by the *Bhāgavata* is the *saṃnyāsin* (renouncer), and the *Bhāgavata* allows a young man to pass directly from the student stage to that of the anchorite.[65] The *Bhāgavata* is wary of the householder stage for fear of attachments to wife and family.[66] The *Devī-Bhāgavata*, however, insists that a man must pass through all four traditional *āśramas* (stages of life) in due order and gives a generally positive assessment of the householder.[67] This more positive assessment is due in part, I suggest, to the *Devī-Bhāgavata*'s greater appreciation of the maternal role not only in the divine but also in the human realm.[68] Both *Bhāgavatas* share the same ultimate goal of transcending the limitations of the finite world, yet often the *Devī-Bhāgavata* author seems a bit more comfortable being in the world, a little more able to appreciate, or to be amused by, the mother's play with her children. And he is able to savor with greater relish the pleasures and enjoyments of our finite existence, as we shall see.[69]

In looking at the two *Bhāgavata*'s precreation histories of themselves, I think a historian of religion can accept both *Bhāgavatas* as containing significant and genuine insights into the nature of reality, though not necessarily total and comprehensive views of truth. In my understanding, there is not a real *Bhāgavata* and a false one, but rather two different perspectives on the great (*mahā*) ancient (*purāṇa*) events of the universe, each developed in response to the perceptions of devotees of different times and cultural settings.

The two perspectives, though different, are complementary in many ways. Indeed, the two Purāṇas share many basic assumptions about the nature of the universe and its relation to ultimate reality. Each sees a fundamental ontological unity between the absolute and the finite, as the beginning quotations attest, and as the spider analogy of the *Bhāgavata* shows, an analogy repeated in the *Devī-Bhāgavata*.[70] Both *Bhāgavatas* also view creation as the sport or play of the supreme, confirming the perfection of reality as it is, without any need to become perfect.[71] The human inability to perceive that perfection is merely part of the illusion that constitutes an essential element of the divine play. A central question posed by these two Purāṇas, then, is who is playing with whom? Is the Devī playing with Viṣṇu as she sings lullabies to him in his fig-leaf cradle, or is Viṣṇu merely playing with his own powers, his own *māyā*? Who can answer this, for as the *Bhāgavata* itself says, even Viṣṇu knows not the extent of his *māyā*![72]

The interrelated themes of play (*līlā*) and *māyā* (illusion, delusion) are central to both *Bhāgavatas* not only in a cosmogonic context, but also in terms of the ongoing activity of the God or Goddess within the created universe. Both texts stress the gracious incarnations or *avatāras* of the supreme in this world to punish the wicked and protect the righteous. Both further insist that ultimately such appearances are not a matter of divine necessity but of self-directed play.

Given the similarity of their incarnational perspectives, it is not surprising that the *Devī-Bhāgavata* wishes to differentiate the Devī's *avatāras* from those of Viṣṇu. In fact, a key strategy in the *Devī-Bhāgavata*'s rejection of Viṣṇu's supremacy is its revisionist interpretation of the *Bhāgavata*'s doctrine of Viṣṇu's incarnations. This reinterpretation is the subject of the next chapter, where the situation becomes more serious as the child's play of Viṣṇu and Devī at creation turns into violent horseplay.

Chapter 2

Horsing Around with Viṣṇu: A Case of Capital Murder

Viṣṇu, as the second member of the Trimūrti or cosmic triumvirate, has long been associated with the special role of maintaining and preserving the universe. In this capacity, he early became intimately connected with a large number of incarnations or *avatāras*, whose proper function was to ensure the ongoing stability of the world, ever faced with the threat of the premature outbreak of moral disorder and general chaos. These *avatāras* included not only several human embodiments but also various animal and semi-human forms such as the fish, tortoise, and man-lion.

One of the part-human, part-animal incarnations, whose early fame had become somewhat eclipsed by the time of the *Devī-Bhāgavata*, is the horse-headed form of Viṣṇu, known variously as Hayagrīva (Horse-necked), Hayaśiras or Hayaśīrṣā (Horse-headed), Hayāsya (Horse-faced), and Nṛturaṅga (Man-horse). It is this equine *avatāra* that the *Devī-Bhāgavata* chose for its primary assault upon Viṣṇu's traditional role as world-protector. The *Devī-Bhāgavata*'s rough treatment of this venerable, if somewhat overlooked, embodiment of the god nicely illustrates the Devī's play—in this case clearly horseplay—with Viṣṇu.

We may wonder why such a relatively minor figure should be the focus for the *Devī-Bhāgavata*'s initial attack upon Viṣṇu's *avatāras*. On the one hand, some of the most ancient and authoritative stories about Viṣṇu's horse-headed form were rich in their dramatic potential for embarrassing the god. These stories, though long neglected, were not quite forgotten within the Vaiṣṇava community. This circumstance, far from impeding the basic strategy of the *Devī-Bhāgavata*, helped the Purāṇa to prepare an ambush, as it were, and to present its reinterpretation as a shocking reminder of the "real truth" behind Viṣṇu's incarnations.

On the other hand, the story of Hayagrīva, like the cosmogonic controversy, is intertwined with the questions of scriptural authoritativeness and which of the two *Bhāgavatas* is *the* Mahā-Purāṇa. An old definition of "the *Bhāgavata*" asserts: "That (Purāṇa) verily they call the *Bhāgavata* wherein occurs the Hayagrīva-Brahmavidyā as well as the slaying of Vṛtra."[1] The *Devī-Bhāgavata* is apparently aware of this definition, for it refers to itself as "this holy Purāṇa called the *Bhāgavata*, replete with many ancient tales including the slaying of Vṛtrāsura, and a treasury of Brahmavidyā."[2] The *Devī-Bhāgavata* has prominently displayed the tale of the demon Vṛtra (the subject of our next chapter) and the account of Hayagrīva with its closely related topic of the Brahmavidyā (knowledge of Brahman).[3] In this manner it seems that the *Devī-Bhāgavata* has tried to mold itself to the traditional definition of "the *Bhāgavata*." By placing the story of Hayagrīva early in the first Skandha or book, the Purāṇa may well be reminding its audience right at the start that it is to be considered the Mahā-Purāṇa.

Whether the old definition applies better to the *Devī-Bhāgavata* or to the *Bhāgavata* has been much debated by scholars and devotees alike. Of all the arguments marshalled by both sides, none is particularly convincing, a conclusion that is almost inevitable if our supposition is correct that the *Devī-Bhāgavata* has fitted itself to the definition.[4] In any case, the horse-headed Viṣṇu appears in both Purāṇas, and to the treatment of this equine *avatāra* in the two texts we now turn.

Viṣṇu-Hayaśiras in the *Bhāgavata Purāṇa*

In the *Bhāgavata* Viṣṇu appears in his horse-headed form[5] in two distinct though interrelated aspects, as promulgator and protector of the Vedas, and as the cosmic sacrifice. The first is briefly alluded to in a short prayer addressed to Hayaśīrṣa, the last verse of which reads: "Reverence to him who, at the end of the age (*yuga*), in the form of a man-horse (*nṛ-turaṅga*), retrieved from Rasātala (the underworld) the Vedas concealed by *tamas* (darkness) and restored them to Brahmā."[6] According to the commentator Śrīdhara, the *tamas* is actually darkness in the form of a *daitya* or demon. But who is this demon, and why is he referred to as *tamas*?

Part of the answer is given near the end of the *Bhāgavata* in a summary description of the various *avatāras* of Viṣṇu, wherein the horse-headed form (Hayāsya) by which he recovered the "Śrutis" (Vedas) is called the slayer of Madhu.[7] Elsewhere, the devotee Akrura mentions two demon victims in his praise of Viṣṇu as Hayaśīrṣā: Madhu and his famous sidekick Kaiṭabha.[8] A fuller explanation is provided by another distinguished *bhakta*, the long-suffering Prahlāda. After recounting the well-known story of the Lord's yogic sleep on the cosmic waters and Brahmā's birth on his navel-lotus, Prahlāda concludes: "[O Viṣṇu, the embodiment of] *sattva* (goodness), your favorite form, while bearing the form of Hayaśiras, you slew the two mighty Veda-enemies Madhu and Kaiṭabha, [the embodiments of] *rajas* (energy) and *tamas*, and restored to him [Brahmā] the Śruti-collections."[9]

These several references clearly are based on the Madhu-Kaiṭabha myth found in the Śānti Parva of the *Mahābhārata* briefly summarized in chapter one above.[10] This account already identifies the demons with the two inferior qualities (*guṇas*) of energy and darkness. When the god Brahmā arose from Viṣṇu's navel-lotus, he was endowed with *sattva*. In the lotus were two drops of water: one was bright, resembling honey (*madhu*), and became Madhu, endowed with *tamas*; the other was hard (*kaṭhina*), and became Kaiṭabha, endowed with *rajas*.

The Śānti version also connects Viṣṇu with the horse-head. The Śānti relates that after the two demons seized the Vedas from Brahmā and dove with them to the bottom of the ocean, Brahmā, deprived of his eyes (the Vedas), implored Hari (Viṣṇu) to awaken from his yogic sleep and restore his sight. Hari arose, agreeing to the creator's request, and assumed a horse-headed form (Hayaśiras). The form is described as a cosmic homologue: its head is the heavens with the stars, its long hair like the sun's rays, its ears the upper and lower worlds, its forehead the earth, its eyes the moon and sun, and so on.[11] The Lord then entered the nether world (*rasā*) and sweetly recited the Vedas, thereby distracting the demons who left the Vedas to search for the source of the chanting. Viṣṇu seized the unguarded Vedas, returned them to Brahmā, and went back to yogic sleep. The demons, not finding the source of the sweet voice and discovering the Vedas gone, came upon the sleeping Viṣṇu, shining with *sattva*. The embodiments of *rajas* and *tamas* then awakened Viṣṇu, challenged him to a fight, and were slain by him in his horse-headed form.

By the time of the *Bhāgavata*, Hayaśiras had become fully assimilated into the Vaiṣṇava *avatāra* doctrine.[12] In the *Bhāgavata* itself he appears not infrequently in lists of incarnation-forms.[13] Yet nowhere in the Purāṇa is his story told at length, and in the first great catalogue of Viṣṇu's descents (listing twenty-two *avatāras*), there is no mention of any horse-headed form.[14] It seems that the equine *avatāra* has been quietly forgotten or removed in this list, due to what appears to be a general process of eclipse of Hayaśiras in the *Bhāgavata*.[15] We may note the juxtaposition of the horse-headed and fish (Matsya) forms in many of the lists,[16] and there appears to be a special relationship between these two incarnations. Indeed the eclipse of Hayaśiras seems to be due in part to his replacement by Matsya, as seen in the extended account of the latter's deeds in the eighth Skandha.

To gain a better perspective on the special features of the *Bhāgavata*'s account, let us refer briefly to the story of the fish *avatāra* as found in the beginning of the *Matsya Purāṇa*. There the narrative is concerned primarily with the rescue of Manu from the flood of dissolution at the end of an eon.[17] One significant detail is the fish's declaration that when the flood is over, he will promote the Vedas.[18] The *Bhāgavata*'s account is basically the same as the *Matsya*'s but adds an interesting introduction and conclusion. In the former, we are told that long ago, at the end of a *kalpa* and the start of the flood of dissolution, Brahmā desired to lie down and went to sleep.[19] From his mouth slipped out the Vedas, which were carried off by a demon named Hayagrīva![20] The Lord Hari (Viṣṇu), knowing the demon's behavior, took on the form of a fish. At this point, the traditional account of Matsya and Manu (here in his former incarnation as King Satyavrata) commences. This standard account ends with reference to Matsya's teaching a Purāṇic Saṃhitā (the *Matsya Purāṇa*) to the king while sporting on the ocean of dissolution.[21] The narrator concludes: "Hari, having slain the *asura* Hayagrīva, restored the Vedas to Brahmā rising up (from sleep) at the end of the *pralaya*."[22] Not only has Matsya replaced Hayaśiras, but the demon Hayagrīva has also replaced Madhu and Kaiṭabha.[23]

What underlying motives were responsible for the double substitution of Matsya for Hayaśiras and Hayagrīva for Madhu-Kaiṭabha in the *Bhāgavata* account? O'Flaherty notes the generally negative symbolism of the mare, with its connotations of eroticism without fertility, in post-Vedic times when "the cult of asceticism reared its ugly head."[24] Further, the connotations of the mare as "dangerous seductress begin to pollute the reputation of the stallion" as well.[25] Such trends led to the growing importance of demonic horse-headed figures, which at least in part was responsible for the "turnabout" in the Śānti myth of Madhu and Kaiṭabha that we find in the *Bhāgavata*. O'Flaherty concludes: "In order to rescue Viṣṇu from his equine role when it becomes a negative one, the Paurāṇika draws upon an already available avatar: the fish who rescues the Vedas from the doomsday flood. . . . So the fish who was the enemy of the doomsday mare now becomes the fish who is the enemy of the demonic underwater horse."[26]

While the *Bhāgavata*'s ascetic world view may have contributed to the decline of Viṣṇu's horse-headed form therein, I think there may well be a more immediate cause. This other possibility is that the changes were made in response to the Madhu-Kaiṭabha myth as told in the *Devī-Māhātmya*. As we have seen, the *Devī-Māhātmya* capitalizes on the notion of Viṣṇu's sleep on the cosmic ocean, reinterpreting his yogic trance as ordinary slumber. And Hayaśiras had been associated with the cosmic sleep since the Śānti version of the Madhu-Kaiṭabha myth (though there is no mention of the equine Viṣṇu in the *Devī-Māhātmya*). If the slumbering Hayaśiras was becoming something of an embarrassment, the figure of Matsya was a ready antidote: the fish, far from going to sleep during the *pralaya*, sports on the great ocean the whole night through, a point emphasized in the *Bhāgavata* story. Indeed, it is suggested that Viṣṇu took the form specifically of a fish because he desired to play in the ocean of dissolution.[27] It is now Brahmā, not Viṣṇu, who falls asleep during the cosmic darkness, referred to significantly as Brahmā's night.[28] The substitution of Matsya for Hayaśiras was clearly aided by the fact that both *avatāras* were connected with promulgating or protecting the Vedas.[29]

In substituting Hayagrīva for the two traditional Veda-thieves, the *Bhāgavata* further distanced Viṣṇu from the *Devī-Māhātmya* account, while still retaining the ancient association of the myth with a horse-headed figure. In addition, we find already in the *Mahābhārata* a curious juxtaposition of Hayagrīva and the other two demons: "When sleeping in the one vast ocean he [*Kṛṣṇa*] slew Madhu and Kaiṭabha, and in another birth slew Hayagrīva."[30] This verse associates sleep with Viṣṇu in his role as the slayer of Madhu-Kaiṭabha, and at the same time suggests another demon victim unconnected with sleep. Hayagrīva's specific deeds are not mentioned in the *Mahābhārata*, but by the time of the *Bhāgavata*, he had become a handy, all-purpose foe of the gods, and especially of Viṣṇu.[31] The *Bhāgavata* certainly had good use for him as a Veda-thief, clearing Viṣṇu of unwanted associations. Nonetheless, if the *Bhāgavata* was trying to avoid the embarrassment to Viṣṇu occasioned by the *Devī-Māhātmya*'s interpretation of his sleep, its attempt was not wholly successful. Viṣṇu's slumber was to cause him much greater discomfiture in the *Devī-Bhāgavata*, especially when conjoined with the second aspect of Hayaśiras appearing in the *Bhāgavata*.

This second facet, concerning the role of Hayaśiras as the cosmic sacrifice, is mentioned in the great *avatāra* catalogue provided by Brahmā in Skandha two. Here the creator god enumerates the various incarnations of Viṣṇu and describes the tenth as follows: "In my sacrifice [to start the work of creation] the Lord appeared in person as Hayaśīrṣa, the

Sacrificial-Man (Yajña-Puruṣa) of golden hue, composed of the Vedas, composed of the sacrifice (*makha-maya*), and composed of all the deities; the beautiful pure words [of the Veda] issued from his nose as he breathed."[32] The full story of Brahmā's sacrifice alluded to in the above quotation is told in the preceding chapter, following a typical description of Viṣṇu's cosmic form as Virāj (the Lord's universal form whose limbs and body parts consist of all the worlds, stars, etc.).[33] Brahmā there relates that when he himself was born on the navel-lotus of the Lord, he found no provisions for sacrifice to carry out creation, except for the limbs of the cosmic Puruṣa (that is, Viṣṇu as Virāj). Gathering from those limbs the necessary requisites, the creator performed a sacrifice in honor of the Puruṣa.

The notion of the Sacrificial-Man, of course, goes back to the famous Hymn to Puruṣa of the *Ṛg Veda*.[34] The identification of Viṣṇu with the sacrifice (*makha*) is almost as ancient, being found already in the *Śatapatha Brāhmaṇa*,[35] in a passage of critical importance to the *Devī-Bhāgavata* which we shall consider in a moment. As for the specific identification of the Yajña-Puruṣa with Hayaśiras in the *Bhāgavata*, we may recall that in the Śānti Parva the equine form of Viṣṇu—assumed in order to slay Madhu and Kaiṭabha—is described as a cosmic homologue. This homologue echoes the venerable theme of the sacrificial horse from whose substance the universe is created.[36] The *Bhāgavata* thus weaves together many ancient Vedic and epic themes of the cosmic Puruṣa, the creative self-immolation, and the *aśvamedha* (horse-sacrifice), with Viṣṇu the interlocking warp.

Like Hayaśiras the Veda-protector/demon-slayer, so too Hayaśiras the sacrificial horse seems to be in eclipse in the *Bhāgavata*.[37] At least part of the reason may well be due to the Purāṇa's somewhat negative attitude towards animal sacrifice.[38] More significantly, perhaps, was a new understanding of the nature of sacrifice itself: no longer primarily a transactional rite for the mutual benefit of gods and human sacrificers, nor a reestablishment of cosmic order, but an act dedicated solely to the glorifying and pleasing of God. The equation of Viṣṇu and the sacrifice retained its vitality in the *Bhāgavata* but primarily as adapted to new forms of worship (*pūjā*, *ārādhana*), forms which shared little with the imagery of the *aśvamedha*, whether literally or symbolically interpreted.[39]

While Hayaśiras in both his aspects may be in decline in the *Bhāgavata*, he had not entirely disappeared. The *Devī-Bhāgavata* composer(s), I suggest, noted the remaining fragments of the Viṣṇu-Hayaśiras myth, recalled their ancient roots, searched out other closely associated motifs, and then took great delight in reinterpreting the various interrelated themes in an attempt to show the true meaning of these ancient myths and the final superiority of the Goddess.

Viṣṇu-Hayagrīva in the *Devī-Bhāgavata*

The story of Viṣṇu-Hayaśiras, or Hayagrīva as he is known in the *Devī-Bhāgavata*, is the first major mythological narrative about the gods in the Purāṇa, being inserted into the story of Vyāsa and Śuka in the fifth chapter of the first book or Skandha. This strategic location highlights a number of important themes introduced by the story, which are further developed throughout the rest of the Purāṇa. Sūta, the main narrator, having mentioned Viṣṇu's equine form at the end of the preceding chapter, is queried further about this puzzling subject by the Naimiṣa sages. Sūta then tells the following tale.

Once Viṣṇu, after engaging in a ten-thousand-year-long battle, had grown weary and desired to rest. He assumed the lotus-posture in a level, auspicious place in order to meditate while recovering his strength. Given his extreme state of exhaustion, he propped himself up with his bow, his neck lying against the still strung weapon. Due to his fatigue and the influence of fate, as well as to his own nature being addicted to excessive slumbering (*atinidritaḥ*), Viṣṇu fell into a deep sleep. Meanwhile all the other gods, including Brahmā and Śiva, were preparing for a sacrifice and went to Vaikuṇṭha to see Viṣṇu for ensuring success in their undertaking, as he is the Lord of Sacrifices (*makhānām adhipam*). Not finding him there, they discovered his whereabouts through meditation. Going to Viṣṇu, they found him completely under the control of Yoganidrā, unconscious (*vicetanam*) and paralyzed in sleep (*nidrā-supta*).

The gods were worried: Viṣṇu had to be awakened for the success of the sacrifice, but it is a serious offense to disturb someone's sleep. Brahmā thus created an ant (*vaṃrī*) and ordered it to gnaw through the tip of the bow resting on the ground, which would cause the bow to spring open. Viṣṇu would thereby be wakened and the gods would be absolved of all blame. The *vaṃrī* objected, however, given the sinful nature of the deed. Yet the ant was willing to incur the sin if he could reap some personal benefit from the act. Brahmā promised him a share in the sacrifice (*makha*), specifically whatever falls to the side during the oblation. The ant agreed and at once chewed through the bow tip. The upper arm of the bow rose up with a resounding roar, frightening the gods and causing the world to tremble. A terrifying darkness descended upon the world as the sun disappeared. Also gone was Viṣṇu's head, with its earrings and crown.

When the awful darkness subsided, Brahmā and Śiva made out the disfigured body of Viṣṇu. Seeing the beheaded trunk (*kabandha*), the gods were astonished, wondering: "By what god's illusion has your (Viṣṇu's) head been carried off, for you are ever uncleavable and indivisible. . . . It could not be the Sāttvikī Māyā [Viṣṇu's own deluding power], nor the Rājasī Māyā [of Brahmā], nor the Tāmasī Māyā [of Śiva], by which (or whom) your head was cut off, [for you are] the Lord of Māyā (Māyeśa)."[40] The *devas* were also aggrieved, especially as they realized that it was not the demons, the perennial foes of Viṣṇu, but they themselves, the gods, who were responsible for this beheading of the Lord of Sacrifices, a clear case of capital murder.

A discussion ensued on what could be done in their predicament, the conversation quickly evolving into a debate over the relative strength of fate versus human effort. Brahmā, at first seeming to side with the fatalists, argued that every embodied being must experience pain and pleasure, citing several examples of bodily mishaps that had involved even the gods themselves: his own head, through the force of time, was once cut off by Śiva; Śiva's penis fell off through a curse; and Indra's body had had a thousand vulvas imprinted on it. Similarly, now Viṣṇu's head had fallen into the Salt Ocean. Brahmā next, however, offered a suggestion as to how fate might be overcome: through supplication of the eternal Mahā-Māyā (the Great Illusion), the Devī herself, whom Brahmā refers to as Brahmavidyā. He then petitioned the Vedas to sing hymns of praise to Brahmavidyā to secure her favor.

The Vedas acclaimed the Devī as supreme and proceeded to raise a series of questions as to why she had allowed Viṣṇu's head to be cut off. Perhaps she had wished to ascertain the power (*śakti*) of the Madhu-slayer, or maybe it was due to some sin of Hari, or because she was angry with the gods, or with Viṣṇu's wife, Mahā-Lakṣmī, or she wished to please the demons. Or possibly she was just curious to see how Viṣṇu looked without a head. The Vedas concluded by asking the Devī to save the gods and restore Viṣṇu's life. The Goddess then spoke to them from the sky in a disembodied voice (*vāṇī . . . ākāśasthā 'śarīriṇī*), explaining the reasons for Viṣṇu's decapitation and how to resuscitate him.

Before dealing with the Devī's response, let us interrupt the narrative to consider a number of points. The *Devī-Bhāgavata*'s account of Viṣṇu's beheading is based upon a story from the *Śatapatha Brāhmaṇa*, wherein Viṣṇu is identified with the *makha* or sacrifice.[41] The myth explains the origin of an ancient ceremony, the Pravargya.[42] The gods Agni, Indra, Soma, Makha (whose name is also that of the sacrifice), Viṣṇu, and the rest of the gods except the Aśvins once performed a sacrifice to attain excellence and glory. The gods declared, "whoever of us . . . shall first encompass the end of the sacrifice, he shall be the most excellent of us, and shall then be in common to us all."[43] Viṣṇu was the first to attain it and thus became the most excellent of the gods. But Viṣṇu, who is the sacrifice and also the sun, was unable to control his love of glory, which he was unwilling to share. "Taking his bow, . . . he stepped forth. He stood, resting his head on the end of the bow. Not daring to attack him,[44] the gods sat themselves down all around him. Then the ants (*vaṃrī*) said . . . 'what would ye give to him who should gnaw the bowstring?'" The gods offered food and water, and so the ants ate through the bowstring. "When it was cut, the ends of the bow, springing asunder, cut off Viṣṇu's head. It fell with the sound 'gh*rin*'; and on falling it became yonder sun." From the sound 'gh*rin*' the *gharma*[45] took its name. Since the body "was stretched out (pra-v*rig*), therefrom the Pravargya (took its name)." The gods, dividing among themselves the decapitated *makha* identified with Viṣṇu, continued toiling with that headless sacrifice.[46]

The *Devī-Bhāgavata*'s assimilation of the *Śatapatha Brāhmaṇa* myth has clearly made a number of modifications.[47] The most obvious change is the motive behind telling the story at all. The *Devī-Bhāgavata* is not interested in explaining the origin or details of an ancient Vedic rite, but rather in embarrassing Viṣṇu.[48] This is seen at once in the respective treatments of Viṣṇu's corpse. Whereas the *Śatapatha* uses the stretched-out body to explain the name Pravargya, the *Devī-Bhāgavata* stresses the disfigurement of the cadaver, describing it as inauspicious or disgusting (*vilakṣaṇa*).[49] The reference to the headless body as *kabandha*[50] evokes the *Devī-Māhātmya*'s images of the numerous *kabandhas* of the various demons who suffer decapitation at the hands of the Devī.[51] But whereas the *kabandhas* in the *Devī-Māhātmya* retain life, engaging in further battle, Viṣṇu's *kabandha* is portrayed as a lifeless corpse.

Of interest here is a reference to *kabandha* in the *Bhāgavata*. In the story of Dakṣa's sacrifice,[52] after most of the ruined *yajña* had been restored by Śiva, the assembled Brahmans worshipped Viṣṇu for the successful continuation of the rites. Hari then appeared in their midst, brilliant with a crown shining like the sun and adorned with earrings, and was praised by the several personages gathered there. Dakṣa's wife in her eulogy declared, "O Supreme Head, without you the sacrifice (*makha*), (even though) having all its (other) parts, does not look beautiful, like a man (*puruṣa*) that is headless, a mere *kabandha*."[53] The wife's praise clearly resonates with the themes of the ancient *Śatapatha* myth, and in turn is reechoed in the *Devī-Bhāgavata*, admittedly with new modulations.[54]

Another modification of the *Śatapatha* myth in the *Devī-Bhāgavata* concerns the sacrificial context. In the *Śatapatha* the gods, including Viṣṇu, all strive to "first compass the end of the sacrifice." In the *Devī-Bhāgavata*, Viṣṇu does not participate in the contest because—and now is introduced a favorite leitmotif—he is under the control of the goddess Yoganidrā and fast asleep. Here, in fact, is the first appearance of this theme in the Purāṇa, serving as an introduction to the story of Yoganidrā in the slaying of Madhu and Kaiṭabha, narrated in the following four chapters. In the present story, we find a further indication that Viṣṇu's slumber is not a *samādhic* trance (*yoga-nidrā* as yogic "sleep"): after assuming the lotus-posture, he is unable to meditate because he is exhausted and thus cannot stay awake.

The *Devī-Bhāgavata* further modifies the old *Śatapatha* myth by introducing the concept of *māyā*, which as we have indicated plays an important role in both *Bhāgavatas*. In the *Bhāgavata*, *māyā*, whether as impersonal magical power or as personified goddess, is strictly under the control of Viṣṇu, and he is frequently referred to as Māyeśa, Master of Māyā.[55] In the *Devī-Bhāgavata* story, the gods think the decapitation must be an illusion and wonder whose *māyā* was responsible for the dreadful occurrence, all the more puzzling since Viṣṇu himself is Māyeśa. The commentator, Nīlakaṇṭha adds an interesting note here: "[the gods believe that] Māyā never deludes the Master of Māyā [Viṣṇu], only someone else. This view, even today, is held by those who recognize the 'Māyā-Mastery' of Viṣṇu but who fail to recognize the power of Bhagavatī, the Mistress of all. [The beheading] was due to the absence of Māyā-mastery on Viṣṇu's part, on account of the Māyā-mastery belonging just to Devī."[56] The *Devī-Bhāgavata*'s use of the epithet Māyeśa, then, is clearly ironic: he who is called "Māyā-Master" is really he whose Master is Māyā.

The discussion of Māyā in the *Devī-Bhāgavata* serves to introduce the Goddess herself, who is ultimately responsible for allowing the decapitation to happen. Of equal importance, it is she who knows how to restore Viṣṇu's head, which circumstance leads us back once again to the *Śatapatha Brāhmaṇa*. In the sequel to the beheading of the sacrifice, we discover that while the gods were toiling fruitlessly with the mutilated *makha*, there was someone who knew how to restore its head, the sage Dadhyañc. But Dadhyañc was threatened by Indra with decapitation himself should he reveal the knowledge to anyone. The Aśvins (who had been excluded from the earlier sacrifice) approached Dadhyañc, requesting from him the forbidden secret. The sage then explained why he was afraid to divulge the hidden knowledge, but the Aśvins suggested an ingenious if somewhat sanguinary solution to his predicament: they would cut off his head, storing it safely, and replace it with a horse's head. With this equine head, the sage could teach them the restorative secret. Then, when Indra severed this head, they could replace the original. Dadhyañc agreed, and the plan was executed without a hitch.

The secret knowledge revealed to the Aśvins by the horse-headed sage is referred to as Madhuvidyā, the "sweet wisdom" or "honey doctrine." Eventually, the esoteric teachings of Dadhyañc came to be widely known as Brahmavidyā, the mystical knowledge of the supreme Brahman.[57] It seems then no mere coincidence that Brahmā in the *Devī-Bhāgavata*, in petitioning the Vedas to eulogize Devī, refers to the Goddess by this very name.

The Devī replaces Dadhyañc as discloser of the secret Madhuvidyā or Brahmavidyā. At the same time, she is completely disassociated from his equine form: she presents herself to the distressed gods as a disembodied voice. This incorporeal manifestation safely distances the Goddess from the kind of physical mishap that befell the horse-headed Dadhyañc. It also evokes a motif further strengthening her identification with Brahmavidyā and ultimately with the supreme Brahman of the Upaniṣads. In the famous *Kena Upaniṣad* story of the humbling of Agni, Vāyu, and Indra, the goddess Umā Haimavatī appears in the sky (*ākāśe*) as a mediator between the supreme and the gods and as revealer of Brahman.[58] Śaṃkara, in his commentary on the *Kena*, argues that the above story is meant to eulogize Brahmavidyā, by which Indra, Agni, and other gods attained preeminence, and he specifically equates Umā with Vidyā (i.e., Brahmavidyā). Similarly, Sāyaṇa, the fourteenth-century Vedic commentator, identifies her with Brahmavidyā.[59]

The *Kena Upaniṣad* story is given in typically elaborated form in the twelfth Skandha of the *Devī-Bhāgavata*.[60] There the Devī first appears to Indra as a celestial voice (*vyoma-vāṇī*) and later, after appropriate ascesis on the part of Indra, as a great mass of light. Within that light the Devī manifests herself as the beautiful Umā Haimavatī. Going beyond the Upaniṣad, the *Devī-Bhāgavata* interprets this Umā as no mere mediator: she herself, praised on all sides by the four Vedas incarnate, is the supreme Brahman.[61] The *vyoma-vāṇī* above clearly resembles the *vāṇī* . . .

ākāśasthā that manifests itself to the gods after Viṣṇu's beheading, having been praised by the Vedas. The Devī, then, not only takes over the role of Dadhyañc as revealer of Brahmavidyā, but also, by association with Umā Haimavatī, becomes known as the Brahmavidyā itself,[62] and ultimately as that which is revealed through the divine knowledge: the supreme Brahman.

The role of the Vedas in the Hayagrīva story, incidentally, reveals yet another interesting twist. We have seen that traditionally Viṣṇu was associated with the Vedas as their promulgator and protector; in the *Devī-Bhāgavata* we find the roles reversed: it is the Vedas who come to the rescue of Viṣṇu, petitioning the Devī to revive the Lord.

Dadhyañc's traditional role as horse-headed revealer of the hidden knowledge has become split in the *Devī-Bhāgavata*. His revelatory function has fallen to the Devī while his equine aspect emerges in the figure of Viṣṇu. The parallelism between Dadhyañc and Viṣṇu is suggested by the fate of their severed heads. According to a tradition noted by Sāyaṇa, Dadhyañc's head ends up in Lake Śaryaṇāvat, from where Indra has it retrieved to use in his fight with the demons.[63] As for Viṣṇu, in the *Mahābhārata*'s Śānti version of the Madhu-Kaiṭabha myth, after he restored the Vedas to Brahmā, he placed his equine head in the Northeast Ocean.[64] Elsewhere in the epic a connection is made between the horse-headed Viṣṇu known as Vaḍavāmukha (the famous submarine mare) and the Salt Ocean.[65] In the *Devī-Bhāgavata*, Visnu's (original) head finds its resting place, Brahmā informs us, in the Salt Ocean, evoking images of the ancient submarine horse-head lurking in that ocean, and anticipating Viṣṇu's receiving his own equine head.[66]

With the beheading of Viṣṇu in the *Devī-Bhāgavata*, the discomfiture of the god is well under way, but the Devī's horseplay with him is only about to begin. We need now to return to the narrative and look at the underlying reasons as to why Viṣṇu lost his head, and how he gained the head of a horse. The Devī, in explaining the decapitation, provides two basic reasons, loosely interrelated, the second of which introduces the motif of the horse-head. The first concerns the jealousy of Viṣṇu's wife, Mahā-Lakṣmī. Once Viṣṇu, looking on her beautiful face, had smiled, but she mistook it for mockery, believing he found her appearance for some reason unattractive. She immediately suspected that her husband had chosen another fair-complexioned woman to be a co-wife. Mahā-Lakṣmī, though gentle or *sattvic* by nature, was possessed by Tāmasī Śakti, and becoming angry, she cursed her spouse: "May your head fall off!"[67]

Mahā-Lakṣmī's curse of Viṣṇu, by the way, introduces one more leitmotif in the debasement of his *avatāras*, foreshadowing the imprecation of the sage Bhṛgu. According to a later story in the *Devī-Bhāgavata*, when Viṣṇu kills Bhṛgu's wife, the enraged husband denounces him: "By my curse, may you undergo incarnations in the world of mortals. May you experience the abundant sufferings arising from [birth in] the womb, on account of your sin, O Janārdana [Viṣṇu]."[68] The account of Bhṛgu's curse, though absent (not surprisingly) in the *Bhāgavata*, is not original with the *Devī-Bhāgavata*, as the latter has borrowed it, quite possibly from the *Matsya Purāṇa*.[69] The *Devī-Bhāgavata* once again clearly delights in using established, even if somewhat obscure, traditions to demean Viṣṇu, though it does not hesitate to elaborate the old themes, or to develop new or parallel versions.

Returning to the story of Viṣṇu's beheading, we may note that while the immediate cause of the curse is due to the Tāmasī Śakti's entering Mahā-Lakṣmī, her possession by this "dark power" is further accounted for in terms of other more fundamental causes. Three of these are basically just different aspects of fate (*daiva*): time (*kāla*), inevitability (*bhāvitvā*), and inherent nature (*svabhāva*).[70] The term *svabhāva*, in the present context, refers specifically to woman's nature (*strī-svabhāva*) as manifested in Mahā-Lakṣmī's actions. The Devī herself characterizes *strī-svabhāva* as reckless, foolish, deceitful, and cruel. Such an explanation clearly reflects a traditional misogynism, yet even woman's evil nature, according to the story, can be put to good use, as there is yet a higher force directing fate itself. The Tāmasī Śakti, after all, is a manifestation and a tool of the Devī.

Mahā-Lakṣmī's curse, it turns out, is ultimately part of the Devi's plan to rescue the gods from another disaster. As the Goddess declares to the *devas*: "Through the force of time, for the success of the business of the gods, the Tāmasī Śakti entered her [Mahā-Lakṣmī's] body."[71] Though not explicit, the Devī's words suggest that she intends to fulfill the gods' own desires, using fate, time, and woman's inherent nature as the means. Certainly in the end, the successful conclusion of this whole affair is attributed to the grace of the Devī.

What, exactly, is this "business of the gods," to which the Devī has referred? The Devī gives the following account, which also provides the second major explanation for Viṣṇu's decapitation. Formerly, a *daitya* of great arms and high renown, known by the name Hayagrīva, performed *tapas* on the banks of the Sarasvatī for a thousand years. The essence of his ascesis was the recitation (*japa*) of the Devī's one-syllable mantra, the *māyā-bīja*.[72] The demon meditated on the Devī as Tāmasī Śakti, who eventually appeared before him, pleased with his *tapas*, ready to grant him a boon. The *dānava*, filled with love (*preman*) and eyes overflowing with tears, circumambulated the Goddess, bowed to her and offered a brief eulogy. He then requested the boon of immortality, but the Devī refused on the excuse that: "Of the born, death is certain; and of the dead, birth."[73] She asked Hayagrīva to request another boon, and he responded with an appeal for "limited immortality," namely that he could be killed only by one who, like himself, was horse-faced.[74] The Goddess agreed and sent him home to rule as he so willed.

The Devī, in the continuation of her story, suddenly characterizes Hayagrīva as evil-natured (*duṣṭātmā*) despite his earlier devotion. She recounts how the demon began to harass the sages and Vedas[75]—here, incidentally, being the only allusion in the *Devī-Bhāgavata* to Hayagrīva's role as Veda-thief, developed earlier in the *Bhāgavata*.[76] Given the Devī's boon to the demon, there is currently no one in the three worlds capable of slaying him. Accordingly, the Goddess instructs the gods to have the divine craftsman Tvaṣṭṛ affix a handsome horse-head on Viṣṇu's decapitated body, so that "Bhagavan Hayagrīva" (the Horse-headed Lord) could smite the evil and cruel horse-headed *dānava* for the welfare of the gods. The Devī's celestial voice at last falls silent, and the *devas* execute her plan. The *Devī-Bhāgavata* notes in closing, "Hari became Hayagrīva through the grace (*prasāda*) of Mahā-Māyā."[77]

As in the *Bhāgavata*, the horse-headed figure appears in the *Devī-Bhāgavata* as both a form of Viṣṇu and as a demon. But in the *Bhāgavata*, the two are carefully separated: they never appear together in the same story, and they do not share the same epithet. The *Devī-Bhāgavata* has combined the two horse-headed figures in a single myth and repeatedly refers to Viṣṇu as Hayagrīva, the same name used for the demon. R. H. van Gulik refers to the *Devī-Bhāgavata*'s synthesizing account as "one of those paradoxical combinations, much beloved by Indians: Hayagrīva kills Hayagrīva."[78]

Van Gulik wonders if the ancient story of the fight between Rāma and Paraśu-Rāma (the so-called *Rāma-Rāma* battle or *rāmarāma-vivāda*) might have influenced the *Devī-Bhāgavata*'s synthesis, but I think the paradox has a more immediate explanation. The Rāma-Rāma fight involves two forms of the divine, while the Hayagrīva-Hayagrīva battle concerns the divine and the demonic. In the context of the general perspective of the *Devī-Bhāgavata*, the paradoxical convergence of the two Hayagrīvas suggests a parallelism between, or even an intermixture of, deific and demonic nature, of the *sattv*ic and the *tamas*ic. Thus, just as the demon Hayagrīva, *tamas*ic by nature, acts in a largely *sattvic* manner worshipping the Devī, so Viṣṇu, *sattvic* by nature, often engages in *tamasic* activity, a theme developed at length later in the Purāṇa and meant to emphasize Viṣṇu's entanglement in the material qualities or *guṇas* of the world.

In any case, the Hayagrīva paradox is made possible only through the benevolence of the Goddess. It is through her grace that the demon receives his boon, and through that same grace Viṣṇu receives the horse-head and thus is able to slay the *dānava*. In this way, then, the *Devī-Bhāgavata* is able to add the myth of the slaying of the demon Hayagrīva, formerly a Vaiṣṇava story, to the growing list of the Devī's great deeds. As the *Devī-Bhāgavata* concludes: "This (account of the) great act (*caritra*) of Mahā-Māyā, purifying, destroying sin, brings complete prosperity to those who hear or recite it."[79]

One final question remains on the Hayagrīva story before we move on to the other great deeds of the Goddess. What, we may ask, was Viṣṇu's reaction to all this horseplay? Viṣṇu reveals his feelings (as portrayed by the *Devī-Bhāgavata*) in the frame story that introduces the Hayagrīva myth. As this frame story is closely based on the *Bhāgavata* and provides a significant new twist in the reinterpretation of Viṣṇu's incarnations, it deserves a closer look.

The Frame Story of the Hayagrīva Myth: Imitation and Mockery in the *Avatāras* of Viṣṇu

The frame story introducing the Hayagrīva myth in the *Devī-Bhāgavata*[80] borrows much of its basic structure, as well as occasional phrasing, from the *Bhāgavata Purāṇa*. The *Bhāgavata*, in the chapters immediately preceding its account of Viṣṇu's *avatāras* in the second Skandha,[81] tells the following story. The divine sage Nārada once queried his father Brahmā about the identity of the supreme being. The son at first was under the impression that his progenitor, the creator, was this highest reality and thus praised him as the god of gods (*devadeva*), the source of all beings, the Lord of past, present, and future (*bhūtabhavyabhavat-prabhu*) and who, though one, produces all creatures through his own *māyā*. The son knew of nothing higher than his father, yet he was puzzled and anxious as he recalled that formerly Brahmā had once undertaken severe austerities, suggesting that there is someone superior to him. But who could be more preeminent than the creator?

The sage's father replied that people, deluded by *māyā*, say that he, Brahmā, is the supreme deity (*jagad-guru*). In reality, however, it is Nārāyaṇa (Viṣṇu) who is supreme, for it is Nārāyaṇa who creates and motivates the creator. The supreme Lord, who is Master of Māyā (Māyeśa), is beyond the three *guṇas* of *sattva, rajas,* and *tamas;* his *māyā* assumes these three forms for the sake of preservation, creation, and destruction. By Viṣṇu's order, Brahmā creates the world and Śiva destroys it, while the bearer of the three *śakti*s (Nārāyaṇa himself), in the form of Puruṣa, protects the universe. Brahmā goes on to describe at length the creative process, including the evolution of Nārāyaṇa into the cosmic man or Yajña-Puruṣa, whose cosmogonic immolation has already been recounted. In this manner Brahmā sets the context for his enumeration of the Puruṣa's *līlāvatāra*s ("play-incarnations"), including the sacrificial horse Hayaśiras as the tenth.

The *Devī-Bhāgavata,* in taking over many features of the above account, adds another layer to the divine hierarchy.[82] In so doing, the *Devī-Bhāgavata* is able to preserve many of the motifs of the *Bhāgavata,* but these motifs now have an inverted theological significance. The *Devī-Bhāgavata* story begins with Nārada's relating a conversation between his father Brahmā and Viṣṇu, which Brahmā later told to his son. The conversation focusses on the question of who is the supreme refuge in the universe. Brahmā had assumed Viṣṇu was the supreme god of gods (*devadeva*), the Lord of past, present, and future (*bhūta-bhavyabhavat-prabhu*), but was startled when he saw Hari meditating and practicing austerities. Brahmā asked, "I know, O Lord of the world, that you are the primal cause of all, the creator, preserver, and destroyer. . . . By your desire I create all this world and Śiva destroys it by your command. . . . But what god do you meditate upon, for in the three worlds I see no god superior to you?"[83]

Viṣṇu answered that although all beings consider Brahmā, himself, and Śiva to be the creator, preserver, and destroyer, it can be inferred from the Vedas that they are such only through the power of Śakti. The *rājasī śakti* abides in Brahmā during creation, *sāttvikī śakti* in Viṣṇu during preservation, and *tāmasī śakti* in Rudra during destruction. Without Śakti, all three are incapable of carrying out their functions.

Viṣṇu then turned to consideration of his own incarnations: "I go to sleep on the couch of Śeṣa,[84] dependent on another (*paratantra*); I get up, subservient to another, subject to time. Ever dependent, I perform austerities; at other times I sport with Mahā-Lakṣmī. Sometimes I engage in terrible battles with demons—why, before your [Brahmā's] very eyes I fought a great battle for five thousand years with the two demons born of my earwax, and by Devī's grace Madhu and Kaiṭabha were slain. . . . By her will I became a man, wandering on the great ocean, and in age after age I become a tortoise, a boar, a lion, a dwarf. No one likes birth in the wombs of inferior animals (*tiryac*). . . . What independent (*svatantra*) man would abandon pleasures with Lakṣmī to go into the vile wombs of fish etc.?"[85] Viṣṇu concludes his list of incarnational agonies by referring to his own beheading before Brahmā's own eyes—how could Brahmā forget!—when the bowstring snapped: "Then you took a horse-head (*vāji-śiras*) and with the master artisan [Tvaṣṭṛ] joined it [on my body]. Thus I am known as Hayānana (horse-faced). . . . If I were independent, how could such an embarrassing accident (*viḍambana*) have happened in front of everyone! Therefore I am not independent but completely subservient to Śakti."[86]

The *Devī-Bhāgavata* is clearly having fun with the term *viḍambana*, which can mean not only an embarrassment or mockery, but also an imitation, illusion, or deception. It is in these latter senses that we find it used in the *Bhāgavata* to express something of the mystery (*guhya*) of Viṣṇu's incarnations. Thus Kuntī, mother of the Pāṇḍavas, praises Kṛṣṇa in the following words: "O Lord, no one knows the purpose of your coming here into the world in imitation (*viḍambana*) of mortals. . . . You are the self of all, unborn and non-acting. Thus your births and actions in lower animals, in men, seers, and in large aquatic creatures are a mighty disguise or deception (*viḍambana*)."[87]

The docetic quality of Viṣṇu's incarnation in the *Bhāgavata* is made even clearer in the introduction to the story of the fish incarnation in the eighth book. King Parīkṣit is puzzled about the nature of the fish *avatāra* and asks the sage Sūta: "O Sir, I wish to hear the story of the first descent of Hari, of wondrous deeds, in his illusory disguise as a fish (*māyā-matsya-viḍambana*). Why did he take on that piscine form, despised in the world (*loka-jugupsita*), as it is of lowly *tamas*ic nature?"[88] Sūta assures the king that though the Lord wanders like the wind or breath within various beings, high and low, he (like the wind) does not partake of their highness or lowness, as he is *nirguṇa* (without qualities). Elsewhere the *Bhāgavata* further explains the mystery of Viṣṇu's incarnations in high and low forms: "There is no body, no birth, no action of him [the Lord]; yet for the sake of play, to protect the righteous, he enters into wombs, good, bad, and mixed."[89]

For the *Bhāgavata*, then, *viḍambana* signifies the divine imitation of creaturely beings, an imitation which is ultimately a beneficent and salvific illusion or deception.[90] This salvific deception creates the paradoxical tension between Viṣṇu's supreme nature as the quiescent spirit (Puruṣa), without qualities, beyond all birth, and his active incarnational roles, including the most humble and despised, within the world. *Viḍambana* thus highlights the compassionate play of the Lord, whereby he protects, even entertains, his devotees, and evokes in them a sense of love and wonder that he is willing to enter into our world, on our terms.

The *Devī-Bhāgavata,* while interpreting *viḍambana* in the sense of mortification or mockery, also uses the term to bring out certain paradoxical tensions within Viṣṇu's *avatāric* activity. Here, too, the idea of *viḍambana* evokes wonder, but in an ironic way. It is indeed amazing that the *sattvic* Viṣṇu can descend into impure wombs, but this "enwombment" of god is no longer a salvific illusion whereby Viṣṇu manifests his compassionate play. Rather, it is a shocking revelation of Viṣṇu's subjugation to powers beyond his control.

One striking presentation of this view is found in the *Devī-Bhāgavata*'s description of life in the womb. The Purāṇa first points out the belief of some people that through Viṣṇu's will all beings take birth in various sorts of wombs, good and evil. But why, the text goes on to ask, does Viṣṇu himself undergo births in age after age? What sane person would abandon the pleasures of Vaikuṇṭha (Viṣṇu's heaven) to dwell in the hell of a womb, hanging head downwards, entrapped in feces and urine, eating and drinking the same, tormented by worms, and scorched by the digestive fire?[91]

Such a view of fetal existence hardly seems to accord with the *Devī-Bhāgavata*'s high praise of motherhood elsewhere. Yet this disparagement of pregnancy is not the unique creation of our text but has ancient, perhaps Buddhistic, roots. The composer of the *Devī-Bhāgavata,* however, did not have far to look to find a model for this detraction. The *Bhāgavata* itself describes the month-by-month development of the fetus and the various agonies it suffers, including hanging with its head bent down to its stomach, lying in a receptacle filled with urine and feces where worms breed, enduring the bites of those same worms, and being scorched by the mother's gastric fires.[92] Once again, it seems, the *Bhāgavata* has provided the *Devī-Bhāgavata* with the means for its own discomfiture. To the wonder of Viṣṇu's enwombment, the *Devī-Bhāgavata* has added that of his decapitation. In the latter case the marvel is that, as noted above, though he is uncleavable and indivisible, he still lost his head. What greater *viḍambana* or humiliation could there be?

The story of Viṣṇu Hayagrīva reveals many of the basic strategies of the *Devī-Bhāgavata* in its abasement of Viṣṇu. Little is invented, much is assimilated, often from the best of authorities. The beheading of Viṣṇu, though of rare occurrence in the Purāṇas generally, is well attested to in the Brāhmaṇas, especially in the venerable *Śatapatha*.[93] His equine heroics are already proclaimed in the great epic. The *Bhāgavata* provides the necessary links for connecting these motifs in its identification of the Yajña-Puruṣa with Hayaśiras, an identification which echoes the ancient theme of the cosmic horse-sacrifice. The *Bhāgavata* in addition dwells on the mystery of incarnation as beneficent deception. All these notions and ideals the *Devī-Bhāgavata* accepts; but with a slight twist, it turns them all upside down, like the fetus in the womb.

The Hayagrīva story, however, hardly exhausts all the traditional Vaiṣṇava themes inverted by the *Devī-Bhāgavata* composer(s). One major theme, not developed in the case of Hayagrīva, is the potential moral aspect of *viḍambana*, that is, its aspect as deception or deceit. After all, Viṣṇu as a lifeless, headless corpse is hardly capable of being a moral agent, and his moral character is not really brought into question (though the Vedas wonder if Viṣṇu suffered his capital punishment as the result of some sin). Yet the *Devī-Bhāgavata* does not fail to notice the debasing potential of the incarnational deception. It is time, then, to turn to Viṣṇu's role in the nefarious Vṛtra episode, where embarrassing accidents give way to deeds of moral turpitude.

Chapter 3

Who Slew Vṛtrāsura? Deception, Redemption, and Grace in the Two *Bhāgavatas*

We have seen that according to an old definition of "the *Bhāgavata*"[1] the story of the slaying of Vṛtra, along with the Hayagrīva episode, is one of the identifying characteristrics of that work. The compiler(s) of the *Devī-Bhāgavata*, as already noted, may well have been aware of such a definition and consciously composed this Purāṇa to conform to it.[2] In any case, both the *Bhāgavata*[3] and the *Devī-Bhāgavata*[4] narrate the Vṛtra-vadha (Vṛtra-slaying) affair in considerable detail. We can be thankful to the old definition in calling our attention to the two Vṛtra stories, for it thereby suggests at once another interesting and illuminating comparison of mythic motifs in the two Purāṇas. The elaborate development of the Vṛtra myth in each text allows us to probe deeply into their respective theological viewpoints. Indeed, each *Bhāgavata*'s version of the ancient battle between Indra and Vṛtra serves as a kind of mythico-theological paradigm for that Purāṇa, revealing much of its basic model of reality, of the world mired in ignorance and deception, and of redemptive grace.

In dealing with the Vṛtrāsura episode in the two Purāṇas, we shall focus on the basic, but deceptively simple, question of who slew the mighty demon. That is, who is ultimately responsible for his death? In Vedic times, Indra, king of the gods, is solely or chiefly responsible for the *asura*'s demise. Indra's main weapon is the thunderbolt, but he is also a master of illusion and increasingly relies on guile to overcome his foes. By the early epic-Purāṇic period Śiva and Viṣṇu, the great gods of the new *bhakti* movement, have taken general precedence over Indra, who is often ridiculed for his clumsiness and impotence, and castigated for his immorality. He is now often just "the hit man of the gods."[5] Indra then still delivers the actual blow that dispatches Vṛtra, but he is able to do so only with the aid of others, of the higher gods or even merely of various seers and sages. At the same time, Indra's wily ways have been heartily embraced by certain of his allies, not the least of whom is Viṣṇu. Deceit and delusion abound, and it is not always clear who is deceiving whom.

Integral to the question of who slew Vṛtra is the matter of the demon's true identity or nature. Originally an archetypal foe of the gods threatening the world with chaos, and ever the enemy of Indra, Vṛtra in time lost his demonic pride and ferocity, attaining a noble status through a new-found humility. These developments in his character transformed the basic reasons behind his death, with further reverberations for the aftermath of his destruction. We shall then need to look not only at how and why he was killed, but also at the consequences of the execution, both for Vṛtra and for his slayer.

The situation is thus rather convoluted, with many divergent and often seemingly contradictory versions of the Vṛtra story appearing in the older complex of Hindu mythology. Several of these variants occur in the *Mahābhārata*, the basic source of Vṛtra legends for both the *Bhāgavatas*.[6] The ways in which the two Purāṇas selected, utilized, and interpreted the epic materials nicely illuminate the distinct spiritual perspectives of each text. Accordingly, before comparing the two Purāṇic interpretations of Vṛtra's death with each other, it will be helpful to consider how each work availed itself of the Vṛtra materials in the great epic. For both *Bhāgavatas*, the various elements selected from the epic are amazingly well suited to the particular theological thrust of each, as though the *Mahābhārata* had anticipated equally the peculiar needs of the Vaiṣṇava and of the Śākta Paurāṇikas.

The Slaying of Vṛtra in the *Mahābhārata*

The several versions of the Vṛtra story in the epic, though varying remarkably in their individual details and completeness, generally share similar patterns.[7] The most representative, overarching framework is the following:

1. Indra slays Tvaṣṭṛ's son, Triśiras (Viśvarūpa); Tvaṣṭṛ creates another son, Vṛtra, dedicated to avenging the death of his brother.
2. Vṛtra attacks Indra and the gods, overwhelming them.

3. The gods retreat, taking refuge in some higher providential power.
4. The supreme refuge provides the aid/advice necessary to overcome Vṛtra.
5. The gods utilize the aid/advice and Indra slays Vṛtra.
6. The gods rejoice, but Indra flees, fearful of the consequences of his acts.

This outline for the most part fits the basic structure of *surāsura* (god/demon) conflicts in the epic: enmity between the gods and demons arises for some reason; the *asuras* take control of heaven and rout the *suras*; the latter retreat for refuge to the supreme lord of the universe; the supreme lord responds favorably to their plea to help overthrow the demons; the demons are conquered or killed; and the gods and all creatures rejoice at the restoration of cosmic-political order.[8]

A major departure in some of the Vṛtra myths from this general structure concerns the aftermath of the whole affair. While order of a sort is reestablished with Vṛtra's death, a new element of discord is introduced, namely the sin of Brahmanicide. For Vṛtra and his elder brother Triśiras are Brahmans in the epic, and Indra is thus guilty of a heinous crime.[9] This outrage against Brahmanical sanctity is graphically represented in the Śānti Parva by the arising of the fierce hag, Brahmanicide, from Vṛtra's corpse, and her relentless pursuit of his slayer.[10] Only through the grace of Brahmā and the performance of a horse-sacrifice is Indra able to rid himself of this terrible nemesis. The main point of such episodes in the epic, accordingly, is less the *surāsura* conflict than the priestly contention that Brahmanicide is the worst of sins, and "the affirmation of the manifest destiny of the brahmin to impose drastic penalty on anyone, however powerful, who wrongs him."[11]

Indra's sin of Brahmanicide figures prominently in both *Bhāgavata*s, and each attempts to resolve the matter in its own particular way. The epic's introduction of the Brahmanicide motif implicitly raises the question of moral responsibility not only on the part of Indra but also on the part of all those who assisted him. The problem of moral complicity on the part of Indra's allies is of special concern to the *Devī-Bhāgavata*.

Indra's allies in the epic include especially the three gods of the Trimūrti, who provide diverse sorts of advice and assistance. On certain occasions it is Śiva who plays the chief supporting role. In one instance, Śiva furnishes a coat of armor (*varma, kavaca*) along with a mantra, protected by which Indra is able to slay Vṛtra.[12] In another Śiva supplies his energy in the form of a fever, which enters Vṛtra and causes him to yawn. At this point Indra throws his bolt (*vajra*), pervaded by the energy of Viṣṇu, at the gaping demon, thereby slaying him.[13]

In other accounts, it is Brahmā who counsels the desperate gods and reveals the winning strategy: the securing of the bones of the venerable sage Dadhīci, wherewith to forge Indra's bolt to slay the demon.[14] In one version, even after Indra secures the bone-forged *vajra*, he cringes before Vṛtra's mighty onslaught, until Viṣṇu infuses into him his own shining power (*tejas*).[15]

Viṣṇu's role, as seen in certain versions above, is often that of strengthening Indra's weak or flagging powers through entering or imparting his own energy into the god directly, or into his bolt. In similar fashion, in yet another account, Viṣṇu suffuses himself not only into the bolt, but also into some lethal foam that Indra hurls at Vṛtra along with the more orthodox missile. In this account, Viṣṇu also provides aid of a quite different sort: he tells Indra to make a false peace treaty with Vṛtra and to slay the demon when the latter's guard is down.[16] This version, from the Udyoga Parva,[17] presents Viṣṇu as the supreme refuge and not just as one of several allies. The prominence of Viṣṇu in the Udyoga account naturally attracted the attention of the *Bhāgavata* composer(s), but the false peace treaty is entirely ignored.[18] It becomes the centerpiece, however, in the *Devī-Bhāgavata*'s retelling.

The epic version most attractive to the *Bhāgavata* appears in the Śānti Parva, in a frame story surrounding an older core in which Śiva's fever causes Vṛtra to yawn, enabling Indra to make the fatal throw.[19] The new framework profoundly reinterprets Vṛtra's *asura* nature, seeing behind the *deva*-despising facade a hidden potential for supreme devotion to the highest Lord of the universe, Viṣṇu.[20] This *bhakti*-inspired interpretation radically breaks with the old *surāsura* conflict structure outlined above.

The frame story, widely known as the "Vṛtra Gītā," is narrated by the wise old warrior Bhīṣma to console the disenfranchised and dispirited King Yudhiṣṭhira. In this "Gītā" Vṛtra appears as an example of someone who overcomes defeat and loss of sovereignty through attaining the highest knowledge. The "Gītā" itself is in the form of a dialogue between Vṛtra and his guru, Uśanas. Vṛtra apparently has just been vanquished by Indra, and Uśanas is asking him if he is in any way disturbed by his defeat. Vṛtra responds that he neither grieves nor rejoices, having realized the inevitable rise and fall of all beings subject to time and according to the fruits of their karma.

Queried further by his teacher as to how he came by such views, Vṛtra replies that formerly, through his own austerities, he had gained great prosperity, but through his own actions he had suffered great losses as well. Enduring such vicissitudes stoically but still desirous of victory, he had become eager to fight with Indra. In that battle, he had seen the Lord Viṣṇu, a frequent associate of Indra in this war. As a result of that gracious vision, Vṛtra had attained the good fortune now of asking Uśanas to explain further about the workings of karma, the gain and loss of sovereignty, as well as about the ultimate source of all beings and the path to the supreme goal.

Uśanas, aided by the sage Sanatkumāra, provides answers to all of Vṛtra's questions, emphasizing especially the greatness of Viṣṇu (*viṣṇor māhātmyam*). The "Vṛtra Gītā" proper ends with the demon acknowledging the truths spoken by his teachers: "Viṣṇu verily is the Mahātmā (Great Soul), the supreme Puruṣa indeed. All this universe is established in him."[21] Bhīṣma adds that Vṛtra then gave up his life, controlling his Self, and attained the supreme state.

Yudhiṣṭhira, needless to say, is amazed by Vṛtra's knowledge and devotion to Viṣṇu.[22] He asks Bhīṣma to clear up two puzzling points: on the one hand, how could Vṛtra, an *asura*, realize the supreme state of Viṣṇu; and on the other, given that the demon was a righteous devotee of Viṣṇu and a truth-knower, how could he be defeated by Indra?[23] At this point the frame story gives way to the old account of Indra's overcoming Vṛtra with the aid of Śiva's fever. This old account, from a different milieu, not surprisingly fails to answer Yudhiṣṭhira's questions. Near the end of the whole episode, the frame story briefly reemerges to try to tie up the loose ends. Bhīṣma explains that after Vṛtra yawned and was split in two by the bolt, "this Mahā-yogī and great *asura* reached the supreme station of Viṣṇu; for through his devotion (*bhakti*) to Viṣṇu, he came to possess this whole universe, and accordingly when he was slain in battle, he attained Viṣṇu's realm."[24]

The epic thus provides only the most general answers to Yudhiṣṭhira's two questions, in terms of Viṣṇu-*bhakti*. As for how the demon acquired this devotion in the first place, the only explanation is the rather vague suggestion early in the "Vṛtra Gītā" that it was due to the seemingly fortuitous sight of Viṣṇu in the battle with Indra. And that Vṛtra's defeat had a happy ending for the demon does not explain how the defeat was possible or why it was necessary. In the *Bhāgavata*, these questions are dealt with at length.

The Slaying of Vṛtra in the *Bhāgavata Purāṇa*

The *Bhāgavata* in its rendering of the Vṛtra-slaying episode uses the *Mahābhārata* materials quite flexibly, melding together aspects and elements from several accounts in a rather innovative and creative manner, though the "Vṛtra Gītā" is clearly the primary source of inspiration for the Purāṇa.[25] The *Bhāgavata*, of course, projects the epic materials through a Vaiṣṇava lens, so that Viṣṇu appears uniformly and unambiguously as the supreme refuge and ultimate cause behind all events. Thus, it is Viṣṇu rather than Brahmā who tells the gods they must secure the bones of Dadhīci to forge the lethal bolt.[26] Similarly, the armor that protects Indra in his battle with Vṛtra is the Nārāyaṇa Varma (shield of Viṣṇu, a protective prayer or mantra), rather than Śiva's old armor.[27] Further, the *Bhāgavata* greatly expands the praises offered to Viṣṇu by the oppressed gods. And naturally, Viṣṇu's association with the empowering energy of the bolt is retained.[28]

We may focus on the *Bhāgavata*'s account of the final struggle between Indra and Vṛtra, for here, in the typical ebb and flow of battle, the Purāṇa has recourse to the themes of the "Vṛtra Gītā."[29] After an initial exchange of blows in which the demon holds the edge, the two combatants close again, whereupon Vṛtra begins to lecture his foe. With characteristic heroic bravado, he taunts Indra for slaying his innocent brother, Viśvarūpa (Triśiras), who was not only a Brahman but also, in the *Bhāgavata*'s account, Indra's guru.[30] He boasts defiantly that he will soon pierce Indra's heart with a spear, but then there is a sudden change in the tone of Vṛtra's speech. It manifests itself first in a kind of fatalistic resignation: perhaps Indra will be the victor, the demon declares, in which case Vṛtra will attain the dust of the feet of the wise. The *asura* continues, "Why do you not throw that unfailing bolt at me, your enemy? . . . That bolt has been sharpened (*tejita*) by the energy (*tejas*) of Hari and the austerities of Dadhīci. Urged on by Viṣṇu, slay your enemy with that. Where Hari is, there is victory, fortune, and virtues!"[31]

The growing acceptance of his impending death matches the increasing devotional fervor of the noble *asura*. He explains to Indra that death by means of the bolt will free him from the snare of sensual, vulgar pleasures, and through concentrating on the lotus feet of the Lord, he will attain the goal of the sages. Vṛtra then expounds on the way the Lord shows his favor: he does not bestow riches on his devotees, as wealth leads only to hatred, fear, anguish, arrogance, and other forms of suffering; rather, he frustrates the efforts of his servants in seeking the first three ends of life (*kāma, artha, dharma*), showering his grace (*prasāda*) on the destitute, not on others. The demon concludes his sermon with a direct appeal to the Lord himself: "O Hari, may I become a servant of those whose sole refuge is your feet. May I serve you alone in mind, speech and body. I wish for nothing apart from you, no heavenly or other realms, no yogic powers, not even freedom from rebirth. . . . May I, caught in the wheel of *saṃsāra* by my own deeds, find companionship (*sakhyam*) with those devoted to you, not with those whose minds are attached to body, sons, wife, and house."[32]

The fight resumes with Indra quickly sundering one of Vṛtra's arms. The demon nonetheless manages with his one remaining arm to knock the *vajra* out of his foe's grasp. When Indra becomes despondent and hesitates to pick up his weapon, Vṛtra addresses him much as Kṛṣṇa speaks to Arjuna in the *Bhagavad Gītā*. He commands Indra to throw off his depression and to slay his enemy (Vṛtra himself). He warns that victory and defeat are never certain for those dependent on others, and all are dependent finally on the supreme Lord in the form of time. People do not recognize the Lord as the controller of all, regarding themselves as independent. Yet all fortune and misery arise in their season, beyond one's personal control. Accordingly, the wise look upon infamy and glory, victory and defeat, happiness and misery, death and life, with indifference. The true Self, Vṛtra continues, is untouched by the *guṇas* of *prakṛti*, and whoever realizes the Self as only a witness (*sākṣin*) is not bound. When the demon is finished, the chief of the gods sings his praise, applauding his wholehearted devotion to the Lord of the world, the true Self and friend of all. Indra recognizes that his enemy has gone beyond the *māyā* of Viṣṇu that deludes the world (*māyāṃ . . . vaiṣṇavīṃ jana-mohinīm*).[33]

One final time the battle resumes. Vṛtra's last arm is cut off. With about the only means left at his disposal, the *asura* attacks Indra opening his monstrous mouth wide as if to devour the three worlds and swallows his foe. Yet Indra does not die in the belly of the demon. He is saved, but not by a yawn as in an epic version;[34] rather, he is protected by the armor of the Mahā-Puruṣa (Viṣṇu) and by the force of *yoga-māyā*.[35] Indra rips open the demon's belly with the bolt and lops off his head. The divine light of the Self (*ātma-jyoti*) then comes forth from Vṛtra's body and, before all the world, attains to him who transcends this world (*aloka*).[36] Thus concludes the *Bhāgavata*'s own version of the "Vṛtra Gītā."

Regarding the aftermath of Vṛtra's slaying, the *Bhāgavata* portrays Indra's sin of Brahmanicide in a rather different light from the epic accounts.[37] The Purāṇa describes Indra as having been a reluctant executioner of Vṛtra, fearful of killing a Brahman. The Brahman sages themselves urged Indra on, despite his misgivings, promising that they would perform a horse-sacrifice on his behalf. Then, in an astonishing turnabout from the epic, they exclaim:

> Worshipping the Lord Nārāyaṇa, the Puruṣa, the Supreme Self, with the horse-sacrifice, you will be freed even from (the sin of) slaughtering the whole world! The murderer of a Brahman, the murderer of one's father or mother, the murderer of a cow or a preceptor, the eater of dog-flesh, and the outcaste, all are purified by praising (*kīrtanāt*) the Lord. Through this great rite of the horse-sacrifice which we shall perform, you shall not be stained, (worshipping) him with faith, even if you slaughtered the whole world including all the Brahmans, let alone chastising this evil (Vṛtra).[38]

Only with such assurances does Indra undertake the task.

The *Bhāgavata* is hardly endorsing Brahmanicide, yet the whole tone is obviously quite different from the epic's stress on the heinous and sinful nature of the act. In the epic versions of the aftermath, the basic point is that violating a Brahman—or even worse, two Brahmans—has severe consequences, which in turn requires the service of Brahmans (as performers of the horse-sacrifice) to absolve. For the *Bhāgavata*, the message is that even the worst of sinners and the ritually impure, including outcastes and Brahman-slayers, can be sanctified and redeemed through devotion to the Lord.[39]

The final and most striking innovation in the *Bhāgavata*'s rendering of the Vṛtra-vadha relates back to Yudhiṣṭhira's questions to Bhīṣma in the Sānti Parva. Yudhiṣṭhira had wondered how Vṛtra, an *asura*, could have attained the supreme end, and how, as a devotee of Viṣṇu, he could have been defeated by Indra. The epic gives only general answers to these queries, namely that Viṣṇu-*bhakti* is the cause. But the Śānti does not clearly explain how Vṛtra attained to such devotion or why devotion ends in defeat. It is at this point that the *Bhāgavata* goes well beyond the Śānti account, providing an explanation for Vṛtra's devotion to Viṣṇu in terms of his preceding incarnation as a pious king named Citraketu. The story of Citraketu is told at some length.[40]

Citraketu's life story offers the *Bhāgavata*'s basic model of spiritual growth. Citraketu was a handsome, generous, and noble king, the ruler of a prosperous kingdom, and surrounded by thousands of wives. Yet despite his good fortune, he took no delight in any of it as none of his wives had borne him a son. Through the aid of the sage Aṅgiras, he was able finally to obtain a son by his eldest wife. But this child was soon murdered by the neglected and jealous co-wives, plunging the king into deep despair. His overwhelming grief, however, prepared the king to understand the deeper truths of existence.

Aṅgiras, realizing his disciple was now ripe for instruction, warned Citraketu that not only sons, but a wife, house, relatives, power, and riches of various sorts all lead to grief, delusion, and fear; and they are no more real than dreams, illusions, or fancies. The sage also admonished the grieving father to abandon his confidence in the abiding reality of the so-called objective world, immersed as it is in duality, and to enquire into the nature of the Self. Aṅgiras' colleague, the sage Nārada, then advised the king to worship the Lord Saṃkarṣaṇa (a form of the supreme Lord).

Citraketu performed a week-long adoration of Saṃkarṣaṇa and soon reached the feet of this divine manifestation. The king, with his hair standing on end, weeping tears of devotion, praised the Lord as the ultimate controller of the universe. Saṃkarṣaṇa then undertook the king's final instruction. In brief, the Lord revealed that he is all beings, the Self of beings, and the source of beings. A wise person will recognize this unity of being, drop his concerns over wordly affairs and become a devotee of the Lord, realizing oneness with the supreme Ātman. In closing, Saṃkarṣaṇa promised that Citraketu would soon attain true knowledge and wisdom.

As a result of his devotion, the king found himself sporting in the celestial realms, where he roamed for millions of years. One day, coming upon Śiva in an assembly of sages with his spouse Pārvatī on his lap, he chided Śiva for embracing his wife openly in public. Śiva laughed at the remark as a joke, but his wife, embarrassed and angered, cursed Citraketu to become a demon. Citraketu as a true devotee—regarding curse and blessing, heaven and hell, pleasure and pain, as all simply part of the round of existence ordained by the Lord—refrained from a countercurse. Indeed, he even apologized to Pārvatī, whereupon Śiva extolled his patience, wisdom, and indifference to his worldly fate and even to final liberation (*upavarga*). Being intent on the Lord alone, then, Citraketu willingly accepted rebirth as the demon Vṛtra.

We can now see how Vṛtra came by his profound wisdom and

devotion to the Lord. Modern commentators on the Citraketu episode have tended to interpret the story as simply an incarnational device to explain the "inconsistency" in Vṛtra's character, demonic by birth but steeped in devotion.[41] O'Flaherty, in considering the doctrine of reincarnation in the Purāṇas generally, writes:

> Though the functions of karma and mechanisms of rebirth are discussed at great length, and though characters in tight spots often blame fate or karma, *while the narrator in a tight spot hastily conjures up a previous incarnation to explain an otherwise awkward twist of the plot or inconsistency of character* [my italics], the major thrusts of the texts is to exhort the worshiper to undertake remedial actions in order to swim like a salmon upstream against the current of karma."[42]

Certainly, as we shall see in relation to both *Bhāgavatas*, the doctrine of karma is radically subordinated to that of *bhakti*, for true devotion undercuts completely the otherwise inevitable process of karmic retribution. Yet the incarnational device in the case of Citraketu is more than a hasty conjuration, being instead a rather carefully worked out model for the functioning of the Lord's divine grace.

The *Bhāgavata*'s particular conception of divine favor is critical for an understanding of the whole Citraketu/Vṛtra story. This conception has already been suggested by Vṛtra in his declaration to Indra that the Lord shows his favor to devotees by obstructing their efforts to obtain the first three ends of life. This notion of grace by deprivation underlies Citraketu's loss of his son, the resulting anguish preparing him to receive the highest knowledge. Similarly, Pārvatī's curse which brought about the demonic birth also appears, in the end, to be an act of divine grace, providing Citraketu with his final challenge.[43] The reason for the defeat of the great devotee Vṛtra is now clear, for his death at the hands of Indra is an act of grace on the part of the Lord. This fitting climax to the chain of gracious intercessions puts an end to his demonic embodiment and effects the mergence of his soul with the supreme, a common motif in the *Bhāgavata*.[44]

Indra and Vṛtra illustrate the working of two different modes of divine grace. Indra, overthrown by *asuras* who threaten the cosmic order, receives the assistance of Viṣṇu in his traditional role as preserver of *dharma* and the protector of the good. It is by Viṣṇu's grace in the form of the Nārāyaṇa Kavaca that Indra is able to burst out of the demon's belly, in imitation of many of Kṛṣṇa's own demon-slaying feats. As Vṛtra himself declares to Indra shortly before his death,

"Where Hari is, there is victory, fortune, and virtues."[45] But Vṛtra goes on to speak of a higher form of grace, the grace of deprivation, of which he is the recipient. This grace does not protect the righteous within the world, but rather rescues the devotee from the world altogether: "Somewhat paradoxically, the major implication that can be drawn from the Lord's deliverance of the world from the forces of disorder and instability within the cosmos is that he is able to rescue the devotee from the cosmos entirely."[46] This paradox is beautifully expressed in the *Bhāgavata*'s rendering of the Vṛtra-vadha, where the two modes of grace converge in a single act.

The *Bhāgavata*, in creating its remarkable version of the Vṛtra myth, ranged widely in appropriating and synthesizing divergent materials from the *Mahābhārata*. At the same time, despite its use of mythic elements from several epic versions, including that of the Udyoga Parva, the *Bhāgavata* makes no mention of the false peace treaty contained therein. This oversight, as it were, did not escape the watchful eyes of the *Devī-Bhāgavata* compiler(s) The *Devī-Bhāgavata* focusses on the deceptive alliance in an effort not only to discredit Viṣṇu, but also to present a different conception of divine grace.

The Slaying of Vṛtra in the *Devī-Bhāgavata Purāṇa*

The *Devī-Bhāgavata* places the story of the Vṛtra-vadha at the start of the sixth book. It is perhaps no mere coincidence that the *Bhāgavata* also tells the story in its sixth book. This placement, in any case, is of significance for the *Devī-Bhāgavata* as it directly follows the narration of the Devī's great deeds in the slaying of Mahiṣa, Śumbha, and Niśumbha in Book V. These latter exploits of the Goddess, made famous in the *Devī-Māhātmya*, provide the general structure for the *Devī-Bhāgavata*'s retelling of the Vṛtra episode. The parallelism helps impress upon the reader or audience that here, too, in the slaying of Vṛtra, is another mighty act of the Devī, though previously not recognized as such by most people.

This lack of recognition of the Devī's role in the slaying of Vṛtra serves as one of two puzzling points that provide the initial inspiration for the telling of the story in the *Devī-Bhāgavata*. The account begins with the Naimiṣa sages querying Sūta about the ancient, auspicious story, told in the Veda, of how Vṛtrāsura was slain in battle by Vāsava (Indra). They are perplexed first by the apparent incongruity that Vṛtra was killed through a deception (*chala*) by Indra, instigated by Viṣṇu, who is the best of those endowed with goodness (*sattva*). For the two Haris (Indra and Viṣṇu) had slain the demon by abandoning truth, violating a truce, with the expedient of foam. The sages here clearly are referring to the version of the slaying given in the Udyoga. The sages are also confused by a statement made earlier in the Purāṇa by Sūta that Vṛtra had been slain by Srī Devī, since it is well known that Vṛtra was slain by Indra.

The earlier statement by Sūta appears in the fourth book, where there is a brief reference to Yogamāyā as "the Goddess by whom the *daitya*s, Vṛtra and others, were slain."[47] The *Devī-Bhāgavata* here may well be taking advantage of a passing comment in the *Bhāgavata*, for there, as we have seen, when Indra is rescued from the belly of Vṛtra, he is saved not only by the Mahā-Puruṣa (Viṣṇu), but also by the force of "*yoga-māyā*."[48] For the *Bhāgavata*, "*yoga-māyā*" is simply the inherent, mystical power of Viṣṇu, in this case the magical power that allows Indra to burst forth unscathed from the demonic maw.[49] For the *Devī-Bhāgavata*, Viṣṇu's intrinsic power has become personified as the mighty and independent Goddess, Yogamāyā, hardly the first example of such personification.[50]

While the *Devī-Bhāgavata* may be indirectly indebted to the *Bhāgavata* for the notion that Vṛtra's slayer is the Devī, there are other ancient and more explicit sanctions for such a view, even though such allusions are rare. Already in the *Ṛg Veda* we find the goddess Sarasvatī referred to as Vṛtraghnī (Destroyer of Vṛtra),[51] and in the *Devī-Māhātmya* the Devī is called Vṛtra-prāṇaharā (Stealer of the life of Vṛtra).[52] Similarly, according to the commentator Nīlakaṇṭha, the *Āditya Purāṇa* refers to the Goddess as the slayer not only of Mahiṣa but also of Vṛtra.[53] Yet as the same commentator points out, it is only in the *Devī-Bhāgavata* among all the Purāṇas that the death of Vṛtra by the Goddess is actually described.[54]

The *Devī-Bhāgavata* commences the actual account of the Vṛtra-vadha by quoting a number of lines, often nearly verbatim, from the opening verses of the Udyoga version, the principal source of the Vṛtra legend for the Purāṇa.[55] The Udyoga begins with the initial rivalry between Indra and Vṛtra's elder brother, the great ascetic Triśiras. The god becomes increasingly apprehensive as he watches the demon's power constantly growing through the practice of severe austerities. Indra first tries to distract Triśiras with seductive Apsarases, a common tactic of the god against ascetic rivals, but usually unsuccessful as is the case here. The god is thus forced to take more violent action before it is too late and angrily strikes down Triśiras with his bolt. Indra justifies his deed by the

Machiavellian principle that "a growing enemy, though still weak, is not to be overlooked by the strong."[56]

The *Devī-Bhāgavata* follows fairly closely the Udyoga's rendering of the Triśiras affair, simply accentuating Indra's moral depravity and emphasizing the contrast between the wicked-hearted god and the blameless demon. In the Purāṇa, even Indra recognizes the goodness of his rival, but this in no way deters him.[57] Further, the Purāṇa eagerly anticipates the theme of the false peace treaty: Indra, in rationalizing his slaughter of Triśiras, declares that "an enemy by all means is to be slain, even by fraud (*chalena*)."[58] Yet it is actually Vṛtra, rather than Triśiras, who is slain by fraud. Moreover, the *Devī-Bhāgavata* refers to the amorous gestures and allurements of the heavenly nymphs sent by Indra to seduce Triśiras as a "*viḍambana*."[59] This term, used previously to describe Viṣṇu's beheading as an embarrassing accident, here means a fraud or deception and is still another foreshadowing of the treacherous alliance between the gods and Vṛtra.

After Triśiras' death, his father Tvaṣṭṛ creates the awesome and effulgent Vṛtra to wreak vengeance on Indra. The *Devī-Bhāgavata* elaborates extensively on the preparations for war between the gods and the mighty demon, and adds an initial skirmish not found in the epic in which the gods are thoroughly routed.

The major deviation of the *Devī-Bhāgavata* from the Udyoga at this point, however, is the addition of a boon granted by Brahmā to Vṛtra.[60] After seeing the gods flee in fear, Vṛtra returns home to his father, declaring that he has accomplished what he set out to do. He even brings Indra's elephant as an offering to his father, a sure sign of Indra's complete humiliation. Though he did not slay Indra, the dutiful and righteous son explains that it is improper to kill one who is frightened. Tvaṣṭṛ, unlike his naive son, is ever distrustful of the gods, especially of Indra, whom he refers to as a deceiver (*chalakartā*).[61] Tvaṣṭṛ accordingly advises his son to practice *tapas* for strength in battle and to receive a boon from Brahmā.

Vṛtra, the ever-obedient son, goes off to perform the requisite austerities, and despite Indra's usual attempts to disrupt his meditation with celestial damsels, he eventually wins the favor of Brahmā after one hundred years. Vṛtra requests and receives from the creator the following boon: "May my death not come through any weapons made of iron or wood, that are dry or wet, or shafted, or any other weapon. May my strength increase in battle, so that I am unconquerable by the gods."[62]

Brahmā's boon-granting, especially his conferring of invulnerability on gods and demons alike as a reward for their *tapas*, is notorious in the epics and Purāṇas. As the father of both gods and demons, his impartiality is understandable. Yet he is not totally indiscriminate: "He gives immortality [to the good demons]. . . . To sinful demons he refuses immortality. He allows the Asuras to grasp the shadow, not the substance."[63] Frequently the "shadow" consists of a series of conditions of invulnerability that at first sight appear to insure immortality. But inevitably there is found a loophole in the boon that the gods exploit. As the gods themselves declare in the *Devī-Bhāgavata*, "an enemy is to be slain by any weak point or loophole (*chidreṇa*); this is the eternal law (*sanātana-dharma*)."[64] The boon given to Vṛtra in the *Devī-Bhāgavata* contains just such a loophole.

The idea of Brahmā's granting a boon to Vṛtra, while absent in the Udyoga, is not original with the *Devī-Bhāgavata*. In the Śānti, Śiva explains to Indra the reason for his early defeats in battle against Vṛtra: "[That demon] practiced austerities for sixty thousand years to gain strength. Brahmā then gave to him a boon consisting of yogic greatness, vast powers of illusion, mighty strength and formidable prowess."[65] The *Devī-Bhāgavata* thus may have gotten the general inspiration for Vṛtra's boon from the Śānti, but the specific conditions of the boon anticipate and replicate the terms of the peace treaty as given in the Udyoga.

Why does the *Devī-Bhāgavata* reduplicate the treaty in the form of the boon? This treaty, we may note, originally belonged to the story of Indra's fight with the demon Namuci rather than with Vṛtra. The Indra-Namuci myth, with roots in the *Ṛg Veda*, is briefly told in the Śalya Parva of the epic.[66] Indra enters into friendship with Namuci, agreeing not to slay him with anything wet or dry, in the night or the day. Eventually, however, Indra slays his "friend" with foam, which is neither wet nor dry.[67] The Indra-Namuci myth also appears in the *Bhāgavata*, but the *Bhāgavata* transforms the original treaty into a boon, whereby all notions of deceit vanish.[68] The *Devī-Bhāgavata* thus has a certain precedent for converting the treaty into a boon, while still retaining the treaty with its deceitful implications.

The *Devī-Bhāgavata*'s interest in the boon, while possibly stimulated by the *Bhāgavata*'s example, is not fully explained by that alone. A comparison of the various demon-slaying myths in the *Devī-Bhāgavata* shows that most were patterned quite uniformly. This pattern includes the granting of a boon, usually by Brahmā but occasionally by the Devī, even in myths which in their earlier versions outside the *Devī-Bhāgavata* lacked this motif. The insertion of the boons appears to be part of a strategy to conform the Devī's heroic deeds to the traditional pattern of certain of Indra's and especially Viṣṇu's great demon-slaying exploits. In the typical epic-Purāṇic pattern, the reception of the boon by a demon is followed by his becoming puffed up with pride as he experiences increasing success against the gods. The arrogance and success eventually require the action of the supreme ruler of the universe to curb.

The motif of demonic arrogance is of critical importance to the *Devī-Bhāgavata*, for it is this pride that makes a demon subject to the self-delusions that bring about his downfall. This arrogance and the ensuing susceptibility to delusion constitute the real weaknesses in a demon's defenses, rather than the loopholes in the conditions of a boon, for the gods can take advantage of the loopholes only when the demons have waxed proud. While demons frequently withstand the onslaught of deceptive and alluring maidens who threaten their austerities, there is none who does not succumb to the seductive delusion of pride brought about by a sense of invulnerability. The inclusion of the boon in the Vṛtra episode, accordingly, serves as an opening for the introduction of the Devī into the mythic action, for she is the Goddess of delusion, Yogamāyā herself.

Following the grant of the boon in the *Devī-Bhāgavata*'s account, Vṛtra proceeds to battle against Indra and the gods at his father's urging. The Purāṇa once again follows, often quite literally, the Udyoga's description of the ensuing struggle, including the swallowing of Indra by Vṛtra, the rescue of the *deva* chief by means of "the Yawn," and the subsequent rout and retreat of the gods. The epic, however, emphasizes the demon's burgeoning strength in battle, while the Purāṇa points to the growing pride of the *asura*, "filled with the arrogance of the boon."[69] The Purāṇa is clearly preparing the way for the entrance of the Goddess, whose deluding power will curb the demon's pride.

In both the Udyoga and the Purāṇa, Indra and the other defeated celestials now seek refuge with Viṣṇu. In the Purāṇa, however, they first go to Śiva, who advises them all to go to one who can really help in this situation, namely, that "wise Janārdana [Viṣṇu], . . . expert in fraud (*chala-jña*)."[70] Then, in both versions again, the gods offer praise to Viṣṇu. They appeal to his track record in overcoming demons, specifically his defeat of Bali (in his dwarf incarnation) and his recovery of the elixir from the *daityas* (as the temptress Mohinī).

The epic Viṣṇu responds briefly with a plan to conciliate Vṛtra and to make a truce with him. Viṣṇu promises in addition to enter unseen into Indra's bolt, which will then have the necessary power to destroy the demon. The Purāṇic Viṣṇu offers the same basic strategy, but is much more explicit about the deception involved, repeatedly stressing the necessity of the fraudulent truce (*sāma-pratāraṇam*) and justifying the plan by arguing that there is no sin in practicing deceit (*śāṭhyam*) on a deceiver.[71] In any case, Viṣṇu continues, he has practiced such deception in the past, referring back to the two *avatāras* just mentioned: the dwarf and the temptress. By contrast, the epic seems little concerned to implicate Viṣṇu in the fraud beyond his role as supreme adviser.

At this point we come to the *Devī-Bhāgavata*'s second major departure from the Udyoga with the long-anticipated introduction of the Devī directly into the myth. She is introduced by Viṣṇu himself, who in concluding his advice to the gods tells them to take refuge in the supreme Goddess and worship her. When pleased, she will delude Vṛtra, who then will easily be conquered. Viṣṇu then recalls his own five-thousand-year-long battle with Madhu and Kaiṭabha. On that occasion, after he had sufficiently propitiated her, the two demons had become deluded (*mohitau*), puffed up with pride (*madagarvitau*), and were slain by Viṣṇu with a trick (*chalena*).[72] Thus does Viṣṇu finish his counsel, and the gods go off to worship the Devī.

The *devas* appeal to the Goddess not only as the remover of all sorrows, but also as their mother. They point out that a mother protects her sons even if they are at fault. Why, then, does she not rescue the gods now, who are faultless? Perhaps, they wonder, she thinks they have abandoned real devotion to her and have come to her simply out of greed for wealth and pleasures. But if this is the reason she is disregarding them, it goes against the natural maternal instinct which she herself ordained. In any case, even if they are immersed in wealth and have abandoned her worship, they are not to be blamed for they have been overpowered by her delusion (*moha*). They plead with her to use that very power of delusion against the arrogant (*mattam*) Vṛtra so that he will be no more, just as she once slew Mahiṣa, Śumbha, and Niśumbha.

A new line of argument is next employed by the gods. If she is to show mercy (*dayā*) to Vṛtra, then she should slay him at once as he has inflicted misery upon the world. Her purifying arrows can save him from his sin and from the darkness of hell. Those enemies of the gods in the past who were slain by her in battle, being sanctified by her arrows, attained the heavenly groves. Did she not kill them out of fear that they would otherwise fall into hell? Changing their tack once again, the gods insist that Vṛtra is really her enemy as he torments those [themselves] who are devoted to her feet. They conclude their appeal by praising her as the creator of all wealth who out of compassion (*kṛpayā*) gives prosperity to those who worship her.

The Devī, moved by their prayers, appears before the gods in her four-armed, beautiful form, richly dressed in all sorts of erotic apparel (*sarva-śṛṅgāra-veṣāḍhyā*),[73] ready to grant them a boon. The *deva*s repeat their request that she delude Vṛtra, here specifying so that he will come to trust the gods. They also ask her to strengthen their weapon (the word *vajra* is not used, but rather the more general term, *āyudha*).[74] She consents to their requests and disappears.

Once more the *Devī-Bhāgavata* returns to the Udyoga account in describing, with typical elaborations, the peace treaty that the seers, acting as spokesmen for the gods, are able to contract with Vṛtra. The Purāṇa has the seers, in their conciliation of the demon, pointedly observe that while there is atonement for drunkards and Brahman-slayers, there is no absolution for those who betray their friends, despite the fact that this is precisely what they know Indra intends to do.[75] The actual terms of the truce are copied nearly verbatim from the epic: Vṛtra will agree to peace if he is not to be slain "by anything dry or wet, made of wood or stone, by a bolt, either by day or night, by Indra with the gods."[76] These conditions, of course, simply reiterate for the most part the terms of the boon Vṛtra had already received from Brahmā according to the Purāṇic version.

The betrayal and slaying of Vṛtra proceed along similar lines in the Purāṇa and epic. While the demon basks in his apparent new-found security, Indra is constantly looking for a means to betray him, searching for some loophole in the truce. One evening, the god finds Vṛtra alone on the seashore. Recalling the boon,[77] he realizes that it is the hour of the terrible twilight,[78] neither day nor night. The time is now or never to kill the demon, through deceit.

In the Udyoga, Indra calls Viṣṇu to mind and then sees a pile of foam in the ocean. Reckoning it to be neither dry nor wet, nor a weapon, he throws the foam at Vṛtra with the *vajra*. Viṣṇu, entering the foam, slays the *asura* (although Viṣṇu had earlier promised to enter the thunderbolt, not the foam).[79] In the *Devī-Bhāgavata*, when Indra remembers Viṣṇu, the latter enters invisibly into the thunderbolt. This, of course, is more consistent with Viṣṇu's earlier words, but more importantly, leaves the foam "unoccupied" as it were, ready for a different infusion of energy. Thus, when Indra takes the frothy mass from the sea to cover his weapon, he recalls the supreme Śakti, who imparts a portion (*aṃśa*) of herself into the foam, thereby fulfilling the request of the gods to strengthen their "weapon" (*āyudha*). Finally, with his foam-smeared bolt, Indra smites the demon and is praised by the seers.

The *Devī-Bhāgavata* adds its own little flourish to the finish.[80] The gods now all honor the Devī, as it was through her grace (*prasāda*) that the demon was vanquished. They set up an image of the Goddess in the celestial gardens and offer *pūjā* to her thrice daily, as she is now their tutelary deity. Peace and order are restored to the cosmos, and the Purāṇa concludes: "In this manner, Vṛtra was deluded by her and was killed violently by Indra with the foam penetrated by the supreme Śakti. Thus, Devī is sung in the worlds as 'Vṛtra-nihantrī' [Vṛtra-slayer]; and since the slaying was actually carried out by Indra, it is also said that [Vṛtra] was slain by Indra."[81] The statement that Devī is celebrated in the worlds as the slayer of Vṛtra helps to set this act of the Goddess alongside her other better-known deeds. Thus, elsewhere in the Purāṇa we find the Devī praised as "Crusher of Niśumbha and Śumbha, Destroyer of Raktabīja, Remover of Dhūmra-*locana, Slayer of Vṛtra* (Vṛtrāsura-nivarhiṇī), Killer of Caṇḍa and Muṇḍa."[82]

The aftermath of the slaying (Indra's flight from Brahmanicide) is told in some detail in the *Devī-Bhāgavata*. For our purposes we may simply note that here, unlike in the Udyoga (and other epic versions), Viṣṇu shares the blame with Indra for the double crime of Brahman-murder and for betrayal of friendship.[83] Although no specific punishment is mentioned for Viṣṇu's role in this affair, it is clear that similar acts of his in the past have resulted in various karmic retributions, often in the form of having to undergo *avatāras* in undesirable forms.[84]

In the end it seems that the *Devī-Bhāgavata* has created an immense dilemma for itself. The Purāṇa wishes to make clear that the Devī is the final refuge of the universe and the power ultimately responsible for overcoming demonic threats to cosmic order, including quite naturally the threat posed by Vṛtra. Yet the Purāṇa also portrays Vṛtra's slaying as an act of cold-blooded murder, a Brahmanicide as well as a heinous betrayal of friendship, in an attempt thoroughly to discredit Indra and particularly Viṣṇu. By insisting on Devī's role as the real power behind the act, the *Devī-Bhāgavata* appears to have implicated her in the very treachery it so vigorously condemns in relation to the two Haris. Is the Purāṇa letting her get away with murder?

One possible justification for her actions has already been suggested by the gods themselves when they plead with her that out of compassion and to save the demon from his own bad karma, she should slay him, purifying him with her arrows. But in that case, Indra and Viṣṇu as well should be praised as Vṛtra's benefactors. Moreover, the Goddess does not actually use her arrows to slay the demon, but rather deludes him and then finally "foams" the hapless *asura*. If Viṣṇu is to be condemned for concealing himself in the bolt, how can she be excused for entering into the foam? Even more, if he is depraved for counselling the false treaty, how can she escape guilt for deluding Vṛtra into accepting that same truce? A further explanation requires a more careful look at her deluding power (*māyā, moha*). Viṣṇu also, as we have seen, wields his own *māyā*, and thus a comparison of their uses of delusion and illusion in the two *Bhāgavata*s will be quite instructive. We shall at the same time need to consider the closely related concepts of responsibility and grace.

Delusion, Responsibility, and Grace in the Two *Bhāgavatas*

In looking at the uses of *māyā* and *moha* (illusion and delusion) in the two *Bhāgavata*s, we shall focus on their incarnational aspects. In the *Bhāgavata*, when the gods appeal to the supreme refuge for help in vanquishing Vṛtra, they refer to the Lord's *māyā* as the mysterious power by which he manifests himself in his several *avatāra*s in age after age to protect the gods and punish the demons.[85] Closely related to this magical power of incarnation is the notion of *viḍambana*. As we saw in the preceding chapter, this term in the *Bhāgavata* signifies the Lord's ability to imitate creaturely beings, such illusory imitations being regarded ultimately as beneficent and salvific deceptions.

From the standpoint of his devotees, the Lord's deceptive illusions naturally appear benign, but how do they appear to the victims of these *avatāri*c apparitions, the *daitya*s themselves? The line betweeen a playful deception (*viḍambana*) and an outright fraud is a thin one. In the *Bhāgavata*, in fact, the Lord is occasionally accused of being a cheat by his demon adversaries. Thus, the demon Hiraṇyakaśipu, grieving and maddened by Viṣṇu's slaying of his brother Hiraṇyākṣa, calls the Lord a fraudulent, scheming (*kūṭa*) enemy, having assumed the form of a wild animal (boar) through his *māyā*.[86] Nor is it simply a matter of the Lord's assuming illusory disguises. He also acts in a deceiving manner.

Probably the most famous of Viṣṇu's deceptive tricks is his request for three paces of land from Bali. In the *Bhāgavata* the dwarf (Viṣṇu himself in disguise) refers to Viṣṇu as the best of conjurers (*māyāvināṃ varaḥ*),[87] while Bali's adviser Śukra warns the demon king of Viṣṇu's intended deception. But Bali, the righteous demon, having promised the Brahman dwarf his request, refuses to go against his word, declaring: "There is no greater breach of *dharma* than untruth (*asatya*)."[88] After the dwarf grows to cosmic size and takes his three steps, the *asuras*, seeing everything taken away by the deceitful begging (*vyāja-yācñayā*), protest: "He [the dwarf] is no associate of Brahmans but Viṣṇu himself, the best of conjurers, disguised in the form of a Brahman."[89]

The *Devī-Bhāgavata* picks up on these suggestions and repeatedly censures Viṣṇu for his deceptions. Thus the sage Sumedhas declares: "Deceiving the *daityas*, without fear of sin, Hari incarnates in various wombs."[90] Similarly, the demon Mahiṣa, after condemning Indra for his adulterous ways and for having broken a treaty with Namuci, proceeds to denounce Viṣṇu as a master of fraud (*kapaṭācāryaḥ*), a cheat (*kuhakaḥ*), learned in deceit (*daṃbha-paṇḍitaḥ*), who takes various forms at will, such as the boar to slay Hiraṇyākṣa and the man-lion to slay Hiraṇyakaśipu.[91] Viṣṇu's role in the ocean-churning, during which he seized the elixir from the demons by fraud (*chalena*), is likewise noted.[92] But it is especially his dwarf form that draws the attention of the *Devī-Bhāgavata* composer(s): "Viṣṇu, the embodiment of *sattva*, was born as the deceitful dwarf (*kapaṭa-vāmana*) and took [Bali's] kingdom by fraud (*chalena*)."[93] "For the purpose of deception (*chalārtham*) Viṣṇu became a dwarf, by whom Bali was deceived (*vañcito*). . . . Bali was virtuous and truthful. . . . Who was the victor, the deceiver or the deceived? . . . Bali was the victor, by whom the earth was given [as alms to the dwarf]."[94]

The *Devī-Bhāgavata* introduces a new element not just in taking these accusations seriously, but also in interpreting Viṣṇu's deceptions as the result of his being deluded by the Devī in the first place. Elaborating, as it were, on Sumedhas' words above, Vyāsa declares in introducing the Vṛtra episode, "Viṣṇu indeed always slays the *daityas* with deception (*kapaṭena*), even though he is *sattvic*, having suffered delusion (*moha*). . . . Who then can overcome even in their minds the Bhagavatī, the deluder of the entire world (*samastajana-mohakarīm*)?"[95]

We can also begin to see that the *Devī-Bhāgavata* makes a distinction, somewhat loosely drawn at times, between delusion (*māyā, moha*) on the one hand and deception (*chadman, chala, dambha, kapaṭa, pratāraṇa, śaṭh, vañc,* etc.) on the other. The Devī may delude demons, gods, the whole world, even Viṣṇu, but she does not practice deceit. Accordingly, Devī's deluding Vṛtra so that he will place trust in the gods is not quite the same thing as the actual urging upon the hapless demon the fraudulent treaty.[96] This may at first appear a bit sophistic, especially given that Viṣṇu's behavior is itself the consequence of her deluding him. Nonetheless, the tension between delusion and deception highlights important aspects of the problem of moral responsibility as well as helping to illuminate the various modes of Devī's divine grace.

When we look closely at the notion of delusion in the *Devī-Bhāgavata*, we find mentioned two different "sources" of *moha*. Often, as we have seen, it is the Devī herself, but also, quite frequently, *moha* is said to arise from *ahaṃkāra*, the principle of egocentricity. These two sources, while seemingly distinct, are actually complementary, for the Devī's deluding power simply acts upon the egoistic impulses already inherent in creatures. Thus, Viṣṇu's deceptive acts are ultimately due to his own egoistic nature, which made him subject to her *moha* in the first place. How, then, does egocentricity originally arise, and what constitutes its specific nature?

According to our text, following general Sāṃkhyan ideas, *prakṛti* (the impersonal, material force of the universe) evolves out of itself the ego-principle in three modes according to the three strands or *guṇas*; from the resulting threefold *ahaṃkāra* arises the whole world and its various qualities.[97] Out of the *sattvic ahaṃkāra* come forth charity and sacrifice; out of the *rajas*ic and *tamas*ic spring quarrelsomeness and delusion. This *tamas*ic, *ahaṃkāra*-based delusion is defined as the false sense of agency: "I am the doer, by me this is done."[98] Such a perception is false, within the Sāṃkhyan perspective, because the real Self (*puruṣa*) is not an agent.

From the theistic perspective of the *Devī-Bhāgavata*, however, the false sense of agency stems from ignorance of the Devī as the real agent responsible for all actions.[99] Such ignorance gives rise to lust, anger, and greed,[100] and to a general possessiveness: "This body, house, relatives, sons, wife are mine."[101] This possessiveness in turn leads to acts both good and bad, including deceit. So long as one insists on being the agent responsible for such acts, then so long will there be appropriate karmic consequences.[102]

Viṣṇu is portrayed ambivalently by the *Devī-Bhāgavata* in the Vṛtra episode: he appears both as an arrogant, Machiavellian schemer, and as a devotee of the Devī. In the former role he is held accountable for his misdeeds. In the latter, he recognizes that even his own delusion is a part of Devī's play and transcends the relative notions of right and wrong. The gods were quite correct in suggesting that even if they were sunk in pleasures and the seeking of wealth and fame, it was not their fault, as it was the result of her own deluding power.[103] This higher theistic perspective thus deemphasizes moral responsibility and even sees the Devī's delusion as a kind of gracious act: one's inherent egocentricity is momentarily strengthened and brought to the surface by her delusion so that it finally can be overcome, thereby short-circuiting the normal karmic process.

Within the *Devī-Bhāgavata* a recurring theme is the contrast between the inexorability of karma and the graciousness of the Devī. The tension between karma and grace, while disconcerting to those who seek a logical and consistent explanation of life's vicissitudes, is not without purpose. From the devotional standpoint of the *Devī-Bhāgavata*, the stress on karma's inevitability is a confession of one's own dependence and helplessness: against the dark and fearsome cloud of karmic vulnerability, the loving grace of the Devī shines all the more brilliantly. The starkness of the contrast between karma and grace thus heightens the anxiety, the anticipation and relief in giving up one's sense of self-sufficiency and surrendering oneself to the supreme.[104]

Both *Bhāgavatas*, of course, hold that the power of grace is ultimately greater than that of karma. But the relationship between karma and grace is envisioned somewhat differently in the two texts. As we have seen, the *Bhāgavata* declares that Viṣṇu favors his devotees frequently by "granting" them poverty, or grief, as in the case of Citraketu. Sons, wife, home, relatives, all these ensnare the mind. To be sure, on a lower level of grace, Viṣṇu may bestow such wordly benefits. But his higher form of grace acts to take them away. As Viṣṇu himself says in responding to the gods' plea for help against Vṛtra:

> When I am pleased, what difficult thing cannot be attained? But he who knows the truth desires nothing other than me. . . . The ignorant person knows not his own good, taking the *guṇas* as real. Whoever bestows [the objects of sense] on one desiring them is a fool of like sort. One who knows his own good does not teach the path of action (karma)[105] to the ignorant, just as a doctor does not give unwholesome food to a patient, even if desired.[106]

Viṣṇu, in the *Bhāgavata*, is the supreme physician whose grace is the medicine that cures the disease of karmic entrapment.[107]

The *Devī-Bhāgavata* agrees with the *Bhāgavata* that humankind's basic predicament is attachment to things and persons that causes one to turn away from or forget the supreme. But what is needed is not the medicine of a doctor but the patience and love of a mother. We can now begin to see some of the theological dimensions reflected in the different attitudes of the two Purāṇas towards the stages of life. Earlier, we noted that the *Bhāgavata* is wary of the householder *āśrama,* in contrast to the *Devī-Bhāgavata*'s insistence that a man must pass through all four stages. The *Devī-Bhāgavata* emphasizes that sons, house, wives, and the like are not in themselves what bind; rather it is *ahaṃkāra* that binds creatures to *saṃsāra.*[108] It is the mistaken sense that one has somehow achieved one's wealth, success, and happiness by one's own doing that is the problem. The Devī, like Viṣṇu, grants wealth and pleasure on a "lower" plane. But her higher form of grace does not necessarily deny these creature comforts; rather, it provides insight to allow one to enjoy prosperity and good fortune as her gifts without the egocentric delusion of taking personal credit for them. Her gifts are simply to be enjoyed for what they are, the beneficence of the divine mother.

Accordingly, even the fearful law of karma can take on a benign aspect: the *Devī-Bhāgavata* at times suggests, not that we can evade our karma, but rather that karma is the mother's way of working out our own destiny. As Vyāsa explains:

> Māyā, the very form of the supreme Brahman, ceaselessly directs (or impels) [all] beings in accord with karma previously done. There is no harshness or cruelty ever on the part of the Bhagavatī; she strives only to free the soul (*jīva-mokṣārtham*). If she did not create this whole world, moving and unmoving, then, without Māyā, the world would ever be unconscious. Therefore, ever resorting to compassion, she creates the worlds and *jīvas*, directing them on.[109]

Here, it seems, is the *Devī-Bhāgavata*'s most profound attempt to reconcile the notions of karma and grace.

It is a tribute to the Paurāṇikas of both *Bhāgavatas* that the Vṛtra myth could be molded and shaped so nicely to express the varied concerns of each group, to portray the problems of human existence that each sees as most compelling, and to suggest the appropriate solutions. Despite genuine differences, the two *Bhāgavatas* are not totally at odds with each other.

The complementary differences of the two Vṛtra episodes can

well be summarized in the words of the Purāṇas themselves. In the *Bhāgavata* Indra, upon hearing the wise words of Vṛtra, declares to the demon: "It is indeed a great wonder that you, *rajas*ic by nature, have set your heart firmly upon the Lord of *sattv*ic essence."[110] Similarly, King Parīkṣit wonders: "How could the sinful Vṛtra, *rajas*ic and *tamas*ic in nature, have such firm devotion to the Lord? Devotion to the Lord's feet does not arise, as a general rule, even in the hearts of the purely *sattv*ic gods or the untainted sages."[111] The *Bhāgavata* thus not only stresses that devotion can overcome sinful or demonic nature but also undermines the stereotypic norms of society. The divisions of class and rank are deceptive, for true wisdom and faith transcend such norms. Pride in one's social status or learning is merely delusion. Association with the outcaste, the ritually impure, is not to be avoided, for among them may be those especially blessed by God.

For the *Devī-Bhāgavata*, the real wonder of the Vṛtrāsura episode is that even a *sattv*ic being like Viṣṇu can commit *rajas*ic or *tamas*ic acts. As the seers say to Sūta: "The gods are born of *sattva*, humans of *rajas*, and animals of *tamas*. . . . There is a great wonder then in that the mighty Vṛtra was slain by Indra with a trick, impelled by Viṣṇu, the best of those endowed with *sattva*."[112] The conclusion here is that if even Viṣṇu, the very embodiment of *sattva*, can commit such heinous deeds, then anyone in the world is capable of unlawful acts. Pride in one's own righteous character or *sattv*ic nature is wholly misplaced, since even *sattva* is one of the *guṇa*s and subject to *moha*.

Thus both *Bhāgavata*s stand in awe of the confusion of *guṇa*s that constitute this world. Both acknowledge the difficulty of overcoming the supreme's deluding power, and the final goal for both, from our human perspective, is to cross over the web of *māyā*. But the *Devī-Bhāgavata* Paurāṇika seems more entranced by the supreme Māyā, more willing to appreciate the playful aspects of delusion, to delight in the garden of this world, even with its barren and bitter trees.

* * *

The composer(s) of the *Devī-Bhāgavata* exhibited little hesitation in searching out the varied dimensions of the enchanting power of Māyā, even at the risk of succumbing to her alluring charms. This is perhaps most evident in the Purāṇa's treatment of the erotic features of the Devī, a motif already hinted at from time to time. It is a motif occasionally juxtaposed with the Devī's role as mother, as seen in her manifestation to the gods in the Vṛtra story when she appears before her "sons" dressed in seductive attire. More commonly, however, her erotic side is interwoven with her martial aspect, a combination that is one of the intriguing features of the Purāṇa, as well as of Māyā itself! This feature will become a recurring theme in the next part.

In Part I, we have concerned ourselves primarily with the relationship between the two *Bhāgavatas*, both in terms of their canonical status and textual models, and in terms of their theological insights. We have seen that the *Devī-Bhāgavata* is not content to glorify the universal power of the Goddess as simply a kind of alternative vision to the *Bhāgavata*'s view of Viṣṇu as supreme, but also insists upon demoting and embarrassing this rival deity. In the process, the *Devī-Bhāgavata* has attempted to wrest not just ultimate power from male divinity, but final authority as well. Power, *śakti,* had long been associated with the feminine side of divinity. But this power had been largely controlled by masculine authority, reflective of the norms of Hindu society especially as they pertain to the husband-wife relationship. The power of Hindu goddesses, at times highly dangerous and destructive, was thus often limited and channeled by their male consorts. When the various goddesses merge in the figure of the dominant Goddess, she comes to wield both power and authority.[113]

The *Devī-Bhāgavata* in celebrating the all-powerful and authoritative Goddess is indebted in many ways to the *Devī-Māhātmya*'s vision of the ultimate as feminine, further elaborating, clarifying, and interpreting the nature of the Devī from its own cultural, historical, and theological perspective some five or six centuries later. The relationship between the *Devī-Bhāgavata* and the *Devī-Māhātmya* will thus be the focus of Part II, in which we examine the Goddess more on her own terms, rather than in relation to Viṣṇu.

her manifestation to the gods in the Vṛtra story, where she appears before the gods dressed in seductive attire. More commonly, however, her erotic side is interwoven with her martial aspect, a combination that is one of the intriguing features of the Purāṇas, as well as of Māyā itself. This feature will become a recurring theme in the next part.

In Part I we have concerned ourselves primarily with the relationship between the two *Bhāgavatas*, both in terms of their canonical status and textual models, and in terms of their theological insights. We have seen that the *Devī Bhāgavata* is not content to glorify the universal power of the Goddess, simply a kind of alternative vision to the *Bhāgavata*'s view of Viṣṇu as supreme, but also insists upon demoting and embarrassing the rival deity. In the process, the *Devī Bhāgavata* has attempted to wrest not just ultimate power from male deity, but final authority as well. Power, *śakti*, had long been associated with the feminine side of divinity. But this power had been largely controlled by masculine authority, reflective of the norms of Hindu society, especially as they pertain to the husband-wife relationship. The power of Hindu goddesses, at times highly dangerous and destructive, was thus often limited and channeled by masculine authority. When the various goddesses merge in the figure of the dominant Goddess, she comes to wield both power and authority.[10]

The *Devī Bhāgavata*, in celebrating the all-powerful and authoritative Goddess, is indebted in many ways to the *Devī-Māhātmya* for much of its vision of the ultimate as feminine, further elaborating, clarifying, and interpreting the nature of the Devī from its own cultural, historical, and theological perspective some five or six centuries later. The relationship between the *Devī-Māhātmya* and the *Devī Bhāgavata* will thus be the focus of Part II, in which we examine the Goddess more in her own terms, rather than in relation to Viṣṇu.

Part II

The Two Devī-Māhātmyas: *Revisions Within the Tradition*

Chapter 4

The Three Great Adventures of the Devī: Heroic Eroticism and Maternal Compassion

The mythological core of the *Devī-Bhāgavata* is undoubtedly the account of the Devī's three great demon-slaying exploits given in the *Devī-Māhātmya* of the *Mārkaṇḍeya Purāṇa.* The *Devī-Māhātmya* nestles the three episodes within a frame story that provides one of several important links between the activities of the Goddess on the cosmic plane and the world of ordinary human affairs. This frame story, recounting the quest of a king and merchant to understand the reasons for their worldly misfortunes and mental sufferings, will be dealt with in detail in chapter six.

These three main exploits of the Goddess in the *Devī-Māhātmya* concern the slaying of the demons Madhu and Kaiṭabha, the killing of Mahiṣa, and the destruction of Śumbha and Niśumbha, each story told with increasing elaboration. Interspersed with the narrative accounts and integral to them are various hymns of praise by the gods to the Devī glorifying her demon-slaying prowess. Brief reference is made to future deeds of the Devī, against such demons as Durgama and Aruṇa. The Devī herself then praises the preceding accounts or glorification (*māhātmya*) of her exploits. The *Devī-Māhātmya* closes by returning to the frame story.

The *Devī-Bhāgavata* recounts the frame story and the three chief adventures of the Devī on two separate occasions. The first retelling, in considerably more detail than in the *Devī-Māhātmya*, changes the overall structure of the narrative in two major ways. First, the frame story is given only as a final commentary or conclusion to the three *caritras* (stories). Second, the initial episode with Madhu and Kaiṭabha has been split off and placed much earlier in the text. Thus, the myth of Madhu and Kaiṭabha is given in the first Skandha, while those of Mahiṣa and of Śumbha and Niśumbha occur in the fifth, along with the frame story.[1]

Despite this splitting off of the first adventure, the reasons for which we shall consider in a moment, the *Devī-Bhāgavata* in general clearly considers the three episodes to be an interconnected whole. Not only does the second retelling[2] retain the *Devī-Māhātmya*'s basic structure of the three myths, but even the first retelling, in introducing the frame story, has King Janamejaya request, "By whom was she [the Devī] worshipped in ancient times by means of the three stories (*caritra-traya*)?"[3] Janamejaya seems to have no trouble connecting the three, even though several thousand verses and various other episodes have intervened between the narration of the first and of the other two great deeds of the Goddess. Similarly, the sage of the frame story (Sumedhas in the *Devī-Bhāgavata*), in describing the proper form of worship of the Devī, includes "the daily recitation of the three adventures" (*caritra-traya-pāṭham*).[4] This is a tribute to the influence and success of the *Devī-Māhātmya*, for it is the text that first links the three stories into an interrelated unit.

As we shall see in the next chapter, the notion that there are *three* great deeds of the Devī is not particularly emphasized in the *Devī-Māhātmya*. The Devī herself, to be sure, does summarize her exploits by referring to the three sets of demons indicated above,[5] but the explicit division of the text into three acts is the product of later interpretation and editing. In any case, by the time of the *Devī-Bhāgavata*, the interconnection of the three deeds is already so well known that even when one of the episodes is separated off by itself, it is still assumed to be one of the three.

It has been indicated above that the *Devī-Māhātmya* provides the mythological core for the *Devī-Bhāgavata*. Lalye suggests much the same thing by stating that "The Saptaśatī[6] or Devī Māhātmya is the primary source of the DB [*Devī-Bhāgavata*]."[7] Although both retellings in the *Devī-Bhāgavata* share occasional verbal similarities with the *Devī-Māhātmya*, Lalye's assertion needs some qualification and clarification, for the *Devī-Māhātmya* at times serves more as an inspirational seed than as the actual primary textual source for the *Devī-Bhāgavata*. For example, the Mahiṣa episode in the first retelling is primarily indebted, from a textual and thematic point of view, not to the *Devī-Māhātmya* but to the *Vāmana* and *Varāha* Purāṇas—we shall analyze these textual relationships later.[8] Nonetheless, the presence of the *Devī-Māhātmya* can always be felt in the background of the *Devī-Bhāgavata*'s narratives.

In this regard, it is of interest that the two accounts of the frame story in the *Devī-Bhāgavata*, which themselves seem to be fairly directly derived from the *Devī-Māhātmya*, each mention the supreme or unequaled "Devī-Māhātmya."[9] These references, however, seem to be generic, signifying the glorification of the Goddess in general rather than a specific text, and can as easily refer to the *Devī-Bhāgavata*'s own recountings of the three stories as to the *Mārkaṇḍeya*'s.[10] Indeed, it is unlikely that the *Devī-Bhāgavata* composer made any great distinction in his own mind between the "Devī-Māhātmyas" of the *Mārkaṇḍeya* and of his own Purāṇa.[11] (For the sake of clarity, I shall set off with quotation marks any mention of a "Devī-Māhātmya" that is not specifically referring to that of the *Mārkaṇḍeya* alone. This latter, having become a text in its own right, will always be italicized.) In any case, the "Devī-Māhātmyas" of the *Devī-Bhāgavata* are not simply summaries of the *Devī-Māhātmya*, but reenvisionings of the Devī first revealed therein. Such reenvisioning is a "seeing again," though in a different context, the same grandeur of the Goddess in her destructive yet salvific modes that the composer(s) of the *Devī-Māhātmya* had felt centuries before.

We shall begin our investigation of the reenvisioning process by looking carefully at the *Devī-Bhāgavata*'s first retelling of the three adventures and the textual models on which it is based, starting with the myth of Madhu-Kaiṭabha. This myth, to which we have referred on several occasions, introduces most of the major new themes that are developed more fully in the remaining two episodes. Yet these new motifs for the most part are new only relative to the *Devī-Māhātmya*, for our Purāṇa has borrowed them from various sources. The originality of the *Devī-Bhāgavata* lies not so much in these "new" motifs as in the way it has interwoven and synthesized older materials and themes.

The Seduction of Madhu and Kaiṭabha: Heroic and Lustful Pride in the *Devī-Māhātmya* and the *Devī-Bhāgavata*

Of the three great adventures in the *Devī-Bhāgavata*, it is the story of Madhu and Kaiṭabha that adheres most closely to the *Devī-Māhātmya*, despite certain striking departures. Not the least of these is the separation of the story from the other two, as already mentioned. But the story is not simply isolated; it is combined with the immediately preceding myth of the decapitation of Viṣṇu and the slaying of the demon Hayagrīva. Together, these two episodes serve to introduce, in mythological terms, two of the major themes of the Purāna as a whole: the Goddess as the ultimate power and authority in the universe, and the radical dependency of the gods, especially Viṣṇu, upon her. The Madhu-Kaiṭabha myth brings out a cosmogonic perspective that is largely submerged in the Hayagrīva story. This cosmogonic aspect is not unrelated to Devī's role as Mahā-Māyā, in which she creates the universe through her mystical power and simultaneously deludes all worlds. This deluding role appears in both the *Devī-Māhātmya*'s version and the *Devī-Bhāgavata*'s, but the latter adds a new dimension to it. Let us look in some detail, then, at the two versions of the myth.

Summaries of the Madhu-Kaiṭabha myth from the *Devī-Māhātmya* and the *Devī-Bhāgavata*, placed in parallel columns, easily show many of the major innovations of the latter text. I have numbered the individual motifs according to their appearance in the *Devī-Bhāgavata* for ease of comparison.

Devī-Māhātmya[12]	*Devī-Bhāgavata Purāṇa*[13]
1. Viṣṇu lies asleep on the cosmic waters	1. The same
2. Madhu-Kaiṭabha spring from Viṣṇu's earwax	2. The same
	3. Madhu-Kaiṭabha receive a boor from the Devī that they will di only when they so desire
4. Madhu-Kaiṭabha seek to slay Brahmā sitting on Viṣṇu's navel-lotus	4. Madhu-Kaiṭabha see Brahm on Viṣṇu's navel-lotus and offe him a choice: to flee or fight
	5. Brahmā considers the fou means of foreign polity but discards them
	6. Brahmā hymns Viṣṇu to arous him but fails
7. Brahmā praises Yoganidrā and requests her to delude the demons and awaken Viṣṇu	7. Brahmā praises Yoganidrā an requests her to kill him or th demons, or to awaken Viṣṇu
8. The Devī quits Viṣṇu's body and he arises	8. The same[14]

	9. Madhu-Kaiṭabha approach and offer Brahmā a new choice: to become their servant or fight
10. Viṣṇu fights the demons for five thousand years	10. Viṣṇu intervenes and a five-thousand-year-long battle commences
	11. Viṣṇu tires and ponders the situation, while the demons offer him the choice: to become their servant or fight
	12. Viṣṇu insists on a rest, and while reflecting, comes to know of the Devī's boon to the demons
	13. Viṣṇu takes refuge with the Devī, who promises to delude the demons with sidelong glances so that he may kill them
	14. As the battle is about to resume, the demons preach to Viṣṇu on the uncertainty of fate
	15. During the ensuing fight, Viṣṇu again becomes distressed and appeals to the Devī, who deludes the demons with seductive glances
	16. Viṣṇu offers the love-struck demons a boon
17. In their pride of strength, deluded by the Devī, the demons offer Viṣṇu a boon	17. In their amorous pride, deluded by the Devī, the demons refuse Viṣṇu's boon and offer him a counterboon
18. Viṣṇu asks that they be slain by him	18. The same
19. The demons ask in turn to be slain where there is no water	19. The demons, realizing they have been deluded, now ask for their boon: to be slain where there is no water
	20. Viṣṇu offers his thighs as a dry place
	21. The demons expand their size, trying to escape their doom, but Viṣṇu grows as well

22. Viṣṇu places the demons on his thighs and beheads them	22. Madhu-Kaiṭabha give up, place their heads on Viṣṇu's thighs, and he beheads them
	23. Their marrow (*medas*) fills the ocean, becoming the earth (*medinī*)

A number of the changes in the *Devī-Bhāgavata* reflects the text's characteristic emphasis on Viṣṇu's helplessness and merely extends the *Devī-Māhātmya*'s own glorification of the Devī over the Trimūrti. Brahmā's unsuccessful attempt to arouse Viṣṇu from the influence of sleep (#6) and Viṣṇu's weariness in battle (#'s 11-12) are typical of this sort of addition. (The motif of Viṣṇu's battle fatigue, we may recall, is already introduced in the preceding myth of Viṣṇu's losing his head after falling asleep on his bow). Even the little episode of the demons' attempt to escape death by expanding their bodies and Viṣṇu's greater expansion to frustrate their attempt (#21) serves indirectly to subordinate him to the Devī, for his expansive powers, well known from his dwarf incarnation, are seen to be effective only when so willed by the Goddess.

More important for our present purposes are the reinterpretations of key aspects of the mythic action and the introduction of certain philosophical and political themes that intertwine with the mythic events. Five such changes are particularly noteworthy: 1) Devī's boon to the demons (#3); 2) the demons' offering to Brahmā the choice of fleeing or fighting (#4), a choice later modified to becoming their servant or fighting (#9), this latter being repeated to Viṣṇu (#11); 3) Brahmā's consideration of the four means of polity (#5); 4) the demons' brief discussion of fate (#14); and 5) the Devī's seduction of the demons (#'s 13, 15-17). Let us consider each of these in some detail.

The account of the demons' receiving a boon from the Devī is as follows. Before their confrontation with Brahmā, while they are sporting on the primordial waters, Madhu and Kaiṭabha begin to ponder the source of their own origin and on the nature of the supporting force that upholds the cosmic ocean. Kaiṭabha, with sudden insight, realizes that Śakti, the supreme Devī, must be the cause and support of all. The two demon brothers, as they meditate on this insight, hear the beautiful Vāg-bījā (seed-mantra of Sarasvatī). Through repeating the mantra and practicing various other austerities, the demons please the Devī in her form as Vāc, and she speaks to them in disembodied voice, granting them a boon through her grace. They request "death by our own will" (*svecchayā maraṇam*).[15]

This boon provides a clever tie-in with the traditional exchange of boons between Viṣṇu and the demons later in the myth, when the god requests the *asuras* to let him kill them, in effect asking that they will their own deaths. We shall return to this exchange of boons when we come to the Devī's seduction of the demons. The Devī's boon also helps to explain why Viṣṇu's initial five-thousand-year battle with Madhu and Kaiṭabha is so futile, as they are protected by her grant. At the same time, the introduction of the boon is typical of the *Devī-Bhāgavata*'s transformation of the major *devāsura* myths taken over from older sources, as we have already seen in the story of Vṛtra.

There are seven major *devāsura* myths in our Purāṇa, all of which incorporate the motif of a boon that renders the demon or demons apparently invulnerable to the attacks of the gods, usually by granting the *asuras* freedom from death except under the most unlikely of circumstances.[16] Inevitably, the boon creates a false sense of security and pride in the demons and thus serves as a major tool of the Devī in bringing about their delusion and final destruction. In most of the myths, Brahmā is the grantor of the boon. Only in the first two, dealing with the slaying of Hayagrīva and of Madhu and Kaiṭabha, is Brahmā replaced by the Devī. This modification, appearing very early in the Purāna, indicates right away that the Goddess is the ultimate boon-giver in the universe. In the Hayagrīva myth, no reason is given as to why the demon chooses to seek a boon from the Devī. In the Madhu-Kaiṭabha myth, however, it is the result of the two demons' reflection upon the ultimate power of the universe and their realization of the Devī as supreme. This motif of recognition of the Devī, in somewhat altered form, also plays an important role in the other two great adventures of the Goddess.

The significance of the boon in the Madhu-Kaiṭabha story is evident on many levels, from the narrative to the theological. One further function of the boon, perhaps not so obvious as those mentioned above, concerns its role in connecting the myth with one of the major philosophic issues of the text: the tension between fate and will. This aspect is brought out by the particular form of the boon itself. In most of the other boons of apparent immortality granted to various demons, death is to occur only under a set of extraordinary physical conditions, such as by a horse-faced being or during a time that is neither day nor night. Here, the extraordinary circumstance is psychological: the demons can be slain only when they will it. As Viṣṇu himself realizes during his futile battle when he ponders the Devī's boon to his adversaries: "No one willingly desires his own death, even when he is miserable, sick, or destitute. How can it be that these proud fellows will ever desire their own death?"[17] The conflict between Viṣṇu's will (to kill the demons) and the demons' will (to live) is a reflection of the higher tension between the inevitable fate of the demons (death, necessary for the creation of world order) and their ability to live so long as they wish it.

Ironically, it is the demons, puffed up with confidence in their boon, who lecture Viṣṇu on fate and its apparent inevitability. After Viṣṇu's withdrawal from battle to catch his breath, the *daityas* challenge him to one last fight: "Stand up, stand up and fight, Four-armed One, realizing that victory and defeat are ruled by fate. The strong [usually] attain victory, yet through fate, the weak may conquer. Thus the great-spirited neither rejoice nor grieve in either case."[18]

Somewhat similar sentiments are expressed by Manu in his famous *Laws of Manu* regarding the duties and responsibilities of kings (*rāja-dharma*). Manu warns that victory and defeat in battle are uncertain, as experience reveals. His conclusion differs, however, from Madhu and Kaiṭabha's, for he admonishes the king to avoid fighting if at all possible, rather than to be indifferent to the outcome.[19] Of particular relevance to us is that this advice in the *Laws* occurs in the midst of a discussion of the four expedients of polity (*upāya, upakrama*), that is, the various means to be adopted against one's foes. The four are *sāma* (conciliation), *dāna* (gifts, bribery), *bheda* (sowing dissension), and *yuddha* or *daṇḍa* (fighting or punishment).[20]

These are the same four means pondered by Brahmā when challenged by Madhu and Kaiṭabha to step down from his lotus seat (growing from Viṣṇu's navel) and flee or fight. The lotus seat, the demons argue, is to be enjoyed only by a hero (*vīra*), and if Brahmā is cowardly (*kātara*), he must leave. Flight, of course, is dishonorable and a dereliction of duty, but Brahmā also is aware that he ought not risk a fight since he does not know the strength of his enemies, a wise conclusion under the circumstances according to the principles of Manu.[21] The other three expedients, representing the approach of artful statesmanship, are a compromise between the cowardly and heroic responses. But Brahmā also rejects each of the remaining *upāyas* in turn: if he praises the demons (to effect conciliation), they will realize his weakness and even one of them will then be able to slay him; bribes, Brahmā says (but he gives no clear reason why), are not appropriate; and there is no way he can see to sow dissension. The creator, unable to rely on his own strength, realizes he must turn elsewhere and thus resolves to wake Viṣṇu. Accordingly, as the text says, "he went in his mind to Viṣṇu, the destroyer of sorrow, for refuge (*śaraṇa*)."[22]

Seeking the protection of a stronger king or ally is, once again, a sound principle of Manu's political strategy. Seeking protection or refuge (*saṃśraya*) belongs to a second set of expedients, known as the six stratagems (*ṣaḍ-guṇas*), which partially overlap with the set of four. This second set consists of peace or alliance (*saṃdhi*), war (*vigraha*), marching (*yāna*), halting (*āsana*), duplicity (*dvaidhī-bhāva*), and seeking refuge (*saṃśraya*).[23] Manu gives specific advice as to when the various stratagems are to be employed.[24] Only when one is strong relative to one's enemy should one make war. When weak, a king must resort to one or another of the various means, and when in imminent danger of attack, he must seek at once the protection of a righteous and powerful king. The *Devī-Bhāgavata* has clearly portrayed Brahmā as a prudent king as described in the ancient *Laws of Manu.* Brahmā's mental recourse to Viṣṇu, on one level, is simply the adoption of the appropriate means for a king about to be overwhelmed by his enemies.

Brahmā's seeking refuge with Viṣṇu is not just an astute political maneuver, however. It is also a significant devotional act, for *śaraṇa* or refuge in relation to a god implies not only the recognition of the god's superiority, but also a surrender or submission to that god, even when motivated, initially, by fear. It is hardly surprising to find, in the context of the *Devī-Bhāgavata,* that when the creator's seeking protection from Viṣṇu turns out to be unavailing, he next seeks refuge with Yoganidrā. As Brahmā tells the Goddess: "O Devī, seeing the horrendous Kaiṭabha along with Madhu, I am frightened and come to you for shelter."[25] His submission to her will, though not total, is evident later in his petition to her. He declares: "Kill me now, Mother, if you wish. Death [at your hands] will not grieve me. Since I was made the creator by you, it would be a great disgrace if I were slain by these demons. Arise, O Devī, assume your wondrous form and smite me or these two, as you wish, in your little girl's play! Or wake Hari that he may slay them."[26]

The creator's *bhakti*c surrender to the will of the Goddess, consequent upon his recognition of her as the supreme force, stands opposed to his earlier consideration of the four expedients, in which his apparent independence as a free agent, his reliance on his own effort, and his self-interest are paramount. The four means represent, as it were, attempts to save oneself. Seeking refuge, in the devotional sense of surrender to the supreme, is the giving up of that attempt.

There are, of course, other kinds of surrender, as seen in the modified choice or challenge that the demons offer to Brahmā (#9). After Viṣṇu has awakened from his slumber and attempted to console the frightened creator, Madhu and Kaiṭabha approach the two gods and declare to Brahmā: "Why have you fled here to [Viṣṇu's] presence? Fight and we shall kill you while he looks on, and then we shall slay him. . . . Give battle now, or say, 'I am your slave (*dāsa*).'"[27] Viṣṇu steps in at this point and agrees to fight in Brahmā's stead, but he eventually tires (after five thousand years) and withdraws from battle. The demons then offer the same choice to Viṣṇu: "If you are too weak and tired from fighting, then with folded hands upon your head declare, 'I am your slave.'"[28]

Such servitude or surrender out of the desire to save one's own skin is apparently beneath Viṣṇu's sense of dignity, for he resorts to one of the three expedients of artful statesmanship, conciliation. With words charming and conciliatory (*sāma-pūrva*), he reminds the demons that it is not the *dharma* of heroes to fight with those who are tired, frightened, weaponless, fallen, or too young, recalling a similar set of rules in the *Laws of Manu*.[29] With this plea, Viṣṇu is able to gain a respite, during which he discovers the reason for the demons' indefatigability (i.e. the Devī's boon). He too, like Brahmā before, now takes refuge in the Devī, acknowledging her as mother and as the power that made him unconscious through sleep. Viṣṇu, like Brahmā, appears as a prudent king, as well as a devotee of the Goddess.

The interweaving of the several political, philosophical, and theological themes reaches its consummation in the seduction of Madhu and Kaiṭabha by the Devī (the actual death of the demons on Viṣṇu's thighs, from the perspectives of the *Devī-Māhātmya* and the *Devī-Bhāgavata*, is a bit anticlimactic, being secondary to the actions of the Goddess herself). The primary tension, in the *Devī-Bhāgavata* version of the story, is that between the inevitable death of the demons and their ability not to die unless they so will, a tension brought about by the graciousness of the Devī herself through the gift of the boon. It is the resolution of this tension, possible only by the same means that created it, that is the focus of attention of the *Devī-Bhāgavata* composer.

Before considering the *Devī-Bhāgavata*'s account of the seduction, let us look at the parallel story of the delusion of the demons in the *Devī-Māhātmya*. According to the latter, Brahmā, while praising Yoganidrā and just prior to his asking her to quit Viṣṇu's body, requests her to delude the demons. The story proceeds quickly through Viṣṇu's awakening and his five-thousand-year battle with the *asuras*. Then it is simply reported: "Those two [demons], arrogant in their excessive strength and deluded by Mahā-Māyā, declared to Viṣṇu: 'Choose a boon from us.'"[30] Viṣṇu promptly responds: "If you should now be pleased with me, then you both are to be slain by me."[31] The two deluded *asuras*, seeing the whole world in flood and, implicitly, hoping to escape their folly in granting Viṣṇu the boon, ask to be slain where there is no water. Viṣṇu assents to this request and the familiar denouement follows.

The *Devī-Māhātmya* account gives little elaboration to Mahā-Māyā's deluding Madhu and Kaitabha, beyond juxtaposing it to the haughty arrogance of the demons. She is thus seen as the cause of their heroic pride, which in turn induces them to make their foolish offer. The *Devī-Māhātmya*'s major contribution to the myth at this point, compared to earlier versions, is its interjection of the Goddess as the cause of their delusion. In one *Harivaṃśa* version, we find Madhu being charmed by the music of celestial musicians and dancers, and by the "yogic eye" of Viṣṇu, but this account makes no reference to any boons.[32] In certain other *Mahābhārata* and *Harivaṃśa* versions the pride of the demons arises naturally, as it were, from their own egotistical self-deception and false confidence in their warrior's strength.[33]

In adding the Goddess the *Devī-Māhātmya* has partially obscured the full story of the exchange of boons between Viṣṇu and the demons, thereby leaving somewhat unexplained why the demons make their request, and why Viṣṇu agrees to it. The more complete version is found in the *Mahābhārata*.[34] There, after Viṣṇu awakens, he sees the demons and declares to them: "Welcome, O mighty ones, I will give you an excellent boon, for I am pleased with you."[35] The demons, described as great heroes, are apparently too proud to accept the boon. They laugh at Viṣṇu and offer him a boon instead, insisting that they are the donors (*dātārau*) (rather than the other way around). Viṣṇu readily accepts their boon, realizing there is no man equal to them, and demands that they be slain by him. The demons, appreciating their predicament as they will not go back on their word, are then forced to claim their boon, previously promised by Viṣṇu.

This *Mahābhārata* version clears up many, but not all, of the questions relating to the exchange of boons. As Coburn asks, for instance, "Why should Viṣṇu, when awakened, be pleased with the Asuras?"[36] What, indeed, prompts Viṣṇu to make the first offer? It is here that the *Devī-Bhāgavata* is able to tie up various loose ends from both the epic and the *Devī-Māhātmya* and to introduce some of its own favorite themes.

Let us pick up the *Devī-Bhāgavata*'s account where we left it above, with Viṣṇu's taking refuge with Yoganidrā after discovering the reason for his foes' seemingly tireless energy in battle. He concludes his plea for help by pointing out that Madhu and Kaiṭabha, who are eager to kill him, have become arrogant through her boon. The Devī replies, "Go fight again, Viṣṇu. . . . I shall certainly delude the two *dānavas* with a sidelong glance. O Nārāyaṇa, quickly slay those two, deluded by my *māyā*."[37] Viṣṇu once more confronts the demons, once more he begins to tire as they exchange pounding blows. The demons are described exactly as in the *Devī-Māhātmya:* arrogant in their excessive strength (*tāv apy atibalonmattau*).[38] But in the *Devī-Bhāgavata*, the ensuing, deluding activity of the Devī is not simply juxtaposed to the demons' haughtiness but is spelled out in detail.

Viṣṇu in his distress puts on a woeful face and looks to the Devī for her promised help. Seeing him in such a pitiable condition (*karuṇā-rasa-saṃyutam*), she laughs and decides it is time to act. She shoots sidelong glances, like the arrows of Kāma, accompanied by gentle smiles and amorous gestures suggestive of pleasure and delight, at the *asuras*. The two hapless fellows, beholding her face, become utterly infatuated, overwhelmed by the darts of love. Staring at her beauty, they are transfixed. Viṣṇu realizes her intention and observes that the demons are thoroughly deluded. Knowing what needs to be done, Viṣṇu speaks to them with soothing words, offering them a boon and indicating that he is pleased with their prowess in fighting. Never before, in all his fights with demons, has he encountered the likes of Madhu and Kaiṭabha. The *dānavas*, still ogling Mahā-Māyā and afflicted with love, loftily announce to Hari that they are not beggars but rather donors (*dātārau*), in a manner reminiscent of the *Mahābhārata* account. Adding that they are pleased with his fighting, they offer him a boon. Then, in words identical with those of the *Devī-Māhātmya*, Viṣṇu accepts: "If you should now be pleased with me, then you both are to be slain by me."[39] The remainder of the *Devī-Bhāgavata*'s story follows, in its essentials, the *Devī-Māhātmya*.

The *Devī-Bhāgavata* has preserved the *Mahābhārata*'s structure of the exchange of boons, intermeshed with the *Devī-Māhātmya*'s incorporation of the Goddess' deluding activity and its own introduction of her boon to the demons. In the process, the *Devī-Bhāgavata* has reinterpreted the deluding activity of the Devī in terms not just of heroic arrogance, but also of lustful pride, as the demons foolishly flaunt their self-perceived superiority to Viṣṇu in front of a supposedly admiring Devī. The Madhu-Kaiṭabha myth in the *Devī-Bhāgavata* thus serves to delineate two of the three major personalities of the Goddess displayed in her demon-slaying exploits, that of the mother and of the alluring woman. The third personality we shall consider in a moment.

In the major myths of *asura*-slaughter in the *Devī-Bhāgavata*, the Goddess' primary role as mother is as protector, refuge, and counselor of the gods, though her maternal aspect as world creator often resonates in the background. This latter or cosmic maternal aspect emphasizes her power and overlordship, the former her graciousness and mercy towards all beings, deserving or not. Her seductive role in these myths, when present, is simply part of her more general deluding proclivity as Māyā or Mahā-Māyā. In general, she is approached as mother by those who are oppressed and fearful, and as alluring woman by those who oppress and are haughty. Or conversely, the Devī manifests herself as mother to those who are humble, in order to comfort them; as alluring woman to those who are proud, as a means of their own destruction.

In the episode of the slaying of the demon Hayagrīva, the Devī's maternal temperament is paramount. Accordingly, as mother, she does not enter directly into the actual slaughter: she simply provides refuge to the gods along with the wise counsel that will resolve their dilemma. Further, any deluding activity on the part of the Devī is at best implicit; Hayagrīva does become puffed up with pride before his destruction, but the cause of his pride is not specified. In the Vṛtra myth, the Devī's beguiling power is manifested, as it is responsible for the demon's acceptance of the fatal treaty. Her delusive persuasion of Vṛtra, however, is not particularly erotic, despite a hint of her seductive persona in the attire she wears in her appearance before the gods. As in the Hayagrīva myth, the Devī here comes forth largely in her maternal guise, consoling and advising the gods and remaining somewhat removed from the destructive action, though a part of her *tejas* enters into the deadly foam. As she becomes more directly involved in the carnage, her erotic, alluring manifestation comes to play an increasingly important role. Thus, in the Madhu-Kaiṭabha myth, she appears in seductive guise on the battlefield, though still refraining from actual combat.

When the Goddess enters fully into battle, her alluring aspect becomes combined with her third major personality complex, that of the fiery and valorous hero. This paradoxical combination of the seductive hero contains a number of apparently antithetical qualities, including that of womanliness and manliness, an enigma that completely undoes her demon antagonists in her next two great adventures.

The Destruction of Mahiṣāsura: All is Fair in Love and War, but is it Love, or War?

As indicated above, the primary textual models for the Mahiṣāsura myth in the *Devī-Bhāgavata* are the *Vāmana* and *Varāha* Purāṇas rather than the *Devī-Māhātmya*.[40] The *Varāha* account of the Mahiṣa myth, according to Kane, "appears to be the earliest Paurāṇika version of the slaughter of Mahiṣāsura."[41] Kane is almost certainly correct, for the *Varāha*'s account of the origin of the Goddess from the united vision of the Trimūrti seems clearly older than the *Devī-Māhātmya*'s version, which came to be the standard, of the Devī's arising from the accumulated energy or *tejas* of the gods. Further, according to the *Varāha*, the origin story explains the arising of the Goddess in general, not just of the form associated with the slaying of Mahiṣa. The *Vāmana* version,[42] though evidently later than the *Varāha*, still appears to precede the *Devī-Māhātmya*.[43]

The *Vāmana* and *Varāha* Purāṇas preserve a number of ancient themes or motifs in the Mahiṣa myth that were ignored by the *Devī-Māhātmya* but which were revitalized by the *Devī-Bhāgavata*. Yet the Devī mythologies of these two Purāṇas could never serve, by themselves, as primary sources of inspiration for the Śākta composer of the *Devī-Bhāgavata*, for neither the *Vāmana* nor the *Varāha* understands the Goddess as *the* ultimate reality. The *Devī-Bhāgavata* thus remains theologically closer in spirit to the *Devī-Māhātmya*.

To show the major innovations of the *Devī-Bhāgavata* relative to the *Devī-Māhātmya* and the dependency of the former on the *Vāmana* and *Varāha* Purāṇas, I have placed summaries of all four versions of the Mahiṣa myth in parallel columns. Again I have numbered the individual motifs or units according to their appearance in the *Devī-Bhāgavata* for ease of comparison. Given the greater complexity of the Mahiṣa myth, I have often combined related motifs into a comprehensive unit for the sake of brevity. Bracketed [ ] units in the summaries of the *Vāmana* and *Varāha* accounts indicate motifs that are extraneous to the *Devī-Bhāgavata* but which are necessary to the particular story lines of those Purāṇas. Themes or subplots in the *Vāmana* and *Varāha* not vital to the understanding of their stories and which have no parallel in the *Devī-Bhāgavata* have been ignored entirely.

The Destruction of Mahiṣāsura by the Goddess Durgā (Mahā-Lakṣmī, according to the *Devī-Bhāgavata Purāṇa*). Pen and ink drawing on palm leaf strips (c. 35 cm x 42 cm). From the author's collection. Photo by Patricia Ullmann.

Devī-Māhātmya[44]	*Devī-Bhāgavata Purāṇa*[45]
1. A great *devāsura* battle breaks out when Mahiṣa and Indra are lords of the demons and gods	1. A great *deva-dānava* battle arises during Mahiṣa's reign over the world
	2. Mahiṣa formerly attained a boon from Brahmā that he could not be slain by anyone of the male sex, females supposedly being too weak to fear
	3. Mahiṣa's origin from Rambha and a she-buffalo described
	4. Mahiṣa, having conquered the human world, sends an ultimatum to Indra in heaven: flee, serve, or fight
	5. Indra scorns Mahiṣa, and the gods and demons hold councils in preparation for war; Bṛhaspati discourses to the gods on fate; Viṣṇu urges war
6. Mahiṣa defeats the gods and rules heaven	6. A dreadful battle ensues, in which the demons rout the gods
7. The gods headed by Brahmā seek refuge with Śiva and Viṣṇu	7. The gods seek refuge with Brahmā, then with Śiva, and finally with Viṣṇu
8. The gods describe their defeat at the hands of Mahiṣa to Viṣṇu and Śiva, who become angry, their faces furrowed	8. The gods discuss Mahiṣa's boon, and Viṣṇu offers a plan: to create through their collective energies, with the help of their wives, a female being capable of killing the demon
9. Energy masses emerge from the faces of the angered Viṣṇu, Brahmā, and Śiva, and from the bodies of the other gods; the energies merge and form a woman	9. Energy masses emerge from the faces or bodies of the several gods, including a red mass from Brahmā, a silvery *tamas*ic mass from Śiva, and a bluish *sattv*ic mass from Viṣṇu; the energies merge and form a beautiful woman, Mahā-Lakṣmī, who is tri-colored and endowed with the three *guna*s

Vāmana Purāṇa[46]	*Varāha Purāṇa*[47]
[Mahiṣa introduced as one of the demons slain by Kātyāyanī when she was protected by the Viṣṇu-amulet given by Śiva]	2. Cf. 16 below
3. Mahiṣa's origin from Rambha and a she-buffalo described	
5. Mahiṣa defeats the gods, who quit heaven	[The demon Andhaka torments the gods]
7. The gods headed by Brahmā go to Viṣṇu and Śiva	7. The gods headed by Brahmā go to Śiva; Brahmā also remembers Viṣṇu, who appears among them
8. The gods relate their plight brought about by Mahiṣa to Viṣṇu and Śiva, who become furious	8. The Trimūrti merge into one and they look at each other with subtle vision
9. An energy mass arises from the angry faces of the gods, is increased by the energy of the sage Kātyāyana, and from that mass the beautiful Devī Kātyāyanī is born	9. Their subtle vision, itself threefold, becomes one, in which is born a divine maiden of three complexions; she later assumes three forms: Brāhmī, of white color and *sattvic*; Vaiṣṇavī, red and *rajasic*; and Raudrī, black and *tamasic*

10. The woman's (Devī's) body parts correlated with the gods from whose energy they arose	10. The same
11. Weapons and emblems given to the Devī by the gods	11. The same
	12. The gods hymn the Devī and request her to slay Mahiṣa, which she agrees to do
13. The Devī gives forth horrible laughs, shaking the earth; the gods shout "Victory"; the demons mobilize for war	13. Thinking of the gods' helplessness, the Devī gives forth a terrible laugh; the earth trembles, the gods shout "Victory," and the demons are filled with fear
14. Mahiṣa, angered, rushes towards the roar, surrounded by *asuras*	14. Mahiṣa, angered, sends envoys to find the source of the sound and to fetch the fellow responsible so he may be punished and slain
	15. The envoys find the Devī and report her beauty to Mahiṣa; they know not who she is, but she seems unmarried, and she is endowed with the *rasas*[48] of love, heroism, laughter, terror, and wonder
	16. A series of councils between Mahiṣa and his ministers begins, interspersed with missions to the Devī with proposals of marriage; the ministers discuss fate, the four expedients of polity in dealing with the Devī, and debate her true nature, specifically, whether she is passionate or hostile; she rejects all love proposals and gives the demons a choice: flee to Pātāla or fight; the envoys note the contrariety of love and heroism and are confused by her amorous looks that seem to conflict with her warlike talk

10. The same	
11. The same	
13. The Devī, pleased, laughs boisterously and is hymned by the gods; she then rides off on her lion to the Vindhya Mountains	[All three goddesses go off to mountain retreats to practice austerities; Vaiṣṇavī Devī goes off to the Mandara Mountains]
	[During *tapas*, Vaiṣṇavī's mind is disturbed, from which arise millions of maidens; she builds a city with palaces for all]
15. Envoys of Mahiṣa, Caṇḍa and Muṇḍa, see Kātyāyanī on the mountain and report her beauty to their lord; she is well armed, however, and they know not who she is	15. Nārada arrives at the city, is amazed by the Devī's beauty, but also by her dispassion, and goes to tell Mahiṣa his discovery
16. Mahiṣa dispatches his troops from heaven to go to the Devī's mountain and sends the demon Dundubhi to the Goddess, with a proposal of marriage; she agrees to accept Mahiṣa as her husband, if he pays the bride price customary in her family, namely, that she be conquered by him in battle; Dundubhi reports her reply to Mahiṣa	16. Mahiṣa discusses with his ministers the four expedients for securing the lady; an envoy is sent to find out more about her; at the same time, Mahiṣa, insolent from Brahmā's boon that no male can slay him, attacks and defeats the gods; meanwhile, the envoy proposes marriage to the Devī, who only laughs as she is under a vow of perpetual virginity

17. Mahiṣa, rushing towards the roar, sees the Devī and sends his troops into action; masses of demons are slaughtered and one by one the demon generals are killed	17. The missions turn violent as the envoys begin to attack the Devī when their proposals are rebuffed; the envoy-generals are slain, one after another, along with their supporting armies, while Mahiṣa holds further councils
18. Mahiṣa, in his buffalo form, terrifies the Devī's troops, slaying many with his hooves, horns, tail, muzzle, and the blast of his breath	18. Mahiṣa himself finally goes to the front, still with hopes of success in his amorous pursuit as he drops his buffalo form and assumes a handsome, human body; his importunities are rebuffed as the Devī declares that she desires no man but the supreme Puruṣa and in any case she has come to the world to protect the righteous: he must flee to Pātāla or fight
19. Mahiṣa attacks the Devī's lion; she binds him with a noose, but he becomes a lion, then a man, an elephant, and finally a buffalo again	19. Mahiṣa attacks the Devī and more of his troops die; he attacks her lion, becoming a lion himself; he next becomes an elephant, a Śarabha,[49] and again a buffalo, as he attempts to escape her onslaught
20. The Devī quaffs wine, jumps on Mahiṣa's neck and strikes him with her spear; caught under her foot, he half issues forth from his buffalo mouth; she beheads him with a sword; the other demons perish, crying "Alas"	20. The Devī quaffs wine and pursues Mahiṣa, who assumes various magical bodies; she pierces his chest with a trident, knocking him senseless on the ground; he stands up, kicking the Devī, but she beheads him with a discus; the remaining *daityas* flee to Pātāla
21. The gods hymn Devī, who soon vanishes	21. The same
	22. The Devī returns to her home

17. Mahiṣa with his army goes forth to the Vindhyas to fight Kātyāyanī; protected only by the Viṣṇu-amulet, she slays many demons, some with the help of Bhūtas (spirits) that issue from her laughter; she quaffs a drink	17. Nārada informs the Devī of the gods' defeat; she sallies forth with her maidens, all in terrible forms, and falls upon the demon army; many *daitya*s are slain while others retreat
18. Mahiṣa ravages the Bhūtas with his hooves, horns, tail, muzzle, and blast of his breath	18. As the demons retreat to Mahiṣa, he chases the maidens away and comes before the Goddess, who assumes a twenty-armed form and recollects Śiva for the destruction of the demons
19. Mahiṣa chases the Devī's lion, enraging her; she binds him with a noose, but he transforms himself into an elephant, then a buffalo	19. Mahiṣa and the Devī advance against each other; at times he fights, at times he withdraws
20. The Devī hurls a trident, spear, and discus at Mahiṣa, but he shatters them all; she jumps on him and cuts his throat with a spear; a man emerges from the neck, whom she beheads with a sword; the surviving demons enter Pātāla, crying "Alas"	20. The Devī attacks Mahiṣa with her feet and smites him with a spear; she cuts off his head with a sword; a man emerges from the headless body and ascends to heaven due to the touch of her weapon
21. The gods are said to praise the Devī; she, at Śiva's feet, promises to be reborn for their sake and then reenters the gods	21. The gods hymn the Devī; she then dismisses them, remaining where she is

A comparison of the four versions quickly reveals that the *Devī-Bhāgavata* is indebted to the *Varāha* (directly or indirectly) for the following themes: Brahmā's boon to Mahiṣa (DBhP #2; VarP #16); the colorful "*guṇa*-masses" connected with the emergence of the Goddess (#9); Mahiṣa's councils with his ministers and their discussion of the four expedients (#16); and Mahiṣa's sending envoys to the Devī with a proposal of marriage (#16), this latter being found also in the *Vāmana*. The *Vāmana* further has contributed the account of Mahiṣa's birth (#3), the envoys who initially discover the Devī and report her beauty to Mahiṣa (Nārada functions in a similar capacity in the *Varāha*) (#15), and the puzzlement of the envoys as to who she truly is (#15).

The *Devī-Bhāgavata* adds in its own favorite motifs: the discussions of fate (#s 5, 16); the choices of fleeing, fighting, or serving (#s 4, 16, 18); and an extra hymn to the Devī (#12). The *Devī-Bhāgavata* also appends a new conclusion to the story, wherein the Devī returns to her home on the Jeweled Island, thereby making clear that she is in no way subordinate to the gods as is implied in the *Vāmana* account.[50] Perhaps the most striking new feature in the *Devī-Bhāgavata* version, however, is the incorporation of the *rasas*, or aesthetic moods, especially those of heroism (*vīrya*) and love (*śṛṅgāra*), introduced in #15 and permeating the whole series of interactions between the Devī and Mahiṣa with his envoys (#s 16-18). This series of interactions, consisting primarily of alternating councils and missions to the Devī, including Mahiṣa's own entreaties before the Goddess, is the most distinctive part of the Purāṇa's retelling of the story and shall be the main focus of our discussion.

The *Devī-Bhāgavata*'s version of the Mahiṣa myth may conveniently be divided into three parts. The first part of the myth[51] introduces the main protagonists, Mahiṣa and the Devī, balancing the account of her origin with that of the demon's birth and thereby highlighting the contrast between her "high" lineage and his brutish ancestry.[52] This first section further defines their interrelationship within the context of the familiar *devāsura* conflict, and specifically in terms of the boon granted the buffalo demon by Brahmā, namely, that he cannot be slain by any male. It is interesting to note that the *Devī-Bhāgavata* has slightly modified the boon as found in the *Varāha*. In the latter, it is simply stated that Mahiṣa cannot be slain by any male (*puruṣa*).[53] In the *Devī-Bhāgavata*, Mahiṣa requests: "May my death not come from any male (*puruṣa*). What woman can slay me? Therefore let my death be at the hands of a beautiful woman (*kāminī*)."[54] Though in asking for the boon in this manner, Mahiṣa obviously did not intend that he should be slain by a female, this is precisely what his masculine vanity has destined him for, and will subject him to great embarrassment.[55] As in the Madhu-Kaiṭabha myth, a boon serves to create and introduce the central tension, in this case, the paradox within the Devī herself between her delicate, womanly, seemingly passionate and erotic nature and her firm, manly, dispassionate heroic strength.

The second part of the myth[56] works out in detail the relationship and mode of interaction between the Devī and Mahiṣa, to be discussed at length below. The third and concluding part[57] recounts the climactic battle between the two protagonists, the death of Mahiṣa despite his metamorphic attempts to escape, and the restoration of world order.

The sequence of councils and missions, constituting the second part, is introduced by the Devī's boisterous laughing and roaring shortly following her arising from the collective *tejas* of the gods. Mahiṣa, hearing the defiant racket and self-assured in the security of his boon, sends envoys to find out the source of the noise, whether it be a *deva* or *dānava*, and to bring the "evil fellow" back for punishment. Or Mahiṣa will go there himself to slay the trouble-maker. The demon chief is somewhat puzzled as to who the creature can be since the gods are too frightened to roar so loudly, having been utterly vanquished by him, and the demons are all his loyal subjects. But once the cause of the sound is discovered, he will know the proper means (*upāya*) to adopt. Here, then, are introduced the two major questions that run throughout the remaining councils and missions: 1) what should Mahiṣa do against his mysterious challenger, the answer to which depends on: 2) who exactly this adversary is.

The question as to the identity of Mahiṣa's adversary has three distinct but closey interrelated parts. First, what is the gender of his antagonist? This question on the surface may seem self-evident but in fact is more subtle and complex. Second, what is the ancestry or origin of this rival, if he, or she, is not a god or demon? And third, what is the true intention of the challenger in coming before Mahiṣa? Let us deal with each of these questions in turn, treating them in a somewhat more systematic manner than the convoluted and repetitive fashion of the Purāṇa, though we shall miss something of the particular dramatic flavor in the process.

The question of the adversary's gender is implicitly raised in Mahiṣa's initial response to the Devī's roar. He assumes that the source of the noise must be some evil and foolish fellow, a male, and thus his only thought is to chastise and slay his apparent enemy. The first envoys quickly discover their leader's mistake when they realize that the cause of the sound is a radiantly charming woman, fair in all her limbs, eighteen-armed, bearing various weapons and drinking wine. On receiving the report of his messengers, Mahiṣa immediately changes his whole attitude and approach, being entranced by the description of the Devī's beauty. Punishment (*daṇḍa*) or fighting (*yudhha*) are now the farthest things from his mind, as he commands his prime minister to bring the lady to him by any of the first three means of polity (conciliation, gifts, sowing dissension) so that he can make her his principle consort (*paṭṭa-mahiṣī*). If she does not come by these means, she is still to be brought but without hurting her, so that there is no interruption of the mood of love (*rasa-bhaṅga*). Mahiṣa, in thinking that he can easily fetch the object of his love, assumes that she is "just a woman," an assumption shared by his prime minister.

The prime minister goes to the Devī, tells her of his master's greatness and invulnerability to all males due to Brahmā's boon, and of his passionate desire to see her. She rebuffs the invitation, insisting that she has come to slay Mahiṣa at the request of the gods, and that she has assumed the incomparable female form (*strī-rūpa*) so that the words of Brahmā may be fulfilled. The minister protests: "O noble lady (*devī*),[58] boastful from wine (or haughty with pride), you speak words suitable to a woman (*strī*). How can you, a young maiden alone and weak, fight with the mighty Mahiṣa with all his troops, elephants, horses, chariots, and the like?"[59] Fearful of breaking the erotic mood, the minister refrains from harsh words, trying conciliation and gifts. He advises the Devī to accept the submissive Mahiṣa, who is willing to become her servant (*dāsa*) if she will become his queen.

The Devī retorts: "Think over what it meant, fool, when you said I have the nature of a woman (*strī-svabhāvā*). I am not a man (*pumān*) [in my present form], but I have that nature (*tat-svabhāvā*), having [merely] donned the guise of a woman. Since your master requested death by a woman, he is a fool who knows not the heroic sentiment. Only eunuchs, not heroes, take pleasure in such a death. Thus I have come to carry out this business, assuming the form of a woman."[60] The Devī then gives the minister a message for Mahiṣa: he must abandon heaven, leaving the gods their share of the sacrifice, and go to Pātāla if he wishes to live; otherwise, he must fight with her and die.

What are the theological implications of the Devī's statement that she is "*tat-svabhāvā*"? Nīlakaṇṭha glosses the phrase as "*puruṣa-svabhāvā*," "having the inherent nature of Puruṣa." "Puruṣa," of course, means "man," but it also refers, in the Sāṃkhya, to the cosmic principle of spirit over against the material principle of matter. Is the Devī denying, then, her material, feminine nature as Prakṛti? Our commentator insists not, explaining from the point of view of the Goddess: "My form as Brahman, endowed with *māyā*, has the double nature of both the male principle and Prakṛti; therefore there is Puruṣa-nature inherent [in me]." Nīlakaṇṭha's interpretation clearly goes beyond the literal meaning of the text itself but is in accord with the general spirit of the Purāṇa, namely that the Devī on the highest level encompasses and transcends the distinctions of gender.

Just as the demons have a hard time determining the real nature of the Devī's gender, they also have difficulty discerning her true ancestry and origin. Mahiṣa at the start suspects his adversary is apparently neither a god nor human, and his first messengers report to him that the beautiful woman they found is neither human nor demonic. They, in fact, had been unable to discover who she is or who she belongs to, since they had not even been able to see her well, being overcome by her splendor (*tejas*).[61] These uncertainties persist throughout the councils, and despite the Devī's own revelation above that she is not "merely a woman," the demons continue to debate whether she is an ordinary, even lowly woman (*nārī varākī*),[62] or something else.

Mahiṣa himself, after receiving the report of his prime minister's futile mission, wonders, "Is this woman an illusion (*māyā*) projected by the gods, like the illusions of the demon Śambara?"[63] In the ensuing discussion, the demon Tāmra answers his leader's question in the following manner: "She is neither a human, nor a Gāndharvī (celestial musician), nor a demoness. She has been created by the gods as an illusion (*māyā*), spreading delusion (*moha-karī*)."[64] Tāmra hardly realizes the full implications of what he has said, thinking the "illusion" of the mysterious lady to be merely a kind of deceptive trick of the gods to scare the demons, like the illusive tricks of Śambara mentioned by Mahiṣa. Tāmra is not yet aware that she is the great Māyā who deludes the entire universe. Accordingly, he advises his chief not to show cowardice but to fight, though he is not quite sure of the outcome, which is in the hands of fate.

Mahiṣa at this point deludes himself in still aspiring to win over the Devī, but he begins to understand that a fight may be inevitable. He sends Tāmra to fetch the lady by whatever means necessary, even slaying her. But since Tāmra is skilled in Kāma-Śāstra (Science of Love), the demon leader hopes he may succeed with gentler methods. Mahiṣa does advise Tāmra, however, to try to find out whose *māyā* she is before fighting her. Tāmra, incidentally, appears to fulfill many of Manu's criteria for the ideal ambassador: he is versed in various sciences, is supposedly adept at understanding the expressions and gestures of an adversary, knows the proper time and place for action, and whether to pursue peace or war.[65]

Tāmra, however, is no match for the Goddess, and when he returns in terror, frightened by the mere roar of the Devī, Mahiṣa again wonders who this mighty woman (*yoṣā*) is that the gods have created. The demon Viḍāla provides an answer that is even more detailed, more on the mark, than Tāmra's, but still only partial: "The gods, realizing that your death is to come from a woman, have created this lotus-eyed beauty from their *tejas* and sent her forth. They will lay in wait, hidden, until the battle begins, but will then come to her aid, putting her in front. They will slay us all, and she will slay you. That, at least, is what the gods desire, but what will actually happen I cannot say. It is simply our duty as servants to obey you, even unto death."[66]

As the demons surmise more and more about the Devī, they become increasingly hesitant about the outcome, some of them turning quite fatalistic and convinced that they will all be killed. Others, though, cling to the opinion that she is merely an arrogant woman and an illusory "construct" of the gods to create fear, but of no real substance. One of the most obtuse demons, in this regard, is Bāṣkala, who volunteers to go slay the helpless woman, and it is only fitting that he is the first to die at the hands of the Devī. Others quickly follow. While matters have clearly taken a violent turn, the demon envoys to the Devī still present their master's proposal of marriage at the beginning of each encounter. Only after it is rejected and there is no help but to break the erotic sentiment, does the heroic mood become dominant as battle commences. In the final mission of envoys, however, a new mood is interjected.

When Asilomā and Viḍāla, the last of the envoys, come before the Goddess, the former asks her: "You ought always to be resolute in *dharma*, so why do you kill demons without fault, O Mother? Compassion (*dayā*) is *dharma*. . . . Compassion and truth are always protected by the wise."[67] Here, for the first time in the myth, a demon approaches the Devī in a spirit of humility and addresses her not as "Beautiful Woman" (*sundari, kāmini*, etc.), but as "Mother." And at the same time the mood changes, if only for a moment, from the erotic and heroic to the sorrowful and tender (*karuṇa*). We shall deal with the Devī's answer to Asilomā later on, but will note here that the demons, or at least one, has at last recognized something of the real nature of the Devī. She is not simply the *māyā* of the gods, but as she revealed to the prime minister much earlier, she is also the mother of the gods (*surāṇaṃ . . . jananī*).[68] Indeed, as Asilomā perceives, she is mother of the demons as well. Thus, though she arose out of the *tejas* of the gods, she was not "constructed" by them. It was unfortunate for the demons, though seemingly inevitable, that they should not awaken to this truth sooner.

Mahiṣa, dull-witted brute that he is, despite the endless councils and futile missions, never seems to realize who his adversary really is. In seeking her hand, he thinks he is following Manu's ancient principle that kings "should marry a woman of the same class (*savarṇā*), endowed with auspicious marks, born in a great family, charming, beautiful and virtuous."[69] His only mistake here, as it were, is in believing that she belongs to his class. He assumes to the very end that he and she are of like nature and thus would make an excellent pair. When he himself comes before the Devī, he argues that she should marry him on the grounds that the best union is between equals, or where the two strive to surpass each other in cleverness, beauty, family connections, conduct, and the like.[70] He actually considers himself to be her superior and thus to be affording her a chance to improve herself.

The Devī accepts the same principle that a woman should marry her equal or someone superior, but she repeatedly contrasts her own qualities with the buffalo-demon's vulgar, brutish nature. In particular, she points out that he is a grass-eater, with horns and a big belly, and frequently disparages his ancestry, reminding him that he is the son of a she-buffalo, *mahiṣī*. We can now see why, in a punning sort of way, she refuses his offer to become his chief consort, also known as *mahiṣī*. Mahiṣa, in proposing marriage to the Goddess, far from elevating her, is actually attempting to reduce her to the status of a she-buffalo.[71]

In fairness to Mahiṣa, it should be noted that he is at least partially aware of his beastly nature. When he is about to go before the Goddess in person, he realizes that she may be put off by his hideous appearance. Accordingly, he transforms himself into a handsome human figure to aid in his suit for her hand, just as later he adopts various animal transformations in his attempt to escape her fierce onslaught. After all, everything is fair in love and war. Unfortunately for the demon king, until the very end he is never able to decide whether the Devī wishes to make love or war, so enthralled is he by her *māyā*. As we have seen, the Goddess early on tells Mahiṣa's prime minister the true reason for her arrival, namely to carry out the request of the gods in conformity with Brahmā's boon. But the demons do not know whether to accept her statement at face value or not. On the one hand, her appearance is that of a beautiful and passionate woman (*kāminī*) that seems to belie her stated mission—though she does roar in a rather unladylike manner and is fully armed, eighteen arms-worth, in fact. On the other hand, Mahiṣa and many of his advisers cannot believe that any woman can truly resist his masculine charms and heroic prowess.

The perplexity of the demons is marvelously portrayed in the first major council session, immediately following the prime minister's futile mission. Mahiṣa summons his wisest and most experienced counselors, requesting that each speak his own mind about the intentions of the Devī, and then he will decide what course of action to follow—here again, the demon king seems to follow the advice of Manu.[72] The demon Virūpākṣa presents the typical "manly-heroic" view: she is merely a lowly woman who speaks as she does because she is puffed up with pride (*mada-garvitā*).[73] The next counselor, Durdhara, grants a certain validity to Virūpākṣa's opinion but sees it as only a half-truth. His view, the "manly-erotic," is worth quoting at length:

> This woman, O King, is tormented by passion. She acts like a mistress proud of her beauty (*rūpa-garvitā*). She frightens you because she desires to make you submissive to her. Such deportment on the part of proud women is known as coquettish flirtation by a man who understands sentiments (*rasa*). The speech of this passionate woman is ambiguous, intent on securing a lover. When she said, "I will slay you with arrows at the battlefront," her words were pregnant with hidden meaning. It is well known that the arrows of proud women are their sidelong glances, their handfuls of flowers, and their words full of innuendo. How can she cast real arrows on you when Brahmā, Viṣṇu, and Śiva are unable to do so? What she really meant, then, was "I shall slay you, King, with my arrow-like eyes." The envoy, not knowing sentiments, understood her words in the wrong or contrary (*viparīta*) sense. Her words to him, "I shall lay your master low on the bed of battle," are to be understood as referring to the love mode of inverted (*viparīta*) intercourse, with the woman on top. When she said, "I shall take away his life force (*prāṇa*)," know that by "life force" she meant "semen virile." That is what she wishes to take from you, nothing else. An excellent woman seeks a husband using words overflowing with innuendo. . . . Knowing this, O King, whatever you do should be in accord with the sentiment of love. Conciliation and gifts are

> the only appropriate means. By such means, whether she is angrv or vain, that proud lady will become submissive to you.[74]

Needless to say, it is Durdhara's "manly-erotic" view that is false or inverted (*viparīta*). Moreover, much of the demons' perplexity throughout the myth is due to their false assumptions that invert the truth. Even when the course of events undermines their assumptions that "she" is merely a woman, and that as a woman, she must be weak, they are slow to awake to the reality. Rather, they attempt to preserve their false assumptions by explaining the unexpected developments as due to another kind of inversion, the adverse nature of the times and of fate.[75]

This explanation, in fact, is offered by Tāmra, the third and final counselor to speak in the first major council session. He rejects Durdhara's view that the lady is at all passionate or enamored of Mahiṣa, or that she has used any insinuating speech. Tāmra attributes the arrival of the strange, eighteen-armed lady, beautiful, alone, but seeking a fight, to the unfavorable (*viparīta*) time.[76] To prove his point, he cites a number of inauspicious omens that he has recently observed. He then presents his opinion, already noted, that she is the *māyā* of the gods and though omens are bad, the demons must not show weakness and thus must fight with her, whatever the outcome.

Tāmra's explanation for the arrival of the mysterious lady contains some truth. When fate is adverse, inverting the normal course of events, even the weak can conquer and the strong can be defeated.[77] As the Devī herself points out earlier to the prime minister, "When fate is adverse (*viparīta*), a blade of grass may become equal to a thunderbolt, and when fate is favorable, a thunderbolt may be like a tuft of grass."[78] What this aphorism does not say, however, and which the demons fail to see, is that the Goddess is the author of fate. Accordingly, the demons consistently fail to discover the appropriate course of action.

At the conclusion of the council, Mahiṣa sends Tāmra on his mission, wishing to avoid bloodshed and hoping at least to clear up the question whether she is motivated by passion (*kāma*) or by enmity (*vaira-bhāva*).[79] Like Durdhara, Mahiṣa cannot yet convince himself that the Devī's intention is war, not love. This ambivalence on the part of the demons persists even after the Devī has begun slaughtering them. When Cikṣura goes to the Devī after the death of Bāṣkala and Durmukha, for instance, he pleads with her: "The fighting of women is with sidelong glances and amorous gestures. Never is a woman like you to fight with actual weapons, for even striking your body with flowers causes pain to such a woman."[80]

The Goddess herself tries to make quite clear to the demons that she is not seeking a husband. Accordingly, she declares to Tāmra on his mission: "I do not desire Indra, Viṣṇu, Śiva, Kubera, Varuṇa, Brahmā, nor Pāvaka. Having rejected the host of gods, how could I choose a beast? I am not a woman seeking a husband (*patiṃ-varā nārī*), for I already have a husband, the Lord who is maker of all, witness of all, yet a non-doer, desireless and steady, omniscient. . . . How could I, abandoning him, bear to serve a dumb buffalo?"[81] The Devī here has described her husband largely in terms of the Sāṃkhyan Puruṣa, who is the inactive witness to the activities of Prakṛti. All this is made quite explicit by the Devī when Mahiṣa himself appears before her. Then she tells the lustful demon: "I desire no man (*puruṣa*) except the Parama Puruṣa, the Supreme Man. I am his will (*icchā*), and I create the whole world. He, the Self of all, beholds me; I am his auspicious Prakṛti. When he approaches, consciousness appears in me. I, ever inert (*jaḍa*), become conscious through union with him."[82]

The Devī's confession to Mahiṣa is effective in putting him in his place. But it seems to subordinate her radically to the masculine, Sāṃkhyan principle of Puruṣa, in apparent contradiction to her earlier statement that she is *tat-svabhāva* ("having that [manhood] as her inherent nature). Further, as we observed in chapter one with reference to the Madhu-Kaiṭabha myth, when Brahmā hymns the Goddess for awakening Viṣṇu, he specifically points out that she cannot be devoid of consciousness, despite what the Sāṃkhya philosophers say,[83] and despite the Devī's assertion above that she is inert. In like manner, when the gods praise her after she has slain Mahiṣa, they declare: "[You] are the *cit-śakti* (power of consciousness) in the supreme Self; this is the cause by which he becomes manifest (*vyakta*) in the worlds [a significant reversal of the Sāṃkhyan notion that it is the unmanifest Prakṛti that becomes manifest]. How can the elements, devoid of [your power of] consciousness and being inert, create the world?"[84]

Nīlakaṇṭha is uneasy with the Devī's apparent contradiction of her own supremacy and repeats his basic contention that she is truly the supreme Brahman, though veiled by *māyā*, and thus has the double nature of both the male and female principles (*puṃ-prakṛti*). He thus explains the Devī's self-identification with Prakṛti in apparent contradistinction to Puruṣa as a "figure of speech" (*alaṃkāra*) on her part.[85]

Confirmation of Nīlakaṇṭha's interpretation is found in the Devī's answer to Asilomā's question as to why she kills the faultless demons.

It is probably no accident that she most fully reveals herself to this demon, who has approached her as a humble son. In her response, she implicitly signifies her oneness with the supreme Puruṣa by identifying herself as the Sākṣin (witness): "I roam through all the worlds, always, O *Daitya*, observing the righteousness and unrighteousness of beings. I have the form of the witness, without desire for enjoyment, without greed, without enmity. For the sake of *dharma*, I wander here in *saṃsāra* to protect the good. This is my eternal vow. The righteous are to be protected, the evil are to be slain, the Vedas are to be safeguarded. Thus I assume countless *avatāra*s in age after age. Mahiṣa is evil, as he desires to slay the gods. Knowing this, I have come here to slay him."[86] This clearly indicates that the Devī's self-deprecating identification with Prakṛti is meant only for Mahiṣa's dull mind and does not represent the ultimate truth about her.

The *Devī-Bhāgavata* here, in the response of the Devī to Asilomā, has synthesized a number of important strands. We see the Devī has taken over the *Bhagavad Gītā*'s doctrine of the incarnation as *dharm*ic defender, fused with the Sāṃkhyan notion of the supreme witness who is beyond enjoyment. In the process, the Devī reveals the futility in trying to ascertain whether she is passionate or hostile, the question that so perplexes Mahiṣa throughout the story. She is neither, for as the supreme witness, she is without desire, and without enmity.

That the Devī can have the appearance of a young woman and yet not be passionate is still one more paradox that befuddles the demon chief. This paradox is highlighted in Mahiṣa's willingness to become the Devī's servant (*dāsa*). While his envoys frequently convey to the Goddess his eagerness to submit to her, Mahiṣa presents his case most persuasively in person: "O beautiful one, I am your slave. I will abandon my enmity towards the gods, as you request. I will do whatever to make you happy. My mind is deluded by your beauty. Tormented, I have come to you for refuge (*śaraṇa*); protect me, submissive, tormented by the arrows of love. The highest duty is to protect those who have come for refuge. I bow at your feet, casting aside my weapons. Be merciful (*dayāṃ kuru*)."[87] Mahiṣa's offer to become the Devī's *dāsa* seems contrary to his heroic and manly self-image and represents an interesting inversion of Madhu and Kaiṭabha's offer to Brahmā and Viṣṇu to become servants as an alternative to fighting. But Mahiṣa's motivation is hardly one of genuine submission. It is simply his attempt to attain by subtler means what he cannot obtain by force. His seeking refuge of the Devī, while outwardly similar to Brahmā's and Viṣṇu's in the Madhu-Kaiṭabha myth, is based not on acknowledgement of her superiority but on *kāma*, passion, which he assumes must be mutually shared.

The Devī does not completely reject Mahiṣa's request to be merciful. She offers him peace (*śama*), the restraint of passion, as a means to happiness (and in the process reverts to ancient, ascetic-misogynistic arguments about women being fetters that bind men more securely than iron chains and keep them from ever attaining freedom). She is willing to be Mahiṣa's friend, not his wife. She thus offers peace as an alternative to love or war, but is rejected. He is too vain and egotistical to accept friendship on her terms. He argues that she has been deceived in thinking the renunciation of enjoyments is advisable. He cannot believe that a woman can be happy without a husband, and cannot understand why she is not afflicted with love's arrows as well. Thinking it may be due to her youth and inexperience, he recounts the story of the unhappy woman Mandodarī. In her youth Mandodarī took a vow of chastity and thus overlooked a fitting husband. But later, overcome by passion, she ended up marrying a wretch. Mahiṣa contends that the Devī will one day regret having passed him up. The Devī responds by calling him a fool, restating her *avatāric* mission, and soon dispatching him in battle.

In this great adventure, the *Devī-Bhāgavata* has brought together from various sources a great diversity of themes and threaded them together on the string of the contrasting *rasas*. Mahiṣa, like Brahmā in the previous myth, is portrayed as knowledgeable in the science of statecraft. The demon chief is also seen as a fierce and mighty enemy of the gods, quick to anger, defiant, in short, a sort of ideal hero. Mahiṣa also falls in love and reveals some familiarity with the science of love (*kāma-śāstra*). But unlike the ideal hero, he has requested to be slain by a woman, thus, in effect, breaking the proper heroic mood. And unlike the ideal lover, he professes his love for the Devī before she has revealed any reciprocal feelings for him, once again breaking the appropriate amorous mood according to the Sanskritic canons of love.

The Devī, by contrast, manifests herself as the moods or *rasas* incarnate; she reveals herself to the demons as endowed not only with the *rasas* of heroism (*vīra*) and eroticism (*śṛṅgāra*), but also of laughter (*hāsa*), wrath (*raudra*), and wonder (*adbhūta*).[88] Indeed, it is the very combination of apparently contradictory *rasas* that helps to create the wonder. She is, as it were, the perfection of all the aesthetic sentiments simultaneously. While certain of the other *rasas*, such as compassionate sorrow (*karuṇa*) and peace (*śānta*), are not emphasized in the mythic action, they are not entirely absent. We have seen Asilomā's request to the Devī to be merciful to the helpless *asuras*, and the Devī's own offer of peace to Mahiṣa.

Although the Devī encompasses several seemingly opposed moods, they all tend to support or nurture the heroic sentiment in the Mahiṣa episode. As Lalye says, with reference to the various *rasas* appearing in the demon myths of the *Devī-Bhāgavata* in general, "Though these Rasas seem to be mutually exclusive they are not contradictory. All descriptions try to nurture the main subsidiary one i.e. Vīra."[89] *Vīra* itself, however, as Lalye's statement indicates, is not the ultimate *rasa* of the Purāṇa. The final aim of the demon legends, according to Lalye, is to delineate not *vīra* but "Bhakti Rasa" (the sentiment of devotion).[90] The subordination of heroism to *bhakti rasa* is a crucial point to keep in mind in interpreting the fierce and terrifying aspect of the Goddess. We shall return to the role of *bhakti* in the demon myths in the concluding section below. Now let us turn to the last of the Devī's three great adventures, the story of Śumbha and Niśumbha, in which the *rasas* and other related aspects are further developed.

The Courting of Śumbha and Niśumbha: Conflicting Moods of Passion, War, and Peace

The myth of Śumbha and Niśumbha in the *Devī-Bhāgavata* follows the general outline of the *Devī-Māhātmya*, interweaving its own familiar and favorite themes into the latter's basic structure. These themes, for the most part faithfully carried over from the Mahiṣa episode, occasionally receive new interpretive twists. We shall focus on these new twists in our analysis below. As before, let us begin with a comparison of the relevant versions of the myth, in parallel columns:

Devī-Māhātmya[91]	*Devī-Bhāgavata Purāṇa*[92]
	1. Śumbha-Niśumbha introduced as tormentors of the gods, invulnerable to all males due to a boon formerly attained from Brahmā that they could not be slain by any male, females supposedly being too weak to fear
	2. Śumbha-Niśumbha gain control of the human world and advance against heaven

3. Śumbha-Niśumbha conquer heaven, routing the gods	3. The demons rout the gods as ordained by fate
	4. The gods consult with Bṛhaspati, who advises the gods to go to the Himālayas to worship the Devī with her seed-mantra
5. The gods recall Devī, go to the Himālayas and praise her	5. The gods go to the Himālayas and worship her as advised
6. Pārvatī comes by to bathe and asks the gods whom they are praising	6. Devī appears, to take her bath, and asks the gods about their distress
7. In answer, as it were, the auspicious goddess Ambikā or Kauśikī emerges from Pārvatī's body sheath (*kośa*); Pārvatī herself turns black and is known as Kālikā	7. The gods explain their plight and request her aid; Devī sends forth from her body a form known as Kauśikī or Ambikā; Devī herself, known also as Pārvatī, becomes the black Kālikā
8. Caṇḍa and Muṇḍa, servants of Śumbha-Niśumbha, see Ambikā and report her beauty to Śumbha, urging him to take her for himself	8. Ambikā takes Kālikā to Śumbha's city and begins to sing enchanting songs; Caṇḍa and Muṇḍa see her and report back to Śumbha, urging him to marry her
9. Śumbha sends Sugrīva as envoy to win the affections of the Devī with a proposal of marriage	9. Śumbha, pointing out that only the first two expedients (conciliation and gifts) are appropriate to the *rasa* of love, sends Sugrīva to win over the Devī by gentle persuasion
10. Sugrīva makes the proposal, pointing out Śumbha's great wealth and power; the Devī is agreeable but reveals a promise she once foolishly made: he who conquers her in battle will be her husband[93]	10. Sugrīva makes the proposal, pointing out not only Śumbha's wealth and power, but also his willingness to be her servant; the Devī indicates that she had come precisely to see her future husband, but first there is the small matter of her foolish promise to marry him who conquers her

11. Sugrīva protests that if she remains so haughty, she will be dragged by the hair to Śumbha; but she says she is helpless because of her promise	11. Sugrīva warns the Devī not to be so haughty, for the love sentiment is the best of the nine *rasas* (and not heroism); if she does not go to Śumbha of her own accord, she will be dragged there by the hair; but she pleads helplessness due to her promise, and in any case, she has come to fight: thus Śumbha must fight or flee to Pātāla
12. Sugrīva reports the Devī's message and Śumbha is angry; he sends a number of envoy-generals to the Devī to bring her back by force if necessary; the first envoy is incinerated, his army killed; with the beginning of bloodshed, thoughts of marriage quickly vanish; succeeding missions become ever more violent, and the Devī sends an envoy to Śumbha-Niśumbha to go to Pātāla or fight and die; the slaughter of demon envoys continues, with the help of the Mātṛs, culminating in the gory death of Raktabīja, whose blood is drunk by Kālī	12. Sugrīva reports to Śumbha about the Devī of unknown ancestry; a series of councils interspersed with missions to the Devī begins; fate, the Devī's true identity, and the appropriate expedients to use against her are discussed; the envoys try hard not to break the mood of love with harsh words or actions, but the Devī's refusal to give in forces each in succession to resort to violent means, resulting in their own deaths; the slaughter of demon envoys continues, with the help of the Mātṛs, culminating in Kālikā's drinking off all of Raktabīja's blood
13. Śumbha-Niśumbha, seeing Raktabīja and other great demon warriors slain, are infuriated	13. The surviving demons report Raktabīja's death to Śumbha-Niśumbha and urge them to give up the fight and to serve the Devī or flee to Pātāla; the two demon chiefs refuse to flee, preferring a hero's death if they cannot conquer her

14. The two demon brothers themselves enter the battle; the Devī knocks unconscious first Niśumbha, then Śumbha; Niśumbha regains his senses and continues the fight, only to be beheaded, while many of his fellow demons also perish	14. Śumbha and Niśumbha go forth to fight the Devī; Niśumbha begins combat with her, while Śumbha observes her simultaneous amorous and fierce aspects, awakening in him the realization of the hopelessness of both marriage and victory; the Devī again offers a choice: live and flee to Pātāla, or die fighting and go to heaven; Niśumbha continues the fight and is soon beheaded
15. Seeing his brother slain, Śumbha is once again angered	15. Niśumbha's fate is reported to Śumbha, with further urgings to give up the fight; knowing he has been the cause of his brother's and other demons' death, Śumbha cannot flee now; realizing that all who are born must die, he heads for battle, leaving victory or death in the hands of fate
16. Śumbha addresses the Devī, taunting her for relying so much on her allies (the *śakti*s or Mothers who had helped her in her previous battles)	16. Śumbha goes before the Devī and is struck with passion by her beauty; he notes various paradoxes within her: delicacy and hardness, budding womanhood and dispassion, alluring charm and demon-slaying prowess; he realizes the first three means (conciliation, etc.) are futile, but there is no fame in death at the hands of a woman either; and it is cowardly to flee; not able to bear the contradictions, Śumbha at last decides to fight, if only she will assume an ugly and fierce form
17. The Devī absorbs all the goddesses into herself and fights singly with the demon chief, finally slaying him	17. The Devī has Kālikā fight in her stead and the latter slays Śumbha

18. World order is restored and the gods, rejoicing, praise the Devī	18. The gods rejoice, world order is restored, and the remaining demons, bowing to the world mother, flee to Pātāla

The *Devī-Bhāgavata* begins, as usual, by inserting and highlighting the boon granted to the demons (#1), around which its version of the story revolves. The boon granted to Śumbha and Niśumbha, of invulnerability to males, is identical to Mahiṣa's boon and is attained under similar circumstances. It nicely prepares the way for the introduction of the erotic interplay between the demon chiefs and the Devī. The erotic element, however, is present explicitly for the first time in the *Devī-Māhātmya*'s version as well as in the *Devī-Bhāgavata*'s (#'s 8-11). Nonetheless, the amorous element is much more emphasized in the *Devī-Bhāgavata* than in the *Devī-Māhātmya*. In the latter, once the blood begins to flow, the mood shifts entirely away from the erotic or romantic, in order to concentrate on the horror and gore of battle (#12). In the *Devī-Bhāgavata*, there is a purposeful balancing and counterbalancing of the erotic and the horrific right up to the very end (#'s 12, 14, 16).

As mentioned above, a number of themes peculiar to the *Devī-Bhāgavata*'s version of the myth are simply carried over from its rendering of the Mahiṣa episode. In addition to the boon motif, there are the series of councils interspersed with missions to the Devī (#12). In the councils, the usual topics are discussed: Who is the Devī and why has she come? Is her bellicose talk to be taken literally, or is it a veiled amorous challenge to participate in the battle of love?[94] Which of the four expedients should be used in dealing with her? Should the demons flee or fight? Is effort and manly determination useless against a lonely woman in the face of time and destiny? In the missions, the demon envoys offer the same mixture of blandishments and protests to the Goddess. The demon chief is ready to become her slave. She will be mistress of the world if she becomes his queen. Her body is too delicate and soft to endure the hardships of battle. A woman's real weapons are her sidelong glances and soft-spoken words. The envoys also hesitate to use sharp words or actions for fear of breaking the amorous mood.

Many of these themes are little developed from the way they appear in the Mahiṣa myth, yet several refinements or elaborations may be noted. First, the demons seem to have an easier time recognizing who the Devī truly is. As soon as the first demon general is slain, along with many of his troops, the mangled survivors realize that they will not attain victory for they correctly perceive that they are up against the world mother (*jagad-ambikā*).[95] Though alone, she is fearless, and although the gods and other celestials are ready to help her, the demons understand that she has no desire for or expectation of any assistance. They conclude: "She by herself is able to destroy the entire universe, let alone the *dānavas*."[96] Again, after the deaths of Caṇḍa and Muṇḍa, the fleeing remnants report to Śumbha: "This Devī is the great Māyā, the supreme Prakṛti, the cause of the destruction of everything at the end of the age. . . . She is Triguṇā, she is Tāmasī, she is endowed with all *śaktis*. . . . She is both Nirguṇā and Saguṇā, bliss and the giver of bliss. . . . Knowing this, abandon your enmity and go to her for refuge; she will protect you."[97] Similarly, after the slaughter of Raktabīja, and once more after the slaughter of Niśumbha, the demons tell Śumbha that she is no "ordinary woman" (*nārī prākṛtā*,[98] *prākṛta-yoṣā*[99]) but rather is Māyā, the unequalled Śakti.

Despite the generally greater awareness of the demons, they remain ambivalent, just as in the Mahiṣa myth. Thus, the survivors who report Niśumbha's death and declare that the lady is not an ordinary woman but the supreme Śakti who bears many forms, go on to blame the demons' misfortunes on the unfavorable (*viparīta*) time.[100] It is interesting that they describe time with the same phrase they have just used of the Devī: "bearing many forms" (*nānā-rūpa-dharā*),[101] referring to their auspicious and inauspicious aspects. Yet they fail to see that the Goddess controls and embodies time (Kāla), especially its destructive aspect as manifested in her horrific form known as Kālī (to be dealt with in a moment). Consequently, they can insist, foolishly, that the cause of their troubles is not Kālī but Kāla.[102]

While Śumbha is not quite sure what to make of the distressing reports from the battlefront, he intuits that his own death is imminent, and here we come to a second interesting elaboration. Śumbha, unlike Mahiṣa, has an overriding sense of his own mortality. The buffalo-demon in contrast often seems to assume that, being protected by the boon, he may truly be immortal. Śumbha refuses to flee for his life out of a sense of kingly duty to those whom he has already sent to their deaths (#15). Most significantly, he recognizes that if he is fated to die in battle, he is no different from all other creatures, including the gods, all of whom will perish sooner or later. The essential similarity of the gods and demons in their dependency on time and in being subject to death is a theme frequently emphasized in the myth. The Goddess herself declares, while propounding an intriguing variation of the traditional *avatāra* doctrine: "Many thousands of Śumbhas and Niśumbhas have been slain by me in the past; in my presence, hosts of gods have perished in *yuga* after *yuga*."[103] The Devī alone is eternal, and if death is inevitable for all other beings, Śumbha can at least preserve his honor by dying courageously in battle.

Another development concerns the Goddess' stance towards the demon chief Śumbha. In the Mahiṣa myth, the Devī assumes the form of the alluring woman in order to entice the demon to her, but she is consistently defiant and hostile in her words and actions. Her appearance alone conveys the erotic mood, and she constantly berates the buffalo-demon for his stupid, ugly, and brutish nature. The contrast between her amorous countenance and belligerent behavior is modified in various ways in the Śumbha episode.

On the one hand, the Devī in her aspect known as Ambikā becomes a thoroughly beguiling temptress. Not only does she appear in ravishing form, she fully acts and talks like a woman seeking a husband (*patikāmā*).[104] She practically begs Śumbha to accept her as his spouse, praising him as a suitable match, extolling his beauty, intelligence, strength, and nobility. She even declares: "I have come from afar to see my own [future] husband (*sva-pati*); I have seen all the proud gods, Gandharvas, Rākṣasas, and others, but they all tremble and swoon in fear at the name of Śumbha."[105] That she must first be conquered in battle initially seems like a small enough matter and adds to her tantalizing allure, playing "hard to get," as it were.

On the other hand, Ambikā can be quite defiant as well. In response to the messenger Caṇḍa, who tries to get her to back off from her "foolish" promise, she retorts: "Having rejected Viṣṇu, Śiva and other gods, why should I choose Śumbha as my husband? I have no need of a husband." This sounds very similar to the Devī's rejection of Mahiṣa's marriage proposal in the previous myth, but there she argued it was because she already had a husband, the supreme Puruṣa. Here Ambikā proceeds on a different note: "I want nothing to do with a husband or master (*pati*), for I am my own master (*svāminī*), lord of all beings."[106] This view is clearly in accord with the general tenor of the Purāṇa as a whole. In any case, Ambikā unites in her speech aspects of the alluring and the defiant woman, a union that, as we shall see, entirely befuddles Śumbha.

In the Mahiṣa myth of the *Devī-Bhāgavata*, the point is often emphasized that the Devī is alone and fights unassisted. This means not only that she is not helped by the gods, but she is also not aided by any female powers that at times issue so freely from her being.[107]

In the Śumbha myth, however, Ambikā is only one of two major forms of the Devī (see #7). The other is Kālikā (sometimes separated from the figure of Kālī, sometimes merged with it).

Kālikā/Kālī is the horrific and bloodthirsty side of the Devī. She is, in many ways, the polar opposite of Ambikā, not least of all in her looks: black in complexion, with protuberant, hanging lips, scrawny limbs, sharp teeth and nails, and yellow eyes like those of a cat. It is she who first shatters the romantic mood, revealing to the envoy Dhūmralocana the Devī's true mission, namely to kill Śumbha and Niśumbha. She first indicates that marriage between Ambikā and Śumbha is out of the question, for why would a lioness choose a jackal, or a she-elephant an ass?[108] And she initiates the first fight, with Dhūmralocana. While Ambikā is the one actually to destroy the demon, incinerating him with her shout of "Hum," this seems to be in deference to the *Devī-Māhātmya*'s version,[109] for twice thereafter in the *Devī-Bhāgavata*, Dhūmralocana's death is attributed to Kālikā.[110] In any case, it is Kālikā/Kālī who predominantly wades in the gore of the demons and delights in the carnage, though Ambikā does not wholly abstain from the bloodshed. The *Devī-Bhāgavata* thus attempts to split the Goddess into two rather sharply distinguished figures, certainly far more sharply than in the *Devī-Māhātmya*.

This splitting of the Goddess allows the myth to attain an intriguing resolution to the paradoxical tension that builds to a head in the climactic encounter between Śumbha and the Devī. When Śumbha confronts Ambikā in person, he is overwhelmed not just by her beauty, but even more by the paradoxical union of opposites he sees in her: she is shining with both the *raudra-rasa* (the sentiment or mood of wrath and fury) and the *śṛṅgāra-rasa* (the erotic mood).[111] His first reaction is to abandon all hope either for marriage or for victory. When he comes before her a second time, after the death of his brother Niśumbha, he is smitten with passion but again is struck by her paradoxical nature. Wondrous is her beauty and her shrewdness combined. Equally amazing is the conjunction of softness and delicacy with durability and fortitude, qualities normally mutually exclusive. Perhaps most amazing of all is that she appears in the bloom of young womanhood, yet she is devoid of passion![112] He, who in his manly firmness ought not to show passion, at least until she reveals her interest in him, is bewildered by his own passion and cannot figure out how to bring her under his control. He realizes that the first three expedients, conciliation and the rest, are futile, and that fleeing the battlefield for Pātāla is unfit for a hero. Yet death at the hands of a woman will hardly bring him glory, especially if the woman is as beautiful as Ambikā.

In desperation, Śumbha decides that it is better to die on the battlefield than to flee, though he pleads with the Devī one last time to refrain from such unwomanly behavior: "a woman's glances are her arrows; her eyebrows, her bow; her amorous gestures, assorted weapons; a skillful man, her target; her fragrant unguents, her armor; her desires (*mano-ratha*), her chariot (*ratha*); and her sweet words, the sounding of war drums. Such are the proper war equipments of a woman, and any others are a matter for laughter (*viḍambana*)."[113] Śumbha uses the word *viḍambana* here for "laughing matter," but the word also suggests that the Devī's bellicose posturing is a "mortification" to the demon king's masculine pride. We may recall a similar sort of embarrassment or *viḍambana* when Viṣṇu lost his head.

When Ambikā insists upon fighting, the only way Śumbha can even partially resolve his dilemma and lessen the degree of his mortification is to plead with her that if she must fight, then would she please assume an ugly appearance, black, ferocious, and cruel, with protruding lips, claws, and the like. Only such a hag fits his preconception of what a destructive female can look like. The *Devī-Bhāgavata* allows him to keep this one last illusion, but without altering Ambikā's general character. Śumbha, in describing the ugly hag, has of course depicted perfectly the appearance of Kālikā. Accordingly, Ambikā, rather than transforming herself into the horrific form Śumbha has requested, merely sends Kālikā in her stead while she remains as a spectator (*prekṣikā*).[114] (Do we have here an evocation of Ambikā as the supreme witness [*sākṣin*]?) The splitting of Devī into Ambikā and Kālikā thus absorbs some of the tension between the erotic and horrific aspects of the Goddess, the most visible of her paradoxes. We shall return to this notion of the split Goddess in our concluding section below.

The final development to be considered concerns the *rasas*. Aside from the usual concerns of the demon envoys not to break the erotic mood with harsh words or deeds, we find them arguing for the actual superiority of the *śṛṅgāra-rasa* over all others. Sugrīva is the first envoy to argue along these lines. Having just been informed by the Devī of her "foolish vow" and hardly believing his ears, Sugrīva protests that she talks this way because of her womanly nature (*strī-svabhāva*)[115]—a charge to which the Devī does not respond, for a change. He continues: "*Śṛṅgāra* is always to be enjoyed with supreme joy by all creatures, as it is the best of the nine [sentiments] according to the wise."[116] It is not just that heroism is unbefitting a beautiful woman, but heroism in general, according to Sugrīva, is subordinate to eroticism.

This argument is further elaborated by the most fearsome of all the demon envoys, Raktabīja. From the time of the *Devī-Māhātmya*, he has been famous for his peculiar and dreadful gift that whenever a drop of his blood touches the ground, another Raktabīja, with the same special qualities, will spring up from that drop.[117] When he comes before the Devī, he is quite prepared to fight, but first he tries to dissuade her from such a violent course of action. After boasting of his own prowess and appealing to her own learning, he asserts: "Of the nine *rasas*, two verily are considered the chief by knowledgeable persons. These two are *śṛṅgāra* and *śānti* (peace). And of these two, *śṛṅgāra* is the better."[118] He then cites a number of examples to show how passion is the law of the universe, from the gods with their wives down to the doves and deer, and even the trees with their entwining creepers. Those who are ignorant of the essence (*rasa*) of life delight in the *śānti-rasa*, deceived by clever words. But, Raktabīja asks, where is knowledge, where is dispassion (*vairāgya*) when love arises in one's mind. Raktabīja thus goes beyond Sugrīva, contrasting the passion of love not with war, but with peace.

The Goddess does, of course, ultimately resort to war in slaying Sumbha and Niśumbha. But in the process, she brings peace to the gods and to the world. It is time, then, to turn to the question raised at so many points by the manifold paradoxes seen in her various manifestations and especially by her frequently bloody deeds. Is she, in short, ultimately benevolent or malevolent?

The Ambivalent Goddess: Theories of Pacification, Bifurcation, and Androgynization

Pacification and domestication. We shall begin by considering the nature of the Goddess in the *Devī-Māhātmya*. Two somewhat different images come into focus, depending on whether one accords primacy to the accounts of the Devī's deeds or to the various hymns of praise offered to her. Her deeds, at least the last two, emphasize quite naturally her destructive and horrific aspects. Lawrence Babb succinctly and vividly describes the impression that these deeds may leave on the reader or audience:

> While the gods of scripture could hardly be called passive, their collective character is different from that of the goddess of the *Saptashati*. The goddess represents a terrible and almost sinister force, all the more sinister

> by comparison with the gods. While the gods are very powerful beings themselves, they seem at the same time to be essentially magnifications of human beings . . . who are often motivated by their emotions, often to anger, but often to mercy and benevolence as well. As she is represented in the *Saptashati*, the only discernible emotion of the goddess is anger—black, implacable, and bloodthirsty. She is something emerging from the highest gods; she is the very essence of their anger. But once unleashed this *shakti* seems to achieve an identity of her own, . . . more powerful, certainly more terrible, than her creators.[119]

Babb acknowledges that a different image of the Devī emerges in the hymns, but starting from the view that she is essentially malevolent or "almost sinister," he sees the hymns as basically a means of pacifying or appeasing the terrible Goddess. He continues:

> We must carefully note that although the goddess emerges in differentiation *from* the gods, in the end she is *of* the gods, an idea suggesting that the goddess is ultimately controllable.
>
> In fact, if approached in the correct fashion the goddess, even in her most terrible manifestations, will serve the ends of men as she did the ends of the gods, and the *Saptashati* includes many hymns designed to flatter her into cooperation with her devotees.[120]

There is undoubtedly much truth to what Babb says, especially in terms of various popular perceptions of the *Devī-Māhātmya*. However, what is lacking in Babb's description above is any sense of gratitude or adoration with which the worshipper may approach the Goddess. If we begin with the hymns themselves, which Coburn refers to as "the devotional core" of the text,[121] and if we remember that the Devī's "origin" from the anger of the gods is merely the manifestation of her who is truly eternal, as the text itself declares in introducing her,[122] then the Devī emerges in a somewhat different light. She is more independent and at the same time less malevolent. The hymns as well appear not just as flattery. They abound and delight in the paradoxical juxtaposition of her auspicious/gentle (*saumyā*) nature with her terrible/horrific (*ghorā, raudrī*) aspect.[123] The hymns, however much they are meant to "pacify" the Goddess, are also joyous celebrations of Devī's ultimacy, transcending yet encompassing all polarities including that of benign and horrific.[124]

It is worth noting in this regard that of the four major hymns to the Goddess in the *Devī-Māhātmya*, two are offered as petitionary prayers,[125] but the other two are offered in the spirit of thanksgiving after she has accomplished her requested tasks.[126] Moreover, while the gods are in part motivated by fear in all four hymns, it is primarily fear of the demons and the cosmic calamities they cause, rather than fear of the Goddess, that is manifest. Accordingly, following the death of Mahiṣa, when the Devī offers the gods a boon after their hymn of praise, they reply: "Everything has been accomplished by you, the Bhagavatī; nothing remains to be done now that our enemy, Mahiṣāsura, is slain. If a boon is still to be given, let it be that whenever you are called to mind, you will destroy our worst misfortunes."[127]

At this point it is instructive to note the parallel situation in the *Devī-Bhāgavata*, where the gods respond in a somewhat different manner: "Everything has been accomplished by you, O Devī; nothing is to be done now that our enemy, Mahiṣāsura, is slain. So that we may always remember your lotus feet, O Mother, allow us to have unswerving devotion to you, the world mother."[128] The *Devī-Bhāgavata* here goes well beyond any fear-and-appeasement model of worship, reflecting instead the ideal of devotion that transcends ulterior motivation. The notion of "disinterested *bhakti*," that devotion to the supreme is the highest goal, has roots going back at least to the *Bhagavad Gītā*[129] and comes to play an especially important role in relatively late Vaiṣṇava Purāṇas like the *Bhāgavata* and the *Brahmavaivarta*.[130] These texts insist that the greatest gift that God can bestow is *bhakti* itself. Such devotion is characterized by loving surrender rather than fear. The *Devī-Bhāgavata* seems to have deeply absorbed and celebrated these Vaiṣṇava devotional ideals. These ideals, though largely undeveloped in the *Devī-Māhātmya*, are frequently implicit in its hymns.

Babb also sees, from his own perspective, another "really different" aspect of the Goddess which is positive and auspicious. The context in which this different aspect appears, according to Babb, is that of marriage and domestication, by which the Devī is tamed or controlled. Let me quote Babb once again, in summary:

> Within the pantheon a very dangerous force is symbolized [by the Goddess], but this is a force that seems to undergo a basic transformation into something almost antisinister, the loving wife, . . . when placed within the context of a restraining social relationship, that of marriage. An appetite for conflict and destruction is thus transformed into the most fundamental of social virtues, that of wifely submission which, on the premises given in Hindu culture, makes the continuation of society possible. The basis for this transformation is a dual notion of divinity, a duality that in turn

> is linked to the opposition between male and female. When female dominates male the pair is sinister; when male dominates female, the pair is benign.[131]

This "marriage control model" of Hindu female divinities is shared by a number of anthropologists. Susan Wadley, for instance, in her study of Karimpur religion, writes: "there is an ever present awareness [in the Hindu cultural context] that female power may become uncontrolled. And when male authority (usually a consort) is absent, the malevolent use of female power is almost assured."[132]

While such an interpretive model seems to fit well the particular social and ritual contexts that Babb and Wadley were studying, we may inquire whether or not it fits the *Devī-Māhātmya*, or the *Devī-Bhāgavata.* In both texts, the supreme Goddess appears basically as the "consort of none" (to use Coburn's expression); rather, she relates "to male deities, as to all that exists, not externally but internally, not as consort, but as *śakti.*"[133] Further, we may note that the three spouses of the Trimūrti in the *Devī-Bhāgavata* hardly fit the model of submissive wives.[134] The pacific and benign aspects of the Goddess, then, hardly seem to be accounted for in terms of her being controlled by male authority.[135]

Bifurcation and isolation. David Shulman, in his marvelous and extensive study of Tamil temple myths, sees the marriage control model as part of a larger strategy for dealing with the tensions inherent in the ambivalent Goddess. Devī, by her very nature as the embodiment of power, is both creative and destructive; dangerous, yet necessary for the dynamic maintenance of life. Life is won out of death. Accordingly, her violent, horrific side cannot be simply jettisoned or ignored, nor can it be wholly subdued through the process of domestication—a process that if fully realized would substantially deprive the Goddess of the power necessary for energizing the life-death-rebirth cycle. At the same time, the Goddess' involvement in death and rebirth surrounds her with blood and pollution. Both power and purity, however, are "two vital religious ideals" in Tamil devotional life.[136] The basic Tamil solution to this dilemma, Shulman argues, is the bifurcation of the Goddess.

"Dichotomy," according to Shulman, "becomes a major technique for handling ambivalence and contradiction."[137] Thus, the Devī in her complex as virgin/bride/spouse, is split into the dark, violent, erotic, and powerful Goddess epitomized in the figure of Kālī, and into the golden, peaceful, nonerotic, and submissive Goddess known as Gaurī. Gaurī is separated from the dangerous, polluting aspects of the Devī and is free to unite with the pure Śiva, as the ideal submissive wife. Kālī, too, may unite with Śiva, but generally speaking only when she is tamed (as in the myths of the dance contest). The more usual pattern is to isolate her in some way: ritually, by setting up her shrine outside the central shrine, wherein Gaurī and Śiva reside in auspicious purity; mythologically, by sending her away (while Gaurī remains behind) to do the dirty work of slaying demons, of whom Mahiṣāsura is the archetype.

The figure of Mahiṣa plays an especially important role in Shulman's analysis, for as he convincingly demonstrates, the buffalo-demon is a surrogate for Śiva himself. Shulman finds, within the Tamil myths, remnants of an early conception of the Goddess as the consort of a buffalo-god; in uniting with him, she slays him, absorbing his power, and finally gives him birth. The god, in seeking the Goddess, sacrifices himself in order to gain renewed strength and vitality through rebirth from her womb. This sacrificial perspective, involving the god in the violence of death and rebirth, was an embarrassment to the Brahmanical Tamil Śaivites, for whom Devī's spouse, Śiva, the supreme reality, could hardly be subject to such polluting processes. The Brahmanical trend away from sacrificial violence thus required reinterpretation of the ancient myth. Introducing a demon-surrogate for Śiva and the splitting of the Devī into dark and light halves were key elements in the reinterpretation.

The sacrificial perspective of the Goddess points to the close interrelation of her virgin/bride/spouse complex and her maternal aspect, since union, death, and rebirth are part of an integrated cycle. Shulman sees the "technique of bifurcation" at work on the mother as well:

> In connection with Devī's maternal aspect, we observe a similar approach to the inherent ambiguities involved. The different components of the divine mother may be combined in a single figure . . . or they may be separated and assigned to distinct carriers. The complex, unitary figure probably represents the more original conception, in which both aspects of the sacrifice—the violent death and the rebirth—are present and appear in association with the goddess. The split image and the accompanying separation of opposing strands reflect the attempt to acommodate a less violent ideology; just as the splitting away of Kālī allows the god to marry the more conventional Gaurī, the separation of the terrifying aspect of the mother allows a more idealized image of the goddess as mother to become dominant.[138]

Certain vestiges of Shulman's ancient sacrificial myth may still be found in the *Devī-Bhāgavata*'s version of the Mahiṣa myth.[139] But the total context is drastically altered: while the surrogate (in the guise of Mahiṣa) is present, the original has vanished. That is, there is no original consort of the Devī (as is also true in the *Devī-Māhātmya* version). While certain features of the Mahiṣa myth in the *Devī-Bhāgavata* may be explained by the sacrificial ideas, especially as they provide background for the juxtaposition of the violent (heroic/horrific) and erotic elements, these ideas in themselves do not provide sufficient insight for a full understanding of the text in its present form. (Nor would Shulman contend that they do.) Nonetheless, his general notion of bifurcation as a technique for dealing with the ambivalence of the Goddess is useful, especially with reference to the myth of Śumbha and Niśumbha.

In this myth, as we have seen, the split of the Goddess is a major feature in both the *Devī-Māhātmya* and *Devī-Bhāgavata* versions, though the bifurcation between Ambikā and Kālikā is more sharply drawn in the latter. In fact, in the *Devī-Māhātmya*, the split is actually reversed and unity restored: when Ambikā confronts Śumbha, he charges her with relying on the strength of others (the various *śakti*s) for her victories.[140] In response, the Devī calls back into herself all of her other manifestations so that she fights alone, and alone she slays him. In the *Devī-Bhāgavata*, Kālikā/Kālī remains separate from Ambikā to the end, and it is the former who slays the demon chief.

We seem to have here, then, an attempt to resolve some of the paradoxical tension in the Devī by reserving the culminating battle and slaughter for Kālikā, thereby removing Ambikā at least some distance from the bloody finale. However, we may observe that the tension is primarily in the mind of the demon and not necessarily in the mind of the Purāṇic composer. Further, the split only resolves the most obvious and visible paradox, between the Devī's erotic, alluring side and her most dark and violent aspect. The psychological paradox within the figure of Ambikā, between her alluring/compliant and defiant moods, remains. For the resolution of this paradox, the *Devī-Bhāgavata* Paurāṇika has proposed another solution.

Androgynization. Let us refer once more to Shulman, who suggests yet another way by which ambivalent or contradictory images of the Goddess may be accommodated. The Devī may be split not only into light and dark aspects, but also "into male and female halves that are united in the androgyne."[141] He finds two sorts of androgynous representations of the Devī in the Tamil materials, only the first of which needs concern us.[142] The Devī's pacific and agressive qualities, he contends, may be seen as feminine and masculine traits: "the goddess is undoubtedly female, but the aggressive, violent side of her nature is easily seen as masculine. Certainly, her menacing, martial behavior clashes with the idealized picture of the submissive, devoted wife."[143]

The *Devī-Bhāgavata*, as we have seen, often presents a similar view. Time and again, the demons protest that strength, valor, fierceness, and determination in fighting are all manly qualities, as the very word *pauruṣa* (manliness, prowess, strength) suggests. The Devī, however, is "only a weak and delicate woman." We may recall the Devī's retort to such accusations, namely that she has "that [manliness] for her inherent nature." O'Flaherty, in her typically vivid manner, comments on the *Devī-Bhāgavata*'s version of the Mahiṣa myth as follows:

> This variant emphasizes the castrating, phallic aspect of the Goddess to such an extent that an actual sex change is suggested. Though she is so beautiful that she inspires the demon with destructive erotic passion, she herself is so devoid of erotic feelings that she insists that she is really a man and, moreover, that her would-be consort is *not* really a man but a mere eunuch. . . . Clearly, only one of them has any balls, and *he* is not the one.[144]

Even the demon counselor Durdhara recognizes something of the Devī's masculine nature. While he cannot accept her manlike behavior on the battlefield, he does accept it on the field of amorous sport: she may act like a man in bed, assuming the *viparīta* position (on top), even though this is an inversion of the normal Hindu pattern of hierarchical authority between male and female. That the Devī ends up "on top" in the actual slaying of Mahiṣa, whatever the sexual overtones, points to the Devī's general inversion of the accepted female role in the heroic as well as the erotic realm.[145] Such inversions nicely reveal aspects of her androgynous nature, which in turn absorbs some of the tensions inherent in the ambivalent Goddess.

The androgynous nature of the Devī first revealed on the mythological level of our text reverberates and ramifies on the theological and soteriological levels as well. But on these higher levels both her masculine and her feminine aspects, as manifested in the notions of Puruṣa and Prakṛti, become increasingly benign. On the one hand, the "Pauruṣic" ("manly") character of the cosmic Puruṣa loses any heroic, aggressive tendencies, becoming absorbed in the image of the quiescent witness. On the other hand, the feminine traits of Prakṛti, at least as they appear in the *Devī-Bhāgavata*, are primarily maternal and nonerotic, lenient rather than lustful. As Prakṛti and Puruṣa fuse in the higher nature of the Devī, she combines the ideals of the dispassionate witness and the compassionate mother.

These ideals are brought together in a number of ways throughout the text. One of the most interesting examples occurs in the eulogy offered to the Devī by the gods after her conquest of Mahiṣa. They proclaim: "It is the mother, indeed, who bears (or forgives) the thousand offenses [of the child]. Knowing this, how can people not worship the womb of the universe (*jagad-yoni*)? Two birds dwell in this body with unceasing friendship between them. There is no third friend who would endure (forgive) the faults. Thus, the soul who abandons you [the Devī], his friend, can hardly attain happiness."[146]

In referring to the two birds, the gods clearly have in mind the famous Upaniṣadic metaphor found in the *Śvetāśvatara*[147] and the *Muṇḍaka*.[148] In these texts it is said that two birds dwell in the same tree, united in friendship; one eats sweet berries (*pippala*) while the other looks on without eating. The bird eating fruit is the human soul experiencing, as it were, the fruits of its actions (another meaning of the word *pippala*). He is deluded and grieves, until he sees the other, the Lord (*īśa*), who does not eat and is thus unaffected by good and evil, the witness of all actions. The *Muṇḍaka* goes on to describe the Lord in androgynous terms, as both Puruṣa and the womb of Brahman (*brahma-yoni*).[149]

The *Devī-Bhāgavata* has replaced the Lord, the womb of Brahman, with the Devī, the womb of the universe, who observes—like the witnessing Puruṣa—the actions of her children. And as mother, she is also their friend who brings them comfort through her patient, forgiving tolerance of their misdeeds.[150] As Nīlakaṇṭha comments, "Not only does the quality of being the womb of the world belong to the Bhagavatī [the Devī], but so also the quality of being the friend of all souls."[151] Nīlakaṇṭha adds that the Devī Bhagavatī "is therefore to be honored by all souls in the capacity of a father, a mother, and a friend."[152]

The Devī as benevolent androgyne on the highest level requires a revaluation of her lower androgynous nature, where the erotic/heroic paradox becomes manifest. It should be clear by now that the erotic and heroic aspects of the Goddess are simply flip sides of her deluding, terrifying, and destructive personality. They stand together, over against the nonerotic and protective mother. And yet her protective and terrible modes are not contradictory. As a contemporary devotee of the Devī writes:

> If She is terrible sometimes, She is so only to the wicked and the bad; and if She is like a warrior at times She is so only to accompish high aims . . . and if She is represented as black in colour She is so represented only to show that She is the deliverer from everything that is fearsome. . . . She is, in a word, the creator, the preserver and the destroyer and it is by virtue of her Sakti that Brahma, Vishnu and Siva carry on their respective duties in the cosmic plane.[153]

A careful distinction needs to be drawn, then, between the Devī's wrathful slaughter of those who oppose world order and a truly sinister or malevolent bloodthirstiness. Destructiveness in itself is not evil. On the one hand, it is part of the natural process of transformation, as seen in the great cosmic cycle. On the other, it may be an act of compassionate grace.

This latter aspect is pointed out by the gods themselves. In the *Devī-Māhātmya*, after the death of Mahiṣa, the deities proclaim that the Devī slays their enemies not only for the benefit of the worlds, but also to save the demons from hell, purifying them by the touch of her weapons and thereby leading them to heaven. Thus she manifests compassion (*dayā*) even towards the sinful.[154] The gods succinctly summarize: "Compassion (*kṛpā*) in the heart and hard-hearted cruelty in battle are seen only in you, O Devī, in all the worlds."[155] Indeed, her compassion and cruelty are one.

The *Devī-Bhāgavata* echoes the *Devī-Māhātmya* in its own hymn celebrating the Devī's victory over Mahiṣa. R. K. Narayan, in his modern retelling of the Mahiṣa myth from the *Devī-Bhāgavata*, nicely summarizes the gods' hymn: "Great Mother. . . . You are all-pervasive, and everything in creation is a part of you. Wild beasts, poisonous trees, and *asuras* are also your creation. Even to them you afford a victory of the moment, and then punish, vanquish, and help them evolve into better beings. Saints who realize your subtle, secret presence attain unshakable peace and understanding, through meditation."[156] In more specific terms, the gods attribute the Devī's gracious slaughter of the demons to her overflowing tenderness (*dayārdra-bhāva*)[157] and her joy in manifesting the sentiment of compassion (*karuṇā-rasa*).[158] In the *Devī-Bhāgavata*, then, it is compassion that finally absorbs and resolves the various tensions in the diverse personalities of the Goddess.

From a somewhat different perspective, the *Devī-Bhāgavata*'s vision of the Goddess as revealed in its version of her three great adventures suggests that the erotic and heroic aspects, as well as the benign and horrific sides of the Devī, do not constitute splits in the divine mother so much as they reflect a split within human consciousness. The ego-driven, domineering consciousness sees in the Goddess a reflection of its own lust and violence. The consciousness that surrenders itself in devotional love discovers absolution and peace, most effectively symbolized or experienced by our Paurāṇika through the image of the compassionate and merciful mother.

Chapter 5

The Great Manifestations of the Devī: Mahā-Kālī, Mahā-Lakṣmī, Mahā-Sarasvatī

In the preceding chapter we looked at a number of ways in which the Devī's activities in her three great adventures were revised and reinterpreted. The resulting new vision of the Devī emphasized her androgynous and ultimately benevolent nature.

Another important reenvisioning concerns the interrelationship between the three great deeds or *carita*s themselves. In the *Devī Māhātmya*, the three *carita*s are presented basically as increasingly elaborate revelations of the power and majesty (*prabhāva*) of the Goddess and her successive manifestations (*utpatti*).[1] There is no emphasis or explicit assertion that there are three great stories. Indeed, were the extant editions of the text not divided into three *carita*s, one would not be especially aware of the "threeness" of the Devī's great deeds. On the one hand, within the three stories, there are more than three major encounters between the Devī and the demons (see especially the third *carita* and her advances against Caṇḍa-Muṇḍa and Raktabīja as well as against Śumbha and Niśumbha). On the other, her future manifestations, though mentioned only briefly by the Devī near the end of the *Devī-Māhātmya*, indicate that the several episodes already related are just part of her ongoing protective activity.[2] The Goddess herself concludes: "Thus, whenever affliction caused by the *dānava*s arises, I shall incarnate (*avatīrya*) to ensure their destruction."[3]

All this does not mean that there is no organic relationship between the three great deeds in the *Devī-Māhātmya*. The first story, for example, sets out the cosmic and transcendent context in which the next two are to be understood and interpreted.[4] Further, the three stories together appear to represent an integration of myths from three major competing religious milieus: the Vaiṣṇava (the Madhu-Kaiṭabha episode), the Śaivite (the Mahiṣa story, which in the epic belonged to Skanda), and tribal (the Śumbha-Niśumbha myth).[5] Nonetheless, the *Devī-Māhātmya* provides no explicit overarching structure that binds the three *carita*s together as a symbolic or metaphysical unit in themselves.

It is just such a structure or symbolic framework that we find in the *Devī-Bhāgavata*'s second retelling of the *Devī-Māhātmya*, in the tenth Skandha. This second retelling adheres quite closely, in terms of the mythic action, to the *Devī-Māhātmya* itself. The *Devī-Bhāgavata*, however, then superimposes a self-conscious, cosmological and theological interpretation upon the interrelationship between the three great mythic deeds. In turning to this interpretive framework, we shall largely leave behind the specific protective acts of the Devī as we focus more on the general cosmic nature of her manifestations; but these protective acts, we should not forget, remain the life and substance of these manifestations.

From *Avatāri*c Descents to Cosmic Manifestations: The Three Primordial *Śakti*s of the Devī

At the end of the first *carita* in the *Devī-Māhātmya*, following Brahmā's successful arousal of Yoganidrā to withdraw from the sleeping Viṣṇu allowing him to slay Madhu and Kaiṭabha, the sage Medhas concludes: "In this way she herself, praised by Brahmā, arose. Now listen as I tell you further of that Devī's majesty."[6] Using nearly identical language, the *Devī-Bhāgavata* in the tenth Skandha finishes its own account of the first episode, but with an interesting addition: "O King, in this way the Devī, praised by Brahmā, arose as Mahā-Kālī, the mistress of all yoga-masters. Hear also, O King, the arising of Mahā-Lakṣmī."[7] Similarly, at the end of the second story, the *Devī-Māhātmya* says that the manifestation of the Devī from the bodies of the gods has been told, and that her appearance as Gaurī is next to be related.[8] The *Devī-Bhāgavata* substitutes: "Thus did Lakṣmī arise, the slayer of Mahiṣa (*mahiṣāsura-mardinī*); hear also, O King, about the manifestation (*prādur-bhāva*) of Sarasvatī."[9] Finally, at the end of the third episode, Medhas in the *Devī-Māhātmya* summarizes: "Thus does the Devī Bhagavatī, although eternal, manifest herself again and again for the protection of the world, O King,"[10] clearly echoing the famous description of Viṣṇu's/Kṛṣṇa's *avatāra*s in the fourth chapter of the *Bhagavad Gītā*.[11] In the *Devī-Bhāgavata*, after Sumedhas[12] has related the episode of Śumbha and Niśumbha, the sage concludes: "Thus has been described to you, O King, the pleasing manifestations of Kālī, Mahā-Lakṣmī, and Sarasvatī in order."[13] The *Devī-Bhāgavata*, then, has identified the successive appearances or incarnations of the Goddess in the three great deeds of the *Devī-Māhātmya* with her cosmic manifestations known as Mahā-Kālī, Mahā-Lakṣmī, and (Mahā-)Sarasvatī.[14]

These three great manifestations, whom I shall refer to as the three Mahā-Devīs, correspond to the interrelated cosmic moments or phases of destruction, preservation, and creation. These cosmic functions, long connected with the masculine Trimūrti of Śiva, Viṣṇu, and Brahmā and their respective *guṇas* or qualities of darkness (*tamas*), goodness (*sattva*), and activity (*rajas*), gradually came to be associated with the personified, female powers or *śaktis* of the gods. Around the time of the *Devī-Māhātmya* (fifth or sixth century A.D.), in fact, the *Ahirbudhnya Saṃhitā* identifies the *śaktis* of Brahmā, Viṣṇu, and Śiva with Sarasvatī, Lakṣmī, and Gaurī, and further sees these *śaktis* as manifestations of the three *guṇas* of the primal creative energy known as Māyāśakti and Mūlaprakṛti (Primordial Nature).[15] A few centuries later (ca. ninth or tenth), the *Kriyāyogasāra* regards Brahmā, Viṣṇu, and Śiva as manifestations of Mahā-Viṣṇu, arising for the continuation of the cosmic cycle. Then from Mahā-Viṣṇu's primal creative energy (*ādyā prakṛti*) evolve the three goddesses Brāhmī, Lakṣmī, and Ambikā to assist their counterparts in their cosmic duties.[16] Yet in both the *Ahirbudhnya* and the *Kriyāyogasāra*, the *śaktis* are subordinate to and at the service of the masculine God or gods.

The *Devī-Māhātmya*, naturally, challenges this masculine interpretation of the cosmic process right from the start. Brahmā, in his eulogy of Yoganidrā, asserts: "By you is this universe supported; by you the world is created; by you it is protected, and in the end you consume it, always. . . . You are the Nature (Prakṛti) of all, stimulating the three *guṇas*. . . . By you the [alleged] creator, maintainer and consumer of the world [Viṣṇu] has been overpowered in sleep . . . and by you Viṣṇu, I, and Īśāna (Śiva) are made to take on embodied forms."[17] The same idea is repeated near the end by the sage Medhas, just after his mentioning that the Devī incarnates herself again and again to protect the worlds: "When it is time, just she [the Devī] is the great destroyer (*mahāmārī*); just she, without beginning, becomes the creation; and just she, eternal, maintains [all] beings at the right time."[18]

The *Devī-Māhātmya*'s juxtaposition of the Devī's cosmic functions next to her protective incarnations is echoed in the *Devī-Bhāgavata*. The latter, in the parallel context, after referring to the Devī's successive incarnations in the three *carita*s (as Kālī, Mahā-Lakṣmī, and Sarasvatī), immediately adds: "The supreme mistress, the Devī, brings about the creation of the world, as well as its protection and destruction."[19] The *Devī-Bhāgavata*'s correlation of the three Mahā-Devīs with the three *carita*s was thus already suggested, in however latent a form, by the *Devī-Māhātmya* itself.

It is difficult to determine the date of the correlations in the *Devī-Bhāgavata*.[20] I have been unable to determine whether it is more likely that they belong to the very latest layers of the text (fifteenth-sixteenth centuries), or to the more basic core of the Purāṇa (eleventh-twelfth centuries). Even in the latter case, however, our text almost certainly was not the first to envision a correspondence between the three *śakti*s or cosmic manifestations of the Goddess and her demon-slaying exploits. One early model for drawing such a correspondence is found in the *Varāha Purāṇa*, in the intriguing section known as the "Triśakti-Māhātmya" (chapters 89-95), whose date is probably no later than the ninth century A.D.[21] In the "Triśakti-Māhātmya" we find an account of the "birth" of the Devī and of her becoming threefold according to the *guṇa*s—already mentioned in connection with the "origin" of Mahiṣāsura-Mardinī in chapter four above.

We may recall that, according to the account, Brahmā and the other *deva*s, being harassed in typical fashion by the demon Andhaka, take refuge with Śiva. Then in a passage reminiscent of the "origin" of the Devī in the second *carita* of the *Devī-Māhātmya*, Brahmā looks at Śiva while remembering Viṣṇu, who appears in their midst. The three then merge into one, though they continue to gaze at one another with "subtle vision." Their threefold vision itself becomes one, in which arises (*samutpannā*) a young maiden (*kumārī*) of divine form.[22] The three gods ask her who she is; and she, described as having three complexions (*trivarṇā*), black, white, and yellow, replies: "I am sprung from the union of your vision. Do you not know me, of fair hips, as your own *śakti*, the supreme mistress (*parameśvarī*)?"[23] The gods then explain to her that she will have various names arising from the [three] *guṇa*s, and request her to assume three forms (*mūrti-traya*) according to the three complexions.[24] The three forms she assumes are: 1) Brāhmī, also known as Sṛṣṭi and Sarasvatī, of white color, who creates beings; 2) Vaiṣṇavī, also called Viṣṇumāyā, of red color, who protects the world; and 3) Raudrī, of black color, who destroys the world.

The *Varāha* then relates an anecdote or episode about each of the three *śaktis*. The first, regarding Brāhmī or Sṛṣṭi, one might have expected to deal with Andhaka, but the demon has vanished completely, never to reappear in the "Triśakti-Māhātmya." Instead, Sṛṣṭi's attainment of omnipresence from Brahmā and his consequent success in furthering creation is told. Sṛṣṭi, incidentally, is later identified as *sāttvikī*.[25] The next two episodes, however, are standard demon-vanquishing tales. The Devī Vaiṣṇavī, who is called the *rājasī śakti*, slays Mahiṣāsura, while Raudrī, the *śakti* born of *tamas*, kills the *daitya* Ruru. At the end of the story of Mahiṣa, the text refers to the appearance of Vaiṣṇavī as "this second birth (*janma*) of the Devī."[26] After the last episode, in the *phala-śruti* (fruits of hearing the preceding accounts), the Purāṇa declares: "Who hears with devotion this arising (*samudbhavam*) of the Triśakti is freed from all sin."[27] In the following verses, similar mention is made of the "origin (*utpatti*) of the threefold Devī"[28] and "the creation (*sarga*) of the Triśakti."[29]

While the "Triśakti-Māhātmya" has been regarded as a relatively late Śākta interpolation into the *Varāha Purāṇa*,[30] its "feminine" aspects are often interwoven with, or overrriden by, a "masculine" orientation. Not infrequently the Goddess and her various forms are treated as subordinate to or dependent on the gods. Thus Sṛṣṭi, after attaining the boon of omnipresence from Brahmā, dissolves back into his body,[31] while Raudrī prays to Rudra to keep from being devoured by her own attendants.[32] Further, near the very end of the Māhātmya, it is said that Rudra becomes the husband and lord (*pati*) of each *śakti*, and that however many forms Mahā-Śakti assumes, Śaṃkaraṇ (Śiva) in the form of their husband enjoys all of them.[33] The final verse adds: "Rudra will be pleased with whoever worships them [the *śaktis*]."[34]

The masculine orientation of the "Triśakti-Māhātmya" seems also implicit in the birth of the original maiden from the union of the threefold vision of the Trimūrti. Unlike the account of the birth of the Goddess from the *tejas* of the gods in the *Devī-Māhātmya*, where it is clear that she is only taking on a new form, having eternal existence, the "Triśakti-Māhātmya" is far more ambivalent, her birth here seeming to be her ultimate origin. Yet even the *Devī-Māhātmya*'s account, as we have seen, has been interpreted (or misinterpreted) as implying a subordination of the Devī to the gods.

All such ambiguities, however, are done away with in the "Prādhānika-Rahasya," one of the Six Limbs that has become attached to the *Devī-Māhātmya*.[35] The "Prādhānika-Rahasya" ("The Preeminent

Mystery," or "The Secret Relating to Pradhāna [Prakṛti]") gives a cosmogonic myth that "explains" the hidden nature of the Devī and her *guṇa*-manifestations. The supreme Devī, here referred to as Mahā-Lakṣmī and as *triguṇā,* evolves from herself a *tāmasī* form, Mahā-Kālī, and a *sāttvikī* form, Mahā-Sarasvatī. This evolutionary development of the Goddess is reversed from that given in the "Triśakti-Māhātmya": Mahā-Lakṣmī is not the result of combining the *guṇa*-energies, but their source.

The "Prādhānika-Rahasya," in reversing the evolution of the Goddess, also inverts the relation of the gods to the Devī: after Mahā-Lakṣmī has evolved the other two Mahā-Devīs, the three goddesses next create a male and female pair of deities each. The males are the gods of the Trimūrti, though they are not matched with their usual consorts. Mahā-Lakṣmī rearranges the pairs, giving the males their appropriate spouses. The creation of the world egg and its various elements is then briefly described.[36]

Another of the Six Limbs, the immediately following "Vaikṛtika-Rahasya" ("The Mystery of the Manifestations"), shifts from a cosmogonic to an "incarnational" perspective. Here we encounter the complete correlation of the three famous demon-slaying incarnations of the Goddess as found in the *Devī-Māhātmya* with the three *guṇa*-manifestations or Mahā-Devīs.[37] The goddess Vaiṣṇavī of the "Triśakti-Māhātmya," connected with the slaying of Mahiṣa, is now identified with Mahā-Lakṣmī, both names being closely associated with Viṣṇu. In accord with the first "Rahasya," the "Vaikṛtika" associates Mahā-Lakṣmī with all three *guṇa*s and Sarasvatī with *sattva*.

That the two "Rahasyas" may have been indirectly indebted to the "Triśakti-Māhātmya" account is suggested by the fact that all three give the somewhat unusual correlation of Sarasvatī with the *sattva guṇa*. As Brahma's wife, she is more often associated with the active, creative quality of *rajas,* while Viṣṇu's spouse is identified with *sattva*. The "Rahasyas," while retaining the association of Sarasvatī with *sattva,* identify Mahā-Lakṣmī not with *rajaṣ,* but rather with all the *guṇa*s.

The exalted position of Mahā-Lakṣmī in the "Rahasyas" is a bit puzzling at first and is almost certainly due in part to Vaiṣṇava influence. Indeed, it is quite likely that the "Rahasyas" are dependent upon the Vaiṣṇava *Lakṣmī Tantra* (ninth to twelfth centuries),[38] where we find perhaps the earliest correlation of the Mahā-Devīs with the three incarnations of the main *carita*s of the *Devī-Māhātmya*. The description of the cosmogonic manifestations of the Goddess is often nearly identical in the Tantra and the "Rahasyas," and there is a general parallel in the structure of the accounts as a whole, including the correlations and enumerations of the Devī's incarnations.[39] It is quite natural in the context of the Tantra that the supreme Devī, identified as "Viṣṇu's supreme being,"[40] be known as Mahā-Lakṣmī. It appears that the author or authors of the "Rahasyas" were quite eager to share in the Tantra's insights into the cosmogonic and incarnational mysteries of the Goddess, whatever her name, while ignoring those aspects of the Tantra that commingled her nature with Viṣṇu's.[41]

In any case, I suggest that these "Rahasyas" may well lie behind the *Devī-Bhāgavata*'s correlations of the three deeds with the three cosmic manifestations. We may note, in particular, that the brief account of the emergence of Mahiṣa-Mardinī in the "Vaikṛtika-Rahasya" contains certain features also found in the *Devī-Bhāgavata*'s extended version of the same event in Skandha V. In the latter, the Devī who arises from the *tejas* of the gods is referred to as Mahā-Lakṣmī.[42] Moreover, she is called *triguṇā*,[43] for she represents the union of the red [*rajas*ic] energy mass of Brahmā, the silvery *tamas*ic mass of Śiva, and the bluish, *sattv*ic mass of Viṣṇu. There are a number of other intriguing verbal similarities in the description of the Devī in the two accounts. For instance, both refer to Mahā-Lakṣmī as being eighteen-armed and at the same time thousand-armed.[44] There are, however, several differences in the details as well, not the least of which is the *Devī-Bhāgavata*'s attribution of *rajas* to Brahmā's energy and *sattva* to Viṣṇu's. This change suggests that the *Devī-Bhāgavata* is further removed from the "Triśakti-Māhātmya" than the two "Rahasyas."

The "Prādhānika-Rahasya's" inversion of the relation between the gods and the Devī, including the account of the Devī's gift of the spouses to the Trimūrti, parallels the *Devī-Bhāgavata*'s version of creation in Book III. According to the latter, shortly after Viṣṇu's victory against Madhu and Kaiṭabha, he and Brahmā, along with Śiva, begin to praise the Devī, who is standing before them. She is pleased and speaks to the gods, commanding them, now that the two demons are slain, to proceed with the work of creation, preservation, and destruction, and to create their own celestial homes wherein to dwell free of affliction.[45] The gods, however, are perplexed about how to begin, since they are powerless (*aśakta*) and there is only one vast expanse of water, without the *guṇa*s, *bhūta*s (elements), or other raw materials needed for creation.[46] The Devī immediately transports them to her celestial home of Maṇi-Dvīpa, the Jeweled Island, and after transforming the gods into females,[47] reveals to them that she is the power behind all actions. She consoles the Trimūrti by telling them that when they become endowed with *śakti*, they will be able to fulfill their roles.[48]

The Devī then gives specific instructions to each of the gods. To Brahmā she says: "O Creator, take this beautiful and sweetly smiling *śakti*, known as Mahā-Sarasvatī, conjoined with *rajo-guṇa*, fair, dressed in white, divine, adorned with divine ornaments, mounted on an excellent seat. [Take her] as your wife, for the sake of play (*krīḍā*). . . . Never is she to be disrespected, for she is most worthy of worship. Go with her at once to Satyaloka [Brahmā's world] and begin creation."[49] In a similar fashion the Devī gives the charming (*manoharā*) Mahā-Lakṣmī to Viṣṇu[50] and Mahā-Kālī (also described as *manoharā*!) to Śiva.[51] The Devī dismisses the gods, advising them that whenever they are in difficulty, if they remember her, she will grant to them *darśana* (her gracious appearance).[52] This promise echoes her boon to the gods in the *Devī-Māhātmya*, where she agrees to destroy their misfortunes whenever they remember her.[53] Her promise here, in the context of the gift of the three Mahā-Devīs, thus anticipates the correspondence between her cosmic manifestations and her protective incarnations.[54]

One of the *Devī-Bhāgavata*'s most succinct acclamations of the superiority of the Mahā-Devī's over the masculine Trimūrti is found in the definitions of *sarga* (creation) and *prati-sarga* (secondary creation), the first two of the *pañca-lakṣaṇa*s (five marks of a Purāṇa). After naming the five characteristics, the *Devī-Bhāgavata* continues: "She who is without qualities (*nirguṇā*), eternal . . . and transcendent [the *turīyā*, or fourth, beyond the three *guṇa*s of *prakṛti*], manifests three powers (*śakti*s) in the female forms known as Mahā-Lakṣmī, Sarasvatī, and Mahā-Kālī. When these three *śakti*s take on divine bodies for the sake of creation (*sṛṣṭi*), that characteristic is known as *sarga*. . . . The arising next of Viṣṇu, Brahmā, and Śiva for the sake of protection, production, and destruction is known as *prati-sarga*."[55]

Commenting on the above definition of *sarga*, Nīlakaṇṭha asserts that the manifestations (*utpatti*) of Mahā-Kālī and the other *śakti*s are given in the first and fifth Skandhas of the Purāṇa, clearly referring to the accounts of the three great adventures of the Devī in I.6-9, V.2-20, and V.21-31. However, neither the first nor third episodes (in I.6-9 and V.21-31) explicitly refer to their appropriate, corresponding

Mahā-Devīs.[56]

It seems reasonable to suppose that the *Devī-Bhāgavata* has utilized the two "Rahasyas," or sources closely related to them, in elaborating its own accounts and definitions of the Mahā-Devīs. The *Devī-Bhāgavata* in many ways appears to have simplified the more complex cosmogonic myth of the "Prādhānika-Rahasya," and as already noted, to have reassigned the *guṇas* to the three goddesses in a more orthodox manner (at least from a Vaiṣṇava point of view). This latter change raises an important issue, for the *guṇa*-correspondences, as well as the related correlation of the Mahā-Devīs with the three *caritas*, may appear to be quite capricious. That is, the specific correlations of Mahā-Kālī with Yoganidrā (in the Madhu-Kaiṭabha myth), of Mahā-Lakṣmī with Mahiṣāsura-Mardinī, and of Mahā-Sarasvatī with the slayer of Śumbha and Niśumbha may seem wholly arbitrary, especially in the last two instances.

The first correlation, to be sure, is somewhat more understandable, for the *Devī-Māhātmya* already identifies Yoganidrā as the "Devī Tāmasī,"[57] a natural enough identification since sleep (*nidrā*) is associated with darkness and inertia, the prime features of *tamas*. Mahā-Kālī, long associated with *tamas*, was thus readily identified with Yoganidrā. This single identification was perhaps sufficient to inspire the correlation of the other two main incarnations with the remaining two *guṇas* and their corresponding Mahā-Devīs, given the Hindu penchant for uncovering hidden or mystical correspondences between all kinds of worldly, cosmic, and divine phenomena.[58]

The three *guṇas*, in particular, have been an important vehicle for making, or rather discovering, triadic correlations throughout the universe.[59] While to outsiders, such correlations may seem quite artificial and superficial, they reflect a basic Hindu intuition that the universe is an interconnected and integrated whole, that the variety and confusion of surface phenomena are ultimately simply the manifestation of a deeper, underlying pattern and structure. Further, the three *guṇas* and associated triads are not merely literary-philosophical ideals divorced from the common life; as the anthropologist Ákos Östör has noted, they also have importance as "ethnographic categories in local systems and contexts."[60] With specific reference to the three Mahā-Devīs, Östör observes:

> According to the Caṇḍī legend, there are three forms of the goddess, corresponding to the three guṇas: Mahā Kālī, or *tama guṇ*, Mahā Lakṣmī, or *raja guṇ*, and Mahā Sarasvatī, or *sattva guṇ*. These three forms issued

> from the goddess as her first creation; they also form the basis of the social order and of the people's participation in the pūjās. . . . The goddess expresses the created world, and the three qualities define the whole of creation. . . . The goddess, the qualities, and the created world (*prakriti*) are different ways of defining the same totality.[61]

My only qualification of Östör's comments would be to clarify that the notion of the three Mahā-Devīs and their arising from the Goddess as her first creation is not found in the Caṇḍī legend as given in the *Devī-Māhātmya* itself, but rather in the "Rahasyas" and other later interpretations of the Caṇḍī myth.[62]

Adding to the impression, for the outsider, that the correlations are largely arbitrary is the fact that the specific correspondences frequently appear to be inconsistent, even within a single text or context. Yet this, too, reflects a basic Hindu intuition, namely the recognition that a single phenomenon can appear in diverse and seemingly contradictory forms according to the perspectives from which it is viewed. This results in a high degree of flexibility within the symbol system. Here again, Östör makes some very pertinent observations in relation to the ways of performing the *pūjā*s of various gods: "Viṣṇu, though the god of mokṣa, may be worshiped for profit; the goddess Kālī, though a tamasik deity, may grant liberation. *Śakti* pūjās of desire, power, and pride may be performed in the way of love and pure devotion (bhakti). The referents of symbols overlap, and categories are not mutually exclusive—they define ideal types of action and can be rearranged within the total system."[63]

With these ideas of multiple perspectives and overlap of symbols in mind, it is easier to see how Kālī, or Mahā-Kālī, usually identified with destruction, is associated with the one *carita* that is intimately connected with cosmogony. In the *Devī-Māhātmya* itself, the name Mahā-Kālī occurs once[64] and is immediately associated with Mahā-Mārī, the great death, who arises at the end of time. In the next verse, however, she is said to be not only the destroyer, but also the creator and maintainer of the universe.

Various creative aspects of the "*tamas*ic" Mahā-Kālī are suggested by Charlotte Vaudeville: "Under her dark aspect the Goddess is conceived as Ādyakālī, the primeval Kālī. She is the 'Mother of Time' (Kālamātā), the night or sleep, the primordial waters from which creation arises, the cosmic Mother from whose womb all beings including the gods arise."[65] Vaudeville's description clearly rings with overtones from the *Devī-Māhātmya*'s myth of Yoganidrā. From the larger, cosmic perspective, the fact that Kālī (the diminutive form of Mahā-Kālī, as it were) manifests herself and performs her great deeds against Raktabīja in the third *carita*, correlated with the manifestation of Mahā-Sarasvatī, is thus basically irrelevant.[66]

In this connection, it is interesting to note that the one reference to Sarasvatī in the *Devī-Māhātmya*[67] contains in the same line the epithet "*tāmasi*," indicating the interchangeability of names, epithets, and forms of the Devī typical of the text as a whole. This fluid, even slippery nature of the identities of the several manifestations of the Goddess makes it highly problematic in most cases to establish "logically strict" or "narrowly rational" correspondences between these manifestations in the *Devī-Māhātmya* and the Mahā-Devīs of the "Rahasyas" or the *Devī-Bhāgavata*.

As already intimated with regards to the last two *caritas*, there is nothing in the actions of the incarnations themselves that is particularly suggestive of the usual functions or characteristics of their corresponding Mahā-Devīs. This lack of obvious or direct connection, however, underscores in one sense the fact that we are not dealing with the surface appearance of events but with their hidden, underlying pattern.

This underlying structure represented by the three Mahā-Devīs is a mystery, as the "Prādhānika" and "Vaikṛtika" Rahasyas indicate, and as acknowledged by later commentators on the *Devī-Māhātmya*. Bhāskararāya (eighteenth century), for instance, in his commentary *Guptavatī*, writes with reference to the identification of Yoganidrā with the "Devī Tāmasī": "Here is this *rahasya* (secret, esoteric teaching; mystery). The *devatās* [divinities][68] of the three stories are Mahā-Kālī, Mahā-Lakṣmī, and Mahā-Sarasvatī in order. She [the supreme Devī] is actually predominantly *sāttvikī*, but for the sake of removing *daityas*, she appears in the forms of *tamas*, *rajas*, and *sattva*."[69] The mystery, then, as suggested by Bhāskararāya, seems to be that the Goddess who is essentially truth and goodness (*sāttvikī*) manifests all her *guṇa*-forms, including the horrific and destructive, to protect the world. Behind the plethora of names and forms appearing in the texts is the trifold mystery of the one supreme reality, a notion already latent in the *Devī-Māhātmya*, developed in the "Rahasyas," and systematized and formalized in the *Devī-Bhāgavata*.

The correlation of the Devī's cosmic manifestations with her protective incarnations was of tremendous importance for later Śākta devotional practices. In the *Devī-Bhāgavata*, the Goddess often grants to the devout a vision (*darśana*) of herself. But she rarely reveals her ultimate and transcendent nature; rather, she manifests herself in some lower, embodied form, frequently in one of her *guṇa*-forms as one of the three Mahā-Devīs. In this connection, we may note Vyāsa's advice to Janamejaya shortly after recounting the story of the gift of the Mahā-Devīs to the Trimūrti. Vyāsa urges the king: "With supreme devotion, go worship the Goddess [who is] Māhā-Lakṣmī, Mahā-Kālī, and also Mahā-Sarasvatī, the mistress of all beings, the cause of all causes, bestowing all desires and wealth, tranquil (*śāntā*), easily served, compassionate."[70] Vyāsa seems to suggest that it is easier to worship the Goddess in one of her more recognizable and better-known forms.

The intimate connection between the Devī's cosmic manifestations and her protective incarnations is in subtle contrast to what we find in the *Bhāgavata Purāṇa*. There we discover a distinction between the Lord's cosmic manifestations as Brahmā, Viṣṇu, and Śiva according to the *guṇas*, referred to as his *guṇāvatāras*[71], and his protective and playful manifestations (what are normally understood as his basic incarnations, such as the fish, dwarf, etc.), called *līlāvatāras*.[72] The *guṇāvatāra* notion in the *Bhāgavata* functions on one level to establish the superiority of the Lord or Kṛṣṇa over the Trimūrti, for "the Supreme Deity . . . is ultimately beyond the process of creation while these gods [of the Trimūrti] are not."[73] On the highest level, of course, given the *advaita* (nondualist) perspective of the *Bhāgavata*, all of Kṛṣṇa's forms are one, but it is a unity that largely transcends the cosmos: "The cosmic manifestations are . . . the mediators of reality from the absolute reality of Bhagavān [the Lord] to the reality of each individual being. Actually they are identical with Bhagavān and an expression of his non-duality."[74]

While the *guṇāvatāras* of Kṛṣṇa may be mediators, they serve as such primarily on a philosophical and theological, rather than on a personal and devotional level, for there often remains, despite the transcosmic unity, a sense of underlying tension between the identity of the Lord himself and that of the three members of the Trimūrti. Thus in the later Vaiṣṇava-Kṛṣṇaite schools, the *guṇāvatāras* are treated, from a devotional standpoint, with a fair degree of circumspection. The attitude of Jīva Gosvāmin, for instance, may be summarized as follows:

> The worship of deities other than the Bhagavat [Kṛṣṇa] is forbidden. Even the Guṇāvatāras, Brahmā, Śiva and Viṣṇu, are not worthy of the highest worship. . . . Deities like Śiva or Brahmā can be worshipped in so far as they are themselves Vaiṣṇavas . . . or in so far as they are particular locations . . . of the Bhagavat himself. . . . But for those who regard them

> as separate and independent objects of worship, there is the terrible curse of Bhṛgu Muni referred to in *Bhāgavata* iv. 2. 27-8.[75]

The Devī, too, of course, is the transcendent "One," but she is also the supreme Prakṛti. Accordingly, she is not just endowed with or united with the three *guṇa*s in the manner of Kṛṣṇa,[76] she is also *triguṇā* and *triguṇātmikā* (she whose essence is the three *guṇa*s). There is thus a greater sense of unity between the supreme Devī and her *guṇa*-forms, and little concern that they may be mistaken as separate and independent entities. The *Devī-Bhāgavata* therefore has no hesitation in affirming that the Mahā-Devīs are most worthy of worship (*pūjyatamā*),[77] an admonition taken to heart by later devotees of the Goddess. While the worship of Kṛṣṇa's *guṇāvatāra*s languished, those of the Devī flourished, for the esoteric identification of her *guṇa*-manifestations with her protective incarnations allowed for her cosmic aspects to become approachable on a devotional level, and conversely, for her attention to the personal matters of the devotee to take on a kind of cosmic significance.

The worship of the Mahā-Devīs in the *Devī-Bhāgavata* is imbued not only with a cosmic but also with a Vedic and a Tantric significance. These aspects are clearly seen in the very latest layers of the text, where the Mahā-Devīs undergo their final evolution, being interpreted as Vedic and Tantric *devatā*s or divinities. These interrelated transformations were especially important given that the Tantricizing tendencies of the Purāṇa were in potential conflict with the Vedic orthodoxy of the times. Let us then turn to this last development.

From Cosmic Manifestations to *Devatās*: Vedicization and Tantricization of the *Devī-Māhātmya*

The eighteenth-century devotee Bhāskararāya, as we have noted, refers to the three Mahā-Devīs or *śakti*s as *devatā*s in his commentary on the *Devī-Māhātmya*.[78] The word *devatā*, derived from *deva* and literally meaning godhood or divinity, may also mean simply a deity, an image of a deity, or one of the several protective deities that may reside in the body—these last having considerable relevance for the Tantric aspects in the *Devī-Bhāgavata*. In addition, *devatā* may refer to the particular gods to whom the various mantras or hymns of the *Ṛg Veda* are addressed. This latter usage is of critical importance here, for it directly relates to how later devotees of the Goddess came to regard the *Devī-Māhātmya* not merely as *smṛti*, an authoritative interpretation of divine truth, but also as *śruti*, the original and eternally immutable revelation of that truth and thus itself "Veda" ("Eternal Knowledge").[79] The *Devī-Bhāgavata* reflects certain important aspects or stages in the later Vedicization of the *Devī-Māhātmya*, not only in its correlation of the three *caritas* with the three Mahā-Devīs, but most specifically in its interpretation of the Mahā-Devīs as Vedic *devatās*.

This interpretation is found in the last chapter of the ninth Skandha, a Skandha, we may recall, that is largely a borrowing from the "Prakṛti Khaṇḍa" of the *Brahmavaivarta Purāṇa* inserted by the late redactor of our text. The "Prakṛti Khaṇḍa" describes the deeds (*caritas*) of the major forms of the Goddess, who is variously identified as Mūlaprakṛti, Rādhā, or Durgā, and is consistently portrayed as ontologically subordinate to Kṛṣṇa. Near the beginning of the "Prakṛti Khaṇḍa," the disciple Nārada asks about how the diverse forms of Mūlaprakṛti were worshipped, by whom, and what were the boons given as a result of worshipping them; Nārada also inquires about the various *kavacas* (amulets), *stotras* (hymns of praise), *dhyānas* (meditations), *prabhāvas* (powers), as well as the *caritas* of the different goddesses.[80] The sage Nārāyaṇa replies first by giving a table of contents of the "Prakṛti Khaṇḍa,"[81] listing all the *devīs* he is going to talk about, ending with the great and extensive *caritas* of Durgā and Rādhā. Nārāyaṇa then proceeds to narrate the stories and worship of the several goddesses.

The *Devī-Bhāgavata* takes over almost verbatim Nārada's questions and Nārāyaṇa's introductory table of contents,[82] and recounts in similar fashion the narratives of the various *devīs*, being careful, however, to remove or recast most of the references that subordinate the Goddess or her forms to Kṛṣṇa. Only in the accounts of the last two goddesses, Rādhā and Durgā, do we find that the *Devī-Bhāgavata* diverges widely from its model in the *Brahmavaivarta*.

The *Devī-Bhāgavata* redactor shows almost no interest in the *Brahmavaivarta*'s account of the *carita* of Rādhā,[83] focussing almost exclusively on her worship. The redactor follows more closely the *Brahmavaivarta*'s account of Durgā, but the latter Purāṇa only briefly mentions her deeds in a description of her *dhyāna*.[84] Accordingly, the discussion of Durgā in *Devī-Bhāgavata* IX concentrates on the various aspects of her *pūjā*, referring to her deeds only in its own description of her *dhyāna*. Here, though, it is not due to lack of interest in those deeds, the slaying of Madhu-Kaiṭabha, Mahiṣāsura, etc., for they are about to be related in the tenth Skandha.[85] At any rate, the interest of the *Brahmavaivarta* in the history and methods of Durgā-worship clearly appealed to and inspired our redactor, who followed the general outline of the Kṛṣṇaite text in describing the methods of worshipping Durgā.

The delineation of the rules for Durgā-worship given in the *Devī-Bhāgavata*[86] begins with a brief introduction of the Goddess,[87] proceeds to relate her mantra, certain preliminary rites known as *nyāsa* (the assignment of deities or other entities to various parts of the body for purification or protection of the worshipper), the *dhyāna* of the Devī, her *yantra* worship (in which she and various surrounding, protective deities are situated on the diverse parts of a mystical diagram [*yantra*] composed of triangles and lotus forms), other assorted offerings and acts pleasing to her, and finally an account of the fruits of worshipping her. All of these general topics are dealt with in the *Brahmavaivarta*, though the details are often quite different. Two such differences are especially relevant to our present inquiry.

The first difference concerns the treatment of the Devī's mantra. Though the *Brahmavaivarta* refers to various mantras in worshipping Durgā, the essential mantra seems to be the one contained in the invocation inviting her to be present in her image: "Oṃ Hrīṃ Śrīṃ Klīṃ Durgāyai Vahnijāyai (the wife of Fire or Svāhā)."[88] With the exception of "Oṃ," the other one syllable utterances (having no ordinary semantic meaning) are typical of the seed syllables (*bījas*) of Tantric mantras.

In the *Devī-Bhāgavata*, a different mantra of the Devī is given, though it also appears in Tantric form. It is referred to as the *kāma-bīja* (the seed mantra of Kāma or Desire) and is said to consist of nine syllables.[89] After extolling the nine-syllable formula as the best of all mantras, the *Devī-Bhāgavata* adds: "Brahmā, Viṣṇu, and Maheśāna (Śiva) are renowned as its seers; its meters are said to be the Gāyatrī, Uṣṇik, and Anuṣṭubh eternally;[90] Mahā-Kālī, Mahā-Lakṣmī, and Sarasvatī are its *devatās*; Raktadantikā, Durgā, and Bhrāmarī are its *bīja*s; Nandā, Śākambharī, and Bhīmā are remembered as its *śakti*s;[91] and *dharma*, *artha*, *kāma*, and *mokṣa* are declared [the fruits of] its application (*viniyoga*)."[92]

What the *Devī-Bhāgavata* has done is to treat this mantra, typical of Purāṇic/Tantric mantras, as a Vedic mantra.[93] The mantras or hymns of the Vedas, especially of the *Ṛg Veda*, had been catalogued or indexed in the early Sūtra period (600-200 B.C.) to help preserve the "oral texts" from loss or change. The catalogues or indices, known as Anukramaṇīs, give the contents of the Vedic Saṃhitās according to various matters such as the author or seer of the mantras or hymns, the deities (*devatā*s) addressed, the meters used, the first words of every hymn, the number of verses in each, and the application or employment (*vidhāna* or *viniyoga*) of the various hymns.[94] The *Devī-*

Bhāgavata, going beyond the traditional Vedic categories, has added two of its own having a distinctly Tantric flavor, the *bīja*s (the "seeds" or "original essences") and *śakti*s (empowering principles). Most significantly for our purposes, the *Devī-Bhāgavata* redactor has in the process effected the transformation of the Trimūrti into Vedic seers and the Mahā-Devīs into Vedic *devatā*s.

A somewhat peculiar feature of the *Devī-Bhāgavata*'s own Anukramaṇī is its trifold character, assigning three seers, meters, etc., to the one mantra. While somewhat artificial in this context, it is reflective of the late redactor's fascination with triadic correspondences.

The triadic perspective of the redactor also manifests itself in regards to the second significant difference or modification of the "Prakṛti Khaṇḍa's" account, found in the *dhyāna* or meditation of the Goddess. This *dhyāna* as given in the *Brahmavaivarta*[95] begins with a general eulogy of Durgā, emphasizing her relation to Viṣṇu (as Viṣṇumāyā, Vaiṣṇavī, etc.), her dearness to Kṛṣṇa, but also her ontological subordination to the latter. Next is given a description of her physical form, her color, the beauty of her limbs, the sweetness of her smiling face, her ornaments and dress, and the like. The *dhyāna* concludes with references to her demon-slaying exploits: the destruction of Niśumbha-Śumbha, Mahiṣāsura, Tripura, Madhu-Kaiṭabha, Raktabīja, Hiraṇyakaśipu, and Hiraṇyakṣa. The *Devī-Bhāgavata* reduces the exploits to the essential three *carita*s belonging to the three Mahā-Devīs and then furnishes not one but three *dhyāna*s, one for each Great-Goddess.

The three *dhyāna*s are quite similar in form, each giving the various emblems (mainly weapons but also other objects like garlands and water pots) held in the several hands of the goddess, her color, name, deed, and associated mantra-*bīja*. Thus one should meditate on Mahā-Kālī, who was praised by Brahmā for the destruction of Madhu-Kaiṭabha, as holding ten weapons in her ten hands (she also has ten feet and ten mouths), having the color of Nīlañjana (a dark blue or black pigment), and whose essential nature is the Kāma-bīja. One should meditate on Mahā-Lakṣmī, known as Mahiṣāsura-Mardinī, as holding eighteen emblems, of reddish color, and whose mantric identity is the Māyā-bīja. Finally, one should meditate on Mahā-Sarasvatī, the slayer of Śumbha and other *daitya*s, as holding eight emblems, of the color of jasmine (white), and having the mantric form of Vāṇa-bīja.[96]

These *dhyāna*s, with their focus on the forms and colors of the goddesses, are suggestive of the Tantric emphasis on visualization of the deity within one's mind, to be attained with the help of reciting the appropriate *bīja*-mantras. The significance of these *bīja*-mantras for Tantric practitioners is nicely summarized by Kane:

> All the *mantras* . . . are deemed (by Tāntrikas) to be living conscious sound powers. It is the bīja mantras like hrīm, śrīm, krīm that make visible the form of the Devatā. . . . It is wrong to suppose that mantras are mere letters or words or language. . . . The bījamantras like Hrīm (representing Tribhuvaneśvarī or Māyā), Śrīm (representing Lakṣmī), Krīm (representing Kālī) cannot possibly be called language, since they convey no meaning to ordinary men. They are the Devatā [the chosen deity of the worshipper].[97]

The inner vision of the chosen deity manifested through the *bīja*-mantra, of course, may well be derived or abstracted from an actua physical image or icon (*mūrti, devatā*) of the deity.[98] The *dhyānas* on the Mahā-Devīs thus fuse together Vedic and Tantric notions of *devatā*.

The *Devī-Bhāgavata*'s addition of a Vedic-like Anukramaṇī to the Devī's mantra, combined with its three meditations on the Mahā-Devīs reflects trends that were becoming increasingly popular among late interpreters of the nature and function of the original *Devī-Māhātmya* itself. The three *dhyānas* are very similar to the meditations affixed at the beginning of each of the three *caritas* in modern editions of the *Devī-Māhātmya*.

These latter *dhyānas*, with slight variants, are already given by one of the earliest commentators on the *Devī-Māhātmya*, Nāgojībhaṭṭ (A.D. 1700-1750),[99] in his rules for the use or recitation of the text Following his presentation of the "*mahākāly-ādi-devatā-traya-dhyānam* ("the meditation on the three *devatās* beginning with Mahā-Kālī", Nāgojībhaṭṭa adds: "In the first *caritra* [variant of *carita*] of the *Saptaśat* Padmabhū (Brahmā) is the muni, the meter is said to be Gāyatr Mahā-Kālī the *devatā*; Vāk is the *bīja*, Fire the essence (*tattva*), *dharma* th fruit of its use. In the middle *caritra*, here the muni is said to be Viṣṇu Uṣṇik the meter, Mahā-Lakṣmī the *devatā*, Adrijā (Pārvatī) the *bīja*, Win the essence, and wealth the fruit of its use. Of the last *caritra*, Śaṅkar (Śiva) is declared the seer, Triṣṭubh the meter, Mahā-Pūrvā Sarasva the *devatā*, Kāma the *bija*, Sun the essence, and pleasure the fruit c its use."[100]

Despite the addition of a new category (the *tattvas*) and a few mino variations, the parallels with the *Devī-Bhāgavata*'s Anukramaṇī a striking. The major difference is that Nāgojībhaṭṭa has applied h index not to the Devi's mantra, but directly to the three *caritras* themselves, a logical step given the correlation of the three episodes with the Mahā-Devīs/*devatās* already in the *Devī-Bhāgavata*. We thus see here a major step in the Vedicization of the *Devī-Māhātmya* itself.

I do not wish to imply that the *Devī-Bhāgavata* was necessarily the immediate or direct source of inspiration for writers like Nāgojībhaṭṭa. It is possible that the late redactor of the *Devī-Bhāgavata* was merely expressing a certain mood or tendency prevalent among Śāktas of his time, but he at least attests to the fact that the process of Vedicization of the *Devī-Māhātmya* was already well under way by the fifteenth-sixteenth century, if not earlier. Nāgojībhaṭṭa himself refers to the *Kātyāyanī Tantra*[101] (of unknown date) for another variant Anukramaṇī, one that has some features closer to the *Devī-Bhāgavata*'s and other features closer to Nāgojībhaṭṭa's given above.[102] We may also note the Anukramaṇī given by the "Tithitattva" of Raghunandana (sixteenth century), which is in some respects even closer to the *Devī-Bhāgavata*'s.[103] The historical relationship between these various Anukramaṇīs awaits further research. The one seeming invariable in all of these Anukramaṇīs is the identification of the three Mahā-Devīs as the chief *devatās* associated with the three *caritas*, even if only indirectly in the case of the threefold *dhyāna* of the *Devī-Bhāgavata*.

The Vedicization of the *Devī-Māhātmya* can be observed not only in the creation of the Anukramaṇīs but also in the composition of Six Limbs (Ṣaḍaṅgas) that came to be attached to the text. The famous Six Limbs of the Vedas (Vedāṅgas or Ṣaḍaṅgas), dealing with phonetics, metrics, grammar, etymology, ritual procedures, and astronomy, were closely related to the Vedic Anukramaṇīs.[104] The purpose of the Vedāṅgas was to provide for the proper recitation and understanding of the mantras and their appropriate use in ritual.

The Six Limbs of the *Devī-Māhātmya* have the same general purpose, though conceived in a very different manner. They are divided into two sets of three: the first triad consists of a Devī-*kavaca* (armor, or protective mantra), *argala* (bolt or fastening), and *kīlaka* (pin, or the inner syllables of a mantra);[105] the second triad, of three "Rahasyas" or "Secrets" that explain the esoteric meaning of the text. The first two "Rahasyas," the "Prādhānika" and "Vaikṛtika," we have already had occasion to mention. The importance of these Limbs in the eyes of devotees is given in the *Kātyāyanī Tantra*: "Just as an embodied being, without limbs, is useless for all activities, so is the *Saptaśatī* eulogy without its Six Limbs. Therefore reciting them, one should chant the supreme *Saptaśatī*; otherwise one meets with trouble and failure at every step. Rāvaṇa and others used this eulogy without the Limbs and they were slain by Rāma. Therefore do not recite [the *Saptaśatī*] without them."[106]

The Ṣaḍaṅgas of the *Devī-Māhātmya* are of relevance for us not simply because of their function as Vedic analogues, but also because of their contents as these relate to the *Devī-Bhāgavata*.[107] Of special interest for us in the present context are the portions of the "Vaikṛtika-Rahasya" that deal with the worship of the Devī. The "Vaikṛtika" describes various parts of the "service" (*upāsana*) of the Devī, including: a) the visual forms of the three Mahā-Devīs, emphasizing their colorful appearance and the emblems they hold in their hands; b) the worship of the Trimūrti and their consorts in particular arrangements, along with the worship of other deities and beings, including Mahiṣāsura himself; c) the presentation of diverse offerings such as incense, flowers, water, food, wine, and blood; d) instructions for the recitation of the three *caritas* of the *Devī-Māhātmya*; and e) a declaration of the fruits of worshipping the Devī: "Whoever thus worships the supreme mistress with devotion every day, enjoying all pleasures as desired, will attain Devī-*sāyujya* (absorption into the Devī, one of the four main types of *mokṣa*)."[108]

The "Vaikṛtika-Rahasya" provides us with a model for Devī-worship very close to that given by the late redactor of the *Devī-Bhāgavata*, already partly summarized above. Both in overall structure and in specific details, the "Vaikṛtika" is closer to the *Devī-Bhāgavata*'s "Rules for Durgā-worship"[109] than is the "Prakṛti Khaṇḍa." The *Devī-Bhāgavata* describes in the following order: a) the threefold *dhyāna* of Durgā, with its meditation on the three Mahā-Devīs; b) the various deities to be worshipped on the *yantra*, including the Trimūrti and their spouses, and Mahiṣa; c) the offerings to be made to the Goddess; d) instructions for chanting the *Saptaśatī-stotra* of the Devī; and e) an affirmation of the benefits resulting from such worship: "A man should please the Goddess daily with this [*stotra*; such a] man wins *dharma, artha, kāma,* and *mokṣa*."[110] The *Devī-Bhāgavata* redactor, in closing, refers to the accounts of all the goddesses (in the whole of Skandha IX) as a "most mysterious secret" *rahasyātirahasyakam*).[111]

The *Devī-Bhāgavata*'s "Durgā-Rahasya," if I may so designate its account of Durgā-worship, has added a number of distinctly Tantric elements to the procedures outlined in the "Vaikṛtika Rahasya." These include the *nyāsa* rites,[112] the seed-syllables or *bija*-mantras connected with the *dhyānas* of the three Mahā-Devīs, and the specific and detailed use of the *yantra* for positioning the various deities to be worshipped. Also new, apparently, is the *Devī-Bhāgavata*'s addition of the Vedic-like Anukramaṇīs to the Devī-mantra.[113] What is clear in all of this, at least, is that the *Devī-Bhāgavata*'s late redactor has attempted some sort of accommodation between its Vedic and Tantric aspects.

As mentioned earlier, the Tantricizing tendencies of the Purāṇa were in potential conflict with several aspects of Brahmanical-Vedic orthodoxy. Already by the seventh century A.D., Tantric ritual practices had gained considerable popularity among all levels of Hindu society, and they continued to flourish during the seventh to eleventh centuries.[114] Certain of these practices, especially those associated with the Vāmācāra or Left-Handed forms of Tantricism, espoused an antinomian attitude towards many of the Brahmanical ideals of *varṇāśrama-dharma* (the ideals of social order based upon the four classes and stages of life).

Particularly offensive to orthodox minds were the rites involved in the famous five *makāra*s, including the consumption of flesh and wine, and the indulgence in sexual intercourse between unmarried partners, in which the woman was often of low caste. These rites, regarded by the Tantrics as a quick but dangerous path to realization, required both the supervision of qualified spiritual leaders and an advanced understanding of the inner significance of the rituals on the part of the participants.

Whatever the merits of the Vāmācāra path and whatever validity there may be to the arguments of the Tantric apologists, the orthodox proponents of *varṇāśrama-dharma* roundly condemned such practices. A modern Indian scholar whose sympathies lie with the orthodox view, while recognizing some positive aspects to the Tantric path on its highest levels, asserts that "it very often degenerated into magic and moral depravity."[115] Regarding the social consequences of Tantricism, this same scholar writes: "The teaching of Tāntrika texts about the five *makāra*s must have created a very unhealthy and debased state among all classes, particularly the lower orders of Society."[116] The desire to instill "social discipline" according to the Vedic-orthodox ideals in the face of such "degrading" forces as Vāmācāra Tantricism was one of the reasons for the composition of new Purāṇas, in particular the Śākta Purāṇas including the *Devī-Bhāgavata*.[117]

At the same time, the Śākta Paurāṇikas could not simply ignore the developments occurring in the Tantric schools. Different Śākta Purāṇas varied in the degree of their acceptance of Tantric ideas, some being more open to Vāmācāra influence; others, like the *Devī-Bhāgavata*, looking with favor only on the Dakṣiṇācāra or Right-Handed Tantric path.[118] Those Purāṇas more open to Vāmācāra ideas tend to regard the Vedas and Tantras as of comparable authority. Thus, the *Mahābhāgavata* has the Devī herself state: "the Āgama [Tantra] and the Veda are my two hands with which I sustain the whole universe. . . . If, out of ignorance, anybody violates [the directions of] these two, he is sure to slip down from my hands."[119] The *Devī-Bhāgavata*, however, clearly subordinates the Tantras to the Vedas. Its basic attitude is that the Veda is the one, true, and final authority. Tantra may also be accepted as authoritative, but only where it does not conflict with the Veda.[120]

Both the *Devī-Bhāgavata*'s original composer(s) and its late redactor felt little hesitation in incorporating many Tantric elements, like the *nyāsas*, *yantras*, *dhyānas*, and *bīja-mantras*, which were not in outright contradiction to their Brahmanical-Vedic ideals. This assimilation was not just a matter of acquiescing to the popular demands of the masses, however. Both on the ritual and on the philosophical levels, Tantricism offered insights that could deepen and enrich the Purāṇic tradition.

Its Tantricizing perspective allowed the *Devī-Bhāgavata* to affirm that the "truth" revealed in the *Devī-Māhātmya*, in addition to being "heard" and "recited," is also to be "visualized," whether with the help of concrete *mūrtis* (images) or with Tantricized *dhyānas* and "Rahasyas." The late redactor provides vivid images of the Goddess in her three cosmic manifestations and emphasizes the mental interiorization or visualization of these forms with the aid of mantra and *yantra*. The mantra and *yantra* are the sound form and diagrammatic, visible expression of the Devī herself, identical with her essence. Mantra and *yantra* are thus the means of providing even greater accessibility to the Goddess, allowing the various senses to apprehend the divine, who reveals herself in the mind or heart of the devotee in meditation.[121] By transforming the Mahā-Devīs into Vedic *devatās*, the *Devī-Bhāgavata* extends a Vedic sanction to the Tantric elements incorporated into their ritual worship.

The Tantricization process in the *Devī-Bhāgavata* is not just a matter of introducing new techniques into the worship of the Goddess, for it also represents new ways of understanding her and the Mahā-Devīs. We may note, in particular, the evolving symbolic interpretation of the Goddess developed in connection with the "hidden" or "secret" explanations of the meaning of her incarnations, especially prominent in later Tantric writings but already present in seed form in the *Devī-*

Bhāgavata.

For example, the various weapons and emblems held in the arms of the Mahā-Devīs, enumerated in the threefold *dhyāna* of the Goddess, are seen as symbolic of her various powers and attributes. Thus, in his commentary on the *Lalitāsahasranāma*, Bhāskararāya reveals "the symbolic meaning underlying the *pāśa* [noose], the *aṅkuśa* [goad] and the other weapons and emblems which are usually carried by the goddess. . . . What we are led to see is that these weapons and emblems symbolize the powers of Nature and also of this goddess as the Supreme Mistress of Nature."[122] Such symbolic interpretations go back much earlier: the *Varāha Purāṇa* indicates that "the *śaṅkha* [conch] is the destroyer of *avidyā* or ignorance, the *khaḍga* [sword] is the sunderer of *ajñāna* or unwisdom, the *chakra* [discus] is the wheel of time, and lastly the *gadā* [club] is the destroyer of *adharma* or unrighteousness."[123] Given such an interpretive climate, the weapons of the Mahā-Devīs, so prominent in their *dhyāna*s, are no longer mere reflections of martial exploits but reminders of the higher identities of the goddesses.

The Tantric philosophical reinterpretation of the true nature of the Mahā-Devīs is frequently reflective of Vedāntic perspectives as well. This is brought out, for instance, in Nīlakaṇṭha's interpretation of the nine-syllable mantra of the Devī ("Aiṃ Hrīṃ Klīṃ Cāmuṇḍāyai Vicce"). Commenting on the *Devī-Bhāgavata*'s statement that this mantra should be recited with knowledge of its meaning,[124] Nīlakaṇṭha explains its esoteric significance in the following manner: the three *bīja* syllables represent Mahā-Sarasvatī, Mahā-Lakṣmī, and Mahā-Kālī; the three parts of "Vicce" ("*vit-ca-i*") signify *cit*, *sat*, and *ānanda*, corresponding to the three *bīja*s; and Cāmuṇḍā signifies Brahmavidyā. Nīlakaṇṭha then gives another meaning: for the sake of obtaining Brahmavidyā, one should meditate on Cāmuṇḍā who in the form of *cit* is Mahā-Sarasvatī, in the form of *sat* is Mahā-Lakṣmī, and in the form of *ānanda* is Mahā-Kālī. Nīlakaṇṭha, interestingly enough, bases his interpretation on Bhāskararāya's explanation of the mantra in the *Guptavatī*, which he quotes.[125] While such interpretations go beyond the explicit statements of the *Devī-Bhāgavata* itself, it is not against the spirit of the Purāṇa, which at the end of the *dhyāna* of Mahā-Sarasvatī declares that one should meditate on her, the embodiment of *sat*, *cit*, and *ānanda*.[126]

We have come a long way from the terrible, blood-drinking incarnations of the Goddess in the second and third *carita*s of the *Devī-Māhātmya*. What a discovery to find in Yoganidrā the Vedāntic bliss (*ānanda*) of Brahman, to see in Mahiṣāsura-Mardinī the manifestation of infinite being (*sat*), and in Śumbha's slayer the unchanging consciousness (*cit*)!

We may note in conclusion that the late *Devī-Bhāgavata* redactor participated in significant ways in the Vedicization and Tantricization of the *Devī-Māhātmya* and the reinterpretation of its vision of the Goddess. This process, we have seen, is intertwined at many points with the careers of the three Mahā-Devīs. Through them, the often fierce goddesses of the three *carita*s were transformed into cosmic manifestations of the Devī, which in turn, with *bhaktic* insight, were conceived as largely benevolent aspects of the one supreme mother. Through Vedicization, the Mahā-Devīs came to be regarded as the direct revelations of eternal knowledge and truth. Finally, through Tantricization and the accompanying Vedāntic interpretation, they were transformed into the inner truth of one's own being, consciousness, and bliss. Yet we must remind ourselves that what is explicit in the *Devī-Bhāgavata* and later interpretations of the Goddess is often implicit already in the *Devī-Māhātmya*.

Chapter 6

Of Merchants and Kings: Worship and Its Fruits in the Frame Stories of the *Devī-Bhāgavata* and *Mārkaṇḍeya* Purāṇas

In this chapter we turn to the frame story of King Suratha and the merchant Samādhi that surrounds the account of the Devī's three famous deeds. In the preceding two chapters, we examined various ways in which the *Devī-Bhāgavata* reinterpreted and reenvisioned the mighty acts of the Goddess originally disclosed in the *Devī-Māhātmya*. The general focus in chapter four was on the revelation of the Devī's splendor or power, what the *Devī-Māhātmya* refers to as *prabhāva*.[1] The revelation of her power, however, is only one of three great moments in the interaction between the Devī and human beings. In response to the revelation of her splendor, humans are moved to worship her; and she, in response to our worship (*ārādhana*), graciously confers the various fruits (*phala*) that humans may desire.

These three moments are briefly alluded to in the *Devī-Māhātmya* when the sage Medhas, having just finished his account of the deeds of the Devī, addresses King Suratha: "This most excellent 'Devī-Māhātmya' has been told to you, O King. Such is the majestic power (*prabhāva*) of the Devī. . . . Take refuge in the supreme mistress, for when she is worshipped (*ārādhitā*), she bestows enjoyment, heaven and release on men (*bhoga-svargāpavarga-dā*)."[2]

Similarly in the *Devī-Bhāgavata* the three moments serve as a basic structuring device. After Vyāsa has concluded his account of Devī's destruction of Mahiṣa and of Śumbha and Niśumbha in Skandha V, King Janamejaya says to him: "The greatness (*mahimā*, a synonym for *prabhāva*) of Caṇḍikā has been completely described by you, O Muni. Now tell by whom was she worshipped earlier with the threefold story; by whom was she, the giver of boons, pleased and by whom was the great fruit received?"[3] In answer to these questions, Vyāsa recounts the story of Suratha and Samādhi. As these passages suggest, it is the last two moments, of worship and the bestowal of fruits, that are highlighted in the frame story of the king and merchant. *Ārādhana* and *phala* (worship and fruits), accordingly, will serve as our main focal points in this chapter.

The three moments are clearly interrelated and closely intertwined.[4] Thus, in chapter five we have seen that the *Devī-Bhāgavata*'s reenvisioning of the divine *prabhāva* provided new insights into the Goddess' cosmic functions and manifestations, with significant consequences for the *ārādhana* of the Devī. In this chapter, our examination of the worship of the Goddess will be from a different perspective, concentrating more on the Purāṇa's understanding of certain historical aspects of her cult, rather than on the actual ritual details. Further, we shall explore the *Devī-Bhāgavata*'s interpretation of the Goddess' role in human history and the mundane affairs of the world. The way in which the three moments are related is a key to the *Devī-Bhāgavata*'s understanding of history.

In a moment we shall compare the *Devī-Bhāgavata*'s and the *Devī-Māhātmya*'s versions of the frame story in detail, but first we should note that the *Devī-Bhāgavata* retells the story twice. Each retelling modifies the *Devī-Māhātmya*'s version in its own ways. The first actually serves as a concluding commentary on the Goddess' last two great deeds rather than as a proper framing device.[5] It is thereby less an introduction to the power of the Devī than an endorsement of the efficacy of her worship. The second recounting,[6] although following more closely the general structure of the *Devī-Māhātmya*, also serves in its own manner primarily as an endorsement of Devī-*ārādhana*. Its major narrative departure from the *Devī-Māhātmya* is its deletion of the merchant Samādhi from the tale. We shall deal with the case of the vanishing merchant in our last section below, on *phala*. Both accounts of the frame story in the *Devī-Bhāgavata* will be utilized throughout the following analysis, as both offer suggestive insights into the Purāṇa's view of history.

Let us now turn to a summary of the *Devī-Māhātmya*'s frame story. In so doing, we shall have to look not only at the frame story proper, but also at its context or framework within the *Mārkaṇḍeya Purāṇa* as a whole in order to gain a better understanding of the role of the

Devī-Māhātmya in its original Purāṇic and historical setting. Then we can proceed to the interpretation of the development of Devī-*ārādhana* given by the *Devī-Bhāgavata* in its own historical context some six centuries later.

Of Manus and Men in the *Mārkaṇḍeya Purāṇa*

The frame story of the *Devī-Māhātmya* is introduced by the sage Mārkaṇḍeya while describing the ruler of the eighth *manvantara* or period of a Manu. In each cosmic cycle of creation there are fourteen Manus or world sovereigns, whose collective reign extends for a day of Brahmā (each Manu thus ruling for 1/14th of a "day," each such day being equal to 4,320,000,000 human years). These Manus represent par excellence kingly power and authority in the human realm, and as such their relation to divine power is a model for all worldly rule. Mārkaṇḍeya briefly indicates that the eighth Manu of the present cycle, the illustrious son of the Sun known as Sāvarṇi, attained his high position through the authority or grace (*anubhāva*) of the Goddess Mahā-Māyā.[7]

Mārkaṇḍeya then recounts the story of Sāvarṇi in a prior life, as the king Suratha. Despite his dutiful attention to protecting his subjects, Suratha loses his kingdom to internal and external enemies. Buffeted by events in the world, he seeks refuge in the forest near the ashram of the sage Medhas. He is soon joined by a merchant, Samādhi, who has lost his wealth and the affections of his kin. The two dispossessed gentlemen hope to find peace in the calm environs of the ashram, as they struggle to understand the reasons for their worldly misfortunes and mental sufferings. The forest offers them little consolation, however, for their apparent renunciation of the world is premature and self-deluding. They both are amazed to find that instead of peace, they encounter merely their own mental agitation as their thoughts cling to the affairs of family and state back home. Failing to understand why they remain anxious over and attached to the very things that had caused them such pain in the first place, they turn for advice to Medhas. The sage explains that their minds, like everyone else's in the whole universe, are deluded by Mahā-Māyā. He then proceeds to recount the mighty deeds of Mahā-Māyā, the supreme Goddess.

After the three deeds are described, the *Devī-Māhātmya* returns to the frame story.[8] The sage Medhas recommends that the two distraught refugees from the world propitiate the Devī to secure her blessings. The king and merchant worship the Goddess for three years to obtain a vision of her. She at last appears before them and grants each the boons they desire. Suratha wishes for a kingdom that does not perish in the future life and for the restoration of his own kingdom, free from enemies, in this life. The Devī assures him that he shall conquer his enemies in a few days and regain his realm, and in a future birth will be the world sovereign or Manu called Sāvarṇi. Samādhi, despondent and disgusted with the world, requests the knowledge that removes attachment, which the Devī grants.

The frame story of the *Devī-Māhātmya* serves to link the great cosmic deeds of the Devī with mundane human affairs. She is involved not only in creating and maintaining the grand order of the universe, destroying those demons who threaten world order, but also in providing comfort and help to people in all walks of life, including such ordinary persons as the merchant. Her bestowal of Manuhood on Suratha further reveals that the exercise of political power and authority in the world is ultimately derived from the Devī herself.

The frame story in addition serves textually to situate the glorification of the Goddess within the larger context of the *Mārkaṇḍeya Purāṇa* as a whole. The *Devī-Māhātmya* is widely recognized as an interpolation in the *Mārkaṇḍeya.*[9] Nowhere else in the *Mārkaṇḍeya* do we meet with the Śākta themes articulated so artfully and forcefully in the *Devī-Māhātmya.* The Śākta redactor spliced his document into the Purāṇa in the midst of an account of the ages or periods of the fourteen Manus, these *manvantaras* being one of the renowned *pañcalakṣaṇas* (five characteristics of a Purāṇa).[10]

In the original account, Mārkaṇḍeya's disciple Krauṣṭuki asks to hear about the various Manu ages, their duration, their gods, seers, and kings.[11] Mārkaṇḍeya tells of the first Manu, Svāyambhuva, and of his descendants who populated the various continents of the world. This leads to a lengthy digression on world geography,[12] after which the sage duly describes the rest of the first seven Manus, the last of whom is the present Manu. None of these Manus has any apparent connection with the Devī. Then Mārkaṇḍeya refers to Sāvarṇi, who is to become the eighth Manu. It is here that the *Devī-Māhātmya* is inserted, with its account of this eighth Manu in his earlier life as King Suratha. This frame story thus embeds the glorification of the Goddess within the well-established Purāṇic confines of the *manvantaras*. The stories of the future ninth through fourteenth Manus are related following the conclusion of the *Devī-Māhātmya,* again without reference to the Goddess.[13]

While from a text-critical viewpoint the insertion of the *Devī-Māhātmya* into the *Mārkaṇḍeya*'s account of the *manvantaras* may be obvious and the seams of the interpolation may appear ill-disguised, the initial impact upon the original audience or readers may well have been heightened by the abrupt intrusion. An audience long acquainted with the general Purāṇic format and account of the ages of the Manus would find little surprising in the stories of the first seven Manus. Suddenly, with the eighth Manu, there is the startling revelation that within the familiar patterns of history there is a hidden power at work. This power, the *prabhāva* of the Devī, accordingly appears in the *Mārkaṇḍeya* as a force previously little recognized.

Certainly Mārkaṇḍeya's disciple Krauṣṭuki seems to have had no inkling about the Devī, judging by his questions mentioned above about the Manu ages. Krauṣṭuki's queries, in their innocence of any knowledge about the Goddess, stand in sharp contrast to those of his counterpart in the *Devī-Bhāgavata*, King Janamejaya. At the start of the eighth Skandha in the *Devī-Bhāgavata*, King Janamejaya declares that, having heard about the doings of the kings of the lunar and solar dynasties (another of the *pañca-lakṣaṇas*, related in the preceding Skandhas), he now wishes to hear from Vyāsa about "that Devī, Jagad-Ambikā, the world mother, and in what form she is worshipped in all the *manvantaras*."[14] Janamejaya also wishes to learn in what holy places (*sthāna*), by what rites, seed-mantras, and meditations, she has been worshipped. A lengthy account of the fourteen Manus then follows, loosely based on the *Mārkaṇḍeya*'s framework. It is time, then, to turn to the *Devī-Bhāgavata*'s own reworking of the *manvantaras* and its understanding of the Devī's role in history.

The History of Devī-*Ārādhana* in the *Manvantaras* According to the *Devī-Bhāgavata*

At the beginning of Skandha eight, in response to Janamejaya's questions concerning the various forms of the Devī worshipped in all the *manvantaras*, Vyāsa narrates what the Lord Nārāyaṇa once told Nārada on these points.[15] Nārāyaṇa, after a brief introduction of the Devī as the supreme creator, maintainer and destroyer of the universe, proceeds to describe the history of her worship, beginning with the story of Svāyambhuva, the first of the Manus and son of Brahmā. As the first he holds a special place, for he is regarded not only as a great world sovereign but also as a creator, instrumental in completing the work initiated by his father Brahmā. According to the *Devī-Bhāgavata*, prior to the reestablishment of the earth in the present cycle, Brahmā urged his son to perform Devī-worship in order to ensure the success of his creative enterprise. Svāyambhuva hymned the Devī in typical *Devī-Bhāgavata* fashion, receiving from her the boon that through her favor (*anugraha*) the work of creation would move forward without hindrance and his creatures would flourish.

After the Devī disappears, the story takes a puzzling turn. The first Manu requests of his father a solitary place where he can establish himself to create beings and to perform sacrifices to the Lord of gods. Brahmā in response begins to worry about the lack of progress of creation, noting especially that the earth, flooded over with water, has sunk to Rasātala (the nether world). He concludes: "The Lord, the Primal Puruṣa, my friend and helper, will accomplish what is necessary; I am dependent on his advice."[16] The *Devī-Bhāgavata* next relates that as Brahmā reflects on the problems of creation, a young boar the size of a thumb suddenly issues from his nostrils. This boar, who is none other than the famous Varāha-*avatāra* of Viṣṇu, rescues the earth from the bottom of the sea, thus providing Svāyambhuva with a solid base for his work.

This whole episode of the boar is rather curious given the Devī's boon to Svāyambhuva immediately preceding. Why is Brahmā still worried, and why does he mentally seek refuge with the Primal Puruṣa (Viṣṇu) rather than with the Devī, having just told his son to worship her to ensure the success of creation? We shall return to these puzzling matters in a moment.

The *Devī-Bhāgavata* proceeds to give an account of the first Manu's progeny, which leads into a lengthy description of geography.[17] Following a brief exposition of the rules of Devī-worship,[18] we find in the extant text the long interpolation of the "Prakṛti Khaṇḍa" from the *Brahmavaivarta Purāṇa*, constituting the ninth Skandha. In Skandha ten, the *Devī-Bhāgavata* resumes its account of the fourteen Manus.

The beginning of the tenth Skandha echoes the start of Skandha eight. Here in the tenth the sage Nārada repeats to Nārāyaṇa the questions Janamejaya had posed to Vyāsa regarding the various forms that the Devī assumed in each of the *manvantaras*, as well as how and by whom she was worshipped.[19] Nārāyaṇa retells the account of the first Manu, including the latter's worship of the Devī and his receiving her boon assuring that there would be no obstacles to his creative work. She adds that he will also enjoy a kingdom free from "thorns." No reference is made to the boar *avatāra* of Viṣṇu. Instead, when the Devī disappears from Svāyambhuva, she is said to go to the Vindhya mountains. At this point is inserted the story of the lowering of the Vindhya by the sage Agastya, who is portrayed as a faithful devotee of the Devī.[20]

The *Devī-Bhāgavata* continues with its chronicle of the Manus, recounting how each attained his Manuhood through worshipping the Devī.[21] The stories of the second through seventh Manus are rather formulaic and relatively brief.[22] With the eighth Manu, Sāvarṇi, we find introduced the account of his former life as King Suratha.[23] The Devī's great deeds are next told, after which the frame story of Suratha is concluded. In the final chapter of Skandha ten, the account of the remaining six Manus is quickly told, the *Devī-Bhāgavata* emphasizing that each became a Manu through the grace of the Devī.[24]

It should be clear by now that the composer(s) of the *Devī-Bhāgavata* wished to smooth over the rough edges that were left in the *Mārkaṇḍeya Purāṇa*'s account of the *manvantaras* by the insertion of the *Devī-Māhātmya*. The eighth and tenth Skandhas of the *Devī-Bhāgavata* revise the *Mārkaṇḍeya*'s version of the Manu ages by introducing the worship of the Devī right at the start, with the first Manu, while still following, albeit somewhat loosely, the general structure of the earlier Purāṇa, including its digression on geography. The *Devī-Bhāgavata* composer, however, was not primarily concerned with textual emendations, but rather in establishing the ancient primacy of the Devī-cult. Indeed, this concern seems to account for the frequently repeated question in this text as to how and by whom the Devī was worshipped in ages long past, a question never asked in the *Mārkaṇḍeya*.

In this connection it is worth noting an interesting difference regarding the specific manner in which the *Devī-Māhātmya* and *Devī-Bhāgavata* connect the Goddess to their frame stories. The former text, while recounting the history of the Manus, offers to explain, through the words of the wise Mārkaṇḍeya, how Sāvarṇi became the eighth Manu by the grace or power (*anubhāva*) of the Devī. The latter text, however, actually introduces the frame story into an ongoing account of the Devī.[25] The key, connecting question here, as we have emphasized, concerns the history of her worship. There is, then, a subtle shift between these two texts, from a primary concern with the power (*prabhāva, anubhāva*) of the Devī herself to the power of the rituals and rites used to worship her.[26] The shift in part seems to point to a later historical context when her cult was well established but in danger of neglect and possible decline, this development being the subject of our next section. A reasonable antidote to this decline would be to demonstrate the long-term historical success and even inevitability of Devī-worship, despite any temporary setbacks. Certainly the *Devī-Bhāgavata* understands that Devī-*ārādhana* reaches back to the very beginning of the present world cycle, and will continue till its end.

The question about the Devī's forms worshipped or manifested in the *manvantaras*, first raised by Janamejaya at the beginning of Skandha eight, has an intriguing parallel at the start of the *Bhāgavata Purāṇa*'s eighth Skandha. There King Parīkṣit asks the sage Śuka: "The lineage (*vaṃśa*) of Svāyambhuva has been heard in detail . . . ; tell us about the other Manus, in whose ages occur the birth and deeds of Hari; tell what he has done, is doing, and will do, in each [*manvantara*]."[27] It seems not improbable that the similarity between the opening verses of the *Devī-Bhāgavata*'s and the *Bhāgavata*'s eighth Skandhas is more than fortuitous.

Such a conclusion is strongly confirmed when we look at the *Bhāgavata*'s account of Svāyambhuva Manu, referred to by Parīkṣit and given in Skandha three. The *manvantaras* as a whole are introduced with the assertion that in each Manu age the Lord protects the universe by means of the Manus and others, who are his own inherent forms (*sva-mūrti*).[28] The story of the first Manu commences with Brahmā's urging his son Svāyambhuva to beget progeny through his wife, to rule the earth righteously, and to worship the [supreme] Puruṣa with sacrifices. The first Manu dutifully agrees but notes that the earth is submerged in water. Brahmā, seeing this to be the case, thinks long and hard as to how to raise up the earth and finally requests in his mind the help of the Lord. At once from his nostrils issues forth a small boar, the size of a thumb. The boar then rescues the earth from the depths of the ocean.

The resolution to the puzzle of the *Devī-Bhāgavata*'s inclusion of Viṣṇu's boar *avatāra* in its version of the *manvantaras* is now apparent, at least on one level. The *Devī-Bhāgavata*, while conforming to the *Mārkaṇḍeya* in its general structure, has followed in specific content the *Bhāgavata* for its account of the first Manu, with its story of the boar.[29] Likewise, the *Devī-Bhāgavata* has followed the *Bhāgavata* for its geographic section.[30] But why did the *Devī-Bhāgavata* composer(s) see fit to borrow from the *Bhāgavata* in the first place, especially since the borrowed passages frequently portray Viṣṇu in a very positive light? To answer this question, a careful look at the *Devī-Bhāgavata*'s view of history will be helpful.

Frustration and Hope in the Kali Yuga: The *Devī-Bhāgavata*'s Interpretation of History

Our Śākta Paurāṇika, I have argued, was fully aware of the existence of the *Bhāgavata*. He did not reject it out of hand for it was seen as containing much "historical" truth regarding the actual deeds of the gods, and of Viṣṇu in particular. But the Śākta author was convinced that the *Bhāgavata* had misinterpreted history by failing to recognize the larger theological context within which those deeds took place. The *Devī-Bhāgavata* thus quite reasonably appropriated portions of the *Bhāgavata* text, precisely to put them in this larger context, namely of the Devī's all encompassing authority and power. For behind all acts, mundane and cosmic, lies the guiding hand of the Devī.

According to our Śākta composer, the misinterpretation of history on the part of other Paurāṇikas, Śaivite as well as Vaiṣṇava, had serious negative consequences for the Devī-cult. These unfortunate developments are spelled out in the eulogy of the Devī offered by the gods after her defeat of Mahiṣa:

> Alas! The corrupt Kali Age has arrived and men do not worship you. They have been misled by those mischievous deceivers who are clever in misrepresenting past events [or clever in manipulating the Purāṇas]. Men are thus deceived into serving Viṣṇu and Śiva, even though these gods were created by you. Everyone knows that the gods, when tormented by the *asuras*, are submissive to you, yet men still worship those gods. . . . Brahmā, Viṣṇu, Śiva, and other deities all worship your lotus feet. . . . Those who do not worship you are ignorant of the supreme truth, the essence of the Vedas, though it is revealed in hundreds of *śruti* passages. Those who teach the people to turn away from your feet and to worship Viṣṇu, Śiva, the Sun, or Gaṇeśa, with sweet-sounding sayings from the Tantras[31] are nonetheless not subjected to your wrath. Instead, you take compassion on them and make them famous as skillful spell-binders.[32]

This passage reveals a certain sense of frustration with historical developments on the part of the *Devī-Bhāgavata* composer. The worship of the Goddess has not evolved into universal practice, even though her fame as the power behind all cosmic and worldly happenings is well known.

The sense of frustration is muted by a number of factors, however, that are typical of a general Hindu attitude towards history. Most obviously, we are living in the Kali Yuga, the Age of Discord, when the historical process is "naturally" a bit out of joint. Moreover, the untoward developments are in fact countenanced by the Devī herself, who, through her compassion, actually commends and rewards on a mundane level those of her children who have been led astray.

The above passage further indicates that the growing popularity of various "heterodox" works, including certain Purāṇas and Tantras, is simply one aspect of a deeper scriptural crisis: the neglect of the Vedas and ignorance of the teachings revealed in *śruti*. Indeed, the decline in Devī-worship is often accounted for in terms of disrespect for the Vedas. The *Devī-Bhāgavata* emphasizes that the Vedas not only teach that the Devī is the highest reality, but also inculcate her worship, rather than that of the other gods. The close connection between Vedic practice and Devī-worship for the Śākta author is well illustrated in the story of Gautama and the Jealous Brahmans.[33]

The story is introduced by Vyāsa's declaration that "neither Viṣṇu-worship (*upāsana*) nor Viṣṇu-initiation (*dīkṣā*) is said to be obligatory (*nityā*) anywhere in the Veda, and the same is true for Śiva as well; only the worship of Gāyatrī is confirmed as obligatory by all the Vedas."[34] This Gāyatrī, the most celebrated and holy of the sacred mantras of the Veda and to be recited thrice daily according to orthodox practice, is here also personified as a form of the Devī herself. The recitation of the Gāyatrī mantra is thus equated with Devī-worship. The story of Gautama is then told to illustrate the dire consequences of neglecting to worship the Gāyatrī.

According to the tale, some starving Brahmans seek refuge with the noble sage Gautama, who, through the help of the Devī Gāyatrī, is able to feed them for twelve years. But the Brahmans, growing jealous of Gautama's increasing glory and prestige, attempt to dishonor him with a trick. When the sage discovers the deception, he is moved to anger and curses them: they will become averse to performing any Vedic sacrificial acts and will fall away from worshipping the Devī Gāyatrī, mother of the Vedas. In particular, Gautama condemns the resentful Brahmans "to have faith in gods apart from the Devī, to wear on your bodies the marks of the conch and discus, to follow the path of the Kāpālikas and to delight in the scriptures of the Buddhists and other heretics.[35] You will sell your fathers, mothers, brothers, sons, daughters, and even your wives, as well as the Vedas and your own virtue. . . . You will go to your own mothers and daughters, and lust after the wives of others. You and your descendants will burn from my curse . . . and finally you shall all go to hell."[36]

As is typical, the curse is somewhat mitigated in the end. The Brahmans will have to stay in hell until the beginning of the Kali Yuga, at which time they will be born on earth and commit the various atrocities already enumerated. But if they then wish to be released from the curse, they must worship the lotus feet of Gāyatrī Devī. Gautama is at last pacified, reflecting that the course of events is due to ripening karma. Unfortunately for the jealous Brahmans, when the Kali Age does arrive and they are born on earth, they neglect the thrice-daily worship of the Gāyatrī, being bereft of faith in the Vedas. They become Kāpālikas, Kaulas,[37] Buddhists, and Jains, lusting after others' wives, and thus ensuring that they will return to hell. The story concludes with Vyāsa's reiterating that only the worship of Śakti is obligatory, not that of Viṣṇu or Śiva.[38]

This tale of the jealous Brahmans explains that the calamitous decline of the Devī-cult in the Kali Yuga is due to a curse, which in turn is the result of unfavorable karma.[39] The adverse karma, however, not only entails painful consequences for the individual but also produces unfortunate repercussions throughout society as a whole.[40] At the same time, the story suggests that the social evils of the Kali Age are not necessarily inevitable, for worship of the Gāyatrī could alleviate many of its afflictions.

The *Devī-Bhāgavata*'s hope for the restoration of the ideal Brahmanical social order in the present Kali Age and its apprehension over the actual state of affairs seems to be reflected in its rendering of the frame story of Suratha and Samādhi. First we may note the more detailed description of King Suratha's character. In the *Devī-Māhātmya*, the king is simply portrayed as a dutiful protector of his subjects.[41] The *Devī-Bhāgavata* depicts Suratha as a generous and truthful sovereign, energetic, respectful of Brahmans, and devoted to his guru. Further, he is said to take sexual pleasure only with his own wife (*svadāra-gamane rataḥ*).[42] Suratha is thus portrayed as the ideal king subscribing to the Brahmanical ideals of *varṇāśrama-dharma*. In particular, his marital discipline contrasts with the alleged licentiousness of the more liberal Tantric schools. Suratha seems to be offered as a model to counteract those trends in society which the Paurāṇika perceived as leading to corruption and chaos.

Internal corruption, though, was apparently not the only concern of the Paurāṇika. Foreign invaders seem also to have been a cause of anxiety to him. In the *Devī-Māhātmya*, Suratha departs for the forest after losing a battle against enemies who are described as "destroyers" of the Kolās."[43] The *Devī-Bhāgavata* further characterizes these same enemies as Mlecchas residing in the hills.[44] The term Mleccha refers to barbarians or foreigners in general and may merely refer to hill tribes, yet as Hazra says, "The way in which the Mlecchas and the Yavanas [Greeks or foreigners in general] have been mentioned repeatedly in the Devi-bhāgavata [sic], tends to show that the author of this Purāṇa was quite familiar with the spread of the Muhammadans in India."[45] While many of Hazra's citations are to verses in the late ninth Skandha, there are other references in the older core. Among these, the most suggestive refers to the many villages, towns, and cities on the banks of the Ganges wherein dwell various foreigners, Mlecchas, and Hūṇas.[46] Thus Suratha could serve not only as a model of a king beyond personal moral reproach, but also as a courageous conqueror of external enemies.

We can now begin to understand more clearly the reasons behind the *Devī-Bhāgavata*'s deep interest in the history of Devī-worship. The *Devī-Māhātmya*, by contrast, concentrated on the revelation of the Devī's *prabhāva*, assuming that *ārādhana* would be the natural consequence once her power was well known. By the eleventh or twelfth century, however, it was apparent that such an expectation was hardly to be taken for granted. The *Devī-Bhāgavata*, while continuing to glorify the Devī's power, also focusses on the revelation of the efficacy of her worship and the dire personal and social consequences of its neglect. Accordingly, our Śākta Paurāṇika attempts to establish various historical precedents for the legitimacy, propriety, and necessity of Devī-worship, especially in the present Kali Age.[47]

Since King Suratha's reputation as a devout worshipper of the Devī was well established by the time of the *Devī-Bhāgavata*, it is not surprising that many of the kings whose stories are told in the Purāṇa seem to be modeled upon him. The other thirteen Manus of the present world cycle, for instance, appear largely as clones of Suratha. Of special interest among the other rulers who emulate the Suratha ideal are three kings of Ayodhyā, the most famous of whom is Rāmacandra of the Solar Dynasty, the renowned incarnation of Viṣṇu. The three taken together suggest that Ayodhyā played a special role in the *Devī-Bhāgavata*'s view of the development of the Devī-cult. This role is deserving of closer inspection.

The Kings Rāma, Sudarśana, and Śatrughna and the Regeneration of the Devī-Cult in Ayodhyā

The story of Rāma in the *Devī-Bhāgavata* in many ways is molded to fit the pattern of the frame story of the *Devī-Māhātmya*.[48] The *Devī-Bhāgavata* specifically calls attention to the parallel in introducing a brief summary of the development of the Devī's cult in India: "Durgā, the remover of difficulties, was first worshipped by Suratha; then by Śrī Rāmacandra for the destruction of Rāvaṇa; after that, the mother of the universe was worshipped in the three worlds."[49] In Vālmīki's *Rāmāyaṇa*, of course, there is no reference to Rāma's worshipping the Devī, but the Ayodhyān prince's worldly misfortunes, particularly the loss of his kingdom and his wife, already suggested a certain parallel with Suratha.[50] In the *Devī-Bhāgavata* it is hardly surprising that Rāma, like Suratha, finds the solution to his problems in Devī-worship, given the Śākta perspective of our text.

The *Devī-Bhāgavata* adds a number of other features to the traditional Rāma story that echo themes from the *Devī-Māhātmya*. When Rāma, despondent over his exile to the forest and his several losses, is being consoled by his brother Lakṣmaṇa, the sage Nārada suddenly appears from the sky. Like Medhas in the *Devī-Māhātmya*, Nārada is steeped in knowledge about the Devī.[51] He advises Rāma to perform the Navarātra (Nine-night ceremony) in honor of the Goddess in order to slay the demon Rāvaṇa, the abductor of Sītā, and to secure all his other desires. By way of recommending the rite Nārada adds: "The Nine-night ceremony of the Devī . . . has been performed previously by Viṣṇu, Śiva, Brahmā, and Indra, . . . by Indra for the destruction of Vṛtra, by Śiva for the destruction of Tripura, and by Viṣṇu for the destruction of Madhu."[52]

Rāma has apparently never heard of the Devī before and thus he asks the sage, "Who is this Devī? What is her power (*prabhāva*), whence was she born, and what is her form? And how are her rites (*vrata*) to be duly performed?"[53] Except for the query on rites, Suratha in the *Devī-Māhātmya* asks nearly identical questions of Medhas upon the latter's mention of the Devī.[54] Nārada in the *Devī-Bhāgavata* goes on to describe the supreme power of the Devī and gives brief instructions on how to perform the worship. Rāma and his brother carry out the instructions, pleasing the Devī, who appears before them. She informs Rāma of his previous incarnations which he has forgotten, reveals the purpose of his present life, namely to kill Rāvaṇa, and promises him the recovery of his kingdom. He will rule for eleven thousand years, duly practicing Devī-*ārādhana* during that time, we may assume.

A final intriguing parallel between the story of Rāma in the *Devī-Bhāgavata* and the *Devī-Māhātmya*'s frame story is the Purāṇa's inclusion of the account of Suśīla, a merchant who is clearly modelled upon the figure of Samādhi. The Suśīla episode is used by the *Devī-Bhāgavata* to introduce the story of Rāma. Suśīla's history, however, can best be dealt with in relation to the discussion of fruits in our final section below.

Turning now to the second Ayodhyān king, Sudarśana, we find that his life in many ways resembles that of his great predecessor and ancestor, Rāmacandra himself.[55] Each of course is the eldest son and legitimate heir of his father's kingdom. Each, while still a prince, is forced into exile in the forest in an attempt by hostile in-laws to allow a younger son to inherit the throne. Each suffers the loss of his father, though under different circumstances. Rāma seeks the recovery of his wife, while Sudarśana seeks to win the hand of his beloved in the face of strong opposition from several competing kings. Each wins a great battle with the help of the Devī, though the ways in which they first encounter the Goddess are quite different.

Sudarśana's father, the King Dhruvasaṃdhi, had two wives, Manoramā and Līlāvatī. Manoramā, the first wife, gave birth to Sudarśana, and shortly thereafter, Līlāvatī bore the king a second son, Śatrujit. Unfortunately for Sudarśana, while he was still a young child, his father Dhruvasaṃdhi was killed in a hunting accident. Līlāvatī's father Yudhājit slew Manoramā's father in battle, in the process securing the throne for his own grandson. Manoramā, recalling the banishment of Rāma to the forest through the jealousy and ambition of his step-mother Kaikeyī, fled to the forest with her own small son. There, while living in the hermitage of the sage Bhāradvāja, Sudarśana accidentally (or by fate) pronounced the root mantra "Klīṃ," sacred to the Goddess, and continued to repeat it in his mind. As a result, he eventually attained a vision of the Devī, who assisted him in securing the daughter of Subāhu, the king of Kāśī (Banāras), for his wife despite his impoverished circumstances. The Goddess also helped Sudarśana and his father-in-law defeat and slay various hostile and disappointed suitors, including the ambitious Yudhājit and his son Śatrujit, thereby enabling Sudarśana to regain his rightful inheritance.

In gratitude for her kindness, Sudarśana and Subāhu established images of the Goddess in their respective cities.[56] Quickly the Devī-cult spread throughout Sudarśana's kingdom of Kosala, just as her worship flourished in the neighboring country of Kāśī. It was not long, says our Purāṇa, before the Goddess was honored at all the Navarātras, by all classes of people, in all parts of Bhārata (India).[57] As a consequence, the *varṇāśrama-dharma* became four-footed,[58] and no one on earth rejoiced in *adharma* (unrighteousness).

Little is known of Sudarśana outside the *Devī-Bhāgavata*. The *Śiva Purāṇa*, however, notes:

> King Suratha, son of Viratha, having performed the Navarātra rites, regained his lost kingdom. Sudarśana, the wise son of Dhruvasaṃdhi and King of Ayodhyā, secured his stolen kingdom by means of the power [of the Navarātra]. Performing this king of rites, pleasing the great mistress, Samādhi [the merchant] attained freedom from worldly bonds and enjoyed liberation.[59]

The *Śiva Purāṇa* thus explicitly fits Sudarśana into the general mold of those righteous kings who, deprived of their realms, resort to the Devī for help, a mold originally cast in the figure of King Suratha in the *Devī-Māhātmya*.

The third great Ayodhyān king in the *Devī-Bhāgavata* is the noble Śatrughna. The Purāṇa gives very little information about this king beyond identifying him as a member of the glorious Solar Dynasty,[60] concentrating instead on the conditions of his kingdom during his rule. Since this Śatrughna apparently lives in the Kali Yuga, he should probably not be identified with Rāma's brother of that name, who never came to govern Ayodhyā in any case, according to the *Rāmāyaṇa*.[61]

The description of Śatrughna's kingdom in the *Devī-Bhāgavata*[62] serves as a kind of epilogue to the account of Mahiṣa's defeat. The gods in their praise of the Devī after her victory over the buffalo-demon indicate that the evil time of the Kali Yuga has arrived, when men, deceived by clever Paurāṇikas, worship Viṣṇu and Śiva.[63] After the Goddess disappears from their presence, the gods install on Mahiṣa's vacant throne the mighty Śatrughna, King of Ayodhyā, endowed with all good qualities. A reign of righteousness (*dharma-rājya*) then begins in which all the subjects are happy and the course of natural events reflects the proper order in the political realm. Rains fall in due season, crops are plenteous, trees are fruitful and cows fertile. Brahmans, versed in the Vedas, perform regular sacrifices; the *sattv*ic priests carry out their rites with rice rather than with animals, though the *rajas*ic Brahmans, serving kings, eat meat according to sanctioned rules. Kṣatriyas protect their subjects, are responsible and charitable, and though skilled in arms are fond of peace. The Vaiśyas duly ply their trades, while others fulfill their appropriate roles. Plagues vanish as surely as deceit, vanity, jealousy, and lustfulness.

The *Devī-Bhāgavata* makes very clear what underlay these happy times: "There were no evil men who despised the Vedas. . . . When Mahiṣa was slain, all were happy, being intent on the Vedas."[64] In addition to the universal respect for the Vedas, there was universal love of the Devī: "Brahmans, Kṣatriyas, Vaiśyas, and Śūdras, all on the surface of the earth became intensely devoted to the Devī."[65] The account concludes: "[All] creatures were everywhere intent on the *dharma* enjoined by the Veda (*nigama*), with their hearts given to the service of the lotus feet of Caṇḍikā."[66] The *Devī-Bhāgavata* has thus fused the cosmic and "mythic" events of Mahiṣa's defeat by the Goddess with the mundane and "historic" reestablishment of Brahmanical values based on worship of the Devī.

It is noteworthy that the *Devī-Bhāgavata*'s description of the ideal Brahmanical society in the aftermath of the Mahiṣa episode has no parallel in the *Devī-Māhātmya*. This is natural enough given the latter's primary focus on revealing and introducing, in the Sanskritic tradition, the Devī as the supreme power and authority of the universe. There is, then, in the *Devī-Māhātmya* no sense of disappointment with history, but rather of expectation. Nor is there any expressed concern over the possible decline of Brahmanical ideals; indeed, there is even the suggestion, characteristic of a certain *bhakti*c orientation, that respect for Brahmans is subordinate to the highest devotional acts.[67]

While the ideal moral, social, and political conditions normally prevail in the Satya Yuga or Golden Age, they can occur even in the darkest age, if humans can just be called back to the proper path. As Kane points out, the notion "that the yugas are not watertight parts of Time" goes back at least to Manu who suggests that the king "can by his conduct introduce the characteristics of one yuga into another."[68] The *Devī-Bhāgavata* develops this thought by interjecting the appropriate *bhakti*c ideals into the realm of the righteous King Śatrughna. Devotion to the Goddess (and its corollary of respect for the Vedas) combined with a reigning *dharmi*c king is clearly quite sufficient, in the minds of our Śākta Paurāṇika, to reverse the woeful conditions of the Kali Yuga.

The geographical center where this reversal would begin may well have been, in the eyes of the *Devī-Bhāgavata*'s composer, the ancient city of Ayodhyā, given the special prominence and historical contexts of the three Ayodhyān kings just discussed. Also, there is a suggestion in the text that the composer, an emigrant from Bengal in all probability who came to reside in Banāras, was forced to move once again.[69] If this indeed was the case, perhaps his final destination was the neighboring holy city of Ayodhyā. This legendary city in the eleventh and twelfth centuries A.D. was becoming a major religious center. Although it came to have special importance for the Vaiṣṇavas (and the Rāmaites in particular), there were at that time apparently four Śākta shrines dedicated to various goddesses.[70] The city, which long resisted Muslim invaders, finally came under Muslim rule in the early part of the thirteenth century.

During the preceding two centuries, then, when the major portion of the *Devī-Bhāgavata* was composed, Ayodhyā may well have appeared as a center of both religious and political revival.[71] Here, possibly, the author of our Purāṇa awaited the vindication of the Goddess in the political-historical realm, while devoting himself personally to the pursuit of liberation through the grace of the Devī.

The *Devī-Bhāgavata*'s understanding of history in certain ways runs counter to the usual perception of Hindu attitudes towards history. For instance, W. C. Smith characterizes such attitudes as follows:

> A religious, or anyway moral, significance is given to history in the concept of *karma*; yet salvation lies in extrication from this. For the Hindu, history, *saṃsāra*, is to be transcended. Indeed, this world and all its activity are *māyā*. Protests have been lodged against translating this simply as "illusion"; yet the tangible world and its transient development remain but a veil that religious insight pierces to the motionless truth beyond.[72]

Smith is fully aware that his summary ignores "complexities" and exceptions, and the *Devī-Bhāgavata*'s views represent one of those complexities not embraced by such generalizations.

At the same time, Smith's broad characterizations help to highlight exactly why the *Devī-Bhāgavata* is something of an exception. This Purāṇic text, I would argue, finds the historical process significant to the degree that it does because the Goddess is not, or is not only, "the motionless truth beyond." She is Śakti/Prakṛti, the dynamic principle of the universe, whose love for her creation removes the veil of false understanding that would insist salvation can be had only in extrication from this world. The integration of salvation with responsible political leadership is the subject of our final section below.

The Case of the Vanishing Merchant: Integration of the Fruits of *Ārādhana*

In its tenth Skandha the *Devī-Bhāgavata* tells the story of Suratha, but no mention is made there of the merchant Samādhi. What has become of him? He appears with Suratha in the fifth Skandha's frame story, so why is he absent in the second retelling?[73] We need to look more closely at the role of Samādhi in the frame story.

In the *Devī-Māhātmya*, the presence of Samādhi has a clear purpose in showing that the Devī is involved and concerned with the affairs of various sorts of men, not just with kings. Perhaps more significantly, the appearance of Samādhi and Suratha together allows the text to portray the diverse modes of Devī's grace in concrete terms. The sage Medhas assures the two men that the Goddess, when worshipped, grants enjoyment, heaven, and release from rebirth (*bhoga-svargāpavarga*).[74] When they have propitiated the Devī, she appears before them to give them boons. As we have seen, Suratha requests the recovery of his kingdom and enduring sovereignty in another life. Samādhi, who has become disillusioned with the world, asks not for the return of his wealth but for knowledge that will end all attachment (and thus will also end the cycle of rebirth). The Devī grants both requests and vanishes. The *Devī-Māhātmya* refrains from any judgment about the relative merits of the two requests, or the relative wisdom of the two petitioners, emphasizing instead their common devotion to her.

Suratha and Samādhi thus represent a varied range of devotees, and help to reveal the diversity of the gifts of the Devī, from worldly enjoyment to final liberation.[75] We find in the *Devī-Māhātmya*, then, an early statement of what comes to be a common and oft-noted theme of the later Śākta and Tantric works, expressed in the euphonic formula that the Goddess grants both *bhukti* (enjoyment) and *mukti* (liberation).[76] In certain Tantric works it is even claimed that "of Viṣṇu and Śiva mukti only can be had, but of Devī both bhukti and mukti."[77] While this overstates the case,[78] it does point to some general tendencies. Such tendencies may be reflected in the popular sentiment that the *Bhagavad Gītā* yields only *mukti*, while the *Devī-Māhātmya* yields both *mukti* and *bhukti*. And while Vaiṣṇavas attribute worldly prosperity to Viṣṇu as the supreme Lord, they often radically subordinate this prosperity to "higher" spiritual goals. As we have seen in our discussion of grace in the two *Bhāgavatas*,[79] the Vaiṣṇavas affirm that Viṣṇu bestows poverty and misfortune on those he truly favors, his granting of wealth being a lower manifestation of his grace.

Another Vaiṣṇava Purāṇa, the *Brahmavaivarta*, elaborates upon the *Bhāgavata*'s general viewpoint regarding wealth in an intriguing interpretation of the Devī's twofold power to delude and awaken all beings.[80] This interpretation is especially relevant to us as it is offered in the course of the *Brahmavaivarta*'s own recounting of the frame story of Suratha and Samādhi.[81]

The *Brahmavaivarta* introduces Samādhi as a pious and liberal Vaiṣṇava, an understandable description given the Vaiṣṇava-Kṛṣṇaite nature of the text.[82] Suratha, however, is not portrayed in such positive terms; rather, his enemy Nandi, who ousts him from his kingdom, is presented as a righteous, self-controlled Vaiṣṇava.[83] Suratha, after fleeing to the forest, happens upon Samādhi and becomes his friend. Together, they go to the sage Medhas. The king inquires as to how he may recover his lost domains, and then says of his companion: "This Vaiśya, Samādhi, turned out of his own house . . . free from worldly attachments . . . seeks to serve Hari, though such service is hard to attain. How may he, free of desire, obtain that?"[84]

Medhas responds by revealing that the Goddess Viṣṇumāyā obscures the world with *māyā* at the command of Kṛṣṇa. She bestows her grace on righteous people, to whom she grants devotion to Kṛṣṇa. To others, upon whom she does not bestow her grace, she binds with the snares of delusion. The sage elaborates: "Discrimination (*vivecikā*) and bewilderment (*āvaraṇi*) are the twofold powers of Śakti. The first she gives to a devotee, the second to others. The thought, 'Śrī Kṛṣṇa is the real; all else is impermanent,' characterizes the discriminating mind and belongs to the noble Vaiṣṇavas. The thought, 'This wealth of mine is eternal,' marks the bewildered mind and belongs to the ignoble non-Vaiṣṇavas."[85] Medhas concludes by telling the king to go worship the Devī, who will give him a bewildered mind, as he is filled with desire. To the desireless Vaiṣṇava, Samādhi, she will grant discrimination. In this manner, Suratha regains his kingdom and attains Manuhood, while the Vaiśya attains *mukti*.

That the twofold power of the Devī is interpreted in this text in terms of Kṛṣṇa-*bhakti* is hardly surprising. What is of special interest for us is the way these two powers, of discrimination and bewilderment, are correlated with the Devī's granting of liberation and wealth: she bestows knowledge on those whom she would save, wealth on those whom she would delude. Only her gift of knowledge or discrimination is seen as an act of grace; delusion or bewilderment is the result of her disfavor, as it were. Partially echoing the *Bhāgavata*'s theme of grace by deprivation, the Goddess herself declares to Suratha: "Whom I favor, to him I give pure, unwavering and steadfast devotion to Kṛṣṇa. Whom I delude, to him I give wealth, false and deluding like a daydream."[86] The Devī's granting of wealth (or sovereignty) and knowledge function here in opposed rather than in complementary fashion, as in the *Devī-Māhātmya*. The *Brahmavaivarta* does note, however, that the Devī will grant to the king devotion to Hari at the end of the *manvantara*, after his time of enjoyment is over (*bhogānte*).[87]

In the story of Suratha and Samādhi given in the fifth Skandha of the *Devī-Bhāgavata*, the merchant at times expresses views similar to those of the *Brahmavaivarta*, at least with regards to the disparagement of wealth and worldly life. When granted a boon by the Devī, he declares: "I wish to have nothing to do with home, son, or wealth. All this causes bondage and is impermanent like a dream, O Mother. Give me the calm knowledge that destroys bondage and gives *mokṣa*. Deluded fools drown in this worthless *saṃsāra*; the wise do not desire the worldly course and therefore swim across [the ocean of existence]."[88]

As we have seen, the *Devī-Bhāgavata* often has a much more positive view of worldly life, tempered as it may be by such renunciatory passages. Indeed, in the chapter preceding Samādhi's denunciation of mundane attachments above, the sage Sumedhas gives him advice that seems in striking contrast to the actual boon requested by the merchant: "O most excellent Vaiśya, worship the Devī, the grantor of desires. . . . You will then, having returned home, gain the respect of your relatives and attain once again the wordly (*saṃsārika*) pleasures as you desire. And you will [eventually] go to the auspicious world of the Devī."[89] This passage goes far beyond what Medhas tells the merchant in the *Devī-Māhātmya* and emphasizes the "world-affirming and world-transcending" perspective of the *Devī-Bhāgavata*.

While the Vaiśya Samādhi is ambiguously portrayed in the *Devī-Bhāgavata*, another merchant figure modelled upon him appears to reflect more clearly the fundamental attitude of the Purāṇa toward worldly well-being. This other figure is the trader (*vaṇij, vaiśya*) Suśīla, whose story is told as an introduction to Rāma's worship of the Devī.[90] At the beginning of the story, Suśīla is a poor merchant living in the country of Kosala. He has many children, whom he is barely able to feed. Often they have to go hungry, and the merchant is much troubled by his inability to provide for them. This impoverished trader, however, is ever faithful to *dharma*, calm, of good conduct, truthful, free of anger and pride, and thus fitting his name Suśīla (One of Righteous Character).

After enduring his misfortune for some time, he finally inquires of a Brahman how he might get rid of his poverty. He claims to seek not excessive wealth, but simply enough to maintain his family, to feed his starving children and marry off his daughter. Like Sumedhas, the Brahman counsels Suśīla to perform the worship of the Goddess, for there is no other rite in the world as efficacious as the Navarātra. To substantiate this point, the Brahman reveals that by the power (*prabhāva*) of the Navarātra rite, Rāma had recovered his kingdom and his wife. Suśīla performs the Navarātra and repeats the Devī's mantra for nine years, whereby he attains a great vision of her and the fulfillment of his desires. In certain ways, he is an inversion of Samādhi, starting off poor but ending up, if not wealthy, at least middle class. The story makes clear, in any case, that poverty is not a gift of the Goddess, but rather is the consequence of neglecting her worship.

The Suśīla-Rāma episode as a whole shares too many parallels with the Samādhi-Suratha story to be mere coincidence. The former, though, in stressing the appropriateness of wealth for a householder and the worldly benefits of Devī-worship, neglects the world-transcending aspect of her grace, an aspect illuminated by the traditional role of Samādhi.

The synthesis of the world-affirming and world-transcending perspectives is clearly achieved in the frame story of the tenth Skandha, in spite of, or rather because of, Samādhi's absence from this account! His banishment may be due in part to his rather extreme negative views of the world found in Skandha V. However, the merchant has not disappeared entirely, for in one sense he has been subsumed into the character of Suratha: the king here requests of the Devī not only the return of his own kingdom free of enemies, but also "that supreme knowledge which destroys self-delusion (*nija-moha*)."[91] The Devī grants both requests, as well as future Manuhood. Suratha accordingly combines the dispassion and wisdom of the merchant with his own royal disposition and responsibilities.

The *Devī-Bhāgavata*, then, lends refinement to the *Devī-Māhātmya*'s theme that the Goddess is the power behind both enjoyment and liberation. She may grant *bhukti* and *mukti* to different disciples according to their understanding, and she may lead a devotee from the pleasures of worldly life to eventual liberation (as suggested in the *Brahmavaivarta*), but she may also bestow both simultaneously on the same individual.

Suratha in the tenth Skandha appears in the same mold as King Janaka, the famous *jīvan-mukta* (one who is liberated while still living), who in the first Skandha persuades Śuka to give up his plans to enter directly into the stage of renunciation before becoming a householder. Janaka reminds Śuka: "Look, I am a *jīvan-mukta*, though engaged in government. . . . I enjoy diverse pleasures as I carry out my tasks."[92] While Śuka, like the merchant in Skandha V, finds no pleasure in home, wife, and the like,[93] Janaka points out to him that he (Śuka) is actually bound only by his own thought that he is bound, and for that reason seeks escape from home and wife.[94] Śuka eventually marries, while Samādhi is absorbed into Suratha.

Liberation does not negate or cancel out the temporal order, but exists and is reflected within that very order. This integration of worldly prosperity and liberation is made possible through devotion to the Goddess. At the highest level, this devotion, while encompassing such goals, is without attachment to them. Thus, when Subāhu, King of Banāras and ally of Sudarśana, attains a vision of the Goddess and is granted a boon by her, he responds in an outburst of love: "In comparing sovereignty of the worlds of heaven and earth, on the one hand, and the vision (*darśana*) of you, O Devī, on the other, there is nothing equal [to the latter]. In all the three worlds, there is for me nothing like your *darśana*. What boon should I choose, when all my goals are accomplished . . . ? I only ask this, O Mother, that I may have firm and unswerving devotion to you always."[95] In these lines, Subāhu perfectly expresses the Purāṇa's ideal of selfless devotion.

Part III

The Two Gītās: The Harmonization of Traditions and the Transcendence of Gender

Chapter 7

The *Devī Gītā* and The *Bhagavad Gītā*: Self-Revelations of the Supreme Reality

In Parts I and II of this book we have looked at the ways in which the *Devī-Bhāgavata* respectively reinterpreted ancient themes and motifs of the competing Vaiṣṇava tradition and reenvisioned various ideals of its own Śākta heritage. In this chapter, we find the two processes occurring simultaneously in the Purāṇa's construction of the *Devī Gītā*. This *Devī Gītā*, constituting the last ten chapters of the seventh Skandha,[1] serves as a philosophical-theological consummation of the text, just as its "Devī-Māhātmyas" provide the mythological crux.

The *Devī Gītā* is one of many "imitations" of the famous Kṛṣṇaite-Vaiṣṇava *Bhagavad Gītā*. This latter text, along with the Upaniṣads and the *Brahma Sūtras*, formed one of the three bases (*prasthāna-traya*) of the Vedānta school of philosophy. Any thinker or writer with any Vedāntic inclinations found it imperative to find a sanction for his views in each of the three. On a scholastic level, this usually took the form of commentaries. On a more popular level, especially with regards to the *Bhagavad Gītā*, this often took the form of "Gītā-imitations," several of which are already found in the *Mahābhārata*. Such "Gītās" came to be liberally sprinkled throughout the Purāṇas.

The *Devī Gītā* is more closely modelled upon the *Bhagavad Gītā* "in scheme, form, substance, and language"[2] than many of the other "Gītā imitations" found in other Purāṇas.[3] This accords with the general conservative tendency of our Purāṇa with regards to its following the external forms of its canonical models. The *Devī-Bhāgavata*, however, has not relied solely on the *Bhagavad Gītā* for its own *Gītā*. On the one hand, it has incorporated elements from other Vaiṣṇava Gītās, especially from those in the *Bhāgavata Purāṇa* such as the *Kapila Gītā*.[4] On the other, the *Devī Gītā* has not merely substituted the Devī for Kṛṣṇa or Viṣṇu. She appears in her own Śākta setting, far removed from the battlefield of Kurukṣetra where Kṛṣṇa taught and revealed himself to Arjuna. This new setting, as we might expect, is not original with the *Devī-Bhāgavata*. Rather, it is already found in the *Kūrma* and *Mahābhāgavata* Purāṇas.

Before inquiring into the details of the textual relations between the *Devī Gītā* and its various predecessors, it would be well to examine the general nature of what may be called the "Gītā genre." Gītās usually serve, in a broad sense, as glorifications of a particular deity and thus they parallel another important devotional genre, the Māhātmya. There is no sharp line of demarcation distinguishing the two; indeed, as we shall see, a Māhātmya may evolve into a Gītā, and a Gītā may still be called a Māhātmya.[5] Nonetheless, the two exhibit their own typical forms and function in somewhat different if complementary and overlapping ways.

From Māhātmya to Gītā: Mediated Revelation and Direct Insight

The word *māhātmya* at its most basic level means simply "greatness" or "majesty" and is synonymous with *prabhāva* (splendor, majesty, power). It is frequently applied to deities and to other "sacred" entities as well, such as shrines or scriptures. By extension, it came to refer to a particular genre of works that recount the greatness of a given divine being, place, or object, and in this sense is often translated as "glorification."

As applied to a deity, this glorification is usually accomplished through two basic means: recounting the stories or great deeds (*caritras*) of the god or goddess, and offering eulogies (*stotras*) to the divinity in anticipation of, or grateful thanksgiving for, the great deeds being recited. The emphasis on the mythological events readily reveals the power of the deity, power in which the worshipper may share through appropriate devotional responses. The general perspective is from below up, that is, from the point of view of the devotee (including any subordinate gods directly involved in the mythic events as well as humans to whom the great deeds are recited).

A Gītā or "Song" typically takes the form of a dialogue (*saṃvāda*) between a deity (or a sage in some cases)[6] and a devotee. Unlike in Māhātmyas, the recounting of great mythic deeds is minimized or absent, though the devotee offers occasional *stotras*. What mainly distinguishes a Māhātmya from a Gītā, however, is the perspective a Gītā is the direct revelation of supreme truth from the deity to the disciple.[7] Using the *Bhagavad Gītā* as our basic paradigm, we see that such revelation takes two main forms: personal instruction (*upadeśa*) by the deity and the manifestation (*darśana*) of his/her "cosmic form" or forms.

The didactic discourse in a Gītā typically covers the following interrelated topics: 1) the nature of God including his or her higher and lower forms and various supernal manifestations (*vibhūtis*); 2) the nature and genesis of the world, explained in theistic-Sāṃkhyan terms; 3) the nature of the Ātman and the individual soul (*jīva*); 4) the cosmic functions of the supreme: creation, protection (especially manifest in the *avatāra* doctrine), and destruction; 5) the several paths or yogas leading to the supreme such as *karma, bhakti, jñāna*, each often being analyzed into types according to the *guṇas*; and 6) the ideals of *varṇāśrama-dharma*. All of these topics are dealt with in the *Devī Gītā* at least to some degree.

The granting of a vision to a devotee may be the climactic capstone to previously revealed teachings, an introduction to various theological instructions, or both. Such Gītā theophanies are often unrelated to any ongoing mythic deeds of the deity but are rather gracious gifts of the Lord or Goddess to their devotees for instructional purposes. While these manifestations disclose something of the greatness or power of the deity, their main function is often to reveal other aspects of the divine nature, in particular the ontological relationship between the God or Goddess and the cosmos, and the inherent structure or constitution of the Godhead itself. *Darśana* is thus largely an extension and affirmation of what is revealed in the *upadeśa*.

Māhātmyas, both in form and function, are intimately connected to the *bhakti* ideals of worship and ritual adoration of the deity. Thus a Māhātmya encourages and inspires devotion, often urging its own recitation as an act of deep reverence. In the *Devī-Māhātmya*, for instance, the Devī herself recommends that the account of her great deeds, her Māhātmya, is to be recited on various ritual occasions. This recommendation by the Devī, which constitutes her major speech in the *Devī-Māhātmya*, is itself a brief glorification of her own Māhātmya. Beyond this brief recommendation, the Devī has almost no instructional role in the *Devī-Māhātmya*. She refrains from teaching anything about her inherent nature, except as it relates to her demon-slaying prowess.

While Māhātmyas emphasize *bhakti*, Gītās generally stress the need for some sort of balance between *bhakti* and *jñāna* (knowledge). The inclusion of knowledge is natural enough, given the prominence of *upadeśa* in the Gītās. Even the *darśanas*, however, inspire not only emotional-devotional responses (frequently of fear, trembling, awe, and unworthiness), but also keen insight into the nature of reality. The exact relationship between *bhakti* and *jñāna* is often ambivalently represented and varies from Gītā to Gītā.[8]

As indicated earlier, there is no absolute demarcation between Māhātmyas and Gītās, and many themes or motifs are found in both. Thus, the *Bhagavad Gītā* is renowned for its statement of the *avatāra* doctrine, a motif echoed in the *Devī-Māhātmya*, where the Devī, after slaying the last of the mighty demons, recounts how she will be born or incarnate (*avatīrya*) in future ages to slay further demons and maintain world order.[9] It is not too surprising, then, to find at least one modern edition of the *Devī-Māhātmya* calling itself the *Śrī Saptaśatī Gītā*.

Of special relevance for our present purposes is the ambiguity between Māhātmya and Gītā found in the so-called Devī-Māhātmya of the *Kūrma Purāṇa*.[10] This Māhātmya is in the form of a conversation between the Goddess Pārvatī and her mountain father Himavān. Given that the longest single section of the dialogue is Himavān's eulogy of the Goddess through recitation of her thousand and eight names,[11] it is perhaps natural enough that the *Kūrma* concludes the account by saying, "Now the most excellent glorification of the Devī (*devyā māhātmyam uttamam*) has been told."[12] Except for the lengthy recitation of names, however, the main account consists primarily of instruction by the Goddess on familiar Gītā topics[13] and her granting to Himavān a vision, or rather two visions, of her cosmic forms.[14] (Accordingly, I shall refer to this "Devī-Māhātmya" as a "Devī Gītā," and to avoid confusion with the *Devī-Bhāgavata*'s *Devī Gītā*, I shall call it the *Kūrma Devī Gītā*.)

The *Kūrma Devī Gītā* is an early, probably the first, Śākta adaptation-assimilation of the *Bhagavad Gītā* and provided the model for later Śākta Gītās such as that found in the *Mahābhāgavata Purāṇa*.[15] The latter Purāṇa refers to its account of the Pārvatī-Himālaya (=Himavān) dialogue as the *Pārvatī Gītā*.[16] We shall consider these two early Śākta Gītās in detail when examining the *Devī-Bhāgavata*'s own *Devī Gītā*, which is indebted to them. In dealing with the *Devī Gītā*, we shall analyze it in three parts: the setting or context, the theophanies (*darśanas*), and the teachings (*upadeśa*).

The Setting of the *Devī Gītā*: The Birth of Gaurī (Pārvatī)

The *Devī Gītā* is introduced by Janamejaya's query regarding the supreme light (*mahas*), that is, the highest Śakti, who became manifest on top of the Himālaya mountain (as the Goddess Gaurī).[17] Vyāsa responds with the story of the demon Tāraka, who had received from Brahmā the boon that he could not be slain except by a legitimate son of Śiva. Since at the time Śiva had no such son, Tāraka waxed proud and harassed the gods, displacing them from heaven. To make matters worse, Śiva's wife Satī had immolated herself, and thus Śiva's prospects for a legitimate son were not especially good. The gods fled to Viṣṇu for advice and were told by him to take refuge in the supreme mother. They went to the Himālaya mountain and worshipped her for a number of years, until she finally appeared before them. After offering a eulogy, the gods explained their predicament and requested that she assume a body (to bear Śiva's son). She in turn promised that her *śakti* Gaurī would be born in the house of Himālaya (as a gracious favor to the mountain king, who was mentally worshipping her), and that Gaurī would be given to Śiva in order to accomplish the ends of the gods.

Himālaya became choked with emotion on hearing the news. After expressing his amazement and gratitude that she whose belly contains millions of Brahmāṇḍas (universes) was about to become his daughter, he made a request for yet another favor: "Proclaim to me your nature (*rūpam*) as established in the entire Vedānta, and declare that yoga conjoined with *bhakti* and that *jñāna* in accord with *śruti* whereby you and I will become one."[18] Thus the Paurāṇika sets the scene for the Devī's teachings and the beginning of the *Gītā* proper.

As indicated earlier, the *Devī Gītā*'s setting is derived from older Śākta Gītās such as the *Kūrma Devī Gītā*. This latter was composed by Śaivites with a Śākta orientation and is less insistent than the *Devī-Bhāgavata* on the absolute supremacy of the Devī. The Goddess in the *Kūrma Purāṇa* is said to emerge from the left side of Śiva, who is considered Śaktimat (the possessor of Śakti or Power), though Śiva and Śakti are also affirmed as being nondifferent (*abheda*).[19] Thus, despite the praises of the Devī as supreme, there are frequent suggestions of her ultimate subordination to Śiva.

The narrator of the *Kūrma Devī Gītā*, Lord Viṣṇu in the form of the tortoise (Kūrma), introduces the account with brief mention of the Devī's famous incarnations as the daughter of Dakṣa (Satī) and as the offspring of Himavān (Pārvatī). In the latter case he adds that she was given to Rudra for the benefit of the gods and the three worlds, an oblique reference to her role in providing the gods with the slayer of Tāraka. The sages listening to Kūrma then raise the question as to who this Devī really is, variously called Bhagavatī, the possessor of half of Śiva's body, Śivā, Satī, and Haimavatī.[20] The tortoise next explains her general nature as Śakti and Māyā, and as helpmate of Śiva, before proceeding to the detailed account of her birth as Pārvatī.

Kūrma recounts how Himavān and his wife Menā obtained Pārvatī, the supreme Goddess, as their daughter through performing severe penances. After her birth, both her parents partially recognize her auspicious and divine nature—after all, she is four-faced, three-eyed, and eight-armed—and come to her for refuge. Menā exclaims that their beautiful daughter has been born for the welfare of all beings, while Himavān bows down, perplexed and frightened by her splendor (*tejas*) and addresses her with folded hands. He asks who she is, calling her paradoxically both "lady" (*devī*) and "my little girl" (*vatsā*), realizing that she is no ordinary child. Himavān's question provides the opportunity for the Goddess to begin her didactic discourse and to manifest her divine forms.

The *Mahābhāgavata Purāṇa*'s *Pārvatī Gītā* closely follows the *Kūrma*'s account in describing the setting, frequently borrowing the latter's wording, though the narrator is now Mahādeva (Śiva), rather than Kūrma. The sage Nārada asks Mahādeva to disclose how the supreme Goddess took her birth as Pārvatī in the womb of Menā. Mahādeva then explains that the eternal mother of the worlds was sought both as a daughter by Himālaya and his spouse Menā, and as a wife by Maheśa (Śiva), suffering from the loss of Satī. When Himālaya heard of the birth of his daughter and came to see her, Menakā exalted, in words nearly identical with the *Kūrma*'s: "Behold, O King, your daughter of lotus face, born through our asceticism, for the welfare of all beings."[21]

Himālaya's response is a bit different here, however. He realizes at once that his daughter is the mother of the universe, apparently recognizing the full significance of her multiple limbs and three eyes. As in the *Kūrma*, he bows his head to the ground and with folded palms addresses her. Yet while his speech is stammering, he is shaken not by fear but by devotion (*bhakti*). And though he asserts to her, "I know not who you are, my little girl," his very question to her contains the answer: "Who are you, O Mother!?"[22] While the question is somewhat disingenuous, it is, of course, the required opening for the Devī's self-revelations.

The *Mahābhāgavata Purāṇa* in general is a more thoroughly Śākta text than the *Kūrma Devī Gītā*. Thus in the *Mahābhāgavata* Śiva, as well as all other gods, appears consistently subordinate to her. Early in the Purāṇa it is told how Śiva, along with the other members of the Trimūrti, is created by the supreme Prakṛti, even though the Goddess is pleased to become his wife when she, assuming a dreadful form, is unable to disturb his mind.[23] This Śākta perspective of the Purāṇa as a whole is clearly reflected in the *Pārvatī Gītā*. Mahādeva, in introducing the story of Pārvatī's birth, immediately identifies her as Brahma-rūpā ("the essence of Brahman")[24] and as Pūrṇa-brahma-mayī ("constituting the full Brahman").[25] The major ostensible motive for her birth at this point, further, is the gracious assuaging of Śiva's grief for the loss of Satī (rather than as means to obtain the slayer of Tāraka), thereby emphasizing her active role as the supreme bestower of favors to the distressed.[26] And finally, Himālaya's immediate recognition of his daughter as the mother of the world, while somewhat inconsistent with the plot development, highlights her true identity.

The *Devī-Bhāgavata* clearly shares the *Mahābhāgavata*'s thoroughgoing Śākta outlook and goes even further in demonstrating the Devī's absolute supremacy. The *Devī Gītā*, while set in the familiar surroundings of Pārvatī's birth, is not taught by Pārvatī at all. Pārvatī is merely one of the Devī's Śaktis, and the *Gītā* is taught by the Goddess herself in one of her "higher" states, beyond birth, marriage, and mortal motherhood. This narrative tactic makes any possible subordination of Pārvatī to Śiva irrelevant. At the same time it makes increasingly marginal the specifics of the surrounding context. The *Devī Gītā*'s framework of the Tāraka myth thus merely provides the pretext for establishing the traditional Śākta environment. The sole interest of the *Devī-Bhāgavata* in the Tāraka myth is as a means to introduce the *Devī Gīta*. The whole of the Tāraka myth cycle, including the marriage of Gaurī/Pārvatī to Śiva, the birth of Skanda, and his actual slaying of Tāraka, is told in precisely one line.[27]

It is typical of Purāṇic Gītās, in contrast to the *Bhagavad Gītā*, that they bear little substantive or dramatic relation to their surrounding situation. The lack of significant relationship between Purāṇic Gītās and their larger context is particularly evident in the Purāṇic theophanies, including the *darśanas* of the Goddess in the *Devī Gītā*, to which we now turn.

The *Darśanas* of the *Devī Gītā*

In the *Devī Gītā*, following Himālaya's request to the Devī to proclaim her nature (*rūpam*) according to the Vedānta, she proceeds to describe her essential forms. Though we anticipate some of the *upadeśa* of the Devī, it is necessary here to look at certain aspects of her teachings that relate to the manifestation of these forms.

Prior to the creation, the Devī declares, she is the only existent reality, the one supreme Brahman, in the form of the Ātman, pure consciousness (*cit, saṃvit*).[28] Then in a brief summary similar to compendia like the *Pañcadaśī* and *Vedāntasāra*, she outlines the basic Vedāntic cosmogonic processes, including the evolution of the causal, subtle, and gross bodies of the supreme Self when conjoined with *māyā*. The Self when reflected in the cosmic *māyā* is known as Īśvara, and when reflected in *avidyā* (ignorance, or "individual *māyā*") is known as *jīva*. Each of these has its own causal, subtle, and gross forms. The gross form of Īśvara is also known as the Virāṭ or cosmic body. Īśvara is termed *samaṣṭyātmā* (an aggregate entity viewed as a whole), while *jīva* is termed *vyaṣṭirūpa* (a part of a whole viewed individually).

The Devī follows her Vedāntic summary with a series of self-predications: "I am the Īśvara, and the Sūtrātmā, and I am the Virāṭ-āṭmā.[29] I am Brahmā, Viṣṇu, and Rudra, as well as Gaurī, Brāhmī, and Vaiṣṇavī. I am the sun and I am the stars and also the moon. I am the beasts and the birds, and the Cāṇḍāla am I, and the thief. I am the hunter, I am the man of cruel acts, I am the great man of good acts. I am female, male, and neuter."[30] She then concludes her initial instructions by asserting that whatever is seen or heard is pervaded by her, and that nothing, moving or unmoving, could exist without her, as she is the support of all.

At this juncture, Himālaya makes the request that if she has compassion for him, would she please reveal that marvelous form of hers in which all things appear united as a single aggregate (*samaṣṭy-ātma-vapu*),[31] which she had mentioned earlier. His request is met with approval and joy by the gods, and the Goddess, to fulfill the desires of her devotees, reveals her Virāṭ or gross form.

The description of the Devī's cosmic form that follows consists of two basic parts. The first is a relatively static image identifying the different parts and limbs of the Virāṭ body with the corresponding components of the physical universe, including the various planes of existence—the fourteen lower and upper worlds such as Atala, Mahar, and Satyaloka. The second is a more dynamic image as the

Virāṭ comes to terrifying life: blazing with fire, licking [the whole world] with its tongue, its teeth gnashing and eyes spitting fire, wielding various weapons, powerful, feeding on Brahmans and Kṣatriyas. It is, we are told, possessed of a thousand heads, eyes, and feet, with the brightness of millions of suns and lightning flashes. Needless to say, the gods are terrified, and forgetting that the appearance is just one form of her who is the world mother, they fall into a swoon.

The four Vedas surrounding the Virāṭ awaken the gods, who thereby enlightened, are overcome with emotion. With eyes tearful with love (*premān*), with constricted throats and stammering speech, they begin to praise the Devī. They ask for forgiveness, humbling themselves and eulogizing her greatness, and bowing to her front, back, sides, top, and bottom. They admit their terror and request her to withdraw this unearthly vision and to manifest her beautiful appearance. The Devī respects their request, taking back her horrendous form and showing her pleasing manifestation. Her limbs become soft and delicate; her four hands bear the noose and goad (symbolic of her chastising, protecting functions), and the signs of granting boons and dispelling fears; her eyes are filled with compassion and her face smiles gently.

With the gods restored to calm, the Devī addresses them, telling them they are unworthy to see her wondrous cosmic form, and that only through her affection for her devotees has she shown it to them. She concludes: "Neither study of the Vedas, nor the practice of yoga, nor the giving of gifts, nor penance, nor sacrifice allows one to see this form, without my grace."[32] At this point, the Devī returns to her didactic discourse.

The *Devī Gītā*'s vision of the Goddess, with its introduction and conclusion, shares many of the motifs found in Kṛṣṇa's revelation of himself to Arjuna in the *Bhagavad Gītā*. Among these we may note the following: 1) the prior explanation of the deity's higher and lower natures;[33] 2) the deity's self-predications (the "I am" sayings), referred to in the *Bhagavad Gītā* as *vibhuti*s or supernal manifestations;[34] 3) the disciple's humble request to view the deity's majestic form;[35] 4) the actual revelation of the cosmic form in which the whole world is united;[36] 5) the further description of this form as dazzling, many-armed/faced/eyed etc., with flaming eyes, yawning mouth, devouring and licking up all the world;[37] 6) the trembling, stammering response of the vision's recipient;[38] 7) the offering of a eulogy, including the homage to the front, back, and all sides of the deity;[39] 8) the disciple's request for the deity to withdraw the frightening manifestation in favor of a pleasing, four-armed form;[40] and 9) the deity's closing avowal that such a vision is disclosed only through divine grace and not through works of any sort.[41]

There are, of course, a number of differences between these two Gītās. The *Devī Gītā*'s account of the higher and lower forms of the deity is far more systematic, and it is permeated with the technical concepts and vocabulary of a much later Vedāntic theologizing.[42] The description of the cosmic correspondences is considerably more complete and methodical; in particular we may note the correspondences between the different physical realms, consisting of seven upper and seven lower worlds, and the upper and lower parts of the Devī. The *Bhagavad Gītā* merely says that all the universe is united in Kṛṣṇa, that his eyes are the sun and moon, and that the region between heaven and earth is pervaded by him.[43]

Later Vedāntic cosmogonic discussions, after reviewing the three bodies of the supreme (causal, etc.), often turned to the evolution of the gross elements into the fourteen upper and lower planes of existence.[44] Such discussions may well have served as a general model for the *Devī Gītā*, but the specific source for its correlation of the fourteen worlds with the Devī's Virāṭ form lies elsewhere, in the *Bhāgavata Purāṇa*.[45]

The *Bhāgavata* presents a meditation practice (*dhāraṇā*) in which the devotee concentrates on the gross (*sthūla*) form of the Lord, known as the Vairāja Puruṣa (cosmic man).[46] The text describes in detail this cosmic man, commencing with the soles of his feet, identified with the lowest underworld, Pātāla, working up to the thousand heads, correlated with the highest of the fourteen planes, Satyaloka. There follows a series of more particular correspondences, such as the ears with the directions, the eyelids with day and night, the arms with Indra, and the penis with Prajāpati. This description, with some rearrangement, is followed in considerable detail, often literally, by the *Devī Gītā*.

That the resulting cosmic form of the world mother is masculine may at first seem a bit peculiar. Yet it points in a novel way to the androgynous nature of the Devī, who herself declares, just prior to her manifesting her cosmic form, that she is feminine, masculine, and neuter. Moreover, a major purpose in this obvious borrowing is apologetic: in utilizing the *Bhāgavata*'s description of Viṣṇu's gross, cosmic form, the *Devī Gītā* has assimilated yet another aspect of Vaiṣṇava doctrine into its own.[47] In effect, the *Devī Gītā* has incorporated many of the venerable Vaiṣṇava ideals associated with the cosmic man into its own image of the Goddess as her gross form—a typical manifestation of the Purāṇa's strategy of universalistic inclusivism.[48]

The *Bhāgavata*'s Virāṭ-meditation above is closely associated with cosmogony. After the description of all the limbs of the Vairāja Puruṣa and their cosmic correspondences, the text goes on to say that Brahmā, through meditation on this form, regained the knowledge to recreate the world at the end of the previous *pralaya*.[49] Less benign is the *Devī Gītā*'s setting for its Virāṭ vision. In turning from the relatively static correlation of the body parts to the dynamic characterization of the Devī's gross body, the *Devī Gītā* shifts back to the model of the *Bhagavad Gītā*, with its apocalyptic image of the world-devouring Kṛṣṇa.

The *Devī Gītā*'s theophany of the divine mother's world-shattering Virāṭ form serves a rather different function from Kṛṣṇa's in the epic. This difference is well summarized by James Laine in his study of theophany narratives in the *Mahābhārata*:

> Theophany has been utilized in epic literature as an apt device for presenting the hero's confrontation with fate. Theophany survived the death of epic, for in the *bhakti* literature of the *Purāṇas*, it proved to be an essential device for the glorification of gods. . . . But despite [certain] continuations, one also sees the discontinuities. . . . Whatever eschatological suggestions there are, they are purely pralayic, and there is no hint of the approaching doom of *yugānta*[50]. . . . Most importantly, the witnesses of Purāṇic theophanies are rarely human, and even when they are, they are not heroes; and the theophanies are consequently unrelated to "historically" significant events. In straining for universality, the *Purānas* have avoided the particularity and specificity of epic narrative events in favor of mythic time and space. . . . Thus whereas the epic narratives of theophany preserve older epic themes of moral and martial conflict and the relation of gods to men and women in a specific time of eschatological crisis, Purāṇic accounts of theophany—which began to appear in the epic itself—are the literary counterparts of iconographic images; they are images in words, static images intended to evoke wonder and reverence. Unlike a sacred *mūrti*, however, the narrative of theophany could develop a far more inclusive range of theological attributions, and thus serve as a more sophisticated apologetic instrument.[51]

Laine's characterization of Purāṇic theophanies helps to explain many of the features of the *Devī Gītā*'s own *darśan*ic revelations of the Goddess. The witnesses of the divine visions are the gods and the mountain king, Himālaya, none of them exactly heroes. Himālaya is a model devotee, humble, self-effacing, adept at undisturbed meditation (after all, he is an unmoving mountain), and a truth-seeker. Unlike Arjuna, he plays no other role, and after his initial outburst of gratitude to the Devī for becoming his daughter, even his role as devotee is minimal, extending only to the occasional prompting of the Devī with one line questions or requests.

In the world-devouring imagery of the *Bhagavad Gītā*, not only does Kṛṣṇa show his power to destroy the whole of creation, he also swallows, in a kind of prophetic vision of the *Mahābhārata* war itself, the various heroes assembled on the battlefield, thus revealing to Arjuna that he, Kṛṣṇa, is their real slayer, not Arjuna, who should thus engage in the upcoming slaughter without personal concern. No such specific, practical *dharmic* lesson appears in the *Devī Gītā*. Here there is no "historical" context to the Devī's swallowing Brahmans and Kṣatriyas, and even the "mythical" setting (Tāraka's rise and fall) is peripheral. The *pralayic* imagery of the *Devī Gītā*'s vision serves mainly as a means of portraying one pole of the Devī's character, the horrific.

The motif of two, polar theophanies, that is, the Goddess' revelation of two supernal forms, horrific and benign, is rooted in the *Bhagavad Gītā* but is also reflected in and developed by the *Kūrma Devī Gītā*. There Himavān, having already been somewhat frightened by Pārvatī's original eight-armed, three-eyed, four-faced form, is exceedingly terrified by the Virāṭ form, with multiple hands, feet, and heads. It wears matted locks and a tiger skin, carries a trident and is marked with the crescent moon (symbols of Śiva), but also carries a club, disc, and conch (emblems of Viṣṇu). Despite the gruesome aspects of the image, Himavān manages to stammer out the thousand and eight names of the Devī before finally making his request for her to manifest another form. Pārvatī oblingingly reveals a graceful, two-armed form, thereby calming the mountain king and inducing him to offer another *stotra*.

The *Mahābhāgavata Purāṇa* elaborates upon the *Kūrma Devī Gītā*'s basic theophany narrative. The *Mahābhāgavata*'s original Pārvatī is as in the *Kūrma Purāṇa*, eight-armed and three-eyed. But then it adds another supernal vision by splitting the Virāṭ form into two, the Śiva-like and Viṣṇu-like aspects being separated. The horrible cosmic form that she first reveals is five-headed and three-eyed, with matted locks, bearing a trident, adorned with snakes and a tiger skin.[52] Himālaya immediately asks to see another form and receives a second vision of the Devī, who now holds the conch, disc, club, and lotus (but remains three-eyed).[53] Though this figure is less fearsome (naturally, being for the most part the relatively beneficent Viṣṇu), Himālaya again requests to see another form. The third supernal vision is similar to the second, dark-blue, four-armed, with conch, disc, etc.[54] The polar tension between the horrific and benign of the *Kūrma Purāṇa* has thus been blunted in favor of assimilating the two major figures of the Trimūrti into a triple vision of the Goddess intimating that she is the embodiment of the triumvirate, an intent further suggested by the concluding characterization of the Goddess as "the essence of Brahmā, Viṣṇu, and Śiva."[55]

The *Devī Gītā* has preferred the basic twofold vision of the *Kūrma Devī Gītā*, in part it seems because the emphasis on the horrific-benign polarity follows more closely the pattern of the *Bhagavad Gītā*. Regarding the benign form, however, the *Devī Gītā* has introduced its own iconic ideal, replacing the *Kūrma Devī Gītā*'s beautiful two-armed lady with the charming, four-armed Goddess, wielding noose and goad on one side, and exhibiting the gestures of fearlessness and boon-giving in her other two hands.

This particular four-armed form seems to reflect a well-established iconic tradition. In the *Devī-Bhāgavata*, at least, this image is almost always associated with the benevolent form of the Goddess, and not infrequently is contrasted with the horrific thousand-armed form. It is also this benign four-armed form that seems to express the highest "iconic" manifestation of the Devī, for it is in this form that she occupies her throne in her supreme heavenly world of Maṇi-Dvīpa, the Jeweled Island, which we shall visit in the next chapter.

The *Devī Gītā* includes, in addition to the beautiful, four-armed form and the thousand-armed Virāṭ form of the Goddess, a third, "aniconic" manifestation of the Devī that transcends not only the benign-horrific manifestations, but all other dualities as well, including the masculine and feminine.[56] This aniconic form is "light." We may recall that Janamejaya's original request that introduces the *Devī Gītā* as a whole is to hear about the highest light (*mahas*) that appeared on the top of the Himālaya. While the appearance mentioned here refers specifically to the birth of the Devī as Gaurī on the Himālaya mountain, it also suggests the manifestation of the Goddess as Umā Haimavatī in the story of the humbling of the gods from the *Kena Upaniṣad*.[57] The *Devī-Bhāgavata*, we have seen, in taking over the story, identifies this Umā Haimavatī with the supreme Brahman, in the form of light.[58] At the conclusion of the *Devī Gītā*, Vyāsa explicitly refers to Gaurī as the Devī Haimavatī.[59]

The aniconic, light-form of the Devī thus represents her supreme nature as the highest reality of the Upaniṣads. We may also note that the *Taittirīya Upaniṣad* identifies the transcendent reality (the "fourth"), that is Brahman, with the mystic syllable "*mahas*," ("greatness").[60] The *Devī Gītā*'s use of this ancient mystic utterance, in the sense of light, points to the transcendent nature of the Devī as pure consciousness (the "fourth" level of consciousness beyond waking, dream, and deep sleep).

The *Kūrma Devī Gītā* already presents the aniconic form of the Devī. The Goddess in her instructions to Himavān distinguishes between her composite (*sakala*) and incomposite (*niṣkala*) forms. The latter she describes as void of any characteristics, infinite, pure consciousness, supreme.[61] Similarly in the *Pārvatī Gītā* of the *Mahābhāgavata Purāṇa*, the Devī speaks of her gross (*sthūla*) forms and her subtle (*sūkṣma*) form. She introduces her subtle form in the following way: "Among thousands of men, perhaps one strives for perfection, and among thousands of them, perhaps one knows me truly.[62] My incomposite (*niṣkala*), subtle form, beyond speech, pure, beyond qualities (*nirguṇa*), is the supreme light (*jyotis*) . . . having the form of *sat*, *cit*, and *ānanda*."[63] Pārvatī later adds that she, by her own will, divides her [highest] self into two, female and male, or "Śiva, the chief (*pradhāna*!) Puruṣa, and Śakti, the supreme Śivā!"[64]

The *Devī Gītā* takes over these notions of the incomposite, subtle form of the Goddess and works them into the dramatic action of the Devī's extraordinary revelations. When the gods worship the Devī for help against Tāraka, she first manifests herself in the following way: "That light (*mahas*), made known in *śruti*,[65] became visible before them, praised on four sides by the four Vedas, like millions of suns . . . unlimited, without beginning or end, without hands or other limbs, and neither masculine, feminine, nor both."[66] The gods are momentarily blinded by the dazzling brilliance, but as their vision steadies, they see the light assuming the pleasing form of a divine woman. It is the four-armed, benevolent form of the Goddess.

The double manifestation of the Devī at the beginning of the *Devī Gītā*, first as light and then as a beautiful woman, has a close parallel in the story of the humbling of the gods as given in our Purāṇa: the Devī there first appears to the gods as light (*tejas*, in this case), and then, within that light there is revealed the beautiful young woman, Umā Haimavatī, who is praised on four sides by the four Vedas, and is four-armed, with noose, goad, boon-giving, and fearlessness as the emblems.

We may note another parallel to this double manifestation in the famous "birth" of the Goddess in the Mahiṣa myth. In that myth, she arises first as a mass of light (*tejas*) from the collected energies of the gods. Out of that light is born a beautiful female figure, called Mahā-Lakṣmī in the *Devī-Bhāgavata*. While this general motif has sometimes been interpreted as suggesting some sort of subordination of the Goddess to the gods, I have argued that such an interpretation clearly does not fit the *Devī-Bhāgavata*'s perspective. The birth story, when interpreted in the light of the double manifestation motif of the *Devī Gītā*, suggests not that the Devī is a composite of the gods' energies, but rather that a single energy/light that had become diffused in the various gods suddenly reemerges in its fully transcendent yet all-pervasive unity, before congealing into a more concrete image.[67]

One final motif connected with *darśana* that is worth mentioning is the concept of the "divine eye" (*cakṣus divyam*). When Arjuna requests Kṛṣṇa to reveal his supernal form in the *Bhagavad Gītā*, the Lord responds by saying that the warrior will not be able to see it with his natural eye and thus bestows upon him the divine eye.[68] As Laine has shown, in the epic "'divine eyesight' is more than a simply visual capacity to see the divine supernal form, but is the quality of insight, a faculty which allows the 'the seer' to gain a divine perspective on the nature of things."[69]

The motif of the divine eye/wisdom is a favorite in many later Gītās. The Gītās in the *Kūrma* and *Mahābhāgavata* Purāṇas both refer to the Devī's gift of the *cakṣus divyam* to Himālaya, using nearly the identical wording of Kṛṣṇa to Arjuna.[70] These two Gītās immediately add that the Devī, having given Himālaya discrimination or wisdom (*vijñānam*), revealed her [Virāṭ] form.

In the *Kapila Gītā* of the *Bhāgavata*, the divine eye appears but in a transformed mode. Near the beginning of the *Kapila Gītā*, Devahūti, the mother of the sage Kapila who is the Lord incarnate, declares to her son: "I am depressed by the craving of my senses which has enveloped me in blinding darkness. You, Lord, penetrate that blinding darkness, for you are the true eye (*sac-cakṣus*), which I have received through your grace at the end of [several] births. . . . You are the eye that, like the rising sun, dispels the blinding darkness of the world."[71] In the ensuing conversation, while the Lord does not actually manifest his cosmic form, he does fully describe the Virāṭ Puruṣa in the course of explaining cosmogony.[72] The notion of the divine eye as identified with the Lord reappears later in the *Kapila Gītā* after a disquisition on the eightfold yoga, when Devahūti again declares that the Lord has appeared like the sun of yoga (*yoga-bhāskara*) for those who are eyeless.[73]

It is somewhat surprising, given the conservative tendencies of the *Devī-Bhāgavata*, that the motif of the divine eye has almost entirely vanished in the *Devī Gītā*. Only near the end of the *Devī Gītā*, the Goddess declares in a manner reminiscent of the *Bhāgavata*: "With the light of the sun of *jñāna*, I will destroy the darkness born of ignorance for those who are ever detached."[74] While the gift of the divine eye as such is missing in the *Devī Gītā*, the *Devī-Bhāgavata* elsewhere proposes a radically new, knowledge-inspiring gift of the Goddess. This gift will be the focus of our next chapter. Here, though, it is time to consider the role of *jñāna* in the *Devī Gītā* and its relation to *bhakti*. For this we must turn to the teachings of the Goddess.

The *Upadeśa* of the *Devī Gītā*

Since the teachings in a Gītā cover a wide variety of topics, we must be selective. Here we shall confine ourselves largely to the question of the means of attaining the supreme goal, a question that cannot, however, be entirely separated from the issues regarding the nature of the supreme reality. Similarly intertwined are the several *darśan*ic forms already discussed, for they become the objects of various forms of meditation. Especially relevant is the relationship between devotion and knowledge on the one hand, and meditation on the iconic and aniconic forms of the deity on the other.

In texts that lay heavy emphasis on *bhakti*, an iconic form may take precedence over the aniconic. Thus, in the *Brahmavaivarta Purāṇa*, we find the following description of Kṛṣṇa:

> Kṛṣṇa . . . is both with form and without form.
> Yogis always meditate upon him as formless, as having the
> nature of light (*tejo-rūpa*).
> They say the Lord is the supreme Brahman, the supreme Self.
> Invisible, the end of all forms, without form. . . .
> His devoted followers, however, possessing subtle insight,
> do not think that.
> They say, "How can there be light without someone possessing
> the light?"
> Standing in the middle of the orb of light is the possessor
> of light, the supreme Brahman.[75]

There follows a remarkable description of this supreme Brahman, which consists of a loving portrayal of the blue, two-armed, flute-playing Kṛṣṇa. The *Brahmavaivarta Purāṇa* clearly subordinates the light form of Kṛṣṇa to his most human-like, iconic form.

Another highly devotional text, the *Kapila Gītā*, while not quite so explicit or extreme as the *Brahmavaivarta*, also grants the charming iconic form of the Lord a very high place in meditation practice. In Kapila's exposition of the eight limbs of yoga,[76] the first six are quickly enumerated, while the last two, especially the seventh (*dhyāna*), are dealt with at length. Kapila describes *dhyāna*, which constitutes the supreme means to the final end of *samādhi*, as meditation on the beautiful, four-armed form of the Lord. First one should fix one's mind on the body of God as a whole, and then on each individual limb and part (*sarvāvayava*), from the feet to the knees, thighs, hips, navel, nipples, etc. to the crown of the head. The meditation concludes by fixing one's attention on the laughter of the Lord, in which one sees his teeth like rows of jasmine buds graced with the crimson glow of his full lips. By this means one realizes the Lord in one's own heart and desires to see nothing else.

Through this meditation one's heart melts in devotion, with one's hair standing on end in ecstasy and tears streaming from one's eyes. In this state, the eighth stage of *samādhi*, any sense of duality or separation between the meditating self and the supreme disappears. Now, according to Kapila, echoing his former words as Kṛṣṇa in the *Bhagavad Gītā*, the realized yogi "sees himself (or the Self) in all beings and all beings in himself (or the Self).[77]

Earlier in the *Bhāgavata* the pleasing, four-armed form of God that is the object of the Avayava-yoga ("limb-by-limb meditation" of the deity) above is contrasted with his gross form.[78] Master yogis, it is said, by concentrating their minds on the four-armed form, meditating on each limb, are able to establish this radiant, graceful form in the center of their lotus hearts. But until one is able to fix one's mind on that image through *bhakti*, one should meditate on the [gross] Puruṣa form previously described.

In the *Devī Gītā* the Goddess' benign form becomes the object of meditation in a discussion of the eight-limbed yoga, yet the treatment of this meditation is a bit different from that in the *Bhāgavata*. Following a standard account of the eight limbs, to which is appended a description of Kuṇḍalinī Yoga, the Devī declares:

> The excellent Vāyu-dhāraṇa (holding steady the vital breath) has been related. Now hear [the yoga] called Dhāraṇa (holding steady the consciousness). One should establish one's consciousness on the Devī unlimited by time or space. Quickly he will become united with that [supreme form of the Devī], due to the union of *jīva* and Brahman. If, however, one's consciousness is impure and one does not quickly succeed, then the yogi should practice the Avayava-yoga: he should fix his mind on my sweet body, with its hands, feet, etc."[79]

The Devī's aspect that is unlimited by time or space refers to her light manifestation as pure consciousness. Meditation on this form is what leads directly to the final union. The Avayava-yoga is only a fallback method, and is only summarily described. This yoga clearly holds a less exalted place in the *Devī Gītā* than in the *Kapila Gītā*.

In like fashion, near the end of the *Devī Gītā*, the Goddess discusses various types of worship (*pūjā*).[80] There is internal and external, the latter being divided into Vedic and Tantric, and the Vedic being further subdivided into two types according to the form of the Devī worshipped. The first of the outer, Vedic forms is the countless-armed, Virāṭ manifestation of the Devī;[81] the second is the lovely, four-armed form, with noose and goad, etc.[82] A person should resort to these external forms of worship so long as he is not qualified for the internal. But if he is qualified for the latter, he should abandon the former. The inner worship consists of dissolution into consciousness (*saṃvil-laya*), which the Devī declares is her ultimate form devoid of any limitations.[83]

The supreme place given the Devī's aniconic form as light/consciousness points to the *Devī Gītā*'s overall stress on knowledge. This emphasis is clear in the Goddess' summary discussion of the three main paths to *mokṣa*, *karma-yoga*, *bhakti-yoga*, and *jñāna-yoga*.[84] *Bhakti-yoga* is the easiest, involving the least mental or bodily pain. It is of three kinds, she declares, according to the *guṇas* and the corresponding types of persons:

> The *bhakti* of one who, with a view to hurting others, practices deception and is filled with jealousy and anger, is of the *tamasic* sort. The *bhakti* of one who, without seeking to injure others, pursues his own well-being pleasure and fame, . . . thinking himself different from me, is *rajasic*. That *bhakti* performed with the fruits of action surrendered to the supreme, to cleanse oneself of sin and to fulfill the duties enjoined by the Vedas, . . . but still with the thought of difference [between himself and me] is *sattvic*.[8

This last kind of devotion, while still clinging to the idea of difference, does lead to the supreme *bhakti*.

This supreme *bhakti* consists of listening to the virtues and reciting the names of the Devī. It is characterized by the complete absence of any motivation, self-interest, or even the desire for such states of liberation as *sāmīpya* (being in the presence of the supreme), *sārṣṭi* (sharing divine powers), *sāyujya* (mergence with the supreme), and *sālokya* (dwelling in the same world with the supreme). A person of the highest devotion knows nothing better than serving her and thus has no desire for *mokṣā*. He knows the Devī as nondifferent from himself, sees all souls (*jīva*s) as manifestations of her forms, and takes the same delight in her as he does in himself. Everywhere he sees the same manifestation of her consciousness, and thus treats all beings with respect. He is filled with love (*premān*) for the Devī, his hair standing on end, his eyes brimming with tears of affection, his voice choked with emotion. He in whom the supreme *bhakti* arises will dissolve into her nature consisting of consciousness.[86]

Up to this point in its discussion of the types of *bhakti* and its description of supreme devotion with its ecstatic emotion, the *Devī Gītā* has followed very closely the *Kapila Gītā*—substituting the Devī for Viṣṇu, of course.[87] But then the *Devī Gītā* departs somewhat from its model, as the Goddess declares:

> The supreme limit (*kāṣṭhā*) of *bhakti* and of dispassion (*vairāgya*) is *jñāna*. The climax (*sīmā*) of both is in knowledge. Even when a person performs *bhakti*, if through the strength of *prarabdha* ("leftover") *karma*, knowledge of the Goddess does not arise, such a person will go to the Devī's Jeweled Island. Having gone there he attains all enjoyments, though not desired. In the end, he attains complete knowledge in the form of my consciousness. By that knowledge he is liberated forever; without knowledge there is no liberation.[88]

In light of these remarks of the Devī, we must assume, apparently, that even the supreme *bhakti*, while leading eventually to dissolution in the Devī's consciousness, does so indirectly, and only by instilling supreme *jñāna*. The *Kapila Gītā* holds *jñāna* in high esteem as well, but does not subordinate *bhakti* to it. Rather, the *Kapila Gītā* views the paths of devotion and knowledge as equally leading to the same final goal.[89]

The most striking difference between the *Kapila Gītā* and the *Devī Gītā* regarding *jñāna*, however, concerns the worldly consequences of such knowledge. In the *Kapila Gītā*, knowledge of the Lord who exists in all beings manifests itself in charitable and friendly behavior towards other creatures.[90] At the same time, a wise man leaves behind the world and the life of the householder with all its attachments, preferring the company of like-minded holy renunciates. Knowledge, while instilling a general compassion for all beings, destroys any delight in wife, children, wealth, and the like.[91]

The *Devī Gītā* reiterates the ideal of respect and charity towards all beings, as the Devī, in the form of consciousness, resides everywhere.[92] But as we would expect, the *Devī Gītā* indicates that such realization does not lead to renunciation. The Devī says of the man of knowledge: "Know that I am he and he is I. My *darśana* is there where my *jñānī* resides. I do not dwell in any sacred *tīrtha*, nor in Kailāsa, nor in Vaikuṇṭha, nor in any other place. I dwell in the midst of the lotus heart of my *jñānī*."[93] It is no wonder, then, that this man, whose mind is dissolved in the consciousness of the Devī, purifies his family, blesses his mother, and renders the earth happy and auspicious.[94] Such a man has no need to leave the world behind.

Despite certain disparities that we have noted between the teachings of the *Devī Gītā* and the *Kapila Gītā*, we should not overlook the frequent similarities as well. Except for their respective outlooks on the nature of worldly life and the joys of the householder, the differences between the two texts are often a matter of subtle nuance and emphasis, rather than outright contradiction. Especially is the *Devī Gītā* indebted to the *Kapila Gītā* for its views on the nature of *bhakti*.

There is a similar relationship between the *Devī Gītā* and the *Bhagavad Gītā*. Indeed, regarding the notions of ultimate reality, the views of these two Gītās are on many occasions nearly indistinguishable. Even concerning the gender of the supreme reality, the two are not totally at odds. Kṛṣṇa himself declares in the *Bhagavad Gītā*: "I am the father of this world, and the mother."[95] It is as though the *Bhagavad Gītā* simply concentrated on the masculine side, the *Devī Gītā* on the feminine side of a single reality that all admit transcends gender. In any case, the *Devī-Bhāgavata*'s adaptation and assimilation of the Vaiṣṇava Gītās not only put a Śākta interpretation upon various Vaiṣṇava ideals, but these Vaiṣṇava ideals also put their stamp upon Śākta conceptions of devotion, knowledge, and the goal to which they lead.

There is a unity here, even if not fully acknowledged by the traditions themselves. The *Devī-Bhāgavata* text, interestingly, never refers to its Gītā as the *Devī Gītā*, but rather as *Gītā Śāstra* or simply as

Gītā.[96] The Purāṇa's use of the title *Gītā* without the qualifying "Devī" parallels its preference for its own self-designation as the *Bhāgavata* or *Śrīmad Bhāgavata*. In both cases, there seems to be the implicit claim that here is the work that is truly "the *Bhāgavata*" and "the *Gītā*." While this may appear presumptive from one point of view, at the same time it is an implicit acknowledgement that there is, in the final analysis, only one divine reality, whether Bhagavat or Bhagavatī, and only one "Song" that constitutes the supreme self-revelation of that reality.

Within its own Śākta tradition, the *Devī-Bhāgavata*, in proceeding from Māhātmya to Gītā, has given further stature to the Goddess. While many of the basic theological insights of the *Devī-Bhāgavata* are already found in the *Devī-Māhātmya*, the role of the Goddess as supreme spiritual teacher is largely undeveloped there or merely implied. The basic theological instructions in the *Devī-Māhātmya* are provided indirectly in the *stotras* offered by her devotees. The Devī's actions portrayed therein are for the most part heroic, with her teaching role largely confined to her glorification of her own poem. In the *Devī Gītā*, the Goddess emerges as the great expounder of the secret truths of the Vedānta, the ancient Brahmavidyā. It is here, in the *Devī Gītā*, incidentally, that after explaining the knowledge of Brahman (*brahma-vijñāna*), the Devī declares that this was the same knowledge disclosed by the horse-headed sage Dadhyañc.[97] Like this famous seer, the Devī has become the revealer of Vedic truth. The *Devī Gītā* thus emphasizes her wisdom, in addition to her power.

* * *

The Goddess as the giver of *jñāna* in the *Devī Gītā* has revealed her own highest form that transcends gender. But a question remains regarding our Paurāṇika's views on the relevance of gender for spiritual development within the world. That is, for our author, are women as capable of true insight as men, and as fit for religious responsibilities? Frequently, the *Devī-Bhāgavata* asserts that they are not. Thus, the Devī herself in the *Devī Gītā*, after disclosing the Brahmavidyā, warns: "This is to be told to one's eldest son, who must be devoted and of good conduct, and to a disciple [presumably male] of like character, but to no one else."[98] Similarly, near the end of the *Devī Gītā*, the Goddess declares: "Revealing this Gītā Śāstra . . . [to just anyone] is like uncovering the breasts of a mother. It must be well-guarded always. It is to be given only to a devotee, a disciple, an eldest son."[99] Elsewhere it is said that women and Śūdras may listen to the Purāṇa from the mouth of a Brahman, but they should never recite it themselves.[100]

Such warnings reflect a traditional masculine bias and a fear of women, especially of their sexual, reproductive, and erotic powers. While the composer of the *Devī-Bhāgavata* is willing to explore in depth the erotic play of the Devī with the demons, he is generally unwilling to allow himself to approach the Goddess except as a child, and even then, not so much as a suckling infant, but as an older child whose mother keeps her breasts well covered.

The incongruity between the Paurāṇika's exaltation of the Goddess and his sexist views of women is, to say the least, disconcerting to our contemporary way of thinking. David Kinsley, in noting the various ways in which the author denigrates women, attempts to explain the apparent inconsistency in the following way:

> Denying women importance, equality, dignity, spiritual inclinations; imputing to women base natures, weak intellects, petty concerns, and a wanton desire to seduce men and rob them of their vital fluids (a common male fear in India); effectively stereotyping women into a position of being subhuman vis-à-vis men, the need might well arise to view the feminine in much more positive ways elsewhere in one's view of reality. Mythology and theology are areas conveniently removed from the immediacy of the social sphere, areas in which the feminine may be confronted, even admired, elevated, and extolled quite safely. Denied power in the sphere of sociology, the feminine is elevated to great power in the sphere of theology and mythology.[101]

The split between the sociological and the theological/mythological in relation to the evaluation of women and the feminine is pronounced through much of the text. Yet the Purāṇic author does not completely succeed in keeping the two realms distinct. There is occasionally at least a suggestion that the greatness and positive attributes of the divine feminine overflow into the social realm, even if only somewhat tentatively. One such suggestion, in which femaleness and being a woman appears as a decided advantage, is found in a parallel story to the *Devī Gītā*, in the Journey of the Trimūrti to the Jeweled Island. This story is the subject of our next chapter.

Chapter 8

Gītā-Reflections in the Mystic Isles: Nārada's Journey to the White Island and the Trimūrti's Journey to the Jeweled Island

In the preceding chapter we noted that the traditional Gītā motif of the divine eye had all but disappeared in the *Devī Gītā*, being dissolved into a rather general notion of divine wisdom. But there is another "corporeal" gift that the Devī bestows on those who would partake of her *darśana* at close hand: it is the gift of femaleness. This motif, at least as it is developed in the *Devī-Bhāgavata*, is one of the more original creations of the Purāṇa. It is found, not in the *Devī Gītā* itself, but in a parallel theophany narrative, in the journey of the Trimūrti to the Jeweled Island.[1]

This story is modelled in certain ways upon the journey of Nārada to the White Island recounted in the Nārāyaṇīya section of the *Mahābhārata*.[2] The latter account, with its theophany of Viṣṇu combined with his teachings, is itself an imitation or offshoot of the *Bhagavad Gītā*.[3] In both journeys the theophanies and their accompanying *upadeśa*s complement what appears in the respective Gītās. In the case of the *Devī-Bhāgavata*'s journey, we find the insights into the ultimate transsexual nature of the Goddess that were revealed in the *Devī Gītā* extended into the *saṃsāri*c realm and to the sexual identities of her devotees.

In our discussion below, we shall begin with a brief look at the Nārāyaṇīya prototype. The *Devī-Bhāgavata* offers its own version of Nārada's journey, which introduces the theme of sexual transformation. After considering this story, we shall be better prepared to appreciate the significance of the gift of femaleness in the Trimūrti's journey.

Nārada's Journey to the White Island in the *Mahābhārata*

In the Nārāyaṇīya, the story of Nārada's journey is introduced by the account of another journey by three sages, Ekata, Dvita, and Trita, to the White Island in order to see the Lord in his own form.[4] This story is told in part to illustrate that only "he who is favored by the grace of the Lord is able to see him."[5] After performing *tapas* for thousands of years, the three munis hear the disembodied voice of God, who briefly describes for them a mystical land on the northern shores of the Milk Ocean. This land is the White Island, or Śveta-Dvīpa. The inhabitants of this land, according to the voice, are silver-hued men (*mānavas*, *puruṣas*), intent on the Lord, self-controlled, unwinking, and who [are destined to] merge into the eternal being. The voice concludes, "Go to that island, O Munis, for there I have revealed my Self."[6]

When the three sages arrive on the island, they are able to see nothing, for they are blinded by the dazzling splendor (*tejas*) of the [supreme] Puruṣa. The sages perform more penances and then are able to see the silver-hued inhabitants in their meditations on the Lord. A great light equal to one thousand suns in brilliance suddenly appears once again. The local denizens run toward it bowing, while the sages are deprived of most of their senses by its energy. They are only able to hear a sudden loud sound as the inhabitants shout, "Victory to you, O Lotus-eyed. Honor to you, the world creator."[7] The denizens are able to see the form of the Lord himself within the light, while Ekata, Dvita, and Trita are simply stupefied by the illusion of the Lord. The same incorporeal voice advises them that only through single-minded devotion can one see the supreme.[8]

Nārada's visit as recorded in the epic is more fruitful than that of the three sages. When he reaches the White Island, he too sees the silver-hued denizens, and he worships them, as well as the Lord. After praising the Lord in a lengthy hymn, Nārada attains a vision of the cosmic or universal form (*viśva-rūpa*) of God, with one hundred heads and one thousand eyes, feet, stomachs, and arms. The Lord then explains that Nārada, because of his single-minded devotion, has been able to obtain this vision, unlike Ekata and his companions. In the ensuing dialogue, the silvery saints of the island are further described as realized beings (*siddhas*), freed from the *guṇas* of *rajas* and *tamas*, who will without doubt enter into the supreme Puruṣa and become liberated.[9] That supreme reality, the eternal Self, is not to be seen by the eye or other senses but by knowledge alone. It is without qualities, incomposite, beyond all pairs, and is incomprehensible to Nārada, for he is not [yet] fit to know God completely. While all elements dissolve eventually back into Prakṛti, and Prakṛti into Puruṣa, Puruṣa is eternal, the one, beyond which there is nothing.

The Lord then points out all the deities existing within his cosmic body and enumerates various specific incarnations such as the boar and fish that he will assume in future ages, thus going beyond the *Bhagavad Gītā* in actually naming some of his incarnations. The mood of the vision here is also a bit different from that in the *Bhagavad Gītā*. In the latter the warriors and all the worlds enter into Kṛṣṇa's mouth, revealing his powers to end the Yuga as well as to dissolve the universe in the grand *pralaya*. While *pralay*ic imagery is present in the Nārāyaṇīya theophany, the notion of merging into the Lord's self is primarily salvific. Nārada fails to attain this salvific mergence, no doubt due to his lack of complete understanding. After the Lord finishes his teachings, he vanishes from Nārada's sight, while the sage goes off to a hermitage.

Throughout the account of the White Island in the Nārāyaṇīya, the imagery and atmosphere is thoroughly masculine. The ultimate reality is the supreme Male, Puruṣa, who is above and beyond Prakṛti. His masculine nature is reflected in the blessed, silver-hued denizens of the country, the lesser *puruṣas* who constitute the highest models of devotion and wisdom. Given the affinities of their natures, it is natural enough for these lesser *puruṣas* to dissolve into the great Puruṣa even before the time of *pralaya*. In all of this, it seems to be simply assumed that there are no women in God's highest domain.

Although Nārada is certainly more successful than the three sages, he does not quite reach the final goal. This failure is duly noted by the *Devī-Bhāgavata* in the conclusion to its own story of the Trimūrti's journey to the Jeweled Island. Here Nārada asks his father Brahmā to describe the *nirguṇa* Puruṣa and *nirguṇā* Śakti, whom he had seen during his visit to the Jeweled Island. Nārada adds that despite performing severe *tapas* on Śveta-Dvīpa, he himself had succeeded only in seeing the great-souled *siddhas* living there but did not attain the supreme Ātman itself.[10] The *Devī-Bhāgavata*, as we have noted, gives its own version of Nārada's journey, to which we now turn.

Nārada's Journey to the White Island in the *Devī-Bhāgavata*

According to the *Devī-Bhāgavata*'s version, Nārada at one time went to the White Island to obtain *darśana* of Hari.[11] When he arrived, he found Viṣṇu sporting with his wife Lakṣmī, who promptly departed. When Nārada asked about this, protesting that he was an ascetic who had conquered his passions and *māyā* itself, Viṣṇu responded that it was a rule that a wife was not to stay in the presence of any man except her husband. But even more importantly, Viṣṇu pointed out that no one, not even the gods including himself, had conquered *māyā* (or perhaps we should say Māyā, since the personified power of illusion is now implicit in Viṣṇu's words). Astonished, Nārada inquired about the power of Māyā and demanded to see her. The Lord complied by taking him on his divine bird, Garuḍa, leaving Vaikuṇṭha (apparently identified with Śveta-Dvīpa) for this world and the beautiful country around Kānyakubja. Hari led Nārada to a pond, inviting him to bathe therein. Upon immersion, Nārada at once became transformed into a female, with no memory of his former existence.

As a woman, she soon found herself courted by the king of Kānya-kubja, Tāladhvaja, to whom she was soon wed. Nārada, now known as Saubhāgyasundarī, engaged in amorous sports with her husband for twelve years, during which time she became entirely absorbed in erotic pleasures. She forgot entirely all notions of her previous maleness as well as her former knowledge of Brahman and the scriptures. Eventually she bore Tāladhvaja eight sons and took great delight in the joys of family life.

These joys gradually turned to anxiety and then sorrow. First she grew apprehensive when her sons fell ill. As they grew older, quarrels between her sons and daughters-in-law caused her much pain. But all such sorrows paled in comparison to the grief she experienced when the kingdom was attacked and all her sons and grandsons were slain in the war. At the height of her mourning, as she surveyed the broken bodies in the battlefield, an aged Brahman, the Lord in disguise, appeared to her. He explained that all that had occurred was a misapprehension (*bhrama*) caused by delusion.

The Brahman next advised her, out of respect for the dead, to bathe at a sacred pilgrimage site rather than at home. He led the mourning queen and her husband, to the "Puṃ-Tīrtha" (the "Holy Pool of Manhood"). When Saubhāgyasundarī immersed herself in the waters, she suddenly found herself as Nārada again, much to her own surprise and Tāladhvaja's as well.[12]

The recomposed sage recalled his experiences in a woman's body and came to understand something of Māyā's great power. But he remained puzzled by certain aspects of his experience, including the fact that he was unable to remember his manhood when he was a woman. Viṣṇu explained as best he could, but ultimately concluded that the workings of Māyā are mysterious and unfathomable.

The story of Nārada's transformation into a woman is a popular one in Hindu literature and folklore, with many variants emerging over the centuries.[13] The basic point illustrated in them is the overwhelming power of Māyā to alter our sense of what is real and unreal. Frequently, these themes are developed from an ascetic, *mokṣ*ic point of view which regards *saṃsār*ic existence as not only deluded but painful as well, whatever fleeting joys it may offer. Thus, in most of these stories, the Māyā-induced experience reveals the "illusory nature of apparent happiness and the enlightening power of apparent suffering."[14]

In many of the versions with a world-denying, ascetic orientation, there is the suggestion that femininity represents delusion and entanglement in *saṃsāra*. This is especially evident when the initial transformation is accompanied by a total loss of memory of the preceding male state. With retransformation back to the masculine, there comes an awakening in which the state of deluded femininity is vividly recalled, thus inducing at least a partial realization of the nature of reality.

Most Hindu stories of sexual transformations reflect a traditional cultural view that the female state is an inferior one. W. Norman Brown goes so far as to assert: "it is interesting to note the acceptance by the [Hindu] literature without argument that a change from woman to man is always desirable while the reverse is always undesirable."[15] Brown notes one exception from the epic,[16] and there certainly are others, but his statement is generally valid. In any case, the *Devī-Bhāgavata*'s version of Nārada's sex change seems to be no exception to the usual Hindu point of view.

The main departure of the *Devī-Bhāgavata*'s version from older accounts is its Śākta interpretation of *māyā*. In the earlier Vaiṣṇava variants, Viṣṇu is ultimately responsible for the illusory experiences of his petitioners, as he is the wielder of *māyā*, fully in control of the awesome, deluding power. Thus, in a version from the *Varāha Purāṇa*, Viṣṇu constantly refers to "my *māyā*"[17] and says of it: "Even the gods, deluded, do not know Viṣṇumāyā."[18] In the *Devī-Bhāgavata*, Viṣṇu exclaims: "Neither I, nor Śiva, nor Brahmā know the extent of Māyā and her *guṇas*; who else, then, is able to know?"[19]

The *Varāha*'s version also provides an intriguing alternate conclusion to its story. After the sage-hero (Somaśarma, in this case) has returned to his male state, enlightened as to the illusory nature of existence, Viṣṇu says to him: "O Brahman, you are now perfected and sanctified (*siddha*); giving up your life here [in the world], go to my supreme abode, Śveta-Dvīpa, with me."[20] Somaśarma accepts the Lord's invitation. Thus, in the *Varāha*, the sage's quest culminates in his becoming one of the *siddhas* in Viṣṇu's island paradise. In the *Devī-Bhāgavata* Nārada's quest begins in Śveta-Dvīpa, and though in the end he is invited back to Viṣṇu's heaven (Vaikuṇṭha), he opts to go to his father's world of Brahmaloka instead.[21] After all, even Viṣṇu's world is part of the *saṃsāric* cycle, subject to the deluding power of the Goddess. Once again, Nārada has failed in the ultimate quest.

Despite the implicit ascetic/male interpretation regarding the sexual transformations in the *Devī-Bhāgavata*'s account of Nārada's harrowing experiences, we find that such a perspective does not necessarily represent the Devī's own. Just as the White Island is a lower celestial realm than the Jeweled Island, so also the metaphysical insights into Māyā mediated to Nārada by Viṣṇu are not as complete as those offered directly by the Devī to the Trimūrti in her island home.

The Trimūrti's Journey to the Jeweled Island

Following the death of Madhu and Kaiṭabha, according to the *Devī-Bhāgavata*, Viṣṇu and Brahmā were resting on the cosmic ocean when the third member of the triumvirate, Śiva, happened upon them. All at once the charming Devī appeared self-standing and independent (*svasthā*) before them, who by contrast were dependent (*avasthitān*), reposing on the water. She ordered them to shake off their laziness, now that the two demons were slain, and to commence their cosmic work especially of creation and preservation. They protested that they were unable to begin, since there was only water all around and no other primal elements or raw materials with which to proceed. The Devī in response invited them into an aerial car, promising to show them a wonderful sight.

The divine car carried the gods up through various heavenly worlds, including their own celestial realms wherein they saw duplicates of themselves, thus raising doubts in their minds about their own supposed "reality."[22] At last they reached the Ocean of Nectar, in which nestles the Jeweled Island.[23] On the island they beheld from afar an auspicious couch, on which was seated a charming young lady. She was dressed in red clothing appropriate for lovemaking, while holding a goad and noose in two of her hands and indicating fearlessness and boon-giving with the other two. She was surrounded by various female companions and attendants (*devīs* and *sakhīs*). Very different, then, are the denizens of the Jeweled Island from those of the White Island, where only men are found. *Sakhīs*, not *siddhas*, are predominant in Maṇi-Dvīpa.

The gods failed to recognize the handsome woman, and while they were pondering her identity, she appeared from a distance to possess one thousand eyes, hands, and faces.[24] Then Viṣṇu, seeing her sweetly smiling, remembered: "This is the Devī Bhagavatī, the cause of all, the great knowledge and great illusion, the full Prakṛti, eternal. . . . She it was whom I saw on the great ocean, when I was a baby resting on the fig-leaf for a cradle, sucking my toe . . . while she gently rocked me and sung lullabies to me. I tell you, she is our mother."[25]

The Trimūrti wished to come closer, and as they approached her, she transformed them into beautiful young women. Needless to say, they were greatly astonished as they stared at each other. The Goddess, with a loving gaze, looked at the gods in their feminine forms, standing at her feet. They bowed to her and suddenly beheld the most wondrous thing reflected in a toenail of the Devī. Everything in the universe was contained in that nail: all the gods, rivers, mountains, and even Viṣṇu resting on the cosmic waters, Brahmā on his navel-lotus, with Madhu and Kaiṭabha nearby.

Once again the gods were bewildered by the revelation of their magical doubles, forcing them to abandon all pride in their supposed uniqueness. Combined with the shock of their sexual transformation, they could only doubt the substantiality of their own existence, including their sexual identities. With the normal props of self-identity giving way, one truth became ever more clear: the Devī is the mother of the universe. Clinging to this truth, the gods were able to remain as *sakhīs* for a hundred years on the island paradise, enchanted by the various wonders and sports of the Devī and her other attendants.

The divine toenail-reflection of the Goddess is an arresting parallel to the revelations that Kṛṣṇa provides for his mother in the *Bhāgavata*.[26] There, Kṛṣṇa reveals the universe inside his mouth. The *Devī-Bhāgavata*'s nail-revelation seems a purposeful attempt to supersede Kṛṣṇa's mouth-revelation, for the whole universe appears merely in the Devī's lowest and must humble part.[27]

Returning to the story, we find that during the century the Trimūrti spends on the auspicious isle, each offers a lengthy hymn of praise to the Devī. Viṣṇu, among other things, eulogizes her as the supreme Śakti who displays the whole world to Puruṣa, who is powerless without her. Further, she is praised as the eternal ancient Prakṛti, who out of compassion reveals to the ancient Puruṣa his true nature. Otherwise, deluded by *tamas*, he would imagine that he is the Lord and Master, without beginning, the intelligence of the world soul. Viṣṇu also enquires, rhetorically, how many other universes and how many other Brahmās, Viṣṇus, and Śivas exist. He ends his *stotra* with a plea for the Devī to grant him the illumination of *jñāna*.[28]

Śiva in his praise repeats many of the ideas uttered by Viṣṇu but adds a significant confession:

> O Mother, grant us, who have been transformed into youthful women, constant service to your lotus feet. If we regained our manhood, deprived of your lotus feet, where should we find happiness, indeed!? I have no desire to dwell in the worlds as their Lord, having regained manhood but losing your lotus feet. There is not the slightest such desire for me, having attained the form of a young woman in your presence. How can manhood lead to happiness, if it is unable to lead to the sight of your feet? Always let this glory of mine spread in the three worlds, O Mother, that I became acquainted with your lotus feet having received the form of a young woman.[29]

Śiva's confession represents a radical revaluation of the traditional, ascetic interpretation of sexual transformation. For Śiva, whose primary symbol is the *liṅga*, it is a remarkable confession indeed. He views his transformation into a woman not as something negative, but as a gift of the Goddess herself. It is a foretaste of liberation, at least of that variety known as *sārūpya*, in which one assumes the form of the supreme deity, in this case, the form of the Goddess.[30] It is femaleness that allows Śiva and the other gods to approach the Devī and to worship her in the spirit of true devotion.[31] And like the gift of the divine eye, it allows them to gain insight into her manifold nature.

Part of this insight concerns the real gender of the Goddess. The uncertainty of the gods about their own sexual identity is reflected in doubts about the sexual identity of the Devī. These doubts are nicely expressed in Brahmā's eulogy of the Goddess:

> Some knowledgeable men say that the inactive Lord observes your extended play, and that he, the supreme male (*pumān*), is superior to you in this universe. There is no third that can be discovered. Yet I am troubled in my heart by an apparent inconsistency, for there is the Veda-saying, which cannot be discounted: "That which is Brahman is one alone without a second." Remove this doubt, whether you or he [Puruṣa] are [that one] . . . . Tell me fully, are you a man, or a woman? Thus knowing the supreme power, I shall be liberated from the ocean of existence.[32]

Brahmā's initial puzzlement over whether the ultimate reality is male or female—Puruṣa or Prakṛti to use the standard Sāṃkhyan terminology—dissolves into the doubt as to whether the Devī is male or female. For he already realizes, thanks to the prior display of her magical powers, that she is the ultimate.

The Devī gives the following reply:

> Always there is oneness rather than difference between him and me. That one is I and I am he. Difference is due to error. He who knows our subtle inner nature is wise, and he shall be liberated from *saṃsāra* without doubt. "One alone without a second," verily that is the eternal Brahman. That becomes dual at the time of creation. . . . After the creation ends, I am neither a woman, a man, nor a eunuch.[33]

The Devī's transcendence of gender is here explained in a cosmogonic context, her androgynous sexuality manifesting itself only in creation. But as the *Devī Gītā* makes clear, even during the time of creation, her supreme form as consciousness remains without gender. While sexuality permeates the universe and is intimately bound up with the cosmogonic process, it is not absolute. While it is not unreal, it is not fully substantial either, a lesson more readily comprehended by the gods once they experienced the nonsubstantiality of their own sexual identity.

The Goddess concludes her *upadeśa* in Maṇi-Dvīpa by offering to the gods their respective Śaktis/consorts (the Mahā-Devīs), with whose help the Trimūrti will be able to carry out their cosmic chores. After receiving their wives, the three gods go off some distance and are transformed back into males. The gods climb into their aerial car and descend from the Jeweled Island, landing on the great ocean where Madhu and Kaiṭabha had been slain. They soon commence their cosmic duties.

Although the gods, after their departure from Maṇi-Dvīpa, no longer manifest the feminine within their own physical form, they are now accompanied by their female Śaktis. The gods thus return as "fuller and better males."[34] O'Flaherty offers an insightful analysis of this theme. She writes:

> The exchange of male virility for female powers of revivification may also be seen in some of the episodes of sex reversals: the god turns himself into a woman in order to siphon off male powers . . . ultimately to return to his male condition newly invigorated. . . . The epitome of this Śākta development appears in a myth [the myth we have just been discussing] in which the Goddess turns all three male gods . . . into females in order to teach them how to create; she then turns them back into males, after giving them their three *śaktis*. . . . If one is willing to take the chance of losing one's sexual identity, one can not only survive but return, stronger than before.[35]

The gods are not only stronger (symbolized by their new consorts); they are humbled and enlightened, and perhaps even a little regretful, if we can take Śiva's own words at all seriously.

O'Flaherty above referred to "the exchange of male virility for female powers of revivification." In the *Devī-Bhāgavata* such exchanges take place at the level of the gods, but not on the level of the supreme Goddess. This point is nicely made in another tale of a famous sex change, the legend of King Sudyumna.[36] This tale also provides something of a concluding commentary to the Journey of the Trimūrti, as it is suggestive of the social implications of those celestial events.

The *Devī-Bhāgavata*'s version of the story starts out following the traditional pattern, such as found in the *Bhāgavata*'s account.[37] The story goes that the king, as a result of entering Śiva's enchanted forest, was transformed into a woman, who became known as Ilā. Ilā's surprise quickly turned to anxiety and shame, as he, or rather she, pondered how to govern her kingdom in her feminine condition. Eventually, through the intervention of the sage Vaśiṣṭha, the king's fate was modified so that he was able to live one month as a man and one month as a woman. As a man, he openly ruled his people, but as a woman he retired to the interior of the palace. In time, Sudyumna gave over the reigns of government to his son and left for the forest. At this point, the *Bhāgavata* drops the story and moves on to other matters. The *Devī-Bhāgavata*, however, wishes to delve deeper into the mystery of the sex change and to develop further the intriguing possibilities it offers.

According to the *Devī-Bhāgavata*, then, after the ex-king arrived in the forest, he took up the worship of the Devī. The Goddess soon appeared before him when he was in the form of Ilā. She (Ilā) praised the Devī for her compassion to those who are wretched and miserable, but it is not clear that Ilā included herself among the pitiable. In any case, she was consoled in her ambi-sexual condition by the remembrance of the Trimūrti's experience in Maṇi-Dvīpa. As she says at the end of her eulogy:

> Were not the gods, Brahmā and company, who constantly take refuge in your lotus feet, [transformed into] young women? And I know they were transformed back into men by you. How can I describe your power (*śakti;* feminine energy), O you of infinite virility (*vīrya;* masculine energy). I am not sure whether you are male or female, O Devī, or whether you are *saguṇā* or *nirguṇā.* With love I always bow to you; in the end I want [only] unswerving devotion to you, Mother.[38]

Nīlakaṇṭha interprets Ilā's words to mean: "Although I am now a woman, I am not on that account unfit for your grace. Were not Brahmā and the others . . . who were not born as women, made into women when they went to Maṇi-Dvīpa? Like them, I am worthy of your grace."[39]

The shifting sexuality of the gods, like the king's own, evokes wonder at the greatness of the Goddess, who is the source of and controls both female power and male virility. The devotee is led to an awareness of the irrelevance of gender, both of himself/herself and of the Goddess. Yet, paradoxically, the irrelevance of the Devī's gender only serves to heighten the devotional response to the supreme as mother, from whom both maleness and femaleness arise. The story concludes with the Devī's granting to Ilā liberation in the form of *sāyujya* (mergence into her own self).

The above myths of the Trimūrti and of Sudyumna are examples of what O'Flaherty calls serial androgyny.[40] The ensuing benefits in each case are somewhat different. In the case of the gods, their serial androgyny is primarily of cosmogonic significance, providing them with the feminine creative forces to make fruitful their otherwise impotent virility. The serial androgyny of Sudyumna/Ilā turns out to be an auspicious anticipation of his/her mergence into the Goddess' own androgynous nature. In both cases, what once would have been viewed as a major catastrophe comes to be seen as irrelevant, or more profoundly, as one of the great gifts of the divine mother.

* * *

The revaluation of the motif of transformation into a woman occurred in at least two major ways within the *bhakti* movements of medieval India. In the Vaiṣṇava-Kṛṣṇaite tradition, the basis for the revaluation was largely erotic. For instance, in the *Padma Purāṇa*, there is a variant of the Nārada sex-change legend in which the hero, when transformed into a woman, is taken before Kṛṣṇa. This god, well known for his amorous passion, invites Nārada to embrace him. Nārada makes love with Kṛṣṇa for a year, before he returns as a man to earth.[41] In Kṛṣṇa's case, the positive transformation of male devotees into females allows for the most intense, erotic-spiritual encounter, an encounter, as O'Flaherty points out, that is not entangled in fertility and family life, with its ties to the material world.

The Goddess' devotees, by contrast, have no such divine, erotic union, at least in the *Devī-Bhāgavata*. Though there are suggestions of the Devī's amorous nature as part of her divine sport with Puruṣa that is responsible for creation,[42] and though her seductive enticements play a major role in her relation with demons, her worshippers are shielded from her erotic aspects by her maternal countenance. Devotees who come to share the Devī's feminine form in heaven are simply *sakhī*s, attendants. When they are restored to manhood, as in the case of Trimūrti, they do not seek sexual union with the Goddess. Rather, they return to their former lives better able to carry on the procreative processes that lie at the heart of *saṃsāri*c existence. The Goddess as mother validates the cosmogony and the ongoing cycle of life, as well as those who, by birth, curse, or magical transformation, become women who then participate in the maternal power of the Devī.

On the soteriological level *sārūpya*, the sharing of the Devī's own form, may lead to the quicker comprehension of truth, but ultimately it is superseded in *sāyujya*, mergence into the supreme. In *sāyujya*, the sexual identity of the devotee is immaterial. The knowledge that one may gain through *sārūpya* allows one finally to realize the Devī as pure light, identical with the highest Brahman. With such knowledge, we recognize that we already share in her nature as pure consciousness, her highest form that exists within our own hearts and that encompasses and transcends all gender.

Conclusion

The Triumph of the Goddess

Within the world of Purāṇic discourse the *Devī-Bhāgavata* represents the vindication of the Great Goddess tradition that was first crystallized in the *Devī-Māhātmya.* This study has concentrated on the various strategies adopted by the *Devī-Bhāgavata* composer(s) in pursuit of that goal. Only occasionally did we look forward to later ramifications of the vindicatory vision of the Goddess.

Many questions remain regarding the influence that this Purāṇa exerted in later Śāktism and the role it has played in the lives of Hindus to the present day. Such questions are complex and subtle. On the one hand, the influence of the text may be implicit and unacknowledged.[1] On the other hand, the manner and modes in which the text as scripture has been received by later generations of Śāktas are diverse.[2] It has been regularly chanted, though due to its great length not as frequently as the *Devī-Māhātmya.*[3] It has been commented upon, though not as often as has the *Devī-Māhātmya* or the Vaiṣṇava *Bhāgavata.*[4] In comparison with these texts, the *Devī-Bhāgavata*'s one extant commentary by Nīlakaṇṭha—there were possibly two others, now lost[5]—may seem quite modest. But given the somewhat surprising fact that most Purāṇas lack any commentaries, Nīlakaṇṭha's effort attests to a certain degree of esteem for the *Devī-Bhāgavata.*[6]

The prestige of the Purāṇa is based in large part on its myths of the Goddess. Its stories, with their associated hymns and didactic/philosophical revelations, evoked a vision of the Devī that helped to transfigure its own Śākta heritage and to ensure her victory in the hearts of her devotees, if not always in the historical realm of contending religious perspectives.

The myths of the *Devī-Māhātmya* also are important as transformative narratives. Yet for many Śāktas, the *Devī-Māhātmya* is regarded especially as a unique ritual text, whose verses were particularly formed with intrinsic mystical powers to effect the fulfillment of desired aims. Certain devotees, to distinguish the *Devī-Bhāgavata* from the *Devī-Māhātmya*, refer to the former as "*kathā*," or "story."[7] While such a distinction may not be widespread, and is certainly not absolute, the reference to the *Devī-Bhāgavata* as "*kathā*" is suggestive of the special place that its stories have had in transforming the lives and self-understanding of those who are devoted to the Goddess.

These stories seem to have played a significant role in shaping later conceptions of the Goddess in at least two major areas. The first pertains to the common assumption that the Goddess, in her original and inherent nature, is somehow dark, malevolent, sinister, and only when appeased does she *become* benevolent. This assumption is often supported by reference to the *Devī-Māhātmya*'s description of the Goddess' birth from the anger of the gods. While I have challenged this interpretation, noting the more tender moments of devotion in the *Devī-Māhātmya*, especially in the gods' hymns to the Devī, the text often dwells at length on the more dreadful side of the Goddess. Her supreme nature, as portrayed in the *Devī-Māhātmya*, is thus rather ambiguous in this regard, resting in the paradoxical tension between her terrifying and benevolent aspects. The myths of the *Devī-Bhāgavata* stress to a greater degree the supremely compassionate nature of the Goddess.

The *Devī-Bhāgavata* hardly rejects the harsher and more bloodthirsty side of the Goddess, but the Purāṇa places her horrendous proclivities in an overall context that allows her gentler side to become paramount. We see this in one way in the text's treatment of the *tejas* motif. The aggregation of light/energy (*tejas*) associated with her birth from the anger of the gods in the *Devī-Māhātmya* takes on new meaning as a symbol of her supreme nature as enlightening knowledge or Brahmavidyā. No longer is her manifestation out of this mass of light primarily affiliated with her wrathful role as destroyer of demons, but rather with her embodiment of the pure consciousness that is the highest reality of the Upaniṣads. Thus, in the *Devī Gītā*, it is out of that light that the Goddess emerges to teach the gods the deepest truths of the Vedānta.

Paralleling this Vedāntic mellowing of the Goddess is the *Devī-Bhāgavata*'s treatment of the Devī's maternal character. In the *Devī-Māhātmya* the maternal aspect frequently appears in paradoxical tension with the martial, and in the form of mother (or the "mothers") the Devī enacts some of her most bloodthirsty deeds. In the *Devi-*

Bhāgavata, this paradoxical tension at times remains, but at other times it is dissolved by isolating the maternal from the horrific manifestations. As mother the Devī rises above the erotic/heroic paradoxes that bedevil her demon adversaries, and thus she appears to her devotees more exclusively as the benign and compassionate protectress of the world. For the composer of the *Devī-Bhāgavata*, the mother is most herself when she is at play, rather than at war.

From the *Devī-Bhāgavata*'s perspective, devotion or love does not calm or control the Goddess, but rather it is love such as a child feels for its mother that draws us close enough to her to allow us to gain true insight into her intrinsic nature. The nearer one draws to her, the more clearly one can recognize her benign nature behind the screen of her alluring/terrifying forms. Such an outlook became increasingly important in later Śāktism. A modern devotee, Swami Taṭtwananda, in explaining the nature of "spiritual communion" with the Goddess, nicely reflects this viewpoint:

> When devotion becomes intense . . . the son feels through her grace that he is a child in the hand of the Divine Mother, that she is love personified.... The son then realizes that she assumes name and form.... Creation, preservation and dissolution are but the play of the Mother. Her toy is the thunderbolt charged with the power to shake the world. Though terror is the name given by some because of Her manifestation through famine, epidemic, floods etc. love is the essence of her being. The son ungrudgingly desires to serve Her in all her manifestations both mild and terrible.[8]

The Swami, in the course of his discussion, twice quotes from the *Devī-Māhātmya* itself. Yet his views reflect more immediately the attitude of the *Devī-Bhāgavata* composer(s) towards the Goddess.[9] The *Devī-Bhāgavata* clearly presages the triumph of the Goddess as the benign world mother who succors all of creation and who mercifully absorbs all back into her being.

The second major theological development concerns the ultimate nature of the Goddess in relation to her sexuality. For well over two and a half millennia in India, it has been axiomatic that the ultimate reality cannot be limited by gender. In the case of the transpersonal Brahman of the Upaniṣads, the ultimate is apprehended as being beyond sexual qualities and distinctions altogether. In the case of a supreme personal Lord, gender limitation is transcended by the inclusion of both male and female sexuality. Thus, in the *Śvetāśvatara*, there is already the clear perception that Rudra-Śiva, if truly supreme, cannot be restricted by any singular (masculine) sexual identity: "You are woman, you are man. You are boy and maiden too."[10] Similarly in the *Bhagavad Gītā*, as we have noted, Kṛṣṇa declares: "I am the father of this world, and the mother."[11] These words of Kṛṣṇa are reflected in the *Bhāgavata* by his devotees, who address him as "our mother, friend, lord, and father."[12]

In view of such well-established and enduring traditions, it is rather remarkable that the *Devī-Māhātmya* gives no explicit voice to the androgynous character of the Great Goddess. The *Devī-Māhātmya* delights in many paradoxical assertions about the Devī: she is "both *mahāmāyā* [great illusion] and *mahāvidyā* [great knowledge], both beautiful and grotesque, both maternal and martial."[13] Such paradoxes point to her ultimate transcendency, yet one paradox, one union of opposites, is poignantly missing: male and female. She is, of course, the *śakti* of all beings, of whatever gender, and the mother of the gods. But the sexual imagery and associated symbols used by the *Devī-Māhātmya* to describe and glorify the Devī are all feminine. Every woman, the *Devī-Māhātmya* declares, is a portion of the Goddess,[14] and she abides in all beings in the form of mother.[15] She is the supreme Prakṛti. But nowhere is she called father, nowhere Puruṣa.

The *Devī-Bhāgavata* develops the Devī's androgynous nature not only on the level of her demon conquests, where her erotic and martial aspects correspond to the feminine and masculine, but also on the highest cosmic level, where she is both the supreme, witnessing Puruṣa and the active, energizing Prakṛti. In this respect, the *Devī-Bhāgavata* reflects more the attitude of the *Bhāgavata* than of the *Devī-Māhātmya*. Both *Bhāgavata*s agree that the ultimate encompasses both Puruṣa and Prakṛti, and that the supreme is neither masculine nor feminine exclusively. The *Bhāgavata*, however, ultimately disparages Prakṛti and the whole realm of sexuality in its reproductive, *saṃsāri*c mode as embodied in the householding stage of life, which Prakṛti represents. In the *Devī-Bhāgavata*, the Goddess is both male and female, and transcends the two, but without devaluing either the transcendent or *saṃsāri*c dimensions.

The androgynous image of the Goddess in the *Devī-Bhāgavata* is in many ways the result of fusing traditional Śākta notions of the feminine like Prakṛti with many of the qualities and functions of Viṣṇu. Kinsley interprets this situation rather negatively: "With the exception of the [Purāṇic] author's insistence that the Goddess typically manifests herself through, or is identified with, *prakṛti*, *māyā*, and *avidya* [sic], namely, those principal realities that bind people to unenlightened existence, he tends to portray the Goddess as very much like Viṣṇu."[16] Kinsley sees the *prakṛtic* realm as it appears in the Purāṇa as delusory, threatening, polluting, and thus the Paurāṇika wishes ultimately to elevate the Devī above the material sphere: "When, unavoidably, the Goddess . . . is associated with the material world and its biological rhythms, she takes on dangerous, dark, negative qualities. Ultimately, however, the Goddess, like the remembered idealized mother, is *nirguṇa* (without qualities) in the sense of transcending sexual specificity, or at least female specificity."[17]

While agreeing with much of Kinsley's perceptive analysis, especially his observation that the Goddess transcends female specificity, I would argue that in the *Devī-Bhāgavata* Prakṛti is not only dark, negative, dangerous. It is also the realm in which the Devī bestows many of her gifts, and salvation is not necessarily extrication *from* this world, but realization that this world and its enjoyments are due to her beneficence. The *Devī-Bhāgavata*, while subscribing to much of the traditional Hindu ascetic view of women, departs from an extreme asceticism in its attitude towards the world and history. The *Devī-Bhāgavata*, at least relative to the *Bhāgavata*, is thus moving in the direction of a fuller acceptance of the feminine in the cosmic and historical realms. We need only remember the *Devī-Bhāgavata*'s repeated hope for the restoration of order in the Kali Yuga, its emphasis on the salvific potential of the householding stage of life, and its full legitimation of *bhukti* and *mukti*.

We earlier observed that the *Devī-Māhātmya*, though pervaded by feminine motifs, is not so much concerned with demonstrating that the ultimate reality is feminine as with showing that it is truly ultimate.[18] I then suggested that the *Devī-Bhāgavata*, in contrast, while also wishing to show that the ultimate reality is truly ultimate, in addition feels compelled to establish that this reality is most adequately conceived of, or apprehended as, feminine. This statement now needs qualification.

The *Devī-Bhāgavata* clearly insists that of the two genders, the feminine represents the dominant power and authoritative will in the universe. Yet both genders must be included in the ultimate if it is truly ultimate. The masculine and feminine are aspects of the divine, transcendent reality, which goes beyond but still encompasses them. The Devī, in her supreme form as consciousness, thus transcends gender, but her transcendence is not apart from her immanence. Indeed, this affirmation of the oneness of transcendence and immanence constitutes the very essence of the divine mother, as presented in the Purāṇa. And here we see what may be called "the ultimate triumph" of the Goddess in our text. It is not, finally, that she is infinitely superior to the male gods—though she is that, according to the myths in the *Devī-Bhāgavata*—but rather that she transcends her own feminine nature as Prakṛti without denying it.

Appendix

Three Theories on the Text-History of the *Devī-Bhāgavata Purāṇa*

In the present state of knowledge about Purāṇic literature, and given the fluid nature of the texts themselves, it is extremely difficult to establish anything like a definite text-history for most of these works. Often the most that can be established is the relative dates of the texts, or parts of the texts. Yet even here, establishing the dependency of one text on another, supposedly earlier work, is far from easy. Even where one is comparing two parallel passages or chapters from two different Purāṇas, it is not always clear which borrowed from which, or whether each is dependent on yet a third, common source. It is not surprising, then, that scholars have come up with a number of quite divergent theories regarding the text-history of the *Devī-Bhāgavata*, despite its relatively homogeneous character.

Here I wish to summarize two of the more recent theories, by Nirmal C. Sanyal and P. G. Lalye, followed by my own. While I consider the two former views to have serious flaws, they do point to important facets of the text which must be taken into account in any final assessment.

Let us begin with the theory of Nirmal C. Sanyal.[1] This scholar proposes that a Śākta devotee composed the *Devī-Bhāgavata* during "the age of the Mahā-Purāṇas" in response to the Purāṇic activities of the Śaivas and Vaiṣṇavas. Since these latter sects already had their Mahā-Purāṇas glorifying Śiva and Viṣṇu, it was natural for the Śāktas to want to glorify their own deity in similar fashion. Sanyal gives us no specific dates for the age of the Mahā-Purāṇas, but he seems to have in mind something like the fourth through the eighth or ninth centuries A.D. The *Devī-Bhāgavata*, he argues, could not have been written after this age, for then it would have been too late to fulfill the Śākta need for their own Mahā-Purāṇa.

Sanyal places the *Devī-Bhāgavata* earlier than the Vaiṣṇava *Bhāgavata* and rejects the latter as a Mahā-Purāṇa on the basis of its supposedly late date. He argues that the earliest definite reference to the *Bhāgavata* is Alberuni's inclusion of it in a list of Mahā-Purāṇas, in the eleventh century. He adds: "But long before it [Alberuni's list], the *Devī-Bhāgavata* received similar support to its claim from the Matsyapurāṇa."[2] Sanyal's reference to the *Matsya Purāṇa* is to a two-verse "definition" of "the *Bhāgavata*," which he claims applies in its fullness only to the *Devī-Bhāgavata* (this latter, as we have noted elsewhere, often refers to itself as "the *Bhāgavata*").[3] This definition, and other references to the *Devī-Bhāgavata*, he places in the "early mediaeval age," while the references attesting to the Vaiṣṇava *Bhāgavata* as the Mahā-Purāṇa come from the "late mediaeval age" or later. Again, we must guess at the time frames involved, but perhaps the seventh through tenth centuries covers what Sanyal describes as "early mediaeval." More definite is his claim that the Vaiṣṇava *Bhāgavata* was composed after the *Matsya Purāṇa* definition, or a few years earlier but without sufficient time to become recognized as a major Purāṇa by the time of the *Matsya* verses. He seems to regard the *Bhāgavata* as existing by the year 1000.

Sanyal is fully aware of the anomalous nature of Books VIII (at least the geographical section) and IX of the *Devī-Bhāgavata*. He accounts for this by suggesting that the original text lost its genuine Books VIII and IX in the twelfth century, when zealous Vaiṣṇava kings of Bengal and Orissa may have ordered the manuscripts of the *Devī-Bhāgavata* destroyed, possibly by throwing them in the Ganges. Few manuscripts of the text survived in the lands of its birth (Bengal), and the few manuscripts that were somehow recovered or survived in other parts of India were partially damaged, i.e., without Books VIII and IX. Sanyal does not insist on all the details of his reconstruction, but urges that "certain violent actions taken by certain Vaishṇava kings of Orissa and Bengal seem to be at the root of the mystery relating to the [textual history of the] *Devī-Bhāgavata*."[4]

The loss of most of Book VIII and all of Book IX caused the *Devī-Bhāgavata* to fall far short of its traditional number of verses, eighteen thousand. Accordingly, says Sanyal, a Śākta devotee of the sixteenth or seventeenth century, noticing the discrepancy, interpolated into the text the geographical section from Book V of the Vaiṣṇava *Bhāgavata* ("restoring" Book VIII of the *Devī-Bhāgavata*) and the second Book of the *Brahmavaivarta Purāṇa* (the "Prakṛti Khaṇḍa"), this becoming the extant Book IX of the *Devī-Bhāgavata*. Once again, the text was at its proper length, even if the insertions did not quite always fit the perspective of the rest of the work. We may schematize Sanyal's theory as follows:

SANYAL'S THEORY
[Dates in brackets are inferences
from the meager views expressed by Sanyal]

The original *Devī-Bhāgavata*
(composed during the age of the
Mahā-Purāṇas [c. A.D. 300-800?])

The *Matsya*'s definition of "the
Bhāgavata" and other references to
the *Devī-Bhāgavata* from the "early
mediaeval age" [c. A.D. 600-900?]

The *Bhāgavata* (composed after
the *Matsya*'s definition, or
slightly before [by A.D. 1000])

Loss of Book IX and geographical
chapters of Book VIII (12th cent.)

The *Brahmavaivarta*
[14th-16th cent.]

Restoration of Books VIII and IX
from the *Bhāgavata* and the
Brahmavaivarta (16th-17th cent.)

The extant *Devī-Bhāgavata*
(A Mahā-Purāṇa)

The extant *Bhāgavata*
(Not a Mahā-Purāṇa)

Sanyal's theory maintains, correctly, that the *Devī-Bhāgavata* was composed in response to other sectarian Mahā-Purāṇas. It also points to the existence of heightened sectarian tensions, especially between the Vaiṣṇavas and Śāktas, in northeast India during the first centuries of the second millennium. However, Sanyal's dating of the *Devī-Bhāgavata* seems much too early. It is far more likely that the *Devī-Bhāgavata* was a product of the troubled times of the eleventh and twelfth centuries, and that the main Mahā-Purāṇa it was responding to was the Vaiṣṇava *Bhāgavata*. Sanyal's dating of the *Devī-Bhāgavata* relies far too heavily on controversial interpretations of supposedly early references (such as the *Matsya*'s definition), and there is little justification to speak of an "age of the Mahā-Purāṇas," at least in any absolute or definitive sense. The *Brahmavaivarta* was completed probably no earlier than the fifteenth century, and there is little controversy regarding its acceptance as a Mahā-Purāṇa.[5] But most importantly, Sanyal's theory overlooks the frequent dependence of the *Devī-Bhāgavata* on the *Bhāgavata*. Sanyal notes, of course, the *Devī-Bhāgavata*'s borrowing of the *Bhāgavata*'s geographical section, but the former's indebtedness to the latter is far more extensive, as we have observed on a number of occasions. Far more persuasive is Sanyal's accounting for the late interpolations from the *Bhāgavata* and *Brahmavaivarta* Purāṇas by a sixteenth- or seventeenth-century devotee of the work.[6]

Let us now turn to Lalye's theory, already discussed in some detail in the Introduction.[7] His basic view is that an original Bhāgavata text, composed by the greatest of all Paurāṇikas, Vyāsa, and expanded by Sūta, became split around the ninth century, following a separation within the Bhāgavata sect into Vaiṣṇava and Śākta subgroups. The Vaiṣṇavas developed their version of the Bhāgavata text focussed on Kṛṣṇa, while the Śāktas elaborated on the glorious deeds of the Devī in their version, inspired by the example of the *Devī-Māhātmya*.[8] The Śākta redaction was completed after the Vaiṣṇava and went through five stages in the course of one or two centuries.

In the first stage, various doctrines such as that of *māyā*, *prakṛti*, and karma, along with certain cosmographical materials and legends such as the slaying of Vṛtra were taken from the original Bhāgavata. Also included were several epic legends. The second stage saw the incorporation of the devotional perspective of the *Bhagavad Gītā*, with its synthesis of *bhakti* and *jñāna* ideals, a perspective already influential in the original Bhāgavata and especially apparent in the *Devī-Bhāgavata*'s own Gītā. Next, the "catholic outlook" of the Gupta Age—a respect for all deities, and the amelioration of the conflict between Śaivas and Vaiṣṇavas in particular—found its way into the text. Fourth, the "Prakṛti Khaṇḍa" of the *Brahmavaivarta Purāṇa* was taken over in Book IX, along with Tantric terminology and ideology. Finally, passages were borrowed from the *Śāradātiklaka*, a Tantric work. The whole process was completed, according to Lalye, in the eleventh century. These stages are included in the schema below:

LALYE'S THEORY

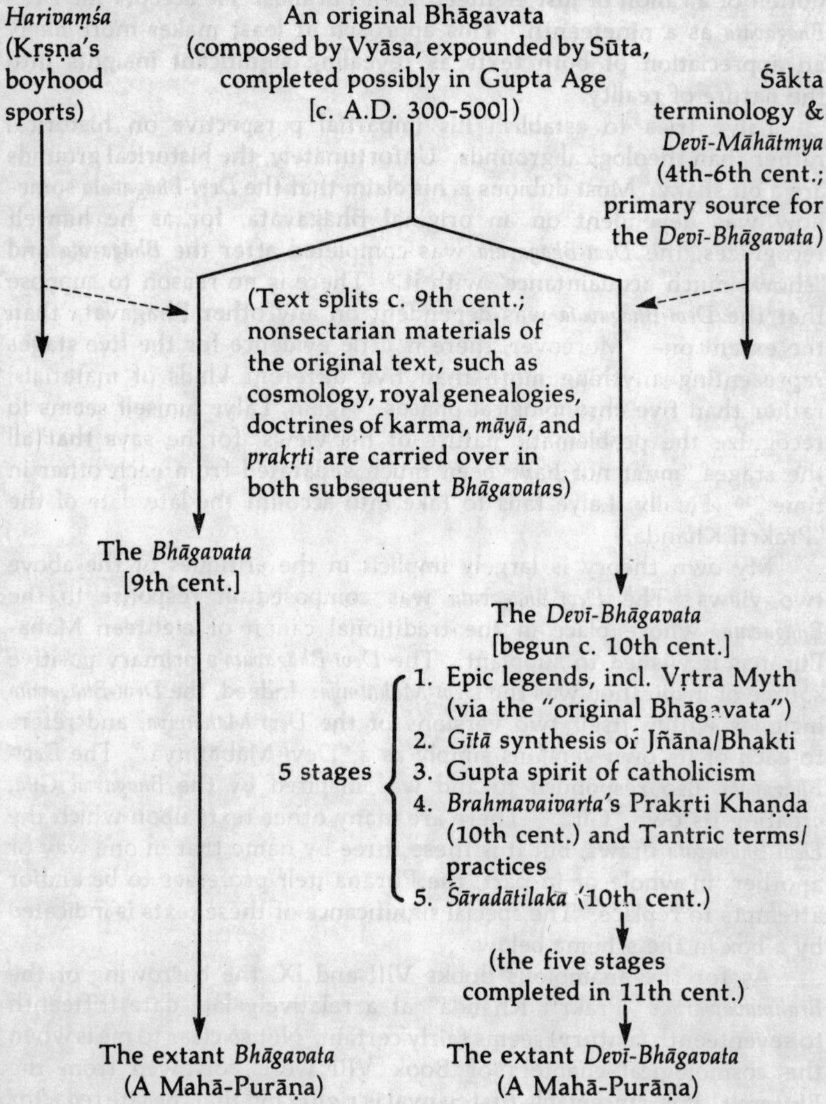

As pointed out earlier, the great virtue of Lalye's reconstruction is that it sidesteps the squabble over which of the two *Bhāgavata*s is the Mahā-Purāṇa, though at the expense of abandoning the classical notion of a canon of just eighteen such Purāṇas. He accepts the *Devī-Bhāgavata* as a nineteenth. This approach at least makes more likely an appreciation of both texts as revealing significant insights into the nature of reality.

Lalye tries to establish his impartial perspective on historical rather than theological grounds. Unfortunately, the historical grounds are a bit shaky. Most dubious is his claim that the *Devī-Bhāgavata* somehow was dependent on an original Bhāgavata, for as he himself recognizes, the *Devī-Bhāgavata* was completed after the *Bhāgavata* and "shows much acquaintance" with it.[9] There is no reason to suppose that the *Devī-Bhāgavata* was dependent on any other Bhāgavata than the extant one. Moreover, there is little evidence for the five stages representing anything more than five different kinds of materials, rather than five chronological phases. Again, Lalye himself seems to recognize the problematic nature of his views, for he says that all the stages "must not have been much separated from each other in time."[10] Finally, Lalye fails to take into account the late date of the "Prakṛti Khaṇḍa."

My own theory is largely implicit in the critiques of the above two views. The *Devī-Bhāgavata* was composed in response to the *Bhāgavata*, whose place in the traditional canon of eighteen Mahā-Purāṇas it wished to supplant. The *Devī-Bhāgavata*'s primary positive source of inspiration was the *Devī-Māhātmya*. Indeed, the *Devī-Bhāgavata* includes within itself two versions of the *Devī-Māhātmya*, and refers to each of its own versions simply as a "Devī-Māhātmya." The *Devī-Bhāgavata* also responded to and was inspired by the *Bhagavad Gītā*, creating its own "Gītā." There are many other texts upon which the *Devī-Bhāgavata* draws, but it is these three by name that in one way or another, in whole or in part, the Purāṇa itelf professes to be and/or attempts to replace. The special significance of these texts is indicated by a box in the schema below.

As for the anamolous Books VIII and IX, the borrowing of the *Brahmavaivarta*'s "Prakṛti Khaṇḍa" at a relatively late date (fifteenth to seventeenth century) seems fairly certain. Not so clear to me is when the cosmological chapters of Book VIII were borrowed from the *Bhāgavata*. It is conceivable that Sanyal is right, and that the late redactor responsible for Book IX also is responsible for Book VIII. However, while Book IX appears somewhat "out of the blue," Book VIII fits its overall context (a section on cosmography would be expected here, as a comparison with the *Mārkaṇḍeya Purāṇa* shows). Further, there is at least the physical possibility, given the earlier date of the *Bhāgavata*, that the original *Devī-Bhāgavata* composer could have been the one who incorporated Book VIII into the text. My schema follows:

AN ALTERNATIVE THEORY

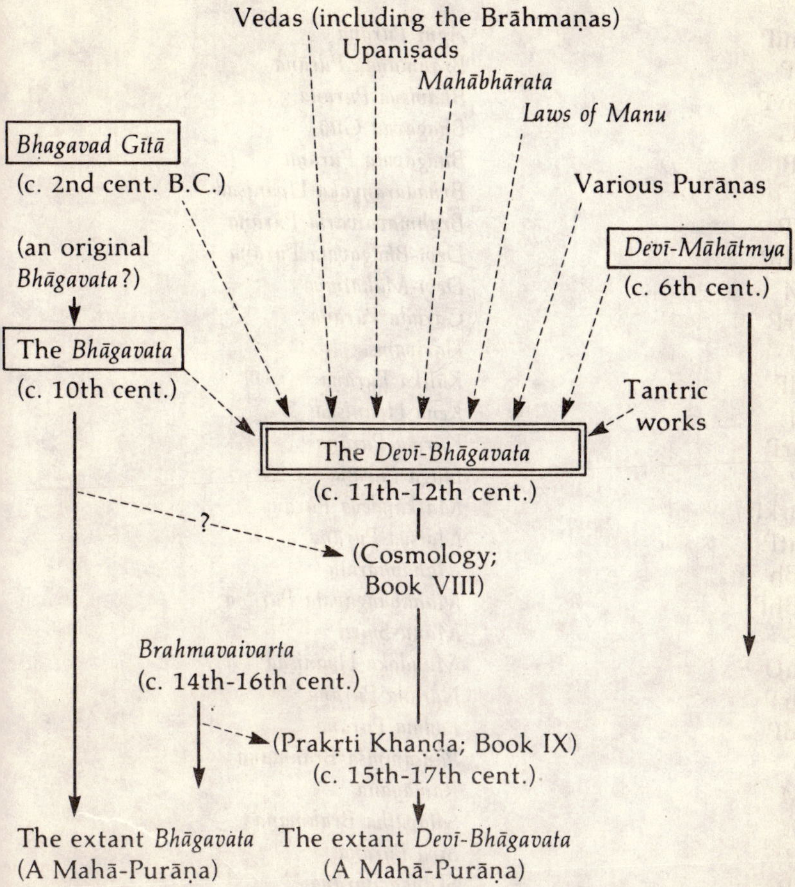

Like Lalye, I accept the notion that both *Bhāgavata*s are Mahā-Purāṇas, though I do not particularly favor abandoning the notion of a canon of eighteen. In chapter one, I suggest an alternative solution, in which the notion of a canon of eighteen is retained but reinterpreted.

Abbreviations

AgniP	*Agni Purāṇa*
BAP	*Brahmāṇḍa Purāṇa*
BhavP	*Bhaviṣya Purāṇa*
BhG	*Bhagavad Gītā*
BhP	*Bhāgavata Purāṇa*
BU	*Bṛhadāraṇyaka Upaniṣad*
BVP	*Brahmavaivarta Purāṇa*
DBhP	*Devī-Bhāgavata Purāṇa*
DM	*Devī-Māhātmya*
GarP	*Garuḍa Purāṇa*
HV	*Harivaṃśa*
KālP	*Kālikā Purāṇa*
KU	*Kena Upaniṣad*
KūrP	*Kūrma Purāṇa*
LiP	*Liṅga Purāṇa*
MārkP	*Mārkaṇḍeya Purāṇa*
MatP	*Matsya Purāṇa*
MBh	*Mahābhārata*
MBhP	*Mahābhāgavata Purāṇa*
MS	*Manu-Smṛti*
MuU	*Muṇḍaka Upaniṣad*
NārP	*Nārada Purāṇa*
PadP	*Padma Purāṇa*
PB	*Pañcaviṃśa Brāhmaṇa*
RM	*Rāmāyaṇa*
ŚB	*Śatapatha Brāhmaṇa*
ŚiP	*Śiva Purāṇa*
SkP	*Skanda Purāṇa*
ŚU	*Śvetāśvatara Upaniṣad*
VāmP	*Vāmana Purāṇa*
VarP	*Varāha Purāṇa*
VāyuP	*Vāyu Purāṇa*
ViP	*Viṣṇu Purāṇa*

Glossary

ahaṃkāra the principle of egocentricity in the Sāṃkhya philosophy; in the *Devī-Bhāgavata*, the cause of self-delusion afflicting both gods and demons and leading to their humiliation or destruction.

ānanda bliss; one of the three fundamental "qualities" of Brahman (the ultimate reality), alongside *sat* (being) and *cit* (consciousness), in the Vedānta philosophy; ascribed to the Goddess in the *Devī-Bhāgavata*.

ārādhana entertaining, serving, or worshipping a deity.

artha prosperity, well-being, success; the second of the four ends of human endeavor, the others being pleasure (*kāma*), moral responsibilities (*dharma*), and liberation (*mokṣa* or *mukti*).

āśrama a stage of life in the orthodox, Brahmanical view; the four stages include that of the student, the householder, the forest dweller, and the renouncer.

asura one of several generic names, like *daitya* and *dānava*, for the enemies of the gods; a demon.

avatāra a descent or incarnation of a god, traditionally associated with Viṣṇu especially; in the *Devī-Bhāgavata*, applied also to the famous demon-slaying exploits of the Goddess.

bhakta a devotee.

bhakti devotion to the supreme personal being; one of the three main traditional paths to the ultimate, alongside *jñāna* (knowledge) and *karma-yoga* (selfless action); *bhakti* and *jñāna* in most schools and texts are seen as complementary, emphasis occasionally being given to one or the other.

bhukti enjoyment; often synonymous with the first three ends of human endeavor and contrasted with liberation (*mukti*); in the *Devī-Bhāgavata*, *bhukti* and *mukti* are not seen as opposed.

bīja seed, source, origin; in Tantra, the initial syllable of a mantra mystically containing the essence of the deity to whom the mantra belongs.

carita or *caritra* deeds, acts; adventures; in the *Devī-Bhāgavata*, refers especially to the demon-slaying exploits of the Goddess.

cit consciousness; one of the three fundamental "qualities" of Brahman (the ultimate reality), alongside *sat* and *ānanda*, in the Vedānta philosophy; ascribed to the Goddess in the *Devī-Bhāgavata* and synonymous with other terms like *caitanya* also applied to the Devī.

daitya one of several generic names, like *asura* and *dānava*, for the enemies of the gods; a demon.

dānava one of several generic names, like *asura* and *daitya*, for the enemies of the gods; a demon.

darśana a vision, especially of a holy person or deity; the granting of such a vision; in the *Devī-Bhāgavata*, refers to the self-revelations of the Goddess to her devotees, particularly in her various, cosmic forms.

deva a god; also referred to as *sura;* opposed to the demons.

devāsura pertaining to the gods and demons; a common adjective applied to the habitual enmity and warfare between the two groups.

devatā a deity or image of a deity; the divinity addressed in a Vedic hymn; in Tantra, the protective deities invoked to reside in the body.

dharma cosmic, social, and moral order; law, virtue, duty, justice; the third of the four ends of human endeavor, alongside *kāma, artha,* and *mokṣa.*

dhyāna meditation, especially on the form and attributes of a deity.

guṇas the three qualities or strands of nature (*prakṛti*) that constitute all phenomena and determine their characteristics: *sattva, rajas,* and *tamas;* in the *Devī-Bhāgavata*, only the Goddess is free from entanglement in the *guṇas*, though they form part of her inherent material nature.

japa recitation, especially of a mantra, prayer, or revealed saying.

jñāna knowledge, especially of ultimate truth; one of the three main traditional paths to the ultimate, alongside *bhakti* (devotion) and *karma-yoga* (selfless action); in the *Devī-Bhāgavata, jñāna* occasionally takes precedence over *bhakti.*

jñānī one who follows the path of knowledge or possesses divine truth.

kāma pleasure, desire, love; the first of the four ends of human endeavor, alongside *artha, dharma,* and *mokṣa.*

kavaca armor; a mantric utterance serving as protective armor.

līlā play, sport; suggests the basic nature of the world as the pastime of the supreme, and expresses the relation between the supreme and his or her devotees; also provides the most profound "explanation" for the incarnations of the supreme; in the *Devī-Bhāgavata,* it is the play of a mother with her children that ultimately characterizes the Devī's interaction with all created beings.

liṅga distinguishing mark or feature; Śiva's distinguishing mark, the phallus.

māhātmya greatness, majesty, dignity; glorification of the greatness or majesty of a sacred object, place, or divine being; a work describing and eulogizing such greatness.

makha a sacrifice, identified with Viṣṇu in the ancient scriptures.

manvantara a cosmic period of time ruled over by a Manu, equal to slightly more than three hundred million human years.

māyā creative, transformative power; illusion, enchanting force; in the *Devī-Bhāgavata*, often used in a positive sense, even when it refers to illusion or the Devī's power of fascination.

moha delusion; in the *Devī-Bhāgavata*, closely linked with the principle of *ahaṃkāra* and with the Devī's power of enchantment.

mokṣa or *mukti* liberation, especially *from* the realm of *saṃsāra* in most traditional Hindu schools; in the *Devī-Bhāgavata*, liberation is more often spoken of as something attained *within* the world.

nidrā sleep; in the compound *yoga-nidrā*, often personified as the Goddess, Yoganidrā.

nirguṇa and *nirguṇā* without attributes or qualities; beyond the three *guṇa*s of nature (*prakṛti*); an epithet emphasizing the transcendent nature of the supreme reality; in the *Devī-Bhāgavata*, the Goddess is paradoxically both *nirguṇā* and *triguṇā* (endowed with the three *guṇa*s), as she is both fully transcendent and immanent.

nyāsa in Tantra, the invoking of protective deities to reside in various parts of the body.

Pātāla the underworld; the appropriate realm of the demons, as opposed to this world or the heavens.

phala fruit; the result or benefit of worship.

prabhāva power, might; splendor, majesty.

prakṛti nature; in Sāṃkhya philosophy, the active but insentient, material cause of the universe, contrasted with spirit (*puruṣa*); in the *Devī-Bhāgavata*, personified as a form or aspect of the Goddess, who is identified with both nature and spirit.

pralaya dissolution; the destruction of the whole universe at the end of a *kalpa* or major cosmic cycle, in contrast to the end of a *yuga* or *mahā-yuga* (age or great-age); during the period of dissolution, the universe exists in mere potentiality, often represented as a cosmic ocean upon which Viṣṇu sleeps, floating on his serpent couch.

prasāda the favor, grace, or compassion of a deity.

pūjā ritual, iconic worship of a deity.

puruṣa conscious spirit; in the Sāṃkhya, the inactive principle that "interacts" with *prakṛti;* in the *Ṛg Veda,* the "cosmic man" that is sacrificed to become the parts of the universe; in the Purāṇas, often identified with Viṣṇu as the cosmic sacrifice; in the *Devī-Bhāgavata,* identified with the Goddess as the supreme conscious spirit, and as part of her androgynous nature.

rajas activity, energy, passion; one of the three *guṇas* of *prakṛti;* adjectival forms: *rajas*ic, *rājasī.*

rasa sentiments, aesthetic moods; traditionally, these include eight or nine; the most prominent ones in the *Devī-Bhāgavata* are those of heroism (*vīrya*) and eroticism (*śṛṅgāra*), though the Devī is said to embody all.

sakhī female companion; attendant of the Goddess.

sākṣin witness, observer; in the Sāṃkhya, an epithet of the quiescent *puruṣa,* who observes the actions of *prakṛti;* in the *Devī-Bhāgavata,* refers to the Devī as the overseeing protector of the world.

śakti energy, power; often personified as a female attendant or partner belonging to or wielded by a god or goddess; also personified as *the* Goddess, the force responsible for all energy and activity in the universe.

sālokya dwelling in the same world with the supreme deity; one of the forms of liberation.

samādhi deep absorption in yogic meditation, the last of the eight limbs of yoga; the trance state in which Viṣṇu resides while resting on the cosmic ocean, according to his followers.

saṃsāra the ongoing cycle of birth, death, and rebirth; the worldly realm.

śānta or *śānti* tranquility, rest, peace; one of the *rasa*s or sentiments.

sat being; one of the three fundamental "qualities" of Brahman (the ultimate reality), alongside *ānanda* (bliss) and *cit* (consciousness), in the Vedānta philosophy; ascribed to the Goddess in the *Devī-Bhāgavata.*

sattva goodness, light, purity; the best of the three *guṇas* of *prakṛti;* adjectival forms: *sattvic, sāttvikī.*

sāyujya absorption into the supreme deity; one of the forms of liberation.

siddha a perfected being of great holiness; one of the denizens in the celestial paradise of the White Island.

śṛṅgāra the erotic sentiment; one of the *rasa*s or aesthetic moods prominent in the Devī's interactions with the demons in the *Devī-Bhāgavata.*

śruti that class of scripture that is "heard," the Vedas, in contrast to *smṛti*, what is "remembered," e.g., the•Purāṇas; the two classes are not absolute, Purāṇas often being called "the fifth Veda."

stotra a hymn of praise.

sura a god or *deva;* an enemy of the demons.

surāsura pertaining to the gods and demons; a more homophonous adjective than *devāsura.*

tamas inertia, sloth, darkness, ignorance; one of the three *guṇa*s of *prakṛti;* adjectival forms: *tamas*ic, *tāmasī.*

tapas asceticism; creative ascetic discipline.

tejas splendor, luster, light, brilliance; prowess, strength, martial valor; energy; in the *Devī-Bhāgavata,* occasionally used interchangeably with *śakti.*

tīrtha a holy site or pilgrimage center.

triguṇā endowed with or possessing the three *guṇas*; a common epithet of the Devī in the *Devī-Bhāgavata*, even though she is also said to be *nirguṇā* (beyond or without *guṇa*s).

Trimūrti the male triumvirate of Brahmā, Viṣṇu, and Śiva, responsible for the creation, preservation, and destruction of the universe, according to traditional, masculine perspectives.

upadeśa instruction, teaching.

vajra thunderbolt; the weapon of Indra, constructed from the bones of the sage Dadhīci.

varma armor; a mantric utterance serving as protective armor.

varṇāśrama-dharma duty as determined by class and stage of life; the responsible ordering of society.

vāṇī speech; the goddess of learning, Sarasvatī; in the *Devī-Bhāgavata,* often the "manifestation" of the Goddess in disembodied form.

veda knowledge, wisdom; the division of sacred learning or scriptures known as *śruti* ("what is heard"); in the plural ("the Vedas"), usually refers to the earliest collections of sacred learning such as the *Ṛg Veda,* to which are formally accorded the highest canonical or scriptural authority.

viḍambana imitation, disguise; deception, deceit, fraud; mockery, mortification, embarrassment, humiliation.

vīra a warrior, hero; heroism; one of the major moods (*rasa*s) displayed by the Devī in her dealings with the demons in the *Devī-Bhāgavata.*

yantra a mystical diagam or arrangement of images used in ritual worship and meditation.

Notes

Preface

1. Parrinder 119.
2. Smith 1974, 29.

Introduction: The Vindication of the Goddess in the Purāṇic Tradition

1. Coburn 1984(a), 304.
2. In the first hymn to the Goddess in the DM, the "creator" Brahmā declares: "By you this universe is supported. By you the world is created, by you it is protected, O Devī, and you consume it at the end, always." (DM 1.75) Then, with ironic reference to the Vaiṣṇava conceit that Viṣṇu is the ultimate agent behind the three cosmic roles, Brahmā continues his praise: "By you, he [Viṣṇu] who is the creator of the world, the protector of the world, who consumes the world, even he is carried off to sleep. . . . Viṣṇu, I, and Śiva have been impelled by you to assume embodied forms. Who then is capable of [adequately] praising you?" (DM 1.83-84)
3. Coburn 1984(a), 303-04.
4. As the DBhP claims to go back to an original utterance by the Goddess during the time of creation, the full text being simply an elaboration of that, a Śākta might well argue that the initial inspiration is as old as creation itself. The tensions between a theological and a text-historical understanding of the "date" of the DBhP will be considered in chapter one below.
5. Dimmitt and van Buitenen 9.
6. Dimmitt and van Buitenen 3.
7. However, the Purāṇas develop their own standards of exclusivity, largely based on the ideals of *bhakti*, rather than of class. That is, many Purāṇic texts declare that they should be shared only with those who are devotees of the gods extolled in the particular Purāṇas themselves. At the same time, it is occasionally said that even the accidental hearing of a Purāṇa, or a part thereof, will have enormous benefits for the hearer.
8. Modern scholars, following the native tradition, often divide Hindu "scriptures" into two major classes: the *śruti* ("that which is heard"),

referring to the Vedas heard by the ancient sages, and *smṛti* ("that which is remembered"), including the later tradition as recorded in such works as the epics, Purāṇas, and law books. It is becoming increasingly apparent to scholars, though, that such a distinction is far from clear-cut. Not only are some works purporting to be *śruti* of relatively late date, but also certain works, which strictly speaking might seem to fall into the *smṛti* class, are accorded the status of *śruti*. Among these, for instance, is the BhG and the DM. And if the Purāṇas as a whole, usually classified as *smṛti*, are the "fifth Veda," then the distinction is becoming rather blurred indeed.

9. One exception is the BVP. It refers to its account of Rādhā (*rādhikākhyānam*) as "not previously heard in the Purāṇas" (*apūrvaṃ . . . purāṇeṣu*; IV.132.15, 17). Similarly, it refers to its third book, the "Ganeṣa Khaṇḍa," as "ever new" or "fresh" (*navaṃ navam*; IV.132.23), and to itself as a whole as "ever fresh" (IV.133.33). What is suggested is not that the events of Rādhā and the like are recent occurrences, but rather that these happenings, many taking place at the beginning of time—at least of the present cycle—have only recently been disclosed. Or that they have been put into fresh, new garb.
10. The phrasing here was suggested to me by Coburn, who asks with reference to the DM, "how is the Sanskritic tradition made contemporary, and how is the worship of the Goddess made traditional?" (1984[a], 9; cf. p. 79.)
11. Rocher 1.
12. The estimate is Haraprasad Shastri's, cited by Rocher (1).
13. We shall consider the Purāṇic definitions of Mahā- and Upa-Purāṇas in chapter one. Such definitions are found only in relatively late Purāṇas, and are not sufficiently rigorous to be useful.
14. A. S. Gupta 1965, 332.
15. Rocher (34) points to the eighteen books of the MBh, the eighteen chapters of the BhG, the eighteen days of the great war, which was fought by eighteen armies.
16. O'Flaherty 1980(b), 80-81.
17. O'Flaherty 1980(b), 81. While the Goddess often appears as a consort in the Purāṇas generally, in the DM she shines forth as superior to all male beings and as the consort of none.
18. Dimmitt and van Buitenen 9. The Mahā-Purāṇas contain some revealing classifications of themselves. The SkP, from a Śaivite perspective, divides them into four groups according to the chief deity they praise: four for Viṣṇu, two for Brahmā, two also for the Sun, and ten for Śiva (text quoted by Gupta 1965, 342). The MatP (53.65) declares that in the Purāṇas there is the glorification of Brahmā, Viṣṇu, the Sun, and Rudra (Śiva). The same text goes on to divide the Mahā-Purāṇas according to the three qualities or *guṇas* and the chief deity of each: the *sāttvika* Purāṇas focus on Viṣṇu, the *rājasa* on Brahmā; the *tāmasa* on Agni and Śiva, and a mixed class on

Sarasvatī and the Pitṛs (53.67-68). The PadP divides the texts into three equal groups of six, according to the *guṇas*, with the *sāttvika* leading to *mokṣa*, the *rājasa* to heaven, and the *tāmasa* to hell. Included in the *sāttvika* are the ViP and the BhP, while the MārkP is in the *rājasa* (text quoted by Gupta 1965, 341). The BhavP has a similar list with the MārkP placed in the *tāmasa* category. It further considers the *tāmasa* to be concerned with "*Śakti-dharma*" (teachings and practice of the Śākta tradition) (text quoted by Gupta 1965, 334). In these classifications, the Goddess is either ignored or severely downplayed, reflecting a Vaiṣṇava or Śaiva orientation. As far as I know, there are no Śākta classificatory schemes of the above sort. Needless to say, such classifications are highly artificial. Cf. Winternitz 532.

19. Rocher 105.

20. Rocher 105.

21. Rocher 113. Cf. Hazra (1963, 1): "There have been Mahāpurāṇas on the rites, customs and faiths of the Brāhmas, Pāñcarātras and Pāśupatas from long before the beginning of the Christian era, but not a single work of this class has ever dealt exhaustively or even principally with Śakti-worship."

22. The other "Śākta Upa-Purāṇas" Rocher mentions are the *Devī*, *Kālikā*, and *Mahābhāgavata* Purāṇas. These, along with the DBhP, are available in printed editions. There are other Śākta Upa-Purāṇas, however, that exist only in manuscript form (see Hazra 1963, 1).

23. Sanyal 142.

24. Kane (V.854-55) suggests that one of the earliest Mahā-Purāṇas, the MatP, comes from the third century A.D., and that most of them were completed between the fifth and ninth centuries. As for the Upa-Purāṇas, Kane says that they "began to be compiled from about the 7th or 8th century A. D. and their numbers went on increasing till about the 13th century or even later." Kane then adds a disquieting note: "After the 9th century no further Mahāpurāṇas appear, but additional matter appears to have been unscrupulously inserted in several Purāṇas." These views are repeated with apparent approval by Gupta (1965, 329).

25. Hardy 486. Cf. Rocher (103), who states that "even for the better established and more coherent purāṇas"—he specifically mentions the BhP—there is little consensus regarding dates.

26. Hazra 1963, 346-47.

27. In chapter one we shall look more closely at the underlying assumptions, historical and theological, as to what constitutes a Mahā-Purāṇa.

28. The evidence for these views will be presented throughout the course of the book. I provide here only a summary of my views in order to give the reader some historical orientation to the text.

29. Hazra 1963, 359.

30. Book VIII of the DBhP deals with cosmography and related topics, including an account of the different forms of Viṣṇu worshipped in the different regions of the world. The DBhP has taken these materials, at times verbatim, from the fifth Book of the BhP, adding a beginning and concluding chapter that attempt to assimilate the intervening subject matter into a Śākta framework. Book IX takes over most of Book II of the BVP. This book, the "Prakṛti Khaṇḍa," which can be dated probably to the fourteenth to sixteenth centuries, is an encyclopaedia of major and minor goddesses, who are all seen as manifestations of the great Goddess Nature (Prakṛti). Yet while Prakṛti is seen in the BVP as the supreme soteriological figure, she is ultimately subordinated in an ontological sense to the male god Kṛṣṇa, as she arises out of his left side at the beginning of creation. The Kṛṣṇaite perspective of the book, while toned down in the DBhP, still is quite evident in the Śākta text.
31. DBhP V.27.21. The epithet, Veda-Mātā, may be rendered not only as "mother of the Vedas," but also as "mother of knowledge."
32. DBhP V.19.32.

Chapter 1. The Origin and Transmission of the Two *Bhāgavata Purāṇas*

1. BhP II.9.32.
2. DBhP I.15.52.
3. By Lalye's count, the BhP has 13,216 verses, the DBhP has 18,276 (34).
4. It is worth noting that the notion of a Mahā-Purāṇa is fairly recent. According to Hazra (1962, 240), it appears only in the relatively late BhP itself (XII.7.10 and 22) and the very late BVP (IV.133.7 and 10). The BhP says that some people make a distinction between great and small Purāṇas (*mahad-alpa*) (XII.7.10), apparently on the basis of whether they contain five or ten topics. The BhP also says that there are eighteen Purāṇas great and small (*kṣullakāni mahānti ca*) (XII.7.22). It seems that for the BhP there is not yet an established tradition of eighteen Mahā-Purāṇas, but only a corpus of eighteen (a traditional, sacred number), generally referred to simply as "Purāṇas" (cf. Rocher 30-34). The earlier Purāṇas also refer to the eighteen only as "the Purāṇas." The DBhP, while to my knowledge not using the term *Mahā-Purāṇa* (the term appears constantly in the chapter colophons of the printed texts), does use the term *Upa-Purāṇa* (I.3.13).
5. See especially Hazra 1953.
6. Hazra 1953, 61-70; Lalye 32.
7. DBhP I.3.13-16. See Hazra 1953, 62-65. Sanyal, in arguing for the earlier date of the DBhP, dismisses its reference to the BhP as a late interpolation, and that therefore the original body of the text "cannot be suspected of

attempting to prove its own superiority" (156-57). However, the DBhP does attempt to prove in more subtle ways its own superiority aside from its one specific mention of the BhP as an Upa-Purāṇa. Moreover, while the reference *may* be late, it may just as well be part of the original core.

8. At I.1.16, the DBhP calls itself: *bhāgavataṃ puṇyaṃ pañcamaṃ vedasaṃmitam* ("the auspicious *Bhāgavata*, the fifth, equal to the Vedas"). That this does not refer to the idea that the Purāṇa is the "fifth Veda"—an important Hindu interpretive concept for understanding the scriptural status and significance of the Purāṇas—but rather to the DBhP as the fifth Mahā-Purāṇa, is made clear in Nīlakaṇṭha's commentary. In glossing the term *pañcamam*, he lists the first five Purāṇas, ending of course with the *Bhāgavata*. In IV.25.83, the DBhP says unequivocally of itself that it is *purāṇaṃ pañcamaṃ nūnaṃ śrīmadbhāgavatābhidham*.
9. DBhP I.2.11; I.3.34; IV.25.83. Rocher (172) asserts that it is only in the chapter colophons and in the last two Skandhas of the text that the self-designation "*Devī-Bhāgavata*" is used. Otherwise, the Purāṇa calls itself the *Bhāgavata* or *Śrīmadbhāgavata* (and once the *Satī-Purāṇa* [I.3.41]). The only references to the "*Devī-Bhāgavata*" in the text itself that I have found are in the last two *adhyāya*s of the very last Skandha: XII.13.8, 17, 24, 26, 30; XII.14.4. Cf. Hazra 1953, 61.
10. For evidence supporting this latter statement, see chapters two and three below.
11. Hazra 1962, 259. Cf. Prasad (307), who sees a possible "three-fold evolution" of the BhP: 1) the four-*śloka Bhāgavata* revealed by Viṣṇu himself; 2) a later expansion [apparently corresponding to Hazra's earlier prototype] referred to in certain ancient definitions of "the *Bhāgavata*," such as that given in MatP 53.20-21, but which do not fit very well the extant BhP [we shall look more closely at some of these definitions in the next two chapters]; and 3) the extant text. Prasad's view represents an interesting blend of theological and historical perspectives.
12. As Hazra (1953, 66) would have it.
13. BhP I.19.
14. MBh I.36.56.
15. DBhP II.8-12.
16. The DBhP may well have been inspired by the BhP in its story of Janamejaya's depression after hearing the MBh. In BhP I.4.25-30, Vyāsa is not at peace with himself, even though he has just finished composing the MBh. We are told in I.5 that it was Vyāsa's failure to sing adequately of the glory of the Lord that caused his discontent, the cure for which is the recitation of the BhP. Both Purāṇas thus see their own recitation as the remedy for the dissatisfaction induced by the inadequacies of the epic.
17. The definition of a Purāṇa as *pañca-lakṣaṇa* was given early in the famous

Sanskrit lexicon, the *Amarakośa* of Amarasiṃha. The author, however, did not specify what the five topics were. The topics are enumerated in the Purāṇas themselves.

18. For a good discussion of the problem of the *pañca-lakṣaṇas*, see Rocher 24-30.
19. Hazra 1953, 64.
20. See note 4 above.
21. A good example is the DM of the MārkP. In the strictest sense, one could argue, such a praise of the Goddess is not properly one of 'he *pañca-lakṣaṇas*. Yet the Māhātmya is woven into the account of Manus (the fourth topic), and itself deals with matters of creation and re-creation.
22. Lalye 26.
23. Lalye 32.
24. See C. M. Brown 205.
25. Ricoeur 274.
26. Ricouer 276.
27. Ricouer 276.
28. From the perspective of the Paurāṇikas, the distinction between history and prehistory, needless to say, is rather arbitrary and meaningless, at least in their specific Western academic senses. I am using the terms loosely to suggest the distinction between those events focussing primarily on the primordial happenings of the gods (prehistory) and the later events more focussed on human events (history). The distinction, of course, is hardly absolute.
29. It would be interesting to investigate the extent to which traditional and modern scholarship on the concept of a canon of eighteen has been influenced by Vaiṣṇava ideas. With reference to the inclusion of the Vaiṣṇava BhP in Alberuni's list of the eighteen Mahā-Purāṇas, Sanyal argues that Alberuni's informants were themselves Vaiṣṇavas (156). Sanyal thereby implies that had Alberuni inquired about the canon of eighteen from Śākta informants, the DBhP would have been included instead of the BhP. While I have some doubts about whether the DBhP already existed in Alberuni's day (eleventh century), Sanyal has a valid point: the answers regarding the canonical status of certain texts depends in part on whom one asks.
30. BhP II.9.5-45; cf. II.4.25; III.4.13; XII.13.10, 19-20.
31. DBhP I.15.50-I.16-32; cf. III.3.63-66; XII.14.1-2.
32. DBhP I.15.52.
33. For the DBhP's extended account of the Madhu-Kaiṭabha legend, see I.6-9; cf. III.2.12-19. This legend, the first of the three great deeds of the Devī in the DM, shall be discussed on a number of occasions, but see especially chapter four below.
34. Brahmā's bewilderment over Viṣṇu's apparent nonsupremacy is a recurring

motif in the DBhP. We shall examine closely one other example of this theme in the next chapter.

35. DBhP III.2.12-19.
36. See DBhP IV.1-25.
37. DBhP III.3.63-67.
38. BhP XII.8-10.
39. BhP XII.9.19.
40. BhP II.8.10.
41. BhP XII.10.1.
42. BhP XII.10.10.
43. BhP X.3.48.
44. BhP X.3.49, 52, 54.
45. BhP VII.9.32-33.
46. For an enlightening discussion of the several variations of the myth and its development from the MBh versions down to the time of the DM, see Coburn 1984(a), 211-21.
47. MBh XII.335.16-64.
48. This version from the Śānti Parva introduces Viṣṇu as the horse-headed god (Hayaśiras). This motif is the main topic of our next chapter, and there we shall give further consideration to this Śānti passage. The myth of Madhu and Kaiṭabha will also figure prominently in chapter four, where we discuss the three great deeds of the Devī.
49. E.g., BhP VII.9.37.
50. The term *yoga-nidrā* has been carefully analyzed by Coburn (1984[a], 191-95) for its significance in the DM.
51. DBhP I.7.20, 24.
52. Paralleling the different mythological evaluations of sleep are various philosophical interpretations. Modern scholars, looking at such Upaniṣadic passages as *Maitrī* VI.25, have sometimes argued that the goal of yoga is exactly what is attained in deep sleep: a natural blissful unity (see e.g., Heimann, 130-45). Commenting on Heimann's interpretation, Fort writes: "While this point-of-view is intriguing and partially convincing, I have found few references in Yoga texts to the blissful unity of sleep or sleep as a model of release; rather, it is referred to as tāmasic-dullness" (chap. V, p. 29, n.55). Fort also points out Rāmānuja's comment on *Brahmasūtra* I.1.1, to the effect that in sleep, one is overcome by *tamoguṇa* (chap. VI, p. 15). Similarly, Fort summarizes Vidyāraṇya's views expressed in his *Jīvanmukti-viveka*: "Vidyāraṇya is quite explicit about sleep's inferiority to samādhi. He notes that bondage and suffering reappear daily after sleep. Sleep is not only not a controlled practice (like samādhi); it stops controlled practice. The fourth (turīya, equivalent to brahman) is more like samādhi; it is obtained when false knowledge (in waking and dream) or ignorance

of reality (in sleep) are destroyed" (chap. VI, p. 24). The BhP seems oblivious to these philosophical/yogic views. Whether or not the DM was aware of or influenced by them, or vice versa, is unclear. The DBhP, in any case, would certainly argue that Viṣṇu is reduced to a *tamas*ic state in his cosmic sleep.

53. Cf. Sheridan 1983, especially pp. 216-22.
54. BhP III.26.9; V.26.36.
55. BhP III.5.49; II.3.9-10.
56. BhP III.31.14; XI.6.14.
57. BhP XI.24.18.
58. BhP I.5.20; I.7.23; I.8.18; XI.11.28.
59. BhP III.26.4; X.80.30.
60. BhP III.27.24.
61. This personifying trend, as we have noted, is already present in the BhP, but there, little is made of such personifications.
62. DBhP I.7.29.
63. Capra 300.
64. BhP I.11.5.
65. BhP XI.17.38.
66. BhP IV.25-29.
67. This is most clearly seen in the DBhP's portrayal of Śuka as a householder, over against the BhP's (and MBh's) portrayal of Śuka as a lifelong celibate. See Hazra 1953, 64-65 and Bedekar.
68. One should be careful not to overstress the DBhP's appreciation of the maternal and/or the feminine, for like most of the Purāṇas, the DBhP shares an ambivalent attitude towards women in general and contains in its more ascetical passages some very strong condemnations of the female sex. See Kinsley 1982.
69. Sanyal (143) indirectly notes the more "world-denying" perspective of the BhP in his explanation of the popularity of the text in relation to the DBhP. In his view, we may recall (see the Appendix), the DBhP is the true *Bhāgavata*. Accordingly, it should have a greater renown than the Vaiṣṇava text, but this is not the case. Sanyal attributes this in part to the greater literary beauty of the BhP, and in part "to the gradual change in the psychology of the Hindus, caused by the Muslim conquest of India, which made them hopeless about worldly prosperity." The DBhP's attitude towards the course of history, and towards material prosperity, is indeed more "optimistic" than the BhP's. Whether or not this had anything to do with the greater popularity of the BhP after the Muslim conquests I would hesitate to say.
70. DBhP III.19.10.

71. BhP I.3.36; DBhP III.5.31, 35.
72. BhP III.6.38.

Chapter 2. Horsing Around with Viṣṇu: A Case of Capital Murder

1. The definition is given by Śrīdhara in the introduction of his commentary to the BhP. Śrīdhara gives as the source for the quotation merely "*purāṇā-ntara*" ("another Purāṇa"), which some Indian scholars have suggested is the SkP (see Sanyal 133; cf. Mahalingam 191). The "Prabhāsa Khaṇḍa" of the SkP (I.2.39-42) does give a definition of "the *Bhāgavata*" that is fairly close to Śrīdhara's, but it contains no reference to the Hayagrīva-Brahmavidyā.
2. DBhP I.16.34-35.
3. Unlike Hazra, I feel the juxtaposition of Hayagrīva witn Brahmavidyā in Śrīdhara's definition is not fortuitous, for the association of the two has ancient roots. Hazra says that the DBhP deals with Brahmavidyā especially in Skandha XII and with the Hayagrīva story in I.5, thus failing to suggest any connection between the two (1953, 63). In any case, the two conjoined came to play a significant role in the canonical controversy. See note 4 below.
4. As a sampling of the intricate and rather obscure arguments often presented, we may consider the following views. In the preface to his commentary on the DBhP, the eighteenth-century scholar/devotee Śaiva Nīlakaṇṭha quotes Śrīdhara's definition of "the *Bhāgavata*" cited above and contends that it supports the claim of the DBhP to be "the Mahā-Purāṇa." Concerning the phrase *Hayagrīva-Brahmavidyā*, he argues: "In the first Skandha of the *Devī-Bhāgavata*, the famous *asura*, Hayagrīva by name, practices a Vidyā treating of Brahman, a Vidyā [by the way] being a mantra with a female being for its divinity. . . . That *daitya* and the Vidyā practiced by him are right there in the first Skandha, as seen in the line [where the Devī herself declares that the demon] 'practiced my one syllable mantra consisting of the *māyā-bīja*.'" The line Nīlakaṇṭha quotes is DBhP I.5.87.

   Nīlakaṇṭha recognizes that supporters of the Vaiṣṇava *Bhāgavata* might claim that the "Hayagrīva-Brahmavidyā" refers to a "Hayagrīva-mantra" occurring in the fifth Skandha of the BhP. The reference apparently is to BhP V.18.3-6, where a prayer, beginning with a mantra, is addressed to Hayaśīrṣa. The "Hayagrīva-mantra" here, then, is addressed *to*, not *by*, the horse-headed one, and this is the basis for Nīlakaṇṭha's rejection of it as fitting the old definition: "We say the definition does not apply to both *Bhāgavata*s for the following reason. In the *Nāradīya* and the *Śāradātilaka*, 'mantras' are explained as having masculine divinities, 'Vidyās' as having feminine divinities. Accordingly, the use of the word

'Vidyā' is appropriate in mantras with feminine divinities, not in mantras with masculine divinities." (NārP I.64.5cd reads: *puṃdaivatās tu mantrā syur vidyāḥ strīdaivatā matāḥ*. *Śāradātilaka* 2.58cd is similar: *mantrāḥ puṃdevatā jñeyā vidyāḥ strīdevatāḥ smṛtāḥ*. Wayman quotes a nearly identical passage from the *Yoginītantra* [73]. This latter text is relatively recent, probably from the sixteenth century [Goudriaan and Gupta 85]). By Nīlakaṇṭha's reasoning, based on a certain presupposition common to Śākta authors, only the *māyā-bīja* uttered by the *daitya* in the DBhP qualifies as a Vidyā, and thus the definition seemingly refers to the DBhP, not the BhP.

The dismissal of the BhP's claim to canonical status on the basis of a Vidyā referring to a female deity is not particularly persuasive. We may question how widely Nīlakaṇṭha's interpretation of Vidyā was accepted outside Śākta circles. Nīlakaṇṭha himself recognized some exceptions to such an interpretation. Further, at least one traditional Vaiṣṇava scholar found support elsewhere in the BhP for the "Hayagrīva-Brahmavidyā." Jīva Gosvāmin (sixteenth century), in his *Tattvasandarbha* (section 20), cites Śrīdhara's definition of "the *Bhāgavata*" and then asserts:

> Since the phrase *Hayagrīva-Brahmavidyā* is here associated with the slaying of Vṛtra, it must refer to the "Nārāyaṇa Varma" (the protective mantra or armor of Nārāyaṇa [described in BhP VI.8.12-34, in the course of the Vṛtra myth]). The term *Hayagrīva* here refers to the horse-headed Dadhīci, by whom was proclaimed the knowledge of Brahman known as the Nārāyaṇa Varma. That he was horse-headed is indicated in the sixth (Skandha of the BhP) by the name *Aśvaśiras* (Horse-headed). (VI.9.52)

The BhP's association of the Nārāyaṇa Varma with the slaying of Vṛtra thus forms part of the basis for Jīva's argument that Śrīdhara's definition applies to the Vaiṣṇava Purāṇa. But what justifies Jīva in equating the Nārāyaṇa Varma with the Hayagrīva-Brahmavidyā?

It is here that the horse-headed Dadhīci plays a crucial role, for he is the chief figure in the original transmission of this Varma or Kavaca, according to the BhP (VI.9.52-53). We shall deal below with the ancient myth of Dadhīci (or Dadhyañc) and his promulgation of secret knowledge, which came to be known as Brahmavidyā. In any case, the BhP, through its transmission history of the Nārāyaṇa Varma, boldly identifies this "Vaiṣṇava Vidyā" with the teachings of Dadhyañc. Jīva Gosvāmin's equation of the Hayagrīva-Brahmavidyā with the Nārāyaṇa Varma is thus quite understandable.

The bearing of all this on the question of canonical genuineness is far from decisive. On the one hand, Sanyal (133-34) points out some obvious objections to Jīva Gosvāmin's identification of the "Hayagrīva-

Brahmavidyā" with the "Nārāyaṇa Varma," including the relative insignificance of the latter in the BhP as a whole (and thus a poor choice for a distinguishing mark). Further, Sanyal deems "Hayagrīva-Brahmavidyā," a phrase not used in the BhP itself, to be a rather "obscure synonym" for the "Nārāyaṇa Varma," raising considerable doubt as to the applicability of the old definition to the BhP. Yet even if Jīva Gosvāmin's identification is far-fetched, the Hayagrīva-Brahmavidyā (as defined by Nīlakaṇṭha) is hardly a major theme in the DBhP either, nor is the mantra uttered by the horse-headed demon in I.5 referred to by that name in the text itself. To be sure, the myth of the demon Hayagrīva is certainly more prominent in the DBhP than in the BhP, but there is the possibility that the DBhP composer emphasized Hayagrīva quite intentionally in order to mold his work to fit the old definition, while this definition may have originally applied nicely enough to an earlier version of the BhP.

On the other hand, even if one accepts the Hayagrīva-Brahmavidyā as referring to Dadhyañc's exposition of the Nārāyaṇa Kavaca in the BhP, we still have little basis for distinguishing between the two *Bhāgavatas* since the DBhP has a parallel story in its famous *Devī Gītā* (VII.36.28-30).

5. It is of interest that in the BhP a number of different names for the horse-headed *avatāra* of Viṣṇu are used, but never Hayagrīva, a name reserved exclusively for a demon, with whom we shall deal later. Accordingly, I have chosen Hayaśiras, one of the more common appellations for Viṣṇu's equine form employed by that text, for general use in this section. I have retained, in specific contexts, the particular name used by the BhP itself.

Most translators of the BhP render Hayaśiras, Hayaśīrṣa, etc., as Hayagrīva. Even the commentarial tradition tends to commingle Hayaśiras/Hayaśīrṣa and Hayagrīva. Similarly, in ViP II.2.50, a reference is made to Hayaśiras, glossed by the modern Hindi commentator as Hayagrīva. However, there is an earlier tradition that sees them as distinct. In VāmP 63.2 and 14, in an account of the geographical distribution of the Lord's forms, Hayaśīrṣa is said to reside in Kṛṣṇāṃśa and Hayagrīva in Mahodaya.

. BhP V.18.6.

. BhP XI.4.17.

. BhP X.40.17.

. BhP VII.9.37.

MBh XII.335.16-64.

A similar cosmic homologue of the horse-headed Viṣṇu appears in HV App. I.41, lines 1421-30.

The seeds for the Hayaśiras *avatāra* are clearly sown in the Śānti account. The specific terminology associated with the horse-headed manifestation, however, is not yet that of the classical *avatāra* doctrine. The Śānti refers simply to Hari's taking on a second form (*"dvitīyāṃ tanum āsthitaḥ"* [XII.335.43;

cf. verses 68 and 69]). Van Gulik (17) finds the oldest *avatāra* list that definitely includes the horse form to be that of ViP V.17.10 (cf. ViP II.2.50-51). Gonḍa (1954, 148) apparently concurs. In the appendix to the ViP, the *Viṣṇudharmottara*, which Kramrisch (1928, 5) dates as no later than the seventh century A. D., the iconic form of Hayagrīva is given, along with a brief reference to his rescuing the Vedas from the two demons (III.80.1-6 [pp. 104-05 of Kramrisch]). This description of Hayagrīva follows those of the man-lion and the boar.

13. E.g., BhP II.7.1 ff.; VI.8.13 ff.; X.2.40; X.40.17 ff.; XI.4.6 ff.
14. BhP I.3.5-28.
15. Prasad (50-51) briefly considers the catalogues in BhP I.3, II.7, and VI.8. He notes the variations in the lists and assumes that two of the three must be "spurious" and "later additions." On the basis of evidence garnered from NārP 96, he concludes that the list in II.7 is the genuine or oldest. I do not think his evidence is persuasive, as the NārP's summary of the BhP is far too scant to draw any firm conclusions. While I agree with Prasad to the extent that I.3 is probably a modification of II.7, this latter list is also relatively late, I suspect, as it alone of all the lists is aware of the mergence of the horse and fish *avatāras* as told in VIII.24.
16. See BhP II.7.11-12; X.2.40; X.40.17; XI.4.17-18.
17. For a brief but clear history of this story from the ŚB up to the Purāṇas see van Buitenen 1975, 203-05. See also Hohenberger, who provides a German translation of the main Purāṇic accounts of the flood, along with those of the ŚB, the MBh, and of Kṣemendra's *Daśavatāracarita* (4-24).
18. MatP 2.15.
19. BhP VIII.24.7-9.
20. This curious development has been noted by many (e.g., Kātre [114]; O'Flaherty [1980(b), 222-23]; S. S. Dange [235]).
21. BhP VIII.24.55.
22. BhP VIII.24.57. Karmarkar (257), taking a rather literal historical approach to the flood legend, sees the two exploits (the rescue of Manu and the recovery of the Vedas) as both being attributed to the fish probably "just after the flood subsided," around the time of the end of the pre-Aryan and the beginning of the Vedic civilization. But as indicated in the next note, the motif of the Veda-stealing demon is clearly a late addition.
23. BhP II.7.12 alludes to this new version of the Matsya story, mentioning the Vedas slipping from Brahmā's mouth and Matsya's recovery of them but without referring to any demon or demons. Other Purāṇas also refer to the BhP's new version. GārP 142.2-3 tells us that Hari, having become a fish, slew the *daitya* Hayagrīva, recovered the Vedas, and protected Manu, etc. Cf. AgniP 2.16-17; PadP VI.230.1-33; cf. also *Śāradātilaka* 17.150. Dikshitar (5-6) acknowledges that the BhP, along with the AgniP and PadP, follows a more recent tradition than the MatP, which adher

more closely to the epic. But elsewhere (53), rather inconsistently, he argues that the MatP "shows its intimate acquaintance with the Bhāgavata Purāṇa." In his ensuing discussion, he suggests that the MatP does not directly give the purpose of the fish *avatāra*, this purpose being given in the BhP's account (namely, the slaying of Hayagrīva to recover the Vedas). He offers two possibilities, either that the BhP supplied the motive that was missing in the MatP, or that the MatP "was aware of the detailed version in the Bhāgavata and did not want to repeat it once again" (54). This latter view is simply not tenable, given the consensus on dating the two Purāṇas today. Dikshitar himself places the MatP among the earliest of the Purāṇas, around the third century A. D. in its final form (71-72). The ninth or tenth century seems the probable date for the BhP. Further, as noted in the text, the BhP's story actually alludes to the "Purāṇic Saṃhitā" taught by Matsya (VIII.24.55), a fairly clear reference to the MatP as pointed out by Prasad (25) and Hohenberger (28), and as already assumed by Śrīdhara. Hohenberger (25-28) argues persuasively that the BhP fish legend adds on to the MatP version, and that the AgniP and PadP accounts are dependent on the BhP's.

24. O'Flaherty 1980(b), 246-47.

25. O'Flaherty 1980(b), 216.

26. O'Flaherty 1980(b), 223.

27. BhP VIII.24.31. Cf. verses 37 and 54.

28. BhP VIII.24.37. An interesting version of the Matsya story relevant to our concerns here is that given in VarP 9.23-35. According to this account, at the end of a *kalpa*, Nārāyaṇa (Viṣṇu) went to sleep, and upon waking after the night had passed, was anxious about the Vedas. He could not discover their whereabouts, however, as he was deluded by the ignorance of sleep (*nidrā*). He finally noticed them lying in the ocean, and assuming the form of a great fish, entered the waters to collect them. Possibly this account in the VarP was the prod for the BhP's Matsya story.

29. Cf. Kātre 114.

30. MBh V.128.49. Van Buitenen's translation (1978, 427). Cf. van Gulik 13.

31. Cf. van Gulik 14-18.

32. BhP II.7.11. Kātre notes that despite the very different details of the Hayaśiras incarnation given here by the BhP, his association with the Vedas remains strong.

33. BhP II.6.22-32.

34. RV X.90.

35. ŚB XIV.1.1.1 ff.

36. See ŚB X.6.4.1, and BU I.1, both quoted in full by Dumont (4-5). The HV, like the Śānti, also portrays Viṣṇu-Hayaśiras as the cosmic sacrificial horse (App. I.41, lines 1421-30), though in both these works, the context

is more that of a divine *darśana* (manifestation or revelation) than of an actual sacrificial immolation.

37. O'Flaherty (1980[b], 216) cites a number of examples from post-Vedic times showing how the horse-sacrifice had actually become an object of ridicule. Yet some sanctity remained to the *aśvamedha*, or else BhP II.7.11 seems inexplicable.

38. Rukmani (295) gives a number of references (I.8.52; VII.15.8; X.10.14; and XI.5.14-15) indicative of the BhP's advocacy of *ahiṃsā*, but he also notes frequent mention of animal sacrifices. He concludes, "society at that time [of the composition of the BhP] was veering towards ahiṃsā. Vaidika sacrifices were accepted but *hiṃsā* was avoided as far as possible" (296).

39. Cf. Clooney, esp. pp. 370-72, where he discusses Rāmānuja's theory of sacrifice, a theory clearly akin to that of the BhP.

40. DBhP I.5.34, 38.

41. ŚB XIV.1.1.1 ff.

42. The story with alternate versions from the *Taittirīya Araṇyaka* (V.1.1 ff. and the PB (VII.5.6) are given in Muir (IV.123-29). See also Hillebrandt (II.419).

43. Quotations in the summary of this story are Eggeling's translation.

44. The PB version (VII.5.6) says that the gods "tried to take it from him by force and hemmed him in" (Caland 144).

45. *Gharma* refers to the milk boiled in the Pravargya ceremony; thus also to the cauldron or pot used to heat the milk, and to the Pravargya itself.

46. For interpretations of *makha* and the beheading of the sacrifice, see Eggeling 1900, xlvi-xlix; Coomaraswamy 1935 (esp. 377-82) and 1944; Gonda 1954 and Heesterman.

47. Sastri (242) calls the DBhP's version of the story of Makha "an improvement." While I admire the playful creativity of the DBhP's composer, I prefer the more neutral term *modification*.

48. There is an interesting version of the myth in the *Tirurvārūrppurāṇam*, quoted by Shulman (1978-79, 109-10), wherein Viṣṇu, due to his conceit at completing the sacrifice, upon entering the city of the Goddess (Śaktipura), lost his strength and fell asleep with his head resting on the bow of Śiva. It is Śiva who informs the gods how to restore Viṣṇu to life, after the inevitable decapitation. Shulman, who also summarizes the DBhP myth, notes the central role played by the Goddess in both accounts (111-12).

49. DBhP I.5.31.

50. DBhP I.5.32.

51. See DM 2.62-64.

52. BhP IV.2-7.

53. BhP IV.7.36.

54. The story of Dakṣa's sacrifice is even more explicitly connected with the ŚB myth in LiP 100.23-32: Vīrabhadra, in decimating the sacrifice and its participants, repeatedly stuns Viṣṇu, whose bow, thrice overcome or hit, breaks into three pieces. Viṣṇu's head is severed by the flying tips.
55. E.g., BhP II.5.21; II.8.10.
56. Nīlakaṇṭha's commentary on DBhP I.5.38.
57. In the BU the meditation on the honey metaphor (II.5) of the Madhukaṇḍa is identified with Dadhyañc's sweet teaching (II.5.16-19). Śaṃkara, in his commentary on this text (II.5.17), divides Dadhyañc's teachings into two parts: one deals with the Pravargya ceremony, the other with the knowledge of the supreme Brahman (Brahmavidyā). Śrīdhara, in his commentary on BhP VI.9.52, refers to Dadhyañc as "expert in the Pravargya and the Brahmavidyā," apparently following Śaṃkara. Cf. Patil 125.
58. KU 3.1-4.3. The full story tells how the gods, having gained a victory through Brahman, began to take credit for the conquest themselves. Brahman, to disabuse them, appeared before them in the form of a Yakṣa or spirit. First Agni, and then Vāyu, tried to discover who or what the apparition was. The two gods approached the spirit and introduced themselves by boasting of their respective powers to burn or blow away anything. The Yakṣa then challenged them to burn and blow away a blade of grass he placed before them. On their subsequent failure, and not finding out the identity of the apparition, they returned to the other gods. Indra went next to the Yakṣa, but the spirit disappeared on his approach. Then, in the same sky, Indra encountered a resplendent woman, the beautiful Umā Haimavatī, who revealed the identity of the Yakṣa as Brahman, the source of all power including that behind their victory.
59. See Muir IV.422-23. Brahmavidyā already appears as an epithet of a goddess in the MBh. There, in the famous Durgā-stotra, Durgā is praised as "the knowledge of Brahman (Brahmavidyā) among knowledges, and the great sleep (*mahā-nidrā*) of embodied beings" (App. I.1 of the Bhīṣma Parva, line 21). The close conjunction of Brahmavidyā and *mahā-nidrā* is of interest, especially in light of the hymn to Nidrā in the HV, where the latter is referred to as "the sleep of all beings . . . the knowledge of Brahman among knowledges" (App.I.8, lines 40-41). A few lines earlier in the hymn (24-25), Nidrā is called "the foremost Yakṣī among Yakṣas and . . . an expounder of Brahman." Sen (29) sees a connection between this and Umā Haimavatī of the KU. Cf. Vimalānanda-Svāmī (17), a modern Tantric teacher, who explains the identity of the world mother, Mahā-Kālī, as follows: "It was this Brahmavidyā who (Yoginī-Tantra, 10th Patala) at the beginning of this Kalpa was heard as a bodyless [sic] voice from the sky of Brahmā, Viṣṇu, and Maheśvara. . . . It was this Aniruddha-sarasvatī [self-willed speech] who . . . appeared in the Heavens before Indra and other proud Devatās in the form of a brilliant Yakṣa, and crushing

the pride of the Devas Agni and Vāyu, in the form of all-beautiful Umā, taught Brahmatattva to Indra."

60. DBhP XII.8.11 ff.
61. DBhP XII.8.62. The ŚiP (V.49) tells the tale in similar fashion, clearly identifying Umā with Brahman. The BVP (IV.49) has a rather different rendering, with Viṣṇu appearing before Agni in the form of a boy, to offer the unburnable blade of grass. For an analysis of the myth in the KU and the DBhP, see Chemburkar.
62. The very first line of the DBhP refers to the Devī as Vidyā, which the English translator has rendered "Brahmavidyā."
63. See O'Flaherty 1975, 58; Bosch 140. O'Flaherty (1975, 317) provides an extensive bibliography of the primary texts and secondary literature on the themes of Dadhyañc's beheading and his revelation of the secret teaching.
64. MBh XII.335.54. The parallelism between this and the fate of Dadhyañc's head has been noted by Bosch (144).
65. MBh XII.329.48. Viṣṇu as the sage Vaḍavāmukha cursed the previously sweet ocean to become salty like perspiration when it refused to respond to his summons. The curse would end only when Vaḍavāmukha would rove within the ocean drinking its waters and returning them to their sweet, honeyed taste. Cf. van Gulik (11).
66. Viṣṇu, especially as he came to be identified with the Puruṣa-Nārāyaṇa of the epic, shared certain key aspects or features of Dadhyañc himself. Weber (384) long ago noted significant parallels between Puruṣa-Nārāyaṇa and Dadhyañc: both proclaimed a holy wisdom (the Vedas in Nārāyaṇa's case) by means of a horse-head. Senart (101-02) followed Weber in seeing the inseparability of the Nārāyaṇa-Puruṣa and Dadhyañc legends, and emphasizing the parallel between the thunderous yet melodic speech (*vāc*) of the two promulgators of divine wisdom. Bosch (141-45) points to further similarities, including their fierce demon-exterminating roles and their ancient association or identification with the cosmic, sacrificial Puruṣa or Prajāpati.
67. DBhP I.5.80.
68. DBhP IV.12.8. See IV.16.1 ff. for the specific *avatāras* mentioned as due to the curse.
69. MatP 47.58 ff. Muir notes in the preface to the second edition of vol. IV of his *Original Sanskrit Texts*, that the story in the MatP "contains a statement (unusual if not altogether unknown in other Indian works) in reference to Viṣṇu's incarnations, which represents seven of them as being the result of a curse uttered against the god by Śukra." Later, in giving the story, he comments: "I have not elsewhere met with an explanation of Viṣṇu's incarnations so dishonourable to the god" (153). Obviously Muir had not encountered the DBhP. The story is also found, however,

in PadP I.13.199 ff. (a nearly literal parallel to the MatP version) (cf. PadP II.121.4-7, where Bhṛgu curses Viṣṇu to ten births for failure to protect his sacrifice); LiP 29.23; BAP I.1.1.126-27 (=VāyuP I.1.1.137) and I.2.27.22. There is also a brief reference to Viṣṇu's slaying Bhṛgu's wife in RM I.24.18 and an account of Bhṛgu's curse in the Uttara Kaṇḍa (App. I.7) to explain why Viṣṇu had to endure separation from a woman. On the RM references, see Vora (206). Cf. ŚiP II.1.4.15-17, where Nārada curses Viṣṇu to suffer, in human form, the loss of a woman (i.e., to incarnate as Rāma). The story as a whole is discussed at length by Goldman (39-40, 49, 81-82, 115-16, 121, 153, 166). Cf. also Kātre (50).

70. Cf. DBhP III.20.35, 37: "This whole world is subject to fate (*daivādhīnam*). . . . This whole world is pervaded by time, karma, and inherent nature." The DBhP tends to use such terms loosely and interchangeably, and it is of interest that in I.5.4, the sages enquire of Suta how Viṣṇu lost his head through the power of fate (*daivayogāt*), a phrase glossed by Nīlakaṇṭha as "through the power of *prarabdha* karma (*prarabdhayogāt*)."
71. DBhP I.5.79.
72. It is this mantra, incidentally, that the commentator Nīlakaṇṭha identifies with the Hayagrīva-Brahmāvidyā. See note 4 above.
73. DBhP I.5.98.
74. This boon is similar to those received by other famous demonic foes of Viṣṇu like Hiraṇyakaśipu. Cf. Rao I.260.
75. The English translator has apparently misrendered "Vedas" as "Devas."
76. DBhP I.5.103.
77. DBhP I.5.109.
78. Van Gulik 19.
79. DBhP I.5.112.
80. The story is found in DBhP I.4.
81. BhP II.5-6.
82. As for the possibility of the BhP's having borrowed from the DBhP and deleting a layer of divine hierarchy, it seems most unlikely. Just as the DBhP explicitly argues for the inferior canonical status of the BhP and not vice versa, so the frame story of DBhP I.4 explicitly argues for the inferior status of Viṣṇu to the Devī, while the parallel BhP passage has no explicit reference to the inferiority of the Devī. It is difficult to see how the BhP composers could have even considered borrowing from the DBhP's account (assuming it had been in existence and available to them), since such a borrowing would appear to anyone at all familiar with both Purāṇas as quite anticlimactic.
83. DBhP I.4.39-40, 42.
84. Śeṣa is the mythological serpent of a thousand heads, upon whom Viṣṇu rests during the period of cosmic dissolution.

85. DBhP I.4.50-58.
86. DBhP I.4.59-61.
87. BhP I.8.29-30. Cf. I.3.29 where the birth of the Lord is said to be a mystery (*guhya*), and I.3.35, wherein is declared: "The poets thus describe these Veda-secrets, the births and actions of the birthless and actionless Lord of hearts."
88. BhP VIII.24.1-2.
89. BhP X.46.38-39.
90. Cf. Kātre 40-41, 52-53.
91. DBhP IV.2.18-26.
92. BhP III.31.1-17.
93. O'Flaherty (1975, 317) cites a number of ancient texts on the theme of the replacement of Viṣṇu's horse-head, but only the DBhP among the Purāṇas. As indicated earlier, the DBhP composer(s) seemed to delight in searching out relatively obscure, ancient traditions about Viṣṇu which could be put to the service of the Devī's glorification.

Chapter 3. Who Slew Vṛtrāsura? Deception, Redemption, and Grace in the Two *Bhāgavatas*

1. Śrīdhara, who provides this definition in the introduction to his commentary to the BhP, citing as his source simply "another Purāṇa," also quotes MatP 53.20-21, which declares that the Purāṇa known as "the *Bhāgavata*" includes the slaying of Vṛtrāsura among its distinguishing features.
2. It is of interest that the reference to the Vṛtra-vadha episode in DBhP I.16.34 uses the exact same phrasing as that given in the MatP: *vṛtrāsuravadhopetam*. Further, in a rather conspicuous place at the end of the first half of the Purāṇa, in the closing lines of Book VI, Vyāsa states: "Thus have I related completely [the first half of the Purāṇa], beginning with the slaying of Vṛtra. . . . The first half of the Purāṇa has been told . . . wherein the greatness of the Devī is given at length." (DBhP VI.31.56-57) (The division of the DBhP into two parts is also relevant to the canonical controversy. Two Purāṇas, the *Saura* [9.8] and the *Skandha* [Revākhaṇḍa 1.37], refer to "the *Bhāgavata*" as divided into two parts, a feature that applies only to the DBhP. Such references are almost certainly quite late, despite Sanyal's [136] suggestion to the contrary.)

   Regarding the possible conforming of the DBhP to traditional definitions of "the *Bhāgavata*," we may also note that the two *Bhāgavata*'s each commence with a verse reminiscent of the Gāyatrī mantra. Both the MatP and Śrīdhara's "other Purāṇa" state that "the *Bhāgavata*" begins with a Gāyatrī. Lalye (27) concludes that the opening verse of the DBhP "seems to have been deliberately composed . . . to conform to the characteristic of a Bhāgavata given in other Purānas—Gāyatryāh Samārambhah."

3. BhP VI.7-12.
4. DBhP VI.1-6. Lalye (28) cites the argument of certain Śāktas that since the Vṛtra story is told in greater detail in the DBhP, it has the better claim to be the "genuine" *Bhāgavata*. Such an argument is hardly persuasive, even though the BhP's version (including the earlier slaying of Vṛtra's brother Viśvarūpa and related matters, but excluding the aftermath of the Brahmanicide) runs to c. 232 verses (VI.7-12), somewhat less expansive than the DBhP's version of c. 362 verses (VI.1-6). Both versions are quite complete in their own contexts, and the BhP's is hardly "just a simple reference," as implied by the Śākta argument. I can only concur with Sanyal (131) that the Vṛtrāsura episode "is not the distinguishing characteristic of either [*Bhāgavata*]."
5. O'Flaherty 1976, 146.
6. For a recent discussion of some of the older Vedic materials, see Bulliet. For the rich flowering of the Indra-Vṛtra theme in post Vedic and epic-Purāṇic times, see van Buitenen 1978, 159-66; O'Flaherty 1976, 104-11, 146-60; Hiltebeitel 231-34.
7. Among the several versions of the Vṛtra story in the epic, the most relevant to our two Purāṇas are those found in Āraṇyaka Parva 98-99, Udyoga Parva 9-18, Droṇa Parva 69.49-65, Śānti Parva 270-74 and again Śānti 329.17-41.
8. Cf. Hospital (1984, 28-29), who gives a slightly modified pattern from mine. This general pattern, he notes, is particularly common in the accounts of Viṣṇu's major *avatāras*.
9. While Indra in the *Ṛg Veda* "has no criminal record" (Dumézil 67), in the Brāhmaṇas various misdeeds are attributed to him, including the slaying of Vṛtra and his elder brother Viśvarūpa (Dumézil 65-70; cf. Hiltebeitel 231). We can feel considerable empathy for Indra, as he is caught in the moral dilemma of trying to fulfill his duty to destroy demons, yet the demons are not remaining just demons but becoming Brahman priests, who thus under no circumstances should be killed. Ruben (116-19) examines various pre-epic texts that reveal an ongoing controversy among the ancient Brahmans as to whether or not Indra was a sinner. By epic times, Indra was almost universally regarded as an immoral god. For further discussion, see O'Flaherty 1976, 146; Choudhuri 134-35.
10. Śānti 273.10 ff.
11. Van Buitenen 1978, 166.
12. Droṇa Parva 69.49-65.
13. Śānti Parva 272.7-273.9.
14. Āraṇyaka Parva 98.3-11. Cf. Śānti Parva 329.17-27. In the latter, the story focusses on the slaying of Vṛtra's brother Triśiras, and Brahmā advises securing the bolt from Dadhīci for the destruction of this demon; later it is used on Vṛtra as well. As Hiltebeitel (233) points out, "Indra

was able to overcome a brahmin foe only by having access to another brahmin's (Dadhīca's) 'energy.'"

15. Āraṇyaka Parva 99.1-11. In this version, following Viṣṇu's example, other deities and seers infuse their own energies into Indra as well, before he engages in the final battle with Vṛtra.
16. The motif of the false peace treaty originally belonged to another of Indra's exploits, his slaying of the demon Namuci. Many commentators have thus argued that the epic "confuses" the story of Vṛtra and Namuci (e.g., Kirfel 33; E. W. Hopkins 129). Coomaraswamy (1935, 375), on the other hand, refers to Namuci as one "whose identity with Vṛtra is evident." I think Coomaraswamy's remark is far closer to the truth in suggesting the attitude of the epic composers.
17. Udyoga Parva 9-10.
18. This avoidance was already noted by Freer (300).
19. The frame story is told mainly in Śānti 270.13-272.6, with a closing reference in 274.58-59.
20. The phenomenon of the good or righteous demon in the epic has long been noted (E. W. Hopkins 129). It is not only Vṛtra but also demons like Namuci and Bali who are similarly viewed. Such interpretations loomed ever larger in the later *bhakti* movements, to the extent that certain demons became the highest models of true devotion. On the "paradox of the good demon" (O'Flaherty's phrase), see Hospital's brilliant study on Bali; see also Ruben 115-16; O'Flaherty 1976, 94-138.
21. Śānti 271.57.
22. E. W. Hopkins (129) comments that Vṛtra's conversion to Vaiṣṇavism "astonished even the late pietist" who composed the Śānti account.
23. Śānti 272.2-4.
24. Śānti 274.57-58.
25. Freer (298-302) long ago compared the accounts in the Āraṇyaka and Udyoga Parvans of the epic with the BhP's version but was apparently unaware of the other epic sources.
26. BhP VI.9.51-54.
27. BhP VI.7.39-40; VI.9.53-54; VI.12.31. Cf. Droṇa 69.62-65.
28. Cf. Śānti 273.9 and 329.27 with BhP VI.10.13.
29. BhP VI.10.14-VI.12.35.
30. BhP VI.11.14. In Śānti 329.17, Viśvarūpa appears as the priest (*purohita*) of the gods. (The BhP relies on the account in Śānti 329.17 ff., as well as on Udyoga 9.3 ff., for its version of the slaying of Viśvarūpa.) In the BhP, Viśvarūpa not only serves the gods as their priest (VI.9.1-2), but also teaches Indra the Nārāyaṇa Kavaca (VI.7.40; VI.8.42). Indra's sin of Brahmanicide is thus magnified by the foul deed of murdering his own guru.
31. BhP VI.11.19-20.

32. BhP VI.11.24-27.
33. BhP VI.12.20.
34. Udyoga 9.45-49.
35. BhP VI.12.31. The text reads: *mahāpuruṣa-sannaddho yogamāyābalena ca*. Śrīdhara glosses "*mahāpuruṣa-sannaddho*" as "armored by Śrī Nārāyaṇa in the form of the Kavaca."
36. BhP VI.12.35. The term *aloka* is glossed by Śrīdhara as "Bhagavat, the Lord."
37. BhP VI.13.
38. BhP VI.13.7-9.
39. It is interesting to note here an ancient parallel to the BhP's absolution of Indra through devotion. In the *Kauṣītakī Upaniṣad* (3.1), Indra declares to King Pratardana that he has slain Tvaṣṭṛ's son Triśiras, has broken agreements (as he does with Vṛtra according to the Udyoga account), and has committed various other sins, yet not a hair of his has been injured. Indra explains: "He who knows me thus is not injured by any act, not by stealing, not by murdering an embryo [as Ruben (118-19) points out in analyzing this passage, commentators have often interpreted *brūṇa* (embryo) to mean a Brahman], nor by slaying one's mother or father." Indra further clarifies that he is the Ātman, the Self, which does not become great by good action nor small by evil action (3.8). Accordingly, one who knows the highest Self is not stained, a familiar doctrine of the Upaniṣads here applied to Indra's infamous misdeeds. The *Bhāgavata*, then, has reinterpreted this mystical, saving knowledge that transcends good and evil in terms of *bhakti*.
40. BhP VI.14-17.
41. See Kurulkar 82-83, Choudhuri 189-90, O'Flaherty 1976, 110.
42. O'Flaherty 1980(a), 13-14.
43. O'Flaherty's interpretation of the curse episode is somewhat different. She summarizes the account (1976, 110): "He [Citraketu] propitiated her [Pārvatī], pointing out that he was a devotee of Viṣṇu, and she mitigated her curse. He was born as Vṛtra, son of Tvaṣṭṛ, but he remained a devotee of Viṣṇu." The text actually does not mention Pārvatī's mitigating the curse, and the tone of the story is quite different. Citraketu says quite specifically that he propitiates Pārvatī not to be released from the curse, but simply to receive forgiveness for what she considered to be unjustly spoken (VI.17.24). It is Citraketu's complete acceptance of the curse, as ultimately the handiwork of Viṣṇu, that marks him as a true devotee. That Vṛtra retains his wisdom and devotion, gained in his life as Citraketu, is not apparently due to any mitigation of the curse but rather, I suggest, to the grace of the Lord. To be sure, the text does not specifically acknowledge this, either, but the underlying current of the whole Citraketu/Vṛtra cycle is the divine grace of the Lord.
44. For an illuminating discussion of this idea of "Killed But Saved" in the BhP, see Hospital 1978, 202-12. Hospital focusses on the demon devotee's

attitude (emphasizing the complementarity of hate and love), but he also points out: "If attachment [to the Lord] can be in positive or negative modes, so also the Lord's favour. To some the gracious act is punishing, taming, humbling; indeed it may be seen as particularly gracious in that the one so treated is liberated from attachment to pride and wealth and other infatuating paraphernalia of the world" (212).

45. BhP VI.11.20.

46. Hospital 1984, 52.

47. DBhP IV.24.46-47.

48. BhP VI.12.31.

49. Śrīdhara glosses the phrase "by the force of *yoga-māyā*" as "*yogabalena māyābalena ca*," interpreting *yoga-māyā* as two distinct powers and thus hardly the name of a single goddess as the DBhP would have it.

50. Cf. e.g., Yoganidrā.

51. RV VI.61.7.

52. DM 11.19.

53. In the preface to his commentary on the DBhP, Nīlakaṇṭha quotes the following line from the *Āditya Purāṇa*, from its introduction to the story of the slaying of the demon Rakta: *yā jaghne mahiṣaṃ daityaṃ krūraṃ vṛtrāsuraṃ tathā/ sādya raktāsuraṃ hatvā svārājyaṃ te pradāsyati//*

54. In the preface to his commentary, Nīlakaṇṭha, writes, *na hi devībhāgavatātiriktasarvapurāṇeṣu devīkṛto vṛtrāsuravadhaḥ kvacit apy asti// indrakṛtasyaiva tasya sattvāt kevalaṃ devībhāgavata eva devīkṛtaḥ so 'sti//*

55. The verbal similarities between DBhP VI.1 ff. and the Udyoga version clearly refutes Lalye's contention (103) that the Vṛtra story in the DBhP "must have been taken from" an original "Bhāgavata" text.

56. Udyoga 9.21.

57. DBhP VI.2.3.

58. DBhP VI.2.18.

59. DBhP VI.1.52.

60. DBhP VI.3.40-VI.4.12.

61. DBhP VI.3.48.

62. DBhP VI.4.8.

63. E. W. Hopkins 194.

64. DBhP IV.11.36.

65. Śānti 272.36-37.

66. Śalya 42.28-37. For discussion of Namuci in the early literature, see Bloomfield; Dumézil 29-32; Hillebrandt II.148-50.

67. It is not clear exactly how the foam works, but it is obviously not your usual kind of weapon and thus does not transgress the terms of the agreement or treaty. For one early and ingenious attempt to explain

the foam, see Lanman, who argues that the foam originally (in RV VIII. 14.13) was not a weapon at all but descriptive of Namuci as a waterspout demon, accompanied by foam (*phenena*), whom Indra slew. The later tradition, Lanman argues, misinterpreted the instrumental of accompaniment as an actual instrumental of means. Bloomfield (156-58) rejects Lanman's naturalistic interpretation and suggests that the foam was indeed a means, employed in ancient witchcraft practices to overcome or kill an enemy, comparable to the use of lead, which is "soft . . . and has much the same color as foam." (158) In the epic, Namuci is slain with the foam alone (IX.42.31), but Vṛtra is slain by the foam along with the thunderbolt (V.10.38), which then seems to violate the terms of the treaty. But, as van Buitenen (1978, 162) points out, "the tradition that Vṛtra was slain and that the deed was accomplished by Indra's thunderbolt was ineradicable." In the Udyoga account, the effective killing power of the foam is related to the notion that Viṣṇu enters into it.

68. BhP VIII.11.19-42.

69. Udyoga 9.50cd reads: *yadā vyavardhata raṇe vṛtro balasamanvitaḥ*. DBhP VI.4.41ab revises: *yadā vyavardhata raṇe vṛtro varamadāvṛtaḥ*.

70. DBhP VI.4.56.

71. DBhP VI.5.19. It is instructive to compare Viṣṇu's advice in the DBhP with Duryodhana's argument in the epic concerning the law of kings (*rāja-dharma*): "In friendship, Indra made a compact with Namuci and then cut off his head. For him, that was the eternal way with a foe." (Sabhā 50.20) (Cf. Dumézil 32.) Similarly, the follower of Kauṭilya, Kāmandaka, maintained "that a king under certain circumstances must even kill his own ally, just as Indra slew Triśiras . . . and a clever king shall never trust his enemy even if he is bound by a treaty, just as Indra slew Vṛtra while openly declaring cessation of enmity." (Quoted by Ruben 120.) The DBhP thus portrays Viṣṇu as a model Kauṭilyan.

72. DBhP VI.5.29-30.

73. DBhP VI.5.55.

74. DBhP VI.5.58.

75. The DBhP inserts another intriguing theme into the seers' arguments. They contend that only heroes with a taste for battle foolishly praise war, not the learned. Those who are expert in love realize how war destroys the body, making it unfit for pleasure. Thus, the wise will not fight even with flowers, let alone with sharpened arrows (VI.6.8-15). This argument, used here to pacify Vṛtra, is the same argument frequently employed by the demons to try to seduce the Goddess in the Mahiṣa and Śumbha-Niśumbha myths, as we shall see in the next chapter.

76. Udyoga 10.29-30; DBhP VI.6.33-34.

77. Both the epic (V.10.34) and Purāṇa (VI.6.50) use the term *boon* (*vara*) at this point. In the former case, it seems it can only refer to the truce itself,

as there is no other "boon" in the Udyoga account. Perhaps this stray reference was yet another suggestive hint to the DBhP compiler(s) to create the full-bodied account of Brahmā's earlier boon to Vṛtra.

78. The "terrible twilight" (*sandhyā . . . raudrā* [Udyoga 10.34; DBhP VI.6.51]) is explained by O'Flaherty (1975, 77): "The twilight, which plays such an important role in Hindu cosmogony, appears here as a moment of mediation and ambivalence, in conjunction with other oppositional pairs including Vṛtra, who . . . is half brahmin and half anti-god." A further ambivalence may be noted, in that the word *twilight* (*sandhyā*) also means an agreement or promise, and is closely related to the actual word often used for the treaty, *sandhi*, which in turn can mean twilight, or an opportune time, as well as a breach or hole. The terrible twilight thus suggests the truce, and at the same time, by its own nature (being neither day nor night), indicates the opening that Indra seeks.
79. Udyoga 10.12; cf. DBhP VI.5.14, 17.
80. DBhP VI.6.62-68.
81. DBhP VI.6.67-68.
82. DBhP X.13.93-94.
83. As Ruben (115, 122) points out, Viṣṇu in helping Indra in the epic accounts acts much like Kṛṣṇa in aiding the Pāṇḍavas, advising them to deceive the enemy. And while Yudhiṣṭhira, leader of the Pāṇḍavas, goes to hell for following Kṛṣṇa's advice, Kṛṣṇa himself suffers nothing. It is not surprising, then, that Viṣṇu remains free from the consequences of Vṛtra's death. In the RM version of the Vṛtra story (VII.75-76), we can perhaps see the beginning of the extrication of Viṣṇu from involvement in the affair. When requested to kill Vṛtra by the gods, he demurs, saying a long-standing tie of friendship binds him to the noble demon, though he will give advice on how to overcome the *asura*. In MārkP 5, the false treaty is mentioned as Indra's idea, with no reference to Viṣṇu. For discussion of the MārkP version, see Dumézil 72-81, who discerns in the three sins of Indra mentioned in the account, as one would expect of Dumézil, offenses against each of the three orders or functions of Indo-European society.
84. There are several other significant revisions that the DBhP makes in the Udyoga's account of the aftermath. In the Udyoga, even after Indra is purified by the horse-sacrifice and returns from the waters where he had hidden in panic to escape his guilt, he is frightened by the ambitious Nahuṣa, who had been installed on the throne of heaven as his replacement during his absence. Indra disappears once again, this time into a lotus stalk. Indra's wife, Śacī, harassed by Nahuṣa, tries to find her husband, and is able to do so after worshipping the goddess Night (Rātri, Niśā), who, as Upaśruti (the nocturnal voice revealing the future), discloses Indra's hiding place to her. In the *Devī-Bhāgavata*, the goddess Night is replaced by the supreme Devī herself, with extensive elaboration of the incident, and

Devī plays a crucial role in the downfall of Nahuṣa, performing the necessary delusion that we have come to expect for overcoming an upstart and arrogant foe. Once again, the DBhP Paurāṇika discovers the hand of the Devī where previously it had been unnoticed.

85. BhP VI.9.26; cf. verse 40. The gods here are clearly echoing Kṛṣṇa's own words in BhG 4.6-8.

86. BhP VII.2.9.

87. BhP VIII.19.8.

88. BhP VIII.20.4.

89. BhP VIII.21.10-11.

90. DBhP V.33.49.

91. DBhP V.3.36-37.

92. DBhP IV.15.49.

93. DBhP III.16.43-44.

94. DBhP IV.4.17-21. See also IV.15.62-63: "By Hari, taking the form of a dwarf, knowing fraud (*chala*), Bali was deceived (*vañcito*)."

95. DBhP VI.1.23.

96. A nice example of the distinction between delusion and deception is found in Viṣṇu's own words to the gods as he explains how the Devī helped him in the past: "Formerly I slew, after a fierce battle of five thousand years, the demons Madhu and Kaiṭabha. [To accomplish this,] I eagerly praised the supreme Prakṛti, who became pleased. Then those two Daityas were deluded (*mohitau*) [by the Devī], and through a fraud (*chalena*) by me they were slain." (DBhP V.5.28-29)

97. DBhP IV.7.40; IV.10.17-23; V.1.35-36.

98. DBhP V.1.39-40.

99. DBhP V.1.47.

100. DBhP IV.4.34-37; IV.7.40.

101. DBhP VI.1.25.

102. DBhP IV.4.34-35; IV.10.21; V.1.35; VI.25.1.

103. DBhP VI.5.39.

104. Regarding the seeming contradiction between the notions of karma and the ideals of *bhakti* that is characteristic of the Purāṇas as a whole, O'Flaherty (1980[a], 13) has pointed out: "The doctrine of karma is a straw man in the Purāṇas: it is set up in order to be knocked down." She further indicates (1980[a], 27) that while the Purāṇas refer to a number of means by which karma may be conquered, including charity (especially to Brahmans), yoga and meditation, pilgrimage and rites, it is devotion to God that becomes the primary means in the later Purāṇic texts, "when *bhakti* is in full flower." It is noteworthy that O'Flaherty draws a number of her illustrations for the themes of karma and fate from the DBhP.

105. Śrīdhara glosses the word *karma* by "*pravṛtti-mārgam*" (the path of active or worldly life).

106. BhP VI.9.48-50.

107. Hospital (1978, 212) also notes the renunciatory emphasis of the BhP as a whole: "[the] *Bhāgavata* continually encourages an attitude of *vairāgya*, detachment, [and] is at pains to free the devotee from attachment to or infatuation by *prakṛti*, the senses, body, home and family, wealth (4.20.6, 4.29.36, 5.9.12, 6.1.56, etc.)."

108. DBhP V.1.38-39.

109. DBhP IV.25.68-71. The BhP, of course, also sees the Lord as the ultimate controller of human destiny, and thus the director of karma, as in IV.11.19-26 (a passage discussed by O'Flaherty [1980(a), 23-24]). But the point of such passages in the BhP tends to be the independence of the Lord as total master of the universe and his freedom from karma, not his compassion in creating the world in the first place.

110. BhP VI.12.21.

111. BhP VI.14.1-2.

112. DBhP VI.1.5-7.

113. Cf. O'Flaherty 1980(b), 77.

Chapter 4. The Three Great Adventures of the Devī: Heroic Eroticism and Maternal Compassion

1. Specifically, the Madhu-Kaiṭabha myth appears in I.6-9, while the remaining two *caritras* and the frame story appear in V.2-20, V.21-31, and V.32-35, respectively.

2. DBhP X.10-12.

3. DBhP V.32.1.

4. DBhP V.34.12; cf. V.35.16.

5. The Devī declares: "Whoever narrates in praise the [story of the] destruction of Madhu and Kaiṭabha, the slaying of Mahiṣa, and the killing of Śumbha and Niśumbha . . . and whoever hears this 'Māhātmya' of mine . . . shall be free of all misfortunes." (DM 12.3-5)

6. See note 10 below.

7. Lalye 52.

8. Sharma, in comparing the verbal similarities between the DM and the DBhP, argues for the fairly evident conclusion that the DBhP is the later text, but on sometimes shaky grounds. He correctly points out many of the themes that are found in the DBhP and not in the DM, but then suggests that wherever the DBhP diverges from the DM "one can almost sense the presence of extraneous matter" (109). He

thus concludes that many of the new themes (relative to the DM) did not belong to the original version. In fact, some of the themes he so regards are almost certainly older than the DM. And further, while they may be extraneous to the DM, they are integral to certain early versions such as those found in the VāmP and VarP.

9. DBhP V.33.65; X.10.20.
10. One clear reference to the DM text itself is found in the ninth Skandha of the DBhP. As already indicated, this Skandha is largely a borrowing from the "Prakṛti Khaṇḍa" of the BVP and is a late addition to the DBhP. In the last chapter (DBhP IX.50), there occurs the typical kind of "patch-work" to smooth over the seams of the interpolation. Within this patchwork is a description of the worship of Devī or Durgā, including the recitation of the "Saptaśatī-stotra" (verse 86), a relatively late designation of the DM referring to its supposed length of seven hundred verses (a rather arbitrary reckoning as a quick perusal of any edition of the text will readily show).
11. In this regard, it is worth noting the similarity of the first DBhP reference to the "Devī Māhātmya" with a parallel remark in the DM. In both cases the sage has just concluded his recitation of the deeds of the Devī: *etat te sarvam ākhyātaṃ devīmāhātmyam uttamam* (DBhP V.33.35); *etat te kathitaṃ bhūpa devīmāhātmyam uttamam* (DM 13.2).
12. DM 1.67-104.
13. DBhP I.6.20-I.9.84.
14. The DBhP inserts one entire chapter (I.8) at this point extolling the Devī as the supreme power, beyond the Trimūrti. As the discussion of Devī's power is carried on only by the final interlocutors of the Purāṇa (the seers and Sūta) and not by the participants within the myth, I have not included it in the summary.
15. DBhP I.6.37.
16. The seven major *devāsura* conflicts concern the slaying of Hayagrīva (I.5), Madhu and Kaiṭabha (I.6-9), Mahiṣa (V.2-20), Śumbha and Niśumbha (V.21-31), Vṛtra (VI.1-6), Durgama (VII.28), and Aruṇa (X.13).
17. DBhP I.9.35-36.
18. DBhP I.9.54-56.
19. MS 7.199.
20. MS 7.198, 200; cf. 7.107-09.
21. Cf. MS 7.105, 169-74.
22. DBhP I.7.6.
23. MS 7.160.
24. MS 7.169-74.
25. DBhP I.7.36.

26. DBhP I.7.46-47.
27. DBhP I.9.10-11.
28. DBhP I.9.23.
29. MS 7.91-93.
30. DM 1.94-95.
31. DM 1.97-98.
32. HV App. I.41 lines 1325-44; cf. Coburn 1984(a), 220.
33. See MBh III.194.8 ff. and HV App. I.41, lines 378 ff., esp. line 384; cf. Coburn 1984(a), 220.
34. MBh III.194.8-30.
35. MBh III.194.21.
36. Coburn 1984(a), 214-15.
37. DBhP I.9.51-52.
38. DM 1.94; DBhP I.9.58.
39. DM 1.97-98; DBhP I.9.72.
40. As always, it is nearly impossible to say whether the DBhP borrowed directly from the extant VāmP and VarP, or from an intermediary or some other common source belonging to the general family of these Purāṇic versions of the myth. Thus my statement should be taken as meaning that the DBhP's Mahiṣa myth is based on models that are related, more or less directly, to the versions of the myth found in the extant VāmP and VarP.
41. Kane V. 155.
42. I here refer to the first *Vāmana* version of the Mahiṣa myth (chaps. 19-21), in which the Goddess slays the demon, rather than to the second version (chaps. 31-32), in which Skanda is the vanquisher.
43. See Kapadia 181. The VāmP knows only the last two great deeds of the Goddess and in general, as Coburn (1984[a], 249) suggests, its Devī mythology appears to represent a transitional stage between epic and DM or post DM phases. Regarding the place of the VarP in these developments, von Stietencron, in a marvelous analysis of the Mahiṣa myths in the Purāṇas, gives a different order from mine. He divides the Purāṇic texts into two basic groups, earlier and later, with the DM, VāmP and DBhP belonging to the earlier, and the VarP to the later (122, 140). He does so on the basis that the earlier group views the Devī as generated from the united energy of the gods and thus implicitly makes her dependent upon them. For the later group, the Devī is uncreated, no mere product of the powers of the gods (122). I disagree with this developmental scheme, for it seems to me that in both the DM and DBhP, the Goddess is clearly uncreated and independent, and that the birth from the energy of the gods is an account only of the origin of one of her manifestations. I accept

that such an origin could be misinterpreted as suggesting a certain subordination, but the fact that a text like the DBhP retains the theme is not proof that it belongs to an earlier developmental stage. In any case, the VarP describes the Goddess as arising out of the united vision of the Trimūrti, and thus, by von Stietencron's reasoning, should belong to the earlier group.

44. DM 2-4.
45. DBhP V.2-20.
46. VāmP 18-21.
47. VarP 89, 91-94.
48. The *rasas* or "sentiments" play an important role in the DBhP, and we shall discuss them in detail below.
49. A fabulous beast with eight legs and more powerful than a lion.
50. Of the four versions, the VāmP's conclusion, in which the Devī reenters the gods, is the least complimentary to the Goddess. But the DM's conclusion is not explicit in showing the ongoing and independent nature of the Devī, though this is clearly the intent given the total context of the DM. As Coburn (1984[a], 247) says: "The DM allows for her on-going and unique reality by saying simply, but suggestively, 'she vanished.'" The DBhP, as usual, is not satisfied with mere suggestion and thus indicates explicitly that the Devī does not just reenter the gods or merely vanish, but goes back to reign in her supreme abode.
51. DBhP V.2.1-V.9.35.
52. For an insightful analysis of the buffalo demon's ancestry, see von Stietencron 124-27. Mahiṣa's ancestry is an important clue to the changing valuation of his relationship to the Devī. Von Stietencron's overall view that Mahiṣa becomes transformed from an enemy of the Goddess to her devotee is certainly correct, but the historical stages he suggests are less certain. A similar change in regards to Vṛtra, for instance, is already found in the late portions of the MBh, and thus the motif of a demon-devotee has quite early roots.
53. VarP 94.13.
54. DBhP V.2.12-13.
55. R. K. Narayan, in retelling the DBhP's version of the Mahiṣa story, refers to this boon of the buffalo-chief as the strangest of all the demonly requests for averting death (50).
56. DBhP V.9.36-V.18.53.
57. DBhP V.18.54-V.20.
58. The demons do not yet recognize her divine stature, and so the word *devī* seems best rendered as "noble lady" rather than "goddess."
59. DBhP V.10.18-19.

60. DBhP V.10.32-35.
61. DBhP V.9.53.
62. DBhP V.11.11.
63. DBhP V.11.3.
64. DBhP V.11.41.
65. See MS 7.63-67.
66. DBhP V.12.33-38
67. DBhP V.15.16-17.
68. DBhP V.10.2.
69. MS 7.77.
70. DBhP V.16.21-23.
71. Cf. O'Flaherty 1980(b), 164.
72. MS 7.56-57.
73. DBhP V.11.11.
74. DBhP V.11.18-29.
75. Compare, for example, the words of Asilomā to the Devī after observing her handiwork in the battlefield: "Fate, indeed, I consider supreme. Fie on our worthless manliness [*pauruṣam*, a word that also means human effort and heroic prowess]; the *dānavas* fall quickly to the ground when struck by your arrows." (V.15.43) See also the words of Śumbha in the next myth: "Fate, indeed, I consider supreme. Fie on our worthless manliness; Niśumbha, conqueror of all the gods, is slain by a woman." (V.31.8)
76. DBhP V.11.36.
77. We may recall the similar words of Madhu and Kaiṭabha to Viṣṇu in the first episode.
78. DBhP V.10.36. In the third great adventure, Śumbha makes a similar comment to his younger brother Niśumbha (V.25.49).
79. DBhP V.11.49.
80. DBhP V.14.15-16.
81. DBhP V.12.4-8.
82. DBhP V.16.35-37.
83. DBhP I.7.29.
84. DBhP V.19.28-29.
85. Nīlakaṇṭha makes this comment on V.16.35 (where the Devī is speaking to Mahiṣa), and a very similar comment on V.12.6 (where she is addressing Tāmra).
86. DBhP V.15.19-24.
87. DBhP V.16.26-32.
88. DBhP V.9.54. The *rasas* are usually eight in number. In addition to the

above mentioned, there is also compassionate sorrow (*karuṇa*), fear (*bhayānaka*), and abhorrence (*bībhatsa*). Sometimes a ninth is added, peace (*śānta*). The DBhP assumes there are nine, as we shall see in dealing with the Śumbha-Niśumbha myth.

89. Lalye 307.
90. Lalye 305. Lalye actually makes this assertion with reference to both *Bhāgavatas*.
91. DM 5-11.
92. DBhP V.21-31.
93. The Devī's condition for accepting the marriage proposal, incidentally, may well be derived from the VāmP's version of the Mahiṣa myth (see the Mahiṣa parallels above, #16), though the VāmP makes the condition of her being conquered in battle a bride price (*śulka*), rather than a promise or vow (*pratijñā*).
94. In the Śumbha episode, the erotic interpretation of the Devī's martial challenge is presented by the demon Dhūmralocana directly to the Goddess herself (V.24.46-57). He insists to her face that what she really means by the word *battle* is not actual combat but amorous fighting, in which his master will conquer her and exhaust her on the bed of pleasure, and will bloody her body with lovers' scratches and lip-bites.
95. DBhP V.25.37.
96. DBhP V.25.44.
97. DBhP V.27.19-23.
98. DBhP V.29.47.
99. DBhP V.30.47.
100. DBhP V.30.55.
101. DBhP V.30.48 and 57.
102. DBhP V.30.60.
103. DBhP V.26.21-22.
104. DBhP V.23.60.
105. DBhP V.23.55-56.
106. DBhP V.26.19-20.
107. This is in contrast to the DM version of the Mahiṣa myth. See, e.g., DM 2.52-53.
108. DBhP V.25.5-6.
109. Cf. DM 6.13 and DBhP V.25.22.
110. DBhP V.25.32 and 47.
111. DBhP V.30.18.
112. DBhP V.31.23.
113. DBhP V.31.36-38.

114. DBhP V.31.48.
115. DBhP V.24.1.
116. DBhP V.24.7.
117. The DM does not say where Raktabīja gained his extraordinary power. The DBhP, typically, attributes it to a boon, in this case received from Śiva (V.29.1-3; cf. V.21.34-37).
118. DBhP V.27.56-57.
119. Babb 220-21.
120. Babb 221.
121. Coburn 1984(a), 253.
122. DM 1.64-66.
123. E.g., DM 1.80-81; 4.26; 5.13.
124. Cf. the observations of Payne (40) made over half a century ago: "In it [the DM] there are . . . descriptions of the terrifying appearance of the goddess, but appeals are also made to her tenderer aspects, and a deep faith in her power is evidenced. . . . In this fierce framework [of the bloody exploits of the Devī] there are passages breathing deep religious feeling and enthusiastic adoration."
125. The "Brahmā-stuti" in DM 1.73-87 and the "Yā Devī" hymn in 5.9-82.
126. The "Śakrādi-stuti" in DM 4.3-27 and the "Nārāyaṇī-stuti" in 11.3-35.
127. DM 4.34-35.
128. DBhP V.19.36-37.
129. See BhG 17.11-22.
130. For a discussion of the ideal of "motiveless" *bhakti* in the BhP and the BVP, see C. M. Brown 93-96.
131. Babb 225-26.
132. Wadley 121.
133. Coburn 1982, 163. Coburn is talking of the DM only, but his observation seems to me equally valid for the DBhP, not withstanding the Devī's claim to Mahiṣa that the supreme Puruṣa is her husband. On the one hand, this Puruṣa is rather abstract and does not significantly affect the Devī's actions in any substantial way, the claim being made for Mahiṣa's benefit, primarily. On the other, we have seen the Devī more or less directly identify herself with the Puruṣa, and moreover, in the Śumbha myth she denies quite explicitly that she has any husband.
134. This is made clear in a story about two of the wives of the Trimūrti who are insulted by their husbands, despite the Devī's warning that the goddesses are never to be treated with disrespect (III.6.34 and 51). The story (given in VII.29.19—VII.30.19) begins with reference to the Devī's gift to the Trimūrti of the three *śakti*s, here referred to as Gaurī, Lakṣmī, and Sarasvatī, in ancient times. It is then told how Śiva and Viṣṇu once

conquered some mighty demons, and after the two gods returned home they bragged to their wives about their prowess, when in fact it was the *śakti*s of Gaurī and Lakṣmī who were responsible. (This clearly resembles the story of the humbling of the gods in the KU and its reinterpretation in DBhP XII.8, referred to in chapter two above.) Lakṣmī and Gaurī laughed at their husbands' presumption, evoking abusive contempt in response. Thus insulted, the goddesses vanished, leaving the two gods powerless, bewildered, and finally unconscious, forcing Brahmā, who had not insulted Sarasvatī, to carry out all three cosmic functions. Much distressed by his overload of work, Brahmā appealed to the supreme Devī, who graciously restored Viṣṇu and Śiva to health and sanity, having removed their false pride.

135. For further discussion and critique of the marriage control model, see Gatwood, especially 1-5, 108-20.

136. Shulman 1980. 223.

137. Shulman 1980, 225.

138. Shulman 1980, 226.

139. See, for instance, DBhP V.10.59, where the prime minister reports to Mahiṣa the following words of the Goddess: "That worst of brutes, born of the womb of a she-buffalo, I shall give as a sacrificial victim to the Devī for the benefit of the gods."

140. DM 10.3.

141. Shulman 1980, 141.

142. The second androgynous form of the Devī is suggested by her absorption of the seed/power of her masculine victim, who thereby loses his virility in an exchange of vital power. Given the insistence of our text that the Devī is the source of all power, this latter form of androgyny is less relevant to our investigation. To be sure, there are allusions in the DBhP to the Devī's depriving her male partner/victim of his virility, but these allusions are made only by the demons. Further, it would be a matter more of her withdrawing *her own* inherent power from him, rather than of absorbing *his* power, should such an erotic exchange take place, which does not.

143. Shulman 1980, 295.

144. O'Flaherty 1980(b), 82-83.

145. Cf. O'Flaherty 1980(b), 127.

146. DBhP V.19.38-40.

147. ŚU 4.6-7.

148. MuU III.1.1-2.

149. MuU III.1.3.

150. Cf. BhP XI.11.6-7, where the same metaphor is employed to emphasize the ignorance and knowledge of the two birds, respectively, and their consequent states of bondage and liberation.

151. Nīlakaṇṭha's commentary on DBhP V.19.39. The DBhP's interpretation of the Upaniṣadic metaphor makes me take exception to Lalye's statement that "the Devī is never approached as a friend or lover. The awe and respect created by Her Tāmasa exploits, always keep the devotees at a distance. Sakhya [friendship] is not possible with the Devī. Though She showers kindness on all those who approach Her with humility and submission, She is always an object of fear and reverence" (305). Often, perhaps, but not always. Lalye is quite right, though, in saying that the Devī is never approached as a lover—except, of course, by the ignorant demon suitors.
152. Nīlakaṇṭha's commentary on V.19.40.
153. Chaudhuri 33. I have edited the passage to clean up the grammar and style, but have made no substantive changes to what he has said.
154. DM 4.18-23.
155. DM 4.22.
156. Narayan 62-63.
157. DBhP V.19.21.
158. DBhP V.19.10.

Chapter 5. The Great Manifestations of the Devī: Mahā-Kālī, Mahā-Lakṣmī, Mahā-Sarasvatī

1. For the use of these terms in the text, see DM 1.104 and 1.65, respectively.
2. Desai (149-53) illustrates my point well. Focussing on the births of the Goddess in the DM rather than on her deeds, Desai argues that there are five accounts of the origins or incarnations of the Goddess. The first *carita*, according to her, does not actually "constitute an origin but is only a statement of her [the Devī's] exploit" (149). The five accounts are: 1) the origin of Mahiṣāsura-Mardinī from the combined *tejas* of the gods; 2) the arising of Kauśikī from Pārvatī's body; 3) the springing forth of Kālī from the forehead of Ambikā; 4) the arising of Caṇḍikā-śakti from Devī; and 5) the various future incarnations of the Goddess.
3. DM 11.54-55.
4. As Coburn writes (1984[a], 304), the DM "is explicit about establishing the transcendent status of the Goddess at the very outset of its account, and . . . it does so by incorporating the familiar Madhu-Kaiṭabha myth."
5. See Coburn, 1984(a), 306; Coburn elsewhere (1982, 163-65) provides a somewhat more complex analysis of the relationship between the three *caritas* and various religious movements.
6. DM 1.104.
7. DBhP X.11.33-34.

8. DM 4.40-41.
9. DBhP X.12.35.
10. DM 12.36.
11. Cf. also DM 11.54-55, quoted above.
12. Sumedhas is the DBhP's name for Medhas, the sage of the frame story.
13. DBhP X.12.81-82.
14. The prefix "Mahā-" is occasionally left off, especially with Sarasvatī (in the latter case, often for metrical reasons, as her name already consists of four syllables). The context within the DBhP usually makes it clear whether or not a Mahā-Devī or her "diminutive" counterpart is signified.
15. See Schrader 62, 67 and C. M. Brown 148.
16. See Hazra 1958, 269, 273 and C. M. Brown 148.
17. DM 1.75, 78, 83-84.
18. DM 12.39.
19. DBhP X.12.82-83.
20. As with most matters of Purāṇic chronology, the dating of these correlations in absolute terms is a hazardous venture, though dating relative to other texts is *sometimes* possible. In this regard, we may note the account of the Devī's great deeds in the Umā-Saṃhitā (chaps. 45-50) of the ŚiP. The Umā-Saṃhitā account is quite close to the DBhP's version in X.10-12, and like the latter, correlates the three deeds with the Mahā-Devīs. The Umā-Saṃhitā, however, sees the three Mahā-Devīs as manifestations of Umā. Further, the story of Umā's appearance before the gods to curb their pride (based on the KU myth) is added (in chap. 49) as illustrative of Umā's supremacy. The Umā-Saṃhitā's account of Umā's manifestation again is very close to the DBhP's version in XII.8. It seems that one text has borrowed from the other, though it is possible that they both utilized another, common source. In any case, the DBhP's version is clearly closer in overall structure to the DM's, and my general impression in comparing the accounts in the DBhP and the ŚiP is that the latter has borrowed from the former.

    This impression is bolstered by the fact that just prior to the Umā-Saṃhitā's narration of the three deeds, in a listing of the eighteen Mahā-Purāṇas, the fifth is described in the following terms (chap. 44, verse 129): *bhagavatyāś ca durgāyāś caritaṃ yatra vidyate/ tat tu bhāgavataṃ proktaṃ na tu devī-purāṇakam//* ("Wherein are found the deeds of the Bhagavatī Durgā, that is declared to be the *Bhāgavata*, not the *Devī-Purāṇa*.") This verse is quoted by Nīlakaṇṭha in the preface to his DBhP commentary, ascribing it to the Uttara-khaṇḍa of the (Bengal) ŚiP. (The verse, as found in certain modern editions, substitutes *"nanu"* for *"na tu"* [see e.g., the Nag edition, Umā-Saṃhitā 44.129; cf. Jha, who quotes the latter version from the Veṅkaṭeśvara edition].) Nīlakaṇṭha argues that the ŚiP is here referring to the DBhP. If we accept Nīlakaṇṭha's reading, then the Umā-Saṃhitā seems to reveal its knowledge of the DBhP (though it is always possible that its list of Purāṇas is a very late addition to what is already a late insertion into the ŚiP). Cf. also Hazra (1963, 79, 194, 242), who quotes this verse in contrast to those who claimed the *Devī-Purāṇa* was "the real Bhāgavata." Hazra, however, argues that the verse points to the *Kālikā-Purāṇa*. Sanyal (137), on the other hand, sees it as referring to the DBhP.

21. Hazra dates the "Triśakti-Māhātmya" as no later than 1400 in his discussion of the VarP (1936, 104-05). He gives the same later limit for the Sṛṣṭi Khaṇḍa of the PadP (1936, 125), whose 35th chapter is an adaptation of VarP 91-95, which must therefore be somewhat earlier. The earlier limit for the Sṛṣṭi Khaṇḍa and the VarP chapters Hazra does not state, but A. D. 800-900 seems to be implied. According to Kane (V.155), as we have already noted, the story of Mahiṣa that is found in this "Triśakti-Māhātmya" is apparently "the earliest Paurāṇika version" of the myth, a view which seems to me quite probable. Of course, the "Triśakti-Māhātmya" as a whole may not be as old as some of its parts. Nonetheless, it seems likely that the "Triśakti-Māhātmya" predates the DBhP by at least two or three centuries. O'Flaherty (1975, 17-18) suggests an approximate date of A. D. 750 for the VarP as a whole. Cf. the introduction to the critical edition of the VarP (1981, 27).
22. VarP 89.18.
23. VarP 89.22.
24. VarP 89.25.
25. VarP 95.59.
26. VarP 94.67.
27. VarP 95.55.
28. VarP 95.57.
29. VarP 95.62.
30. Hazra 1936, 101.
31. VarP 89.40-41.
32. VarP 95.33-38.
33. VarP 95.70-71.
34. VarP 95.72. The last part of verse 72 reads: "They will attain those [*saktis*] who know the mantra of the Devī, there is no doubt." As we shall see, the Devī's mantra has particular importance for the DBhP's final development of the Mahā-Devī scheme.
35. We shall deal with these limbs in detail below. The Six Limbs are given in the Delhi and Calcutta editions of the DM.
36. For a fuller summary of the "Prādhānika-Rahasya," see Banerjea 496-97. Bhattacharyya (1974, 130; cf. 1977, 125) summarizes the account given in the "Rahasya," but he attributes it to DBhP I.8. The latter does deal with

the Trimūrti and their helplessness in creation, preservation, etc. without their *śaktis*, but makes no reference to the Mahā-Devīs or the creation of the three pairs of gods by them. Rao (335-37) attributes the myth to the DM. Cf. A. S. Gupta (1978, 4-6). See also Coburn's forthcoming book, *Encountering the Goddess: A Translation of the* Devī-Māhātmya *and a Study of Its Interpretation* (State University of New York Press).

37. "Vaikṛtika-Rahasya" verses 2, 7, 14.
38. These are the dates given by S. Gupta in the introduction (pp. XIX—XXI) to his translation of the *Lakṣmī Tantra*.
39. The manifestation/evolution of the *triguṇā* Mahā-Lakṣmī into the *tāmasī* Mahā-Kālī and the *sāttvikī* Mahā-Sarasvatī (or Mahā-Vidyā) is told in *Lakṣmī Tantra* 4.55-67 and "Prādhānika-Rahasya" 4-15. The creation of the three pairs of gods and goddesses, the bestowing of these goddesses on their appropriate husbands, and the creation and maintenance of the cosmic egg are narrated in *Lakṣmī Tantra* 5.1-17 and "Prādhānika-Rahasya" 16-28. The account of the three main demon-slaying incarnations of the Devī correlated with the Mahā-Devīs appears in *Lakṣmī Tantra* 9.8-27 and "Vaikṛtika-Rahasya" 1-16. The minor incarnations are recounted in *Lakṣmī Tantra* 9.28-46 and in the last of the Six limbs, the "Mūrti-Rahasya," 1-21. The "Rahasyas" add a number of iconographic and ritual details lacking in the Tantra.
40. *Lakṣmī Tantra* 3.1; Gupta's translation.
41. Thus the "Rahasyas" pass over all mention of the Vyūhas, the four primordial emanations of Viṣṇu which intermingle with the various emanations and *guṇa*-manifestations of the Devī in the *Lakṣmī Tantra*.
42. DBhP V.8.44, 52; V.10.2; V.20.13.
43. DBhP V.8.44.
44. "Vaikṛtika" 10; DBhP V.8.46.
45. DBhP III.2.29-33.
46. DBhP III.2.35-36.
47. We shall deal with this sex transformation in detail in chapter eight.
48. DBhP III.6.21-23.
49. DBhP III.6.32-35.
50. DBhP III.6.49-50.
51. DBhP III.6.65; cf. III.6.81-82.
52. DBhP III.6.79-80.
53. DM 4.35 and 5.6; cf. 11.39.
54. In this regard, we may also note that near the end of the DBhP's first retelling of the "Devī Māhātmya," brief reference is made to the Devī's gift of the Mahā-Devīs (here called "Gīr, Lakṣmī, and Girija") to the Trimūrti to help them carry out their cosmic functions (V.33.62-65).

55. DBhP I.2.19-22.
56. In DBhP I.9.39, it is said that Viṣṇu praises Yoganidrā, the mistress of the universe (*bhuvaneśvarī*), for the destruction of the two demons. Nīlakaṇṭha here remarks that although Bhuvaneśvarī in essence is beyond the distinctions brought about by *māyā*, being Brahman itself, when she is conjoined with *tāmasī śakti*, she is regarded as Mahā-Kālī.
57. DM 1.89.
58. That the identification of Yoganidrā with the "Devī Tāmasī" was sufficient inspiration for the remaining correlations is suggested by Bhāskararāya's commentary on the DM, known as the *Guptavatī*. In commenting on the verse containing the reference to the "Devī Tāmasī" (1.68 according to the commentary), Bhāskararāya at once refers to Mahā-Kālī, Mahā-Lakṣmī, and Mahā-Sarasvatī as the three *devatās* of the three *caritras* and associates them with the three *guṇas*. We shall consider Bhāskararāya's comment in more detail below. Cf. DBhP I.9.1-2, where the Tāmasī Śakti is said to have issued forth from Viṣṇu's body, and Nīlakaṇṭha's commentary thereon: "When she who is sleepless, under the guise of Nidrā, came forth as the *devatā*, then she, the Tāmasī Śakti who is Mahā-Kālī, stood in the sky, having taken a form, in order to delude the two demons."
59. See, for instance, BhG 17-18.
60. Östör 222.
61. Östör 53-54. As one example of the way the three Mahā-Devīs are correlated with social phenomena and human activities, we may note that in Mysore the nine-day festival (Navarātra) in honor of the Goddess is divided into three subperiods, each being assigned to one of the Mahā-Devīs. Chaudhuri (30) describes the division as follows: "during the first sub-period the Goddess is propitiated in her manifestation of Mahakali for obtaining immunity from diseases, poverty and grief; in the second she is worshipped in her avatar of Mahalaksmi for securing wealth, happiness and prosperity; and in the third, puja is offered to her incarnation of Mahasarasvati to obtain purity of mind, intellectual eminence and spiritual bliss." A further example concerns the spatial structuring of the pilgrimage center at Vindhyācal in northern India. Humes observes (personal correspondence, April 1989): "The sacred Vindhya area is organized according to a triangle of the three major forms of the Great Goddess, viz., Mahālakṣmī . . . , Mahākālī . . . , and Mahāsarasvatī. . . . The pilgrimage is thus known as the 'Trikoṇa Yātrā' [triangle pilgrimage], and there is a small triangle pilgrimage, paralleling the larger, in the main temple . . . for those who cannot walk the large pilgrimage, which is a trek of about 12 kilometers or so."
62. The attribution of concepts and ideals to the DM that actually belong to later interpretations of that work is not uncommon. Especially is this the case with the Six Limbs of the DM, which though "outside"

the DM have often been identified with it. See, for instance, Chaudhuri (32), who attributes to the DM, rather than to the "Prādhānika-Rahasya," the notion that the three Mahā-Devīs along with all other deities evolve from the supreme Goddess Mahā-Lakṣmī. See also Rao (334-37), upon whom Chaudhuri relies.

63. Östör 55.
64. DM 12.38.
65. Vaudeville 2-3.
66. Despite the basic irrelevance, I have found at least one modern attempt to overcome the surface inconsistency. In a devotional booklet, *Cosmic Shakti Kundalini*, Keshavadas recounts in summary form the DM. At the beginning of the second and third *caritas* he has affixed meditations to "Maha Lakshmi" and Maha Saraswathi" respectively. The meditation on "Maha Kali," however, is given not at the beginning of the first *carita* but in the middle of the third, just prior to the emergence of Kālī. The affixation to the three *caritas* of meditations on the three Mahā-Devīs, incidentally, is an interesting and important phenomenon, with which we shall deal later.
67. DM 11.23.
68. We shall consider the notion of the Mahā-Devīs as *devatās* at some length in our next section.
69. *Guptavatī* 1.68.
70. DBhP III.9.38-40.
71. BhP I.2.23; III.7.28.
72. DBhP II.6.45.
73. Sheridan 1986, 63.
74. Sheridan 1986, 63.
75. De's summary (362-63).
76. See e.g., BhP I.2.23.
77. DBhP III.6.34.
78. *Guptavatī* 1.68. Bhāskararāya, incidentally, was quite familiar with the DBhP. In his *Guptavatī* (12.11), for instance, he refers to the DBhP regarding the twice yearly performance of the Navarātra, and he also quotes verses from the DBhP in his commentary on the *Lalitāsahasranāma*. According to one of his disciples, he helped to popularize the Purāṇa (see Sanyal 144).
79. Coburn points out (1984[a], 64) that the "imputation of Vedic significance to the DM is not solely the work of later devotees of the Goddess, but seems to have been of concern to the author(s) of the DM as well." See, for instance, Coburn's comments (129-31) on the DM's use of the terms *Svāhā*, *Svadhā*, and *Vaṣaṭkāra*, which as he indicates are "drenched in Vedic significance" (130). Nonetheless, the Vedicization process in the DM itself seems largely implicit compared to the developments we are about to examine.

80. BVP II.4.1-3.
81. DBhP II.4.8-10.
82. DBhP IX.4.1-9.
83. The story of Rādhā's origin from Kṛṣṇa and how she came to be born on earth through the curse of Sudāma as the daughter of Vṛṣabhānu, told at length in BVP II.49 ff., is summarily dispensed with by the DBhP in one verse: "For some reason, Rādhā, who dwells eternally in Goloka, was born in the forest of Vṛndāvana as the daughter of Vṛṣabnānu." (IX.50.43)
84. BVP II.64.28-30.
85. Similarly, while the "Prakṛti Khaṇḍa" tells the frame story of Suratha and Samādhi in detail, the DBhP deletes all references to the frame story in Skandha IX, as it is about to be told in X.
86. DBhP IX.50.53-100.
87. In the BVP's introduction of Durgā (II.57.1-44), a brief account of the history of her worship is given (verses 29-43). According to this history, Durgā was first worshipped by Kṛṣṇa in [the celestial] Vṛndāvana, at the start of creation, in the Rāsamaṇḍala in Goloka (cf. DBhP IV.19.5-6, where there is a brief reference to Brahmā's and Viṣṇu's seeing the Devī near the start of creation in the Rāsamaṇḍala in Maṇi-Dvīpa). Second, she was worshipped by Brahmā when he was frightened by Madhu and Kaiṭabha; third by Śiva when harassed by Tripura; and fourth, by Indra when cursed by Durvasas. Mention is next made of how she is worshipped whenever she arises in all the worlds by sages, gods, etc., with specific reference to her appearing from the *tejas* of all the gods, who gave her weapons, and to her slaying of the demon Durga. Finally, reference is made to her worship by the King Suratha and his Vaiśya friend. The DBhP simply says, in the parallel context, that the Devī, well known as Durgā, is to be worshipped always by Vaiṣṇavas and Śaivas (IX.50.55-56). In our next chapter, however, we shall see that the DBhP elaborates extensively in several places on this history of Devī-worship.
88. BVP II.64.37. This mantra is basically untranslatable but represents the offering to Durgā of the various one syllable auspicious sounds, "Oṃ," etc.
89. Only six are stated, viz. "Cāmuṇḍāyai Vicce," the other three being unspecified *bījas* (DBhP IX.50.63). The English translator provides Aiṃ Hrīṃ Klīm.
90. The Gāyatrī, Uṣṇik, and Anuṣṭubh are famous Vedic meters, being the first three catalogued in Śaunaka's *Chandonukramaṇī* (Müller 197).
91. The six goddesses correlated with the *bījas* and *śaktis*, Raktadantikā through Bhīmā, are the names of the future incarnations of the Devī which she herself reveals in DM 11.41-54.
92. DBhP IX.50.59-61. The DBhP has treated a number of other sacred

oral formulae (and oral performances) in similar fashion. Thus, the twenty-four syllables of the Gāyatrī are each assigned seers, meters, *devatās*, *śaktis*, colors, substances (*tattvas*), and *mudrās* (XII.1-2). See also the treatment of the "protective armor" (*kavaca*) of the Gāyatrī (XII.3), its "heart" (*hṛdaya*) (XII.4) and the hymn of 1,008 names of the Gāyatrī Devī (XII.6). In none of these instances, however, do the three Mahā-Devīs as such play a role.

93. In this connection, we may note the similar treatment of the Rādhā-mantra in the *Nārada Pañcarātra* (c. sixteenth century or later): "The Ṛṣi of the mantra, is Mahādeva; Gāyattrī is the Chhanda; and the Devatā is Śrīmatī Rādhikā. This is stated, though in a hidden way, in all the Śāstras" (V.9.8; trans. by Swami Vijnanananda). Cf. also the treatment of the Śrī Sūkta in the *Saubhāgya-Lakṣmī Upaniṣad*, which supplies a *bīja* and *śakti* as well as the other standard categories. In like manner, the *Sarasvatī-Rahasyopaniṣad* provides all these categories for a number of mantras, along with a "linchpin" (Kilaka) category. These Śākta Upaniṣads are late compositions, perhaps from the sixteenth century (see the introduction to *The Śākta Upaniṣads*, pp. vi, ix). As early as the eleventh century, the *Śāradātilaka Tantra* already treats Tantric mantras like Vedic ones by providing Anukramaṇīs (see Ewing 73 and Kane V.1103; cf. Goudriaan and Gupta 114-15 [on the *Ākāśabhairavakalpa*] and 134-36 [on the *Śāradātilaka Tantra*]). Finally, we may note that the KālP, which in its present form is probably from the tenth or eleventh century (Hazra 1963, 245), provides a seer, Brahmā, a meter, Gāyatrī, and a *devatā*, Sarasvatī, for the mantras of the "Mātṛka-nyāsa" (77.3-4).

94. For discussion of the Vedic Anukramaṇīs, see Macdonell 39, 52, 267, 271-74; Müller 191-204; and Winternitz 57-58, 286-87.

95. BVP II.64.9-31.

96. DBhP IX.50.65-72.

97. Kane V.1099.

98. Cf. Gonda (1977, 234).

99. According to the introduction to *Srī Srī Chandi*, trans. by Swami Tattwananda, Nāgojībhaṭṭa is the earliest of the commentators (p. v). Both Kane (I.456; II.xii) and Hazra (1963, 344n) give his dates as 1700-1750.

100. Nāgojībhaṭṭa in *Durgāsaptaśatī, with Seven Sanskrit Commentaries*, p. 37.

101. According to Bhattacharyya (1974, 154), Nīlakaṇṭha, our commentator on the DBhP, also wrote a commentary on the *Kātyāyanī Tantra*. Cf. Goudriaan and Gupta 89-90.

102. The Anukramaṇī according to the *Kātyāyanī Tantra*, as given by Nāgojībhaṭṭa (in *Durgāsaptaśatī, with Seven Sanskrit Commentaries*, p. 36), is as follows: the seers of the three *caritas* are Mārkaṇḍeya, Sumedhas [the same name used for the sage in the *Devī-Bhāgavata*, incidentally, rather than Medhas], and Śiva; the meters are Anuṣṭubh in the first two *caritas* and mixed Anuṣṭubh-Jagatī in the last; the *devatās* are the three Mahā-Devīs; Nandā, Śākhambharī,

and Bhīmā are the *śaktis*; Sauṃ, Hrīṃ, and Klīṃ are the *bījas*, and Agni, Vāyu, and Sūrya are the *tattvas*.

103. According to the "Tithitattva," the seers of the three *caritas* are the gods of the Trimūrti; the *devatās* the three Mahā-Devīs; the meters Gāyatrī, Anuṣṭubh, and Uṣṇik; the *śaktis* are Nandā, Śākhambharī, and Bhīmā; the *bījas* Raktadantikā, Durgā, and Bhrāmarī; the *tattvas* Agni, Sūrya, and Vāyu; and the employment in *japa* for the pleasing of the three Mahā-Devīs respectively. The Sanskrit text of the "Tithitattva" passage is given by Kane (V.172n).

104. See Winternitz I.286.

105. Cf. Kane V. 155n.

106. Quoted in the *Durgā-Pradīpa* of Maheśa Ṭhakkura (sixteenth century) in his comment on the first verse of the first Limb (the "Devī-Kavaca"), in *Durgāsaptaśatī, with Seven Sanskrit Commentaries,* p. 16.

107. We may note, for instance, that in the "Argala Stotra" there is a brief allusion to Kṛṣṇa's worshipping Devī or Ambikā (verse 16). The *Durgā-Pradīpa* comments: "This story is well known in the DBhP [IV.24]" (*Durgāsaptaśati, with Seven Sanskrit Commentaries,* p.22). The *Durgā-Pradīpa,* in commenting on an earlier verse (no. 2), where mention is made of the Devī's giving a boon to Brahmā for the destruction of Madhu-Kaiṭabha, likewise says: "This story is made famous in the first Skandha of the DBhP." Similarly in verse 19 of the "Argala Stotra," reference is made to Indrāṇī's worshipping the Goddess for the well-being of her husband, another story related in our Purāṇa (VI.8). These references suggest that the Six Limbs, or at least the "Argala Stotra," while possibly predating the late redactor of the DBhP, were later than the core text of the DBhP.

108. "Vaikṛtika-Rahasya," verse 37.

109. The "Vaikṛtika Rahasya," in accord with the preceding "Prādhānika-Rahasya," gives preference to Mahā-Lakṣmī, so its rules for worship are not strictly speaking those for Durgā-*pūja*. Nonetheless, the parallels between the DBhP and the "Vaikṛtika-Rahasya" are still quite striking.

110. DBhP IX.50.87. Among other interesting similarities, both texts include in the various beings to be worshipped the lion mount of the Goddess and the great *asura* Mahiṣa himself. Cf. DBhP IX.50.77-78 and "Vaikṛtika-Rahasya" verses 29-30. The latter indicates that Mahiṣa attained *sāyujya* with the Goddess, apparently by being decapitated by her.

111. DBhP IX.50.92.

112. Closely related to, but somewhat distinct from, these rites are the old *kavaca* formulas, in which different forms of the deity, or associated weapons, are invoked for protecting different parts of the body, in various circumstances. One of the Six Limbs, we may recall, is the "Devī-Kavaca." *Nyāsa* assigns different deities to body parts, in a kind of identification of the worshipper and the deity.

113. To be sure, both triadic sets of the *Devī-Māhātmya*'s Six Limbs have come to be provided with their own Anukramaṇīs, with the Trimūrti and the Mahā-Devīs being the seers and *devatās* respectively. But these indices may well be much later additions. In any case, the historical relationship between the *Devī-Bhāgavata*'s "Durgā-Rahasya" and the "Vaikṛtika-Rahasya" will need further investigation before any final conclusions can be drawn.

114. See Kane V.1047-48, 1073.

115. Kane V. 1090.

116. Kane V. 1073.

117. Hazra 1963, 30-35.

118. See Dev, who in comparing the *Devī, Kālikā, Mahābhāgavata*, and *Devī-Bhāgavata* Purāṇas, asserts that "it is the Devī-Bhāgavata Purāṇa only which tries its best to establish the Dakṣiṇācārī style of Śāktism whereas other Śākta Purāṇas are influenced [by] and have followed the Vāmācārī sect to some extent" (114).

119. MBhP 8.77-78. Hazra's translation (1963, 283). The same verses are mentioned by Dev (1987, 113).

120. See DBhP XI.1.24-25; cf. VII.39.15-31. This attitude of our Purāṇa has been frequently noted: Hazra (1963, 334-35), Bhattacharyya (1982, 32), Lalye (121-22), Dev (113-14), among others.

121. Subramanian (55) gives the following relevant explanation: "A *Yantra* is a diagramatic [sic] representation of a *Mantra*, which as a sound-expression conjures up the vision of the Deity, meditated upon. Meditation in an abstract void is well-nigh impossible, especially in the initial stages and needs tools which can give the senses a perception of the Divine. The pictorial symbolism of the *Yantra*, together with the constant repetition of the *Mantra* enables the mind to concentrate on the object of devotion."

122. Rao 294-95.

123. Rao 295. Rao gives other symbolic interpretations from the ViP, Śaivāgamas and Vaiṣṇavāgamas (293-94).

124. DBhP IX.50.85.

125. For Bhāskararāya, see *Durgāsaptaśatī, with Seven Sanskrit Commentaries*, p. 10.

126. DBhP IX.50.72.

Chapter 6. Of Merchants and Kings: Worship and Its Fruits in the Frame Stories of the *Devī-Bhāgavata* and *Mārkaṇḍeya* Purāṇas

1. E.g., DM 1.104.
2. DM 13.2-3, 5.
3. DBhP V.32.1-2.

4. The three great moments, while often appearing in sequential manner are subtly intertwined in many ways. Thus, the revelation of the Devī's power is not infrequently the result of worshipping her and may be considered a kind of fruit. Similarly, her bestowal of other gifts such as wealth or victory is simply one more manifestation of her divine might. Further, worship of the Devī may involve the revelation of her power through ritual recitation. Finally, such worship is not always a means to an end but may well be offered in a spirit of thanksgiving for blessings or fruits previously received.
5. The deeds are related in DBhP V.2-32, the frame story in V.32-35. Sharma (96) has noted this different structuring of the story in the DBhP and surmises that it plays "a subsidiary role" relative to its place in the DM. While this may be true to some extent, the story still has a significant though somewhat different, function.
6. DBhP X.10.3-X.11.2 and X.12.81-93.
7. DM 1.3.
8. DM 13.1 ff.
9. The DM constitutes chapters 81-93 of the extant text.
10. The account of *manvantaras* is given in MārkP 53-80, 94-100.
11. MārkP 53.1-2; cf. 61.3.
12. MārkP 54-60.
13. MārkP 94-100.
14. DBhP VIII.1.2.
15. Here, incidentally, at the beginning of Skandha VIII, is the introduction of the interlocutors (Nārāyaṇa and Nārada) who recite most of the rest of the DBhP, up through XII.7. It is possible, perhaps, that this whole section is the contribution of the late redactor, and not just Book IX (and/or VIII). But the change of interlocutors, by itself, is hardly in a proof for such an assertion.
16. DBhP VIII.1.48.
17. DBhP VIII.3-VIII.23.
18. DBhP VIII.24.
19. DBhP X.1.2-3.
20. DBhP X.2.10-X.7. This ancient tale as it appears in the MBh (III.102) has no connection with the Goddess. There it is told that the Vindhya mountain, expanding its size in an attempt to block the path of the Sun, is approached by Agastya on his way to the south. The sage, having been sent by the gods, demands a passageway and further extracts a promise from the mountain not to resume expansion until he returns from the south. The sage has not returned north to the present day.

The VāmP (19) indirectly relates the story to the Devī in its account of the slaying of Mahiṣa. After the Goddess arose from the splendor of the gods and received their various gifts, the *Vāmana* reports that she rode off on her lion to the lofty Vindhya mountain, which had been made low by Agastya. The story of Agastya that follows merely serves to provide an interesting historical note and colorful backdrop to the mountain home of the Devī.

In the DBhP, as indicated, Agastya appears as a devout worshipper of the Devī (X.6.4), dwelling in the holy city of Banāras. The sage is quite unhappy at the prospect of leaving the city, the favorite dwelling place of those desirous of *mokṣa*. Nonetheless, Agastya dutifully assents to the gods' request to humble the Vindhya and he proceeds south.

One wonders if there is not a hidden autobiographical comment in Agastya's reluctance to leave Banāras. Agastya says specifically that sages have warned him that there will be obstacles for saintly people settling in Kāśī (X.7.6). Hazra (1963, 359) argues, and I think convincingly, that the [main] author of the DBhP "was a Smārta Śākta Brahmin of Bengal and that he migrated to Benares (probaly because it was the best place of residence for a Devī-worshipper), lived there for a long time, and then wrote the Devī-bhāgavata." Agastya's lament may suggest that our Paurāṇika's stay in Banāras was not an entirely comfortable one, and that he may even have had to leave the city before composing or finishing the DBhP.

21. The patchwork passage in DBhP IX.50 that stitches the long interpolation from the BVP into the text makes a similar point: "The fourteen Manus attained their 'Manuhood' by meditating on the lotus feet [of Durgā]" (verse 91).
22. DBhP X.8.1-X.10.2. Only the story of the sixth Manu, Cākṣuṣa, is told in any detail, occupying all of chapter 9. In many ways, it appears to be modelled closely on the story of the famous eighth Manu, Sāvarṇi.
23. DBhP X.10.6 ff.
24. After recounting the story of the last six Manus, the DBhP tells at length the deeds of the Devī as Bhrāmarī (X.13.33-124), which basically concludes the tenth Skandha. The DM only briefly alludes to the incarnation of the Devī as Bhrāmarī (11.53-54).
25. This is true of both of the DBhP's retellings of the frame story.
26. This shift should not be taken as absolute. Already in the DM, in the twelfth chapter, the Devī herself proclaims the great and manifold fruits that result from reciting or listening to her glorification, or the performance of her worship. (Coburn notes [1984(a), 59] that parts of this chapter "may be an addition to the original core." Indeed, the whole chapter may be a later addition, given its self-conscious understanding of itself in a cultic context.) Nonetheless, "power" is explicitly attributed only to the Devī herself, rather than to any ritual performance. See, e.g., 12.29-30, where the Devī explains: "Through my power (*prabhāva*) lions and the like, thieves, as well as enemies, will flee far from the person remembering my deeds."

Cf. 12.13, where the effects of listening to the greatness of the Devī are attributed by her to her own grace (*prasāda*). In the DBhP, on the other hand, we find references to the power of the rites in themselves, as in the case of Rāma's performance of the Navarātra (to be discussed below), by the *prabhāva* of which he was able to recover his wife and kingdom (III.27.50-53). The DBhP, of course, hardly neglects to stress the *prabhāva* of the Devī herself.

27. BhP VIII.1.1-3. The old *pañca-lakṣaṇa* known as *manvantara* clearly is significant in *bhaktic* interpretations of history, in Vaiṣṇavism as well as Śāktism. Thus, a modern Vaiṣṇava devotee/scholar writes: "We learn from different Purāṇas that even in the earliest period of the first Manvantara, Viṣṇu was held as the Supreme God, not only by ordinary people, but even by their mighty rulers" (Siddhantashastree 157).
28. BhP III.11.26.
29. The MārkP also contains the story of the boar *avatāra* (47.3-9) in the description of creation that precedes its account of the *manvantaras*. The MārkP version, however, makes no connection between the boar episode and the story of the first Manu. Further, the boar, along with the fish and tortoise forms, are identified as manifestations of Brahmā (47.7), though previously Brahmā has seemingly been identified as a form of Nārāyaṇa (47.4). While the BhP's account of the boar and the Manus may be related, indirectly, to the MārkP's, its own version is quite distinct. The DBhP has clearly relied on the BhP's version, or one very close to it, as can be seen from the frequent verbal similarities. For instance, compare the following descriptions of the origin of the boar:

    ity abhidhyāyato nāsāvivarāt sahasānagha/
    varāha-toko niragād aṅguṣṭha-parimāṇakaḥ//
    tasyābhipaśyataḥ svasthaḥ kṣaṇena kila bhārata/
    gaja-mātraḥ pravavṛdhe tad adbhutam abhūn mahat//
    (BhP III.13.18-19)

    dhyāyatas tasya nāsāgrād virañceḥ sahasā 'nagha/
    varāha-poto niragād ekāṅgula-pramāṇataḥ//
    tasyaiva paśyataḥ svasthaḥ kṣaṇena kila nārada/
    kari-mātraṃ pravavṛdhe tad adbhutatamaṃ hy abhūt//
    (DBhP VIII.2.2-3)

30. Again, we may note certain similarities between the BhP's account of geography and the MārkP's. For instance, the latter (in 54.31; cf. 59.11, 16, and 26) asserts that Viṣṇu has certain forms in the various *varṣas* or continents of the world, not unlike what we find in BhP V.17-19. But whereas the MārkP correlates only four of the nine *varṣas* with four forms of Viṣṇu, the BhP correlates all nine. The DBhP's version is clearly dependent on the BhP's.

31. Literally, the Āgamas, interpreted by Nīlakaṇṭha as "Tantras causing delusion."
32. DBhP V.19.12-13, 15, 23-25.
33. The story is discussed by Bhattacharyya (1982, 32) to illustrate orthodox (pro-Vedic) attitudes towards the Tantras, and to discount the "popular belief that Tantra is the same as Śāktism" (31). Cf. the version in VarP 71.10-63, where there is no mention of Devī-worship. Cf. also Dev (161-62).
34. DBhP XII.8.88-89.
35. The conch and discus are emblems of Viṣṇu. The Kāpālikas are a Śaivite sect whose members wear garlands made of skulls (*kapāla*) and who use the same for eating or drinking vessels.
36. DBhP XII.9.71-74, 76-77, 79. The story of Gautama is also told in KūrP I.15.91-121, but there the curse is only that the Brahmans will be excluded from the Vedas and will be born again and again (I.15.104). No reference is made to any neglect of the Devī-cult.
37. A Śākta sect following the more extreme left-handed practices denounced by the DBhP.
38. DBhP XII.9.98-99.
39. Cf. DBhP VII.39.28-30, where it is said that due to the curses of Dakṣa, Bhṛgu, and Dadhīca, certain Brahmans were deprived of the Vedas, and for liberating them Śiva framed the five Āgamas (scriptures) of the Śaivas, Vaiṣṇavas, Sauras, Śāktas, and Gāṇapatyas.
40. A similar story is told in the account of the slaying of Durgama by Śatākṣī. Durgama had attained his power over the gods by getting control of the Vedas, depriving the Brahmans of them. When the Goddess finally destroys Durgama, she says to the gods: "These [Vedas] are my highest manifestation, to be protected at all costs. You have just seen what calamity arose when they were lost. I am to be worshipped always." (DBhP VII.28. 76-77)
41. DM 1.5.
42. DBhP V.32.6.
43. Various interpretations have been given for the phrase *kolā-vidhvaṃsinas* (1.5; cf. 1.6). Pargiter construes it to mean enemies "in alliance with the Kolas."
44. DBhP V.32.7 and 10.
45. Hazra 1963, 343.
46. DBhP IV.8.31-32.
47. The DBhP's frustrations with and hopes for the historical process help to explain a feature of the text that stands in contrast to the DM as a whole. The DBhP manifests a much greater sectarian assertiveness, especially with regards to Vaiṣṇavism, as Part I has shown. Sharma has noted (91): "while the *Devī-Bhāgavata* would sometimes, in its desire to impress on the reader the greatness of Śakti, disparage the worship of other

deities, the *Saptaśatī* steers clear of all such controversies." Sharma also calls (97) specific attention to the fact that the DM refers to the Devī as "the *mahāmāyā* of Hari [1.54] and also *Bhagavad-Viṣṇu-māyā* [13.3; cf. 5.7, 14], thereby avoiding all idea of conflict between the worship of the two deities." The DBhP generally avoids such epithets for the Goddess, and one suspects it is precisely because they suggest a possible subordination of the Devī to Viṣṇu. (While such epithets occur on rare occasions [e.g., "Viṣṇumāyā" in DBhP IX.50.81], their overall lack in face of the importance of such epithets in the DM is surely significant.)

Sharma concludes (110) that the DBhP probably grew up with the three deeds of the Devī as its nucleus, but then added new hymns of praise [and new stories] "as the older ones did not have the desired emphasis on the exclusive supremacy of Jagadambā [the world mother]. The *Purāṇa* had to cater to the new sectarian demands of the period and to enunciate its position in clearer and more emphatic terms." Beane, who relies in part on Sharma, argues (62) that two basic characteristics of the Purāṇa are 1) its reflection of "an historical situation (*intra* eighth-twelfth centuries) in which there is a more intense Śākta sectarian consciousness;" and 2) its insistence upon Devī as the supreme deity.

While I basically agree with these comments, I find the notion of "catering to sectarian demands" somewhat misleading. The phrase does not seem to do justice to the DBhP's sense that something has gone wrong with history. From the Purāṇa's point of view, Vaiṣṇavism and other sects, in their failure to recognize the true cause of events, were themselves part of the historical problem. It was the DBhP's taking of history seriously, a natural outcome of its own view of the Goddess' love for the world, that in part led to its exclusivistic tendencies.

48. The story of Rāma is told in DBhP III.28-30.

49. DBhP IX.1.145-46. This passage appears in BVP II.1.151-52 as well.

50. Banerjea points out (492) that in the Vālmiki RM (VI.106), Agastya advises Rāma to worship the sun in order to slay Rāvaṇa. Banerjea adds: "It is only in the Bengali *Rāmāyaṇa* by Kṛttivāsa, that the worship of the Sun is replaced by the worship of Durgā." Kṛttivāsa, however, belongs to the fifteenth century, and we already find versions of Rāma's worship of the Devī not only in the DBhP, but also in two other Śākta Purāṇas, the KālP (60.25-31) and the MBhP (36-48), as well as in the *Bṛhad-Dharma Purāṇa* (1.18-22, according to Kinsley [1986, 109, 234]). Cf. Chakravarti 155-56.

Suratha and Rāma are linked in a special, temporal sense. As Chaudhuri affirms (15): "Tradition has it that King Suratha . . . regained his lost kingdom through the grace of Mother Durgā whom he propitiated by long devoted worship. That was, however, not in autumn but in spring and Durgā Pūjā in autumn came in vogue when Sri Ramachandra invoked the blessings of the Mother in the battlefield of Lanka for slaying Rāvana." See also Östör 17-18; Kinsley 1986, 109; Mukhopadhyay 39.

51. In the KālP (60.25 ff.) Brahmā plays the major mediating role between the Devī and Rāma. In an interesting twist on the Madhu and Kaiṭabha myth, Brahmā wakes up the Devī to assist Rāma in the slaying of Rāvaṇa. See Kinsley 1986, 108-09. In the MBhP Brahmā urges Rāma to worship the Devī when he becomes fearful of Kumbhakarṇa, but it is the Devī herself in this text who first tells Rāma to worship her in the autumn and who provides the details of her worship. Cf. Hazra 1963, 269-72 and Dev 166-67. The DBhP version, with Nārada as the prime mediator, thus seems closest to the structure of the DM's frame story.
52. DBhP III.30.19, 21, 25-26. Cf. the following passage from BVP II.57.29-43: "She [Devī] was first worshipped by Kṛṣṇa, the supreme Self, in Vṛndāvana, at the beginning of creation, in Goloka in the Rāsa-Maṇḍala. Secondly, by Brahmā, fearful of Madhu and Kaiṭabha. Thirdly, by Śiva when harassed by Tripura. Fourthly, by Indra when cursed by Durvasas. . . . By all the gods when she arose from their splendor [to kill Mahiṣa]. . . . And finally by Suratha . . . and Vaiśya."
53. DBhP III.30.27.
54. DM 1.60-61.
55. Sudarśana's story is given earlier in Skandha III, in chaps. 14-25. Skandha III as a whole is dedicated to establishing the historical and divine norms for the Devī-cult. The model for the worship of the Goddess on earth is provided by the "history" of her worship by the gods themselves, beginning with the great Devī-Yajña (sacrifice) carried out by Viṣṇu just after setting the wheel of creation in motion (III.13). By this ceremony, incidentally, Viṣṇu received the Devī's boon of being the world's protector, capable of incarnating in various wombs whenever there is a decline in *dharma* (III.13.43-44). The DBhP repeatedly asserts that all the gods pay homage to the Goddess (e.g., III.18.33-34).
56. Cf. Bakker (I,46), who briefly refers to Sudarśana's installation of the Devī in Ayodhyā as mentioned in the DBhP.
57. DBhP III.25.35-46. Dev (143) refers to the DBhP's account of the spread of the Devī-cult throughout India, but mentions only Subāhu's role, which in many ways is subordinate to that of Sudarśana's.
58. *Dharma* or virtue is thought to decline by one quarter in each of the four successive ages. Metaphorically, *dharma* is often represented by a cow that is four-footed in the Satya or Golden age, with one less foot in each of the following yugas. The four-footed *dharma* is thus symbolic of the ideal conditions of the Satya Yuga.
59. ŚiP, Umā Saṃhitā 51.75-77.
60. DBhP V.20.20.
61. Śatrughna of the RM did become king of Madhuvana after slaying Lavaṇāsura, and did return on occasion to visit his brother Rāma in Ayodhyā, but he, along with Bharata, followed Rāma in death through yogic suicide.

Rāma traditionally is said to have lived in the Treta or second age, long before the fourth or Kali Yuga.

62. DBhP V.20.20 ff.
63. DBhP V.19.12; cf. V.19.26.
64. DBhP V.20.37, 45.
65. DBhP V.20.29.
66. DBhP V.20.50.
67. The Devī herself, for instance, declares: "The delight I have in receiving worship day and night for a whole year with offerings of cattle, flowers, and other offerings, and by the feeding of Brahmans . . . is the same delight I receive when the account of my deeds is heard once." (DM 12.20-22) The DBhP, however, usually insists that the feasting of Brahmans should accompany worship of the Devī (e.g., III.27.11 and 14; V.34.16).
68. Kane III.892. The reference to Manu is to MS 9.301-02.
69. See note 20 above.
70. Bakker I, 46.
71. Regarding this general time period in North India, Bhagowalia remarks (174): "The period 700-1200 A.D. saw the free exchange of ideas between the various religious movements. . . . The Śaiva-Śākta cult, to begin with, proved more popular but by the 12th century, it was gradually losing its momentum so that after the 12th century A.D. the initiative is again taken up by the Vaiṣṇavism which had never lost popular support. . . . Vaiṣṇavism alone was left as the most prominent movement representing Hindu religion. It was certainly an honored position but one beset with a big challenge—the challenge to meet Islam. From the 13th century onwards, the story of Vaiṣṇavism is the story of the process of adjustments between Hinduism and Islam."
72. Smith 1957, 21.
73. Lalye's explanation (55) that the "DB has not brought Samādhi merchant here as his mention was irrelevant to the description of Manu's dynasty" seems unconvincing since the same situation applies to the DM, which saw fit to include the merchant despite any irrelevancy to the account of the Manus.
74. DM 13.5.
75. Cf. Agrawala's typical "archetypal" interpretation of the DM as applied to the three key human figures of the frame story (72): "Now these are the three types of persons who are present everywhere, or the three archetypes of the human temperaments of which life is constituted. They are invariable types of the human soul. The Rishi is the type for whom all problems have been resolved. . . . The king typifies the path of action (*karma*). . . . The rich householder represents the plight of gold, which . . . becomes the cause of unhappiness. . . . The Rishi stands for *Jñāna* and the

king for *Karma* and the Vaiśya for a life of confusion in which utter blindness of delusion prevails." While many of Agrawala's symbolic interpretations of the DM may strike certain readers as excessive or gratuitous, he is clearly right in seeing the human actors as "types," from the DM's own point of view.

76. Woodroffe (150) nicely summarizes the Tantric viewpoint: "The eternal rhythm of the Divine Breath is outwards from spirit to matter and inwards from matter to spirit. Devī as Māyā evolves the world. As Mahāmāyā She recalls it to herself. The path of outgoing is the way of pravṛtti; that of return nivṛtti. Each of these movements is divine. Enjoyment (bhukti) and liberation (mukti) are each her gifts."
77. Cited by Woodroffe (151), apparently from the third chapter of the *Śāktānanda-taranginī*.
78. Within the Vaiṣṇava circle, for instance, see *Agastyasaṃhitā* 28.22-23: "Those who ever repeat 'Śrī Rāma, Rāma, Rāma' will attain *bhukti* and *mukti*, without doubt" (quoted in Bakker: I,78).
79. See chapter three above.
80. Cf. DM 1.77, where the Devī is referred to as Mahā-Māyā and Mahā-Vidyā.
81. BVP II.62-65.
82. BVP II.61.105-06.
83. BVP II.62.2-4.
84. BVP II.62.13, 15, 17.
85. BVP II.62.34-35.
86. BVP II.65.40-41.
87. BVP II.65.38; cf. II.65.20.
88. DBhP V.35.37-39.
89. DBhP V.34.38-40.
90. DBhP III.27.30-57.
91. DBhP X.12.88.
92. DBhP I.18.33-34.
93. DBhP I.19.12.
94. DBhP I.19.33-35.
95. DBhP III.24.2-4.

Chapter 7. The *Devī Gīta* and the *Bhagavad Gītā*: Self-Revelations of the Supreme Reality

1. DBhP VII. 31-40.
2. Aiyar 213.
3. Aiyar also includes the *Gaṇeśa Gītā* and the *Śiva Gītā* as closely following

the *Bhagavād Gītā.* Rocher (1986, 170) states bluntly, and somewhat surprisingly, "The Devīgītā has little in common with the Bhagavadgītā." Similarly, Gonda (1977, 272) argues that certain later Gītās such as "the Devī Gītā, contain hardly any reminiscences of this prototype [the *Bhagavad Gītā*]." I concur basically with Aiyar, though as will be seen there are significant divergencies in the *Devī Gītā* from the *Bhagavad Gītā.*

4. BhP III.25-33.
5. Gonda, in introducing his chapter on "Gītās, Māhātmyas and Other Religious Literature" in his survey of medieval Sanskrit literature, comments (1977, 271): "Poems such as the Bhagavadgītā, though primarily designed to teach religious or philosophical doctrines, often have at the same time the character of devotional hymns. And numerous hymns of praise . . . often take a didactic or moralistic turn."
6. As is the case in the "Vṛtra Gītā," discussed in chapter three.
7. Parrinder points out (112) that the *Bhagavad Gītā* represented something quite "unusual" in the Hindu tradition at the time it was written (c. 400-200 B.C.), in that in the prior scriptural tradition of the Vedas, the "action" is all "godward" (humans praising and petitioning the deities), while in the *Gītā*, the action is reversed, or "manward" (God speaking to humans).
8. Cf. Gonda 1977, 272.
9. DM 11.43.
10. KūrP I.11.1-336.
11. KūrP I.11.75-211.
12. KūrP I.11.336. Similarly, the *Devī Gītā* near its end states: "Thus has the excellent glorification of the Devī (*devī-māhātmyam uttamam*) been told." (DBhP VII.40.42) The *Devī Gītā*, however, goes on to call itself a "Gītā" two lines later.
13. KūrP I.11.63-65, 258-318.
14. KūrP I.11.66-74, 213-18.
15. MBhP 15-19.
16. MBhP 19.8. I shall use the name *Pārvatī Gītā* to refer to the MBhP's "Gītā," though the colophon to the final chapter uses the name *Bhagavatī Gītā*. The names can become confusing, for I have also found one modern edition of the *Devī Gītā* which entitles itself the *Bhagavatī Gītā*, and Miśra, in his listing of Purāṇic Gītās (137), refers to the DBhP's *Devī Gītā* as the *Bhagavatī-gītā*. To avoid confusion I shall refer to the *Devī-Bhāgavata*'s Gītā only as the *Devī Gītā*.
17. DBhP VII.31.1.
18. DBhP VII.31.72-73. The last phrase literally is "whereby you, indeed, will become I" (*tvam evā 'ham . . . bhaveḥ*). Nīlakaṇṭha interprets this to mean that there will be nondifference (*abheda*) between Himālaya and the Goddess.
19. KūrP I.11.43.

20. KūrP I.11.17.
21. MBhP 15.12-13.
22. MBhP 15.15.
23. MBhP 3.
24. MBhP 15.4.
25. MBhP 15.6.
26. Pārvatī's marriage to Śiva, her giving birth to Kārttikeya, and the latter's slaying of Tāraka are hardly neglected by the MBhP, however. These are all told at length immediately following the *Pārvatī Gītā*, in *adhyāya*s 20-34.
27. DBhP VII.40.39cd-40ab.
28. DBhP VII.32.2.
29. These correspond to the causal, subtle, and gross bodies of the supreme Self.
30. DBhP VII.33.13-15.
31. DBhP VII.33.20.
32. DBhP VII.34.2.
33. Cf. BhG 7.4 ff.
34. Cf. BhG 10.19-41.
35. Cf. BhG 11.3-4.
36. Cf. BhG 11.5 ff.
37. Cf. esp. BhG 11.23-30.
38. Cf. BhG 11.35.
39. Cf. BhG 11.36-40.
40. Cf. BhG 11.45-46.
41. Cf. BhG 11.47-48.
42. Cf. Gonda 1977, 274.
43. BhG 11.7, 13, 19 and 20.
44. See e.g., *Vedāntasāra* 104.
45. We may also note the suggestive verse in the *Kūrma Devī Gītā* (I.11.243), where Himavān says to the Devī: "I bow to that form of yours known as the world egg . . . situated in the waters, composed of the twice seven worlds, having Puruṣa for its sole Lord."
46. BhP II.1.23 ff.
47. Again, the seed for this full-blown assimilation seems to lie in the *Kūrma Devī Gītā*, where Himavān declares to the Devī: "I bow to that form [of yours] known as Nārāyaṇa, with a thousand heads, of endless power, with a thousand arms, the ancient Puruṣa." (I.11.245)
48. See Laine 279-82. He characterizes this strategy, following Paul Hacker, as an approach in which the opponents' views are not denied, but rather elements of those views are included in one's own, though the significance of the single elements is transformed.

49. BhP II.2.1.
50. The "pralayic" destruction refers to the end of a major cosmic cycle, when the whole universe dissolves back into nothingness. The "*yugānta*," or end of the age, refers merely to the conclusion of one of the four world ages, the Kṛta, Treta, etc. The *Mahābhārata* war is thought to have marked the end of the Dvāpara and the beginning of the Kali Yuga, with Kṛṣṇa as the agent of the transition. "*Yugānta*-eschatology" is thus more "historical."
51. Laine, 303, 324-25.
52. MBhP 15.22-25.
53. MBhP 15.26-29.
54. MBhP 15.33-34.
55. MBhP 15.36.
56. Cf. A. S. Gupta 1978, 6. He refers to the "individual divine form" and the "universal (Virāṭ) form" of the Goddess as "two sides of the same coin." These two represent her *saguṇā* aspect, while consciousness, identical with Brahman, represents her *nirguṇā* aspect.
57. KU 3-4.
58. DBhP XII.8.12-84.
59. DBhP VII.40.39.
60. *Taittirīya Upaniṣad* 1.5.
61. KūrP I.11.292-94.
62. These are the nearly identical words of BhG 7.3. In BhG 7.5 Kṛṣṇa refers to his "higher" and "lower" natures, a rough parallel to the subtle and gross forms of the Devī.
63. MBhP 18.3-5.
64. MBhP 18.13-14. There is a marvelous intermixing here of the masculine and feminine aspects of Śiva and Śakti. Śiva is called the *pradhāna* Puruṣa, the word *pradhāna* being another name for *prakṛti*, associated with the feminine. Conversely, Śakti is called auspicious (*śivā*), the name given her spouse.
65. Nīlakaṇṭha, in commenting on this verse, quotes KU 3.12, where Umā Haimavatī is specifically mentioned.
66. DBhP VII.31.26-29.
67. An interesting inversion of the "birth-from-the-*tejas*-of-the-gods" motif is found in the DBhP's myth of the slaying of Durgama (whose destruction is merely forecast by the Devī in DM 11.49). According to the DBhP, when the demon and his hordes rush upon the Devī, accompanied by gods and Brahmans, she envelops her frightened followers within a circle of light (*tejo-mayaṃ cakraṃ*) for their protection, while she remains outside (VII.28.51-52).

68. BhG 11.8.
69. Laine 275-77.
70. KūrP I.11.65; MBhP 15.21.
71. BhP III.25.8-9.
72. BhP III.26.51 ff.
73. BhP III.29.5.
74. DBhP VII.39.36-37. Cf. KūrP I.11.289.
75. BVP II.2.12-16. I quoted this passage, with some modifications, in my *God as Mother* (70), in an extended discussion of the formless and formed aspects of Kṛṣṇa in the BVP. The DBhP reproduces the passage nearly verbatim, in IX.2.12 ff., as one might expect.
76. BhP III.28.
77. BhP III.28.42. Cf. BhG 6.29.
78. BhP II.2.8-14.
79. DBhP VII.35.54-57.
80. DBhP VII.39.2 ff.
81. DBhP VII.39.6-8.
82. DBhP VII.39.38-42. Between the first and second form has been inserted a passage based on KūrP I.11.259 ff., which rather confuses the order of things in the extant text.
83. DBhP VII.39.44. We should be careful not to distinguish too sharply between the perspectives of the *Devī Gītā* and the *Kapila Gīta* on these matters. Thus, in the latter, we find Kapila saying: "A man should worship me with images . . . so long as he does not realize me, residing in all creatures, in his own heart." (BhP III.29.25) The DBhP is simply more explicit and more persistent in identifying the Devī's highest form as the aniconic light of consciousness.
84. DBhP VII.37.2 ff.
85. DBhP VII.37.4-9.
86. This description of the supreme *bhakti* is given in DBhP VII.37.11-20.
87. See BhP III.29.
88. DBhP VII.37.28-31.
89. See e.g., BhP III.32.32 ff.
90. See esp. BhP III.29.21-34.
91. See esp. BhP III.30-32.
92. DBhP VII.37.16-18.
93. DBhP VII.36.17-18. Cf. BhG 7.18.
94. DBhP VII.36.19-20.
95. BhG 9.17.

96. DBhP VII.40.34; VII.40.44. It is only the chapter colophons (and subsequent tradition) that refers to this Gītā as the *Devī Gītā*.

97. DBhP VII.36.28-30.

98. DBhP VII.36.21-22. A similar warning is given by Vyāsa at the end of the first half of the Purāṇa (DBhP VI.31.58-59).

99. DBhP VII.40.34-36.

100. DBhP XII.14.24-25.

101. Kinsley 1982, 55.

Chapter 8. Gīta-Reflections in the Mystic Isles: Nārada's Journey to the White Island and the Trimūrti's Journey to the Jeweled Island

1. DBhP III.2.13-III.6.85.

2. MBh XII.325.1-326.101.

3. The account refers to itself as a "great Upaniṣad . . . sung (*gīta*) by the mouth of Nārāyaṇa." (MBh XII.326.100-01)

4. MBh XII.323.19-53.

5. MBh XII.323.18.

6. MBh XII.323.26.

7. MBh XII.323.39.

8. This story, incidentally, suggests that the supreme form of God is not light, but rather an iconic image that lies within the light. Such a view has been highly influential in the Vaiṣṇava tradition and is made fully explicit in the BVP, as we saw in our last chapter. The DBhP, in contrast, we may recall, insists upon the aniconic, light form of the Devī as her supreme form. This "aniconic" view of the supreme is not entirely absent from Vaiṣṇavism, however, especially in contexts that deal with knowledge rather than devotion. Indeed, in the following epic story of Nārada's visit to Śveta-Dvīpa, an aniconic perspective is predominant, for the Lord's supreme form, the Ātman, is said to be known only by *jñāna* and not by any of the physical senses. The visible form that Nārada beholds is only *māyā* (MBh XII.326.43).

9. MBh XII.326.18-24.

10. DBhP III.7.3-6.

11. The story of Nārada appears in DBhP VI.28.1-VI.31.22.

12. On the significance of the king's continuing reality even after Nārada 'awakes' from the delusion of womanhood, see O'Flaherty 1984, 84-87.

13. For summaries and discussion of some of these versions, see Zimmer 27-35; O'Flaherty 1984, 81-89. Zimmer focusses on the symbolism of the water and its transforming powers, whereby one is initiated into the mysteries

of Māyā. O'Flaherty concentrates on the shifting notions of illusion and reality in the stories, and the tension between *saṃsāra* and *mokṣa*.

14. O'Flaherty 1984, 82.
15. W. N. Brown 202.
16. The story of Bhaṅgāsvana in MBh XIII.12. According to the tale, when Bhaṅgāsvana as a woman is offered the opportunity to become a man again, she refuses, on the grounds that a woman has more pleasure in intercourse. For discussions of this story, see S. A. Dange 334; O'Flaherty 1980(b), 305-06, and Vora 112.

    O'Flaherty (1984, 83-84) also notes an exception within the Nārada cycle of myths, from the PadP, which will be discussed below.
17. E.g., VarP 124.9 ff.
18. VarP 124.69. Cf. 124.169.
19. DBhP VI.30.46-47.
20. VarP 124.165. The VarP version, incidentally, has some striking parallels to the DBhP's, despite major differences such as the substitution of the sage Somaśarma for Nārada.
21. DBhP VI.31.5-6.
22. For a discussion of the significance of such "magic doubles," including double universes, see O'Flaherty 1984, 89-109.
23. The text at this point does not actually refer to the island as Maṇi-Dvīpa, though Nīlakaṇṭha makes the identification (comment on DBhP III.3.32). The Jeweled Island is described at length by the DBhP in XII.10-12. There Vyāsa introduces the island home of the Devī in the following words: "Above Brahmaloka is Sarvaloka, according to *śruti*. That indeed is Maṇi-Dvīpa, where shines the Devī. Because it is above all (*sarva*), it is called Sarvaloka." (XII.10.1-2)

    The reference to *śruti* apparently is the Purāṇa's oblique attempt to explain the name of this island. Nīlakaṇṭha, in commenting upon DBhP XII.10.1 above, quotes from the *Subāla Upaniṣad* (10.1), where a series of ever-more-ultimate worlds are named. Near the end of the series, after asking in what world Brahmaloka is established, the Upaniṣad declares. "All worlds (*sarvalokā*), like jewels (*maṇis*) [on a thread, are strung] on the Ātman, on Brahman." Maṇi-Dvīpa is thus a jewel on the thread of Brahman, the ultimate reality.

    Like many celestial realms of the Hindus, Maṇi-Dvīpa has its own terrestial "counterpart" or "manifestation" in the world. Thus, according to Humes (personal correspondence, April 1989), the pilgrims at Vindhyācal frequently testify that the sacred center is none other than the island paradise of the Goddess herself.
24. As Nīlakaṇṭha points out (on DBhP III.3.48), this appearance is the Virāṭ form manifested in Skandha VII (in the *Devī Gītā*).

25. DBhP III.3.50-67.
26. BhP X.8.32-45; cf. X.7.34-37.
27. Cf. O'Flaherty 1984, 109-14, where she discusses the mouth-revelations of Kṛṣṇa to Arjuna in the BhG, to Yaśodā in the BhP, and to Mārkaṇḍeya in the MatP.
28. Viṣṇu's *stotra* is given in DBhP III.4.27-49.
29. DBhP III.5.13-16.
30. Cf. the end of the *Devī Gītā*, where the Goddess declares: "He who thus worships the Devī . . . at the end of his life goes to Maṇi-Dvīpa where he attains the Devī's own form (*devī-svarūpa*)." (DBhP VII.40.30-32)
31. Regarding practical implications, cf. Bhattacharyya (1982, 109), who suggests that stories of sex transformation such as the DBhP's regarding the Trimūrti "may have some bearing on the widespread custom according to which it is compulsory for the priest to use female robes during his priestly function."
32. DBhP III.5.40-43, 46.
33. DBhP III.6.2-4, 7.
34. O'Flaherty's phrase (1980[b], 129).
35. O'Flaherty 1980(b), 129.
36. DBhP I.12. A number of variants of the story are discussed by O'Flaherty (1980[b], 303-05). Cf. Kramrisch 1975, 260.
37. See BhP IX.1.23-42.
38. DBhP I.12.50-51.
39. Nīlakaṇṭha may seem to express a greater appreciation of women than the DBhP. But he only makes explicit what is implicit in the Purāṇa. While sexist elements appear in the DBhP's Ilā myth, the fact remains that the Devī bestows her grace, and liberation, on Ilā as a woman.
40. O'Flaherty 1980(b), 129.
41. The story is summarized in O'Flaherty 1984, 83.
42. Cf. DBhP XII.12.1 ff., where we find a lengthy description of the Devī at home in Maṇi-Dvīpa. She has four great halls in her chief palace, the Ekānta Maṇḍapa, where she consults with her ministers about preserving the universe; Mukti Maṇḍapa, where she grants liberation to souls; Jñāna Maṇḍapa, where she gives *upadeśa* (where we can suppose she instructed the Trimūrti on their journey), and the Śṛṅgāra Maṇḍapa, where she listens to the goddesses and gods sing sweetly (and, we may again suppose, she engages in other more erotic activities). Indeed, the text goes on to describe how, for the sake of her own sport, she is said to become twofold at the beginning of creation, with Maheśvara (*Śiva*) coming into existence from half her body. He outshines the god of love in his beauty, and the Devī, herself exquisitely dressed, sits on his lap.

Conclusion: The Triumph of the Goddess

1. For instance, the pilgrimage route at the sacred center for the Goddess at Vindhyācal is laid out in a triangular arrangement according to the three main forms of the Devī, Mahā-Kālī, Mahā-Lakṣmī, and Mahā-Sarasvatī. Similarly in South India, in Mysore, the first three days of Navarātra are dedicated to Mahā-Kālī, the next three to Mahā-Lakṣmī, and the last three to Mahā-Sarasvatī. To what extent has the *Devī-Bhāgavata*'s glorification of these three Mahā-Devīs contributed, directly or indirectly, to the spatial structuring of the Vindhyācal pilgrimage and to the temporal division of the Navarātra in Mysore? (Cf. chapter five, note 61 above.) And what role has the Purāṇa's elaborate depiction of the Goddess'celestial paradise led to the conceptualization of Vindhyācal as Maṇi-Dvīpa, a realm unknown in the *Devī-Māhātmya*? (Cf. chapter eight, note 23 above.)
2. For a discussion of the ways in which Hindus have dealt with scripture, and with holy words in general (that is, in their spoken as well as their written form), see Coburn 1984(b), esp. 451-53.
3. As early as the sixteenth century, the *Durgā-Pradīpa* of Maheśa Ṭhakkura admonishes: "One should recite the *Devī-Bhāgavata* daily with devotion and concentration, especially in Navarātra, with joy, for the pleasure of Śrī Devī." The verse is cited by Nīlakaṇṭha in the introduction to his commentary. He attributes it to the *Devī-Yāmala* as quoted by Maheśa Ṭhakkura. Hazra (1963, 345) also quotes the verse, and points out that there are no extant manuscripts of the *Devī-Yāmala*. According to Sanyal (144), the *Durgā-Pradīpa* is the only Smṛti Nibandha to refer to the DBhP.

   Nīlakaṇṭha quotes another verse from the *Durgā-Taraṅgiṇi:* "In the Navarātra, O Durgā, one should recite the 'Daurgaṃ Bhāgavatam;' one should chant the *Saptaśati*, or *Caṇḍi*, as prescribed, with devoted attention." While it is not clear that the "Daurgaṃ Bhāgavatam" refers to the DBhP (cf. Hazra 1963, 346), Nīlakaṇṭha apparently assumes that it does.

   In any case, the DM and the DBhP are, at least on occasion, both recited today during the Navarātra. At the temple of the Devī in Vindhyācal there is still a lively tradition of recitation of the DBhP during this festival. The DM, not surprisingly, is the most popular text recited at Vindhyācal, but a fair number of pilgrims also request recitations of the DBhP. Only the more learned pandits at the temple perform these DBhP recitations, according to Humes (personal correspondence), as apparently it is not economically viable for the less skilled. She notes that a poorly educated priest can without much difficulty learn the "700" verses of the DM, with its easy meters and limited vocabulary, and thus make money reciting it for pilgrims. But the eighteen thousand verses of the DBhP require an accomplished Sanskritist to finish the recitation in the normal nine days, and thus to be profitable.

   The great length of the DBhP also means that the cost to the pilgrim for its recitation is much higher. Humes estimates that it is at least one hundred rupees, or nearly ten times what it costs to do the cheapest, plain recitation of the DM, and is probably far more in fact. At any rate, expense is the standard reason given for the lesser popularity of the DBhP. Given that the same fruits are guaranteed by the DM, the greater expense for the DBhP may hardly seem cost-effective. Yet an occasional wealthy patron will arrange for a "one-hundred times recitation" of the *Devī-Bhāgavata*, which takes one lunar month, numerous pandits, and twelve thousand rupees to perform.

As for the pilgrims themselves at Vindhyācal, a substantial minority of over four hundred interviewed by Humes read from the DBhP, as well as from the DM, on a daily basis. How representative such pilgrims are of Hindus generally is hard to say. Humes suggests: "If someone will come to Vindhyācal for nine days to recite DS [*Durgā Saptaśatī*, or DM], it is likely that he will be more religious and wealthy than the average Hindu, so it follows he may have more time and religious impelling to do or to sponsor DB [DBhP] recitations like those I met." Moreover, Vindhyācal may be atypical, with its numerous professional pandits. Humes says: "Vindhyācal may offer recitations like the DB that may not be easily available elsewhere. . . . For DS recitation, I believe it to be unique, and certainly those who come to recite believe there is no place like it."

4. The DM has inspired no less than sixty-seven commentaries. See Coburn 1984(b), 449.
5. See Sanyal 143-44.
6. This esteem is also seen in references to the DBhP as an authority in ritual matters by modern devotees (Humes, personal correspondence).
7. I am relying here on information provided me by Humes regarding the attitude of devotees towards the two texts (personal correspondence). Humes presents her finding—that the DM is seen especially as a ritual text, the DBhP as story—as merely a "strong impression," needing further research to be substantiated. But her tentative interpretation appears to me quite sound and reasonable.
8. Swami Tattwananda 114-16.
9. Of relevance here is Kinsley's insightful account of the "taming" of the fierce Kālī by the two Bengali saints, Rāmprasād and Rāmakrishna (1975, 123): "Through love, through the naive, steadfast devotion of a child, man can make the Mother . . . reveal an aspect of herself that is normally kept well hidden. [Then, quoting Rāmakrishna himself:] 'Prema [devotional love] is the rope by which you can tether God, as it were.'" Kinsley later adds, with reference to both men (1975, 125): "Despite her strange appearance and weird behavior, these two Bengali saints saw in her [*Kālī*] a loving, maternal presence. They saw behind or beneath her ferocity an enduring love. They saw her external appearance as a mask, and by persistently approaching her as children, they succeeded in making

her take off that mask." The DBhP does not go as far as the Bengali saints in adopting an extreme and intimate childlike devotion to the Goddess as mother, but there is certainly a kindred spirit at work.

10. ŚU 4.3.
11. BhG 9.17.
12. BhP I.11.7.
13. Coburn 1984(a), 305. Some of these paradoxes, within the Hindu cultural context, could easily be correlated with a feminine/masculine polarity, but the DM does not do so explicitly.
14. DM 11.6.
15. DM 5.71.
16. Kinsley 1982, 53.
17. Kinsley 1982, 56. Kinsley further argues that the DBhP author ignores or disregards the productive and nourishing aspects of the Devī, portraying the Goddess as "almost entirely removed from agriculture and the fertility of the earth" (53). Similarly, Kinsley says that the Goddess in our text is "almost entirely denied positive nurturing qualities. The process of birth and the womb are said to be filthy and polluting. . . . The Goddess is primarily a powerful authority figure. She is unlike real women, who possess sexual attractiveness, enjoy sex, give birth, and nourish their children with their own milk" (56).

    Kinsley's arguments are generally persuasive, but I would make some modifications of his analysis. For instance, the DBhP's story of Śatākṣī/Śākambharī bears striking testimony to the nurturing quality of the Devī associated with the earth and vegetation. As Śatākṣī ("Hundred-Eyed"), she weeps for a draught-stricken world, her tears filling the rivers and reviving the grasses, crops, and life in general. She bears in one of her four hands flowers, fruits, and vegetables, with which she feeds the hungry, thus becoming known as Śākambharī ("Bearer of Vegetables") (DBhP VII.28.34-47). And while the Goddess of the DBhP is generally not associated with the concrete biological processes of pregnancy, birth and lactation, examples of such are not entirely lacking. As Indra declares to the Devī: "As a mother ever suckles her children with the milk of her breasts, so do you [nourish your children] always, the mother of all. . . . Without a mother, a suckling infant may survive through fate, but without you, certainly no one can live." (DBhP IX.42.63-64)

    Such concrete images admittedly are rare, and the Devī's motherhood is for the most part abstract, representing an all-powerful, protective presence in the universe. Nonetheless, I suggest that the abstraction is not due simply or even primarily to a negative view of Prakṛti, but rather to the fact that we are not dealing simply with a human mother, whose limitations are made quite clear in the quotation above.

18. See the Introduction. We noted there that this interpretation of the DM was put forth by Coburn (1984[a], 303-04).

Appendix: Three Theories on the Text-History of the *Devī-Bhāgavata Purāṇa*

1. His views are found in an article, "The Devī Bhāgavata as the Real Bhāgavata" (1969, 127-58).
2. Sanyal 142.
3. Needless to say, not all scholars agree with Sanyal's interpretation of the MatP verses (53.20-21). Even if his interpretation is correct, the date of the verse is not known and is likely to be a late addition to the Purāṇa, making it virtually useless for dating purposes. These verses are briefly discussed in chapters two and three above.
4. Sanyal 152.
5. To be sure, the extant text of the BVP is almost certainly not the original BVP. Nonetheless, as I have shown in chapter one, age alone is quite an ambivalent criterion for determining the canonical status of a Purāṇa.
6. Sanyal's view provides a necessary correction to some of the conclusions of Hazra regarding the dates of the DBhP and the BVP. Hazra seems to accept the date for the final recasting of the BVP as the sixteenth century (1936, 166). The "Prakṛti Khaṇḍa" undoubtedly belongs to the latest stages of the BVP, that is, to the fifteenth or sixteenth centuries, as I have shown in my study of that text (*God as Mother*, 34, 140-163). Yet Hazra, who was aware of the DBhP's borrowing of the "Prakṛti Khaṇḍa," sees the DBhP being composed or compiled in the eleventh or twelfth century (Hazra 1953, 68, 70; 1963, 343, 346-47). This inconsistency in Hazra's dates is noted by Sanyal (153-54).
7. Lalye's views are found primarily in two places in his book: pp. 31-32 and 102-05.
8. Lalye calls the DM "the primary source" of the DBhP (52).
9. Lalye 104.
10. Lalye 104.

Bibliography

A. Primary Texts with Translations

(References in the notes are to the edition marked by an asterisk [*], unless otherwise indicated. Sanskrit titles beginning with lower case letters have been transliterated from the *devanāgarī* script, as given on title pages.)

Agni Purāṇa

**Agnipurāṇa of Maharṣi Vedavyāsa.* Ed. Āchārya Baladeva Upādhyāya. Varanasi: Chowkhamba Sanskrit Series Office, 1966. Kashi Sanskrit Series 174.

Agni Purāṇam. 2 vols. Trans. Manmatha Nāth Dutt Shastrī. Varanasi: Chowkhamba Sanskrit Series Office, 1967. Chowkhamba Sanskrit Studies, vol. 54.

Amarakośa

Amarakośa with the Commentary of Maheśvara enlarged by Raghunath Shastri Talekar. Ed. Chintamani Shastri Thatte. Bombay: Government Central Book Depot, 1886.

Bhāgavata Purāṇa

Bhāgavata Purāṇa of Kṛṣṇa Dvaipāyana Vyāsa, with Sanskrit Commentary Bhāvārthabodhinī of Śrīdharasvāmin. Ed. J. L. Shastri. Delhi: Motilal Banarsidass, 1983.

**Śrīmad Bhāgavata Mahāpurāṇa (With Sanskrit text and English translation).* 2 vols. Trans. C. L. Goswami. Gorakhpur: Motilal Jalan, 1971.

Bhagavad Gītā

**The Bhagavad-Gītā with the Commentary of Śrī Śankarācārya.* Crit. ed. Dinkar Vishnu Gokhale. Poona: Oriental Book Agency, 1950. Poona Oriental Series, no. 1.

The Bhagavad Gītā. 2 vols. Trans. Franklin Edgerton. Cambridge: Harvard University Press, 1944. Harvard Oriental Series, vols. 38-39. Reprint, rev. 1 vol., Cambridge: Harvard University Press, 1972.

Brahmāṇḍa Purāṇa

The Brahmāṇḍa Purāṇa. 5 vols. Trans. Ganesh Vasudeo Tagare. Delhi: Motilal Banarsidass, 1983-84. Ancient Indian Tradition & Mythology Series, vols. 22-26.

Brahmavaivarta Purāṇa

**brahmavaivartapurāṇam*. 2 vols. Ed. Vināyaka Gaṇeśa Āpte. [Poona:] Ānandāśrama Press, 1935. Ānandāśrama Sanskrit Series, no. 102.

The Brahma-Vaivarta Puranam. 2 vols. Trans. Rajendra Nath Sen. Allahabad: Panini Office, 1920, 1922. Sacred Books of the Hindus, vol. 24. Reprint, New York: AMS Press, 1974.

Bṛhadāraṇyaka Upaniṣad

**The Bṛhadāraṇyaka Upaniṣad with the Commentary of Śaṅkarācārya*. Trans. Swāmī Mādhavānanda. Calcutta: Advaita Ashrama, 1965.

bṛhadāraṇyakopaniṣat śāṅkarabhāṣyayutā. In *Ten Principal Upanishads with Śāṅkarabhāṣya*. Delhi: Motilal Banarsidass, 1964. Works of Śaṅkarācārya in Original Sanskrit, vol. 1.

Devī-Bhāgavata Purāṇa

**śrīmaddevībhāgavatam; mahāpurāṇam*. Varanasi: Ṭhākur Prasād and Sons, n.d.

śrīmaddevībhāgavataṃ saṭīkaṃ samāhātmyam [with the commentary of Nīlakaṇṭha]. [Bombay:] Veṅkaṭeśvara Press, n.d.

The Srimad Devi Bhagawatam. Trans. Swami Vijnanananda [Hari Prasanna Chatterji]. Allahabad: Panini Office, 1921-23. Sacred Books of the Hindus, vol. 26. Reprint, New Delhi: Oriental Books Reprint, 1977.

Devī Gītā (constitutes chaps. 31-40 of the 7th Skandha of the *Devī-Bhāgavata Purāṇa*, for which see above. It has also been published separately.)

śrī bhagavatī-gītā. Comm. Śrī Hari Śāstrī Dādhīca. Allahabad: Śrī Ramādatta Śukla, 1951.

Devī-Māhātmya

**The Devī-Māhātmyam or Śrī Durgā-Saptaśatī (700 Mantras on Śrī Durgā)*. [With Sanskrit text.] Trans. Jagadīśvarānanda. Madras: Sri Ramakrishna Math, 1969.

Durgāsaptaśatī, with Seven Sanskrit Commentaries: Durgāpradīpa—Guptavatī—Caturdharī—Śāntanavī—Nāgojībhaṭṭī—Jagaccandracandrikā—Daṃśoddhāra. Ed. Vyaṅkaṭarāmātmaja Harikṛṣṇaśarma. Delhi: Butala and Co., 1984.

śrī saptaśatī gītā (durgā). Banaras: Śrīmatī Vidyādevī, 1941. Vāṇī-Pustaka-Mālā, no. 3.

Sri Sri Chandi. [With Sanskrit text.] Trans. Swami Tattwananda. Calcutta: Sri Nirmalendu Bikash Sen Gupta, 1962.

Garuḍa Purāṇa

**Śrīgaruḍamahāpurāṇam.* Ed. Rāmatejapāṇḍeya. Kashi: Paṇḍita-Pustakālaya, 1963.

The Garuḍa-Purāṇam. Trans. Manmatha Nath Dutt Shaṣtrī. Varanasi: Chowkhamba Sanskrit Series Office, 1968. Chowkhamba Sanskrit Studies, vol. 67.

Harivaṃśa

The Harivaṃśa, Being the Khila or Supplement to the Mahābhārata. 2 vols. Crit. ed. Parashuram Lakshman Vaidya. Poona: Bhandarkar Oriental Research Institute, 1969, 1971.

Hymn to Kālī; Karpūrādi-Stotra. Ed. and trans. Arthur Avalon [Sir John Woodroffe]. 2nd rev. ed. Madras: Ganesh & Co., 1953.

Jīva Gosvāmin. *Tattvasandarbha.* In *Jīva Gosvāmin's Tattvasandarbha; A Study on the Philosophical and Sectarian Development of the Gauḍiya Vaiṣṇava Movement*, ed. and trans. Stuart Mark Elkman. Delhi: Motil Banarsidass, 1986.

Kālikā Purāṇa

Kālikāpurāṇam. Ed. Biśwanārāyan Śāstrī. Varanasi: Chowkhamba Sanskrit Series Office, 1972. Jaikrishnadas-Krishnadas Prachyavidya Series, no. 5.

Kauṣītakī Upaniṣad

Kauṣītaki-Brāhmaṇa Upaniṣad. In *The Principal Upaniṣads* [with Sanskrit text], ed. and trans. S. Radhakrishnan. London: George Allen & Unwin, 1953. Reprint 1968.

Kena Upaniṣad

Kena Upaniṣad. In *Eight Upaniṣads, with the Commentary of Śaṅkarācārya* [with Sanskrit text], vol. 1, trans. Swāmī Gambhīrānanda. Calcutta: Advaita Ashrama, 1965.

Kūrma Purāṇa

The Kūrma Purāṇa (with English Translation). Crit. ed. Anand Swarup Gupta; trans. Ahibhushan Bhattacharya et al. Varanasi: All-India Kashiraj Trust, 1972.

Lakṣmī Tantra

Lakṣmī Tantra; A Pāñcarātra Text. Trans. Sanjukta Gupta. Leiden: E. J. Brill, 1972. Orientalia Rheno-Traiectina, vol. 15.

Liṅga Purāṇa

liṅgapurāṇam. Ed. Śrījīvānanda Vidyāsāgara Bhaṭṭācāryya. Calcutta: Śrījīvānanda Vidyāsāgara Bhaṭṭācāryya, 1885.

The Liṅga-Purāṇa. 2 vols. Trans. a board of scholars. Delhi: Motilal Banarsidass, 1973. Ancient Indian Tradition & Mythology Series, vols. 5-6.

Mahābhāgavata Purāṇa

The Mahābhāgavata Purāṇa (An Ancient Treatise on Śakti Cult). Crit. ed. Pushpendra Kumar. Delhi: Eastern Book Linkers, 1983.

Mahābhārata

**The Mahābhārata.* 19 vols. Crit. ed. V. S. Sukthaṇkar et al. Poona: Bhandarkar Oriental Research Institute, 1933-59.

The Mahābhārata [Books 1-5]. 3 vols. Trans. and ed. J. A. B. van Buitenen. Chicago: University of Chicago Press, 1973-78.

The Mahabharata of Krishna-Dwaipayana Vyasa. 12 vols. Trans. Kisari Mohan Ganguli. 3rd improved ed. New Delhi: Munshiram Manoharlal, 1972-75. Orig. pub. 1883-96.

Maitrī Upaniṣad

Maitrī Upaniṣad. In *The Principal Upaniṣads* [with Sanskrit text], ed. and trans. S. Radhakrishnan. London: George Allen & Unwin, 1953. Reprint 1968.

Manu-Smṛti

**manusmṛtiḥ (medhātithibhāṣya samalaṅkṛtā).* 2 vols. Calcutta: Manasukharāy More, 1967, 1971. Gurumaṇḍal Series, no. 24.

The Laws of Manu. Trans. Georg Bühler. Oxford: Clarendon Press, 1886. Sacred Books of the East, vol. 25. Reprint, New York: Dover Publications, 1969.

Mārkaṇḍeya Purāṇa

The Mārkaṇḍeyamahāpurāṇam. [Bombay:] Veṅkaṭeśvara Press. Reprint, arranged by Nag Sharma Singh; Delhi: Nag Publishers, n.d.

**The Mārkaṇḍeya Purāṇa.* Trans. F. Eden Pargiter. Calcutta: Asiatic Society of Bengal, 1904. Bibliotheca Indica, New Series nos. 700, 706 etc. Reprint, Delhi: Indological Bookhouse, 1969.

Matsya Purāṇa

**matsyapurāṇam.* Calcutta: Nandalāl More, 1954. Gurumandal Series, no. 13.

The Matsya Purāṇam. Ed. Jamna Das Akhtar. Delhi: Oriental Publishers, 1972. Sacred Books of the Aryans, vol. 1.

Muṇḍaka Upaniṣad

Muṇḍaka Upaniṣad. In *The Principal Upaniṣads* [with Sanskrit text], ed. and trans. S. Radhakrishnan. London: George Allen & Unwin, 1953. Reprint 1968.

Nārada Pañcarātra

Srī Narada Pancharatnam [sic]; *The Jñānāmrita Sāra Saṃhitā.* Trans. Swami Vijnanananda (Hari Prasanna Chatterji). Allahabad: Panini Office, 1921. Sacred Books of the Hindus, vol. 23. Reprint, New York: AMS Press, 1974.

Nārada Purāṇa

*The Nāradīyamahāpurāṇam. [Bombay:] Veṅkaṭeśvara Press. Reprint, arranged by Nag Sharan Singh; Delhi: Nag Publishers, n.d.

The Nārada-Purāṇa. 5 vols. Trans. Ganesh Vasudeo Tagare. Delhi: Motilal Banarsidass, 1980-82. Ancient Indian Tradition & Mythology Series, vols. 15-19.

Nīlakaṇṭha. See under *Devī-Bhāgavata Purāṇa* above.

Padma Purāṇa

Padma Puranam. 5 vols. Calcutta: Manasukharāy More. 1957-59. Gurumandal Series, no. 18.

Pañcaviṃśa Brāhmaṇa

Pañcaviṃśa-Brāhmaṇa; The Brahmana of Twenty Five Chapters. Trans. W. Caland. 2nd ed. Delhi: Sri Satguru Publications, 1982. 1st ed. 1931.

Rāmāyaṇa

The Vālmīki-Rāmāyaṇa. 7 vols. Crit. ed. G. H. Bhatt et al. Baroda: Oriental Institute, 1958-75.

Ṛg Veda

Der Rig-Veda. 4 vols. Trans. Karl Friedrich Geldner. Cambridge: Harvard University Press, 1951-57. Harvard Oriental Series, vols. 33-36.

Śākta Upaniṣads

The Śākta Upaniṣad-s. Trans. A. G. Krishna Warrier. Madras: Adyar Library and Research Centre, 1967. Adyar Library Series, vol. 89.

Śāradātilaka Tantra

Śāradā-Tilaka Tantram. Ed. Arthur Avalon [Sir John Woodroffe]. Delhi: Motilal Banarsidass, 1982. 1st ed. Calcutta: 1933.

Sarasvatī-Rahasyopaniṣad

sarasvatīrahasyopaniṣat. In *The Śākta Upaniṣads with the Commentary of Śrī Upaniṣad-Brahma-Yogin,* ed. A. Mahadeva. Madras: Adyar Library, 1950. Adyar Library Series, no. 10.

Śatapatha Brāhmaṇa

The Satapatha-Brahmana according to the Text of the Madhyandina School. 5 vols. Trans. Julius Eggeling. Oxford: Clarendon Press, 1882-1900. Sacred Books of the East, vols. 12, 26, 41, 43, 44.

Saubhāgya-Lakṣmī Upaniṣad

saubhāgyalakṣmyupaniṣat. In *The Śākta Upaniṣads with the Commentary of Śrī Upaniṣad-Brahma-Yogin,* ed. A. Mahadeva. Madras: Adyar Library, 1950. Adyar Library Series, no. 10.

Saura Purāṇa

Saurapurāṇam. Ed. Vināyaka Gaṇeśa Āpte. [Poona:] Ānandāśrama

Press, 1924. Ānandāśrama Sanskrit Series, no. 18.

Śiva Purāṇa

The Śiva Mahāpurāṇa. Crit. ed. Pushpendra Kumar. Delhi: Nag Publishers, 1981. NP Series, no. 48.

The Śiva-Purāṇa. 4. vols. Trans. a Board of Scholars. Delhi: Motilal Banarsidass, 1970. Ancient Indian Tradition & Mythology Series, vols. 1-4.

Skanda Purāṇa

The Skanda Mahāpurāṇam. 3 vols. Arranged by Nag Sharan Singh. Delhi: Nag Publishers, 1984.

Śrīdhara. See under *Bhāgavata Purāṇa* above.

Subāla Upaniṣad

Subāla Upaniṣad. In *The Principal Upaniṣads* [with Sanskrit text], ed. and trans. S. Radhakrishnan. London: George Allen & Unwin, 1953. Reprint 1968.

Śvetāśvatara Upaniṣad

Śvetāśvatara Upaniṣad. In *The Principal Upaniṣads* [with Sanskrit text], ed. and trans. S. Radhakrishnan. London: George Allen & Unwin, 1953. Reprint 1968.

Taittirīyasaṃhitā

The Veda of the Black Yajus School entitled Taittiriya Sanhita. 2 vols. Trans. Arthur Berriedale Keith. Cambridge: Harvard University Press, 1914. Harvard Oriental Series, vols. 18-19. Reprint, Delhi: Motilal Banarsidass, 1969.

Taittirīya Upaniṣad

Taittirīya Upaniṣad. In *Eight Upaniṣads, with the Commentary of Śaṅkarācārya* [with Sanskrit text], vol. 1, trans. Swāmī Gambhīrānanda. Calcutta: Advaita Ashrama, 1965.

Vāmana Purāṇa

The Vāmana Purāṇa with English Translation. Crit. ed. Anand Swarup Gupta; trans. Satyamsu Mohan Mukhopadhyaya, et al. Varanasi: All India Kashiraj Trust, 1968.

Varāha Purāṇa

The Varāha-Purāṇa (with English Translation). Crit. ed. Anand Swarup Gupta; trans. Ahibhushan Bhattacharya. Varanasi: All-India Kashiraj Trust, 1981.

Vāyu Purāṇa

The Vāyumahāpurāṇam. [Bombay:] Veṅkaṭeśvara Press. Reprint, arranged by Nag Sharan Singh; Delhi: Nag Publishers, n.d.

Vedāntasāra

Vedantasara, or the Essence of Vedanta of Sadananda Yogindra. Ed. and trans.

Swami Nikhilananda. 3rd ed. Mayavati: Advaita Ashrama, 1949. Reprint, Calcutta: Advaita Ashrama, 1968.

Viṣṇu Purāṇa

*śrīśrīviṣṇupurāṇa (with Hindi commentary). Gorakhpur: Motīlāl Jālān, [1934?].

The Vishnu Purana; A System of Hindu Mythology and Tradition. Trans. H. H. Wilson. 3rd ed. Calcutta: Punthi Pustak, 1972. 1st ed., London: 1840.

Viṣṇudharmottara

The Vishṇudharmottara (part III); A Treatise on Indian Painting and Image-Making. Trans. Stella Kramrisch. 2nd rev. ed. Calcutta: Calcutta University Press, 1928.

B. Secondary Works

Agrawala, V. S. "The Glorification of the Great Goddess." *Purāṇa* 5:64-89. 1963.

Aiyar, Parameswara. "Imitations of the Bhagavad-Gītā and Later Gītā Literature." In *Ithihāsas, Purāṇas, Dharma and Other Śāstras*, rev. ed., ed. S. K. De et al, 204-19. Calcutta: Ramakrishna Mission Institute of Culture, 1962. Cultural Heritage of India, vol. 2.

Babb, Lawrence A. *The Divine Hierarchy: Popular Hinduism in Central India.* New York: Columbia University Press, 1975.

Bakker, Hans. *Ayodhyā.* Part I. The history of Ayodhyā from the 7th century to the middle of the 18th century; its development into a sacred center with special reference to the *Ayodhyāmāhātmya* and to the worship of Rāma according to the *Agastyasaṃhitā*. Part II. *Ayodhyāmāhātmya;* introduction, edition, and annotation. Groningen: Egbert Forsten, 1986.

Banerjea, Jitendra Nath. *The Development of Hindu Iconography.* 3rd ed. New Delhi: Munshiram Manoharlal Publishers, 1974. Reprint of the 2nd rev. ed., 1956.

Banerji, S. C. *Tantra in Bengal; A Study in its Origin, Development and Influence.* Calcutta: Naya Prokash, 1977.

Beane, Charles Wendell. *Myth, Cult and Symbols in Śākta Hinduism; a Study of the Indian Mother Goddess.* Leiden: E. J. Brill, 1977.

Bedekar, V. M. "The Story of Śuka in the Mahābhārata and the Purāṇas: A Comparative Study." *Purāṇa* 7: 87-127. 1965.

Bhagowalia, Urmila. *Vaiṣṇavism and Society in Northen India: 700-1200.* New Delhi: Intellectual Publishing House, 1980.

Bhattacharyya, Narendra Nath. *History of the Śākta Religion.* New Delhi:

Munshiram Manoharlal Publishers, 1974.

———. *History of the Tantric Religion (A Historical, Ritualistic and Philosophical Study).* New Delhi: Manohar, 1982.

———. *The Indian Mother Goddess.* 2nd rev. ed. New Delhi: 1977, Manohar.

Bloomfield, Maurice. "The Story of Indra and Namuci." *Journal of the American Oriental Society* 15:143-63. 1893.

Bosch, F. D. K. "The God with the Horse's Head." In *Selected Studies in Indonesian Archaeology,* 137-52. The Hague: M. Nijhoff, 1961.

Brown, C. Mackenzie. *God as Mother: A Feminine Theology in India; An Historical and Theological Study of the Brahmavaivarta Purāṇa.* Hartford, Vermont: Claude Stark & Co., 1974.

Brown, W. Norman. "Change of Sex as a Hindu Story Motif." In *India and Indology; Selected Articles by W. Norman Brown,* ed. Rosane Rocher, 201-11. Delhi: Motilal Banarsidass, 1978.

Bulliet, Lucianne. *The Vṛtra-Myth in the Ṛg Veda.* Ann Arbor: University Microfilms International, 1985.

Capra, Fritjof. *The Tao of Physics: An Exploration of the Parallels Between Modern Physics and Eastern Mysticism.* Boulder, Colorado: Shambhala, 1975.

Chakravarti, Chintaharan. "Purāṇa Tradition in Bengal." *Purāṇa* 7: 150-57. 1965.

Chakravarti, Prabhat Chandra. *Doctrine of Sakti in Indian Literature.* Patna: Eastern Book House [1986]. Orig. pub. c. 1940.

Chaudhuri, Dulal. *Goddess Durgā: The Great Mother.* Calcutta: Mrimol Publishers, 1984.

Chemburkar, Jaya. "Umā Haimavatī Myth in the Devī Bhāgavata—A Study." *Purāṇa* 18:93-100. 1976.

Choudhuri, Usha. *Indra and Varuna in Indian Mythology.* Delhi: Nag Publishers, 1981.

Clooney, Francis X. "Sacrifice and Its Spiritualization in the Christian and Hindu Traditions: A Study in Comparative Theology." *Harvard Theological Review* 78:361-80. 1985.

Coburn, Thomas B. "Consort of None, Śakti of All: The Vision of the *Devī-Māhātmya.*" In *The Divine Consort; Rādhā and the Goddesses of India,* ed. John Stratton Hawley and Donna Marie Wulff, 153-65. Berkeley: Graduate Theological Union, 1982.

———. *Devī-Māhātmya; The Crystallization of the Goddess Tradition.* Delhi: Motilal Banarsidass, 1984(a).

———. *Encountering the Goddess: A Translation of the Devī-Māhātmya and a Study of Its Interpretation.* Forthcoming from State University of New York Press.

———. "'Scripture' in India: Towards a Typology of the Word in Hindu Life." *Journal of the American Academy of Religion* 52: 435-59. 1984(b).

Coomaraswamy, Ananda K. "Angel and Titan: An Essay in Vedic Ontology." *Journal of the American Oriental Society* 55:373-419. 1935.

———. "Sir Gawain and the Green Knight: Indra and Namuci." *Speculum* 19:104-25. 1944.

Dange, Sadashiv Ambadas. *Legends in the Mahābhārata, with (A Brief Survey of Folk-tales).* Delhi: Motilal Banarsidass, 1969.

Dange, Sindhu S. *The Bhāgavata Purāṇa; Mytho-Social Study.* Delhi: Ajanta Publications, 1984.

De, Sushil Kumar. *Early History of the Vaisnava Faith and Movement in Bengal, from Sanskrit and Bengali Sources.* Calcutta: Firma K. L. Mukhopadhyay, 1961.

Desai, Nileshvari Y. *Ancient Indian Society, Religion and Mythology as Depicted in the Mārkaṇḍeya-Purāṇa (A Critical Study).* Baroda: M. S. University of Baroda, 1968.

Dev, Usha. *The Concept of Śakti in the Purāṇas.* Delhi: Nag Publishers, 1987. Purāṇa Vidyā Series, no. 2.

Dikshitar, V. R. Ramachandra. *The Matsya Purana; A Study.* Madras: University of Madras, 1935. Bulletins of the Department of Indian History and Archaeology No. 5.

Dimmitt, Cornelia, and J. A. B. van Buitenen (eds. and trans.). *Classical Hindu Mythology; A Reader in the Sanskrit Purāṇas.* Philadelphia: Temple University Press, 1978.

Dumézil, Georges. *The Destiny of the Warrior.* Trans. Alf Hiltebeitel. Chicago: University of Chicago Press, 1970.

Dumont, P. E. *L'Aśvamedha; Description du Sacrifice Solennel du Cheval dans le Culte Védique d'après les Textes du Yajurveda Blanc.* Paris: Pau Geuthner, 1927.

Eggeling, Julius (trans.). *The Satapatha-Brahmana.* 5 vols. 1882-1900. (See primary works above for full entry.)

Ewing, Arthur H. "The Śāradā-tilaka Tantra." *Journal of the American Oriental Society* 23:65-76. 1902.

Fort, Andrew. *The Self and its States: A States of Consciousness Doctrine in Advaita Vedānta.* Forthcoming from Motilal Banarsidass, Delhi.

Freer, L. "Vritra et Namoutchi dans le Mahābhārata." *Revue de l'Histoire des Religions* 14:291-307. 1886.

Gatwood, Lynn E. *Devi and the Spouse Goddess; Women, Sexuality, and Marriages in India.* Riverdale, Maryland: Riverdale Company, 1985.

Goldman, Robert P. *Gods, Priests, and Warriors; the Bhṛgus of the* Mahābhārata. New York: Columbia University Press, 1977. Studies in Oriental Culture, no. 12.

Gonda, J. *Aspects of Early Viṣṇuism.* Utrecht: A. Oosthoek, 1954.

———. *Medieval Religious Literature in Sanskrit.* Wiesbaden: Otto Harrassowitz, 1977. A History of Indian Literature, vol. 2, fasc. 1.

Goudriaan, Teun, and Sanjukta Gupta. *Hindu Tantric and Śākta Literature.* Wiesbaden: Otto Harrassowitz, 1981. A History of Indian Literature, vol. 2, fasc. 2.

Gupta, Anand Swarup. "Purāṇas and Their Referencing." *Purāṇa* 7:321-51. 1965.

———. "Note on the Devī-Stotra." *Purāṇa* 20:1-6. 1978.

Hardy, Friedhelm. *Viraha-Bhakti; The early history of Kṛṣṇa devotion in South India.* Delhi: Oxford University Press, 1983.

Hazra, R. C. *Studies in the Purāṇic Records on Hindu Rites and Customs.* Dacca: University of Dacca, 1936. Bulletin No. 20.

———. *Studies in the Upapurāṇas.* 2 vols. Calcutta: Sanskrit College, 1958, 1963.

———. "The Devī-bhāgavata." *Journal of Oriental Research, Madras* 21: 49-79. 1953.

———. "The Purāṇas." In *Ithihāsas, Purāṇas, Dharma and Other Śāstras,* rev. ed., ed. by S. K. De et al., 240-70. Calcutta: Ramakrishna Mission Institute of Culture, 1962. Cultural Heritage of India, vol. 2.

Heesterman, J. C. "The Case of the Severed Head." *Wiener Zeitschrift zur Kunde des Süd- und Ostasiens* 11:22-43. 1967.

Heimann, Betty. *Studien zur Eigenart indischen Denkens.* Tubingen: J. C. B. Mohr, 1930.

Hillebrandt, Alfred. *Vedic Mythology.* 2 vols. 2nd rev. ed. Trans. Sreeramula Rajeswara Sarma. Delhi: Motilal Banarsidass, 1980-81. 2nd rev. German ed., 2 vols. Breslau: 1927, 1929.

Hiltebeitel, Alf. *The Ritual of Battle; Krishna in the* Mahābhārata. Ithaca: Cornell University Press, 1976.

Hohenberger, A. *Die Indische Flutsage und das Matsyapurāṇa; Ein Beitrag zur Geschichte der Viṣṇuverehrung.* Leipzig: Otto Harrassowitz, 1930.

Hopkins, E. Washburn. *Epic Mythology.* 1915. Reprint, New York: Biblo and Tannen, 1969.

Hopkins, Thomas J. "The Social Teaching of the *Bhāgavata Purāṇa.*" In *Krishna: Myths, Rites, and Attitudes,* ed. Milton Singer, 3-32. Chicago: University of Chicago Press, 1968.

Hospital, Clifford. "The Enemy Transformed: Opponents of the Lord in the *Bhāgavata Purāṇa.*" *Journal of the American Academy of Religion* 46. Supplement: 200-15. 1978.

———. *The Righteous Demon; A Study of Bali.* Vancouver: University of

British Columbia Press, 1984.

ımes, Cynthia. Letters to author, 26 February 1989, 28 April 1989, and 21 August 1989.

ı, Ganganatha. "Bhāgavatam." In *Mahamahopadhyaya Kuppuswami Sastri Commemoration Volume*, organized by C. K. Raja and P. P. S. Sastri, 1-2. Madras: G. S. Press [1935?].

.ne, Pandurang Vaman. *History of Dharmaśāstra (Ancient and Mediaeval Religious and Civil Law)*. 5 vols. Poona: Bhandarkar Oriental Research Institute, 1930-62.

.padia, Brahmā H. "Some Aspects of Vāmana-Purāṇa." *Purāṇa* 7:170-82. 1965.

ırmarkar, A. P. "The Matsyāvatāra of Viṣṇu (Its Proto-Indian Origin and Location)." In *A Volume of Studies in Indology*, ed. S. M. Katre and P. K. Gode, 253-57. Poona: Oriental Book Agency, [1941]

ıtre, S. L. "Avatāras of God." *Allahabad University Studies* 10:37-130. 1934.

ıshavadas, Sant. *Cosmic Shakti Kundalini (The Universal Mother); A devotional approach*. Washington D.C.: Temple of Cosmic Religion, 1976.

nsley, David. *Hindu Goddesses; Visions of the Divine Feminine in the Hindu Religious Tradition*. Berkeley: University of California Press, 1986.

——. "The Image of the Divine and the Status of Women in the *Devī-Bhagavāta-Purāṇa* [sic]." *Anima* 9:50-56. 1982.

——. *The Sword and the Flute; Kālī and Kṛṣṇa, Dark Visions of the Terrible and the Sublime in Hindu Mythology*. Berkeley: University of California Press, 1975.

rfel, Willibald. *Die Dreiköpfige Gottheit; Archäologisch-ethnologischer Streifzug durch die Ikonographie der Religionen*. Bonn: Ferd. Dümmlers Verlag, 1948.

ʼamrisch, Stella. "The Indian Great Goddess." *History of Religions* 14:235-65. 1975.

——. (trans.). *Viṣṇudharmottara*. 1928. (See primary works above for full entry.)

ımar, Pushpendra. *Śakti and Her Episodes (On the basis of Ancient Indian Tradition and Mythology)*. Delhi: Eastern Book Linkers, 1981.

ırulkar, G. M. "Demons of Hindu Mythology with Special Reference to Their Body Forms." *Journal of the Anthropological Society of Bombay* 1:81-100. 1946.

ine, James William. *The Theophany Narratives of the* Mahābhārata. Ann Arbor: University Microfilms International, 1984.

lye, P. G. *Studies in Devī Bhāgavata*. Bombay: Popular Prakashan, 1973.

nman, Charles R. "The Namuci Myth; or an attempt to explain the text of Rigveda viii.14.13." *Journal of the Royal Asiatic Society of Bengal*

58:28-30. 1889.

Macdonell, Arthur A. *A History of Sanskrit Literature.* New York: D. Appl ton and Co., 1900.

Mahalingam, T. V. "Hayagrīva—The Concept and the Cult." *Ady Library Bulletin* 29:188-99. 1965.

Miśra, Hīrāmaṇi. "purāṇoktā gītāḥ." *Purāṇa* 20:136-38. 1978.

Muir, J. *Original Sanskrit Texts on the Origin and History of the People of Ind Their Religion and Institutions.* Vol. 4. 2nd rev. ed. London: Trubn & Co., 1873.

Mukhopadhyay, Somnath. *Caṇḍī in Art and Iconography.* Delhi: Aga Kala Prakashan, 1984.

Müller, F. Max. *A History of Ancient Sanskrit Literature so far as It Illustrat the Primitive Religion of the Brahmans.* Rev. ed. Varanasi: Chowkhamb Sanskrit Series Office, 1968. Chowkhamba Sanskrit Studies, vo 15. 1st ed., 1859.

Narayan, R. K. *Gods, Demons, and Others.* London: Heinemann, 1965.

O'Flaherty, Wendy Doniger. *Dreams, Illusion, and other Realities.* Chicag University of Chicago Press, 1984.

———. *Hindu Myths; A Sourcebook Translated from the Sanskrit.* New Yor Penguin, 1975.

———. "Karma and Rebirth in the Vedas and Purāṇas." In *Karma ar Rebirth in Classical Indian Traditions*, ed. Wendy Doniger O'Flahert 3-37. Berkeley: University of California Press, 1980(a).

———. *The Origins of Evil in Hindu Mythology.* Berkeley: University c California Press, 1976.

———. *Women, Androgynes, and Other Mythical Beasts.* Chicago: Universit of Chicago Press, 1980(b).

Oldenberg, Hermann. *Die Religion des Veda.* 3rd and 4th ed. Stuttgar und Berlin: J. C. Cotta'sche Buchhandlung Nachfolger, 1923.

Oliphant, Samuel Grant. "Fragments of a Lost Myth,—Indra and th Ants." *American Philological Association, Proceedings of December, 191* lv-lix.

Östör, Ákos. *The Play of the Gods; Locality, Ideology, Structure, and Time i the Festivals of a Bengali Town.* Chicago: University of Chicago Press 1980.

Parrinder, Geoffrey. "Is the Bhagavad-Gītā the Word of God?" I *Truth and Dialogue in World Religions: Conflicting Truth-Claims,* ed John Hick, 111-25. Philadelphia: Westminster Press, 1974.

Patil, N. B. *The Folklore in the Mahābhārata.* New Delhi: Ajanta Publications 1983.

Payne, Ernest A. *The Śāktas; An Introductory and Comparative Study*

London: Oxford University Press, 1933. Reprint, New York: Garland Publishing, 1979.

Prasad, Sheo Shanker. *The Bhāgavata Purāṇa; A Literary Study.* Delhi: Capital Publishing House, 1984.

Rao, T. A. Gopinatha. *Elements of Hindu Iconography.* Vol. 1. Madras: Law Printing House, 1914. Reprint, New York: Garland Publishing, 1981.

Ricoeur, Paul. "The 'Sacred' Text and the Community." In *The Critical Study of Sacred Texts*, ed. W. D. O'Flaherty, 271-76. Berkeley: Berkeley Religious Studies Series, 1979.

Rocher, Ludo. *The Purāṇas.* Wiesbaden: Otto Harrassowitz, 1986. A History of Indian Literature, vol. 2, fasc. 3.

Ruben, W. "Indra's Fight Against Vṛtra in the Mahābhārata." In *S. K. Belvalkar Felicitation Volume*, 113-26. Banaras: 1957.

Rukmani, T. S. *A Critical Study of the Bhāgavata Purāṇa (with Special Reference to Bhakti).* Varanasi: Chowkhamba Sanskrit Series Office, 1970. Chowkhamba Sanskrit Studies, no. 77.

Sanyal, Nirmal Chandra. "The Devī-Bhāgavata as the Real Bhāgavata." *Purāṇa* 11:127-58. 1969.

Sastri, S. Srikantha. "The Two Bhāgavatas." *Annals of the Bhandarkar Oriental Research Institute* 14:241-49. 1932-33.

Schrader, F. Otto. *Introduction to the Pāñcarātra and the Ahirbudhnya Saṃhitā.* Madras: Adyar Library, 1916.

Senart, E. *Essai sur la Légende du Buddha; son Caractère et ses Origines.* 2nd ed. Paris: Libraire de la Société Asiatique de L'école des Langues Orientales Vivantes, 1882.

Sharma, Dasharatha. "Verbal Similarities between the Durgā-Sapta-Śatī and the Devī-Bhāgavata Purāṇa and Other Considerations Bearing on Their Date." *Purāṇa* 5:90-113. 1963.

Sheridan, Daniel P. *The Advaitic Theism of the Bhāgavata Purāṇa.* Delhi: Motilal Banarsidass, 1986.

———. "The Bhāgavata Purāṇa: Sāṃkhya at the Service of Non-Dualism." *Purāṇa* 25:206-24. 1983.

Shulman, David. "The Murderous Bride: Tamil Versions of the Myth of Devī and the Buffalo-Demon." *History of Religions* 16:120-46. 1976-77.

———. "The Serpent and the Sacrifice: An Anthill Myth from Tiruvārūr." *History of Religions* 18:107-37. 1978-79.

———. *Tamil Temple Myths; Sacrifice and Divine Marriage in the South Indian Śaiva tradition.* Princeton: Princeton University Press, 1980.

Siddhantashastree, Rabindra Kumar. *Vaiṣṇavism Through the Ages.* New

Delhi: Munshiram Manoharlal, 1985.

Sinha, Jadunath. *The Cult of Divine Power; "Sakti-Sadhana."* 5th ed. Calcutta: Amiya Kumar Sinha, 1977.

Smith, Wilfred Cantwell. "A Human View of Truth." In *Truth and Dialogue in World Religions: Conflicting Truth-Claims*, ed. John Hick, 20-44. Philadelphia: Westminster Press, 1974.

———. *Islam in Modern History*. Princeton: Princeton University Press, 1957.

Subramanian, S. K. *Saundaryalaharī (The Ocean of Divine Beauty) of Śaṅkarācārya*. Delhi: Motilal Banarsidass, 1977.

Tadpatrikar, S. N. "Devī-bhāgavata or Bhagavatī-purāṇa?" *Annals of the Bhandarkar Oriental Research Institute* 23:559-62. 1942.

Tattwananda, Swami. *Vaisnava Sects; Saiva Sects; Mother Worship*. Calcutta: Firma KLM, 1984.

Tiwari, J. N. *Goddess Cults in Ancient India (With Special Reference to the First Seven Centuries A.D.)*. Delhi: Sundeep Prakashan, 1985.

van Buitenen, J. A. B. (ed. and trans.). *The Mahābhārata*. 3 vols. Chicago: University of Chicago Press, 1973, 1975, 1978.

van Gulik, R. H. *Hayagrīva; The Mantrayānic Aspect of Horse-Cult in China and Japan*. Leiden: E. J. Brill, 1935.

Vaudeville, Charlotte. "Krishna Gopāla, Rādhā, and The Great Goddess." In *The Divine Consort; Rādhā and the Goddesses of India*, ed. John Stratton Hawley and Donna Marie Wulff, 1-12. Berkeley: Graduate Theological Union, 1982.

Vimalānanda-Svāmi. "Introduction." In *Hymn to Kālī; Karpūrādi-Stotra*, ed. Arthur Avalon [Sir John Woodroffe], 15-39. Madras: Ganesh & Co., 1953.

von Stietencron, Heinrich. "Die Göttin Durgā Mahiṣāsuramardinī; Mythos, Darstellung und geschichtliche Rolle bei der Hinduisierung Indiens." In *Visible Religion; Annual for Religious Iconography*, ed. H. G. Kippenberg et al., 2:118-66. Leiden: E. J. Brill, 1983.

Vora, Dhairyabala P. *Evolution of Morals in the Epics (Mahābhārata and Rāmāyaṇa)*. Bombay: Popular Book Depot, 1959.

Wadley, Susan Snow. *Shakti; Power in the Conceptual Structure of Karimpur Religion*. Chicago: University of Chicago Press, 1975.

Wayman, Alex. "The Significance of Mantra-s, from the Veda down to Buddhist Tantric Practice." *Adyar Library Bulletin* 39:65-89. 1975.

Weber, Albrecht. *Indische Studien; Zeitschrift für die Kunde des indische Alterthums*. Vol. 1. Berlin: 1850. Reprint, Hildesheim, New York: Georg Olms Verlag, 1973.

Winternitz, Maurice. *A History of Indian Literature*. Vol. 1. Trans. S. V.

Ketkar and rev. by the author. Calcutta: University of Calcutta, 1927. 1st German ed. 1907.

Woodroffe, John. *Introduction to Tantra Śāstra.* 5th ed. Madras: Ganesh & Co., 1969.

Zimmer, Heinrich. *Myths and Symbols in Indian Art and Civilization.* Ed. Joseph Campbell. New York: Harper & Row, 1962.

[illegible] and rev. by the author. Calcutta: University of Calcutta, 1977. 1st German ed. 1907.

Woodroffe, John. *Introduction to Tantra Śāstra*. 5th ed. Madras: Ganesh & Co., 1969.

Zimmer, Heinrich. *Myths and Symbols in Indian Art and Civilization*. ed. Joseph Campbell. New York: Harper & Row, 1962.

Index